MYSTERIES OF ANCIENT BABYLON

UNVEILING THE SECRETS OF WITCHCRAFT, DIVINATION, HERBALISM, AND MAGIC

PART 1

M.L. Ruscsak

Trient Press
3375 S Rainbow Blvd
#81710, SMB 13135
Las Vegas,NV 89180

Ordering Information:
Quantity sales. Special discounts are available on quantity purchases by corporations, associations, and others. For details, contact the publisher at the address above.
Orders by U.S. trade bookstores and wholesalers. Please contact Trient Press: Tel: (775) 996-3844; or visit www.trientpress.com.

Printed in the United States of America

Publisher's Cataloging-in-Publication data
Ruscsak, M.L.
A title of a book : Mysteries of Ancient Babylon: Unveiling the Secrets of Witchcraft, Divination, Herbalism, and Magic Part 1

ISBN
Hard Cover

Paper Back

Ebook

979-8-88990-115-0
979-8-88990-116-7
979-8-88990-117-4

Unveiling the Secrets of Witchcraft, Divination, Herbalism, and Magic
Part 1

Unveiling the Secrets of Witchcraft, Divination, Herbalism, and Magic
Part 1

Chapter 1: Introduction to Ancient Babylon

Historical Significance of Ancient Babylon

Ancient Babylon stands as a remarkable testament to the cultural, religious, and intellectual achievements of the ancient world. Situated in the fertile lands of Mesopotamia, between the Tigris and Euphrates rivers, the city emerged as a vibrant center of civilization during the early 3rd millennium BCE.

The rise of Babylon was closely intertwined with its strategic geographical location. Mesopotamia, often referred to as the "cradle of civilization," witnessed the development of complex societies due to its fertile soil, which enabled agriculture to thrive. The abundance of resources and the ability to harness water through irrigation systems contributed to the growth of cities like Babylon.

Under the rule of Hammurabi, who ascended to the throne in the 18th century BCE, Babylon experienced a period of significant expansion and cultural development. Hammurabi's Code, a comprehensive legal code inscribed on a stele, is one of the most enduring legacies of ancient Babylon. This legal system provided a framework for governance and justice, emphasizing principles of equity and punishment fitting the crime.

The reign of Nebuchadnezzar II during the 6th century BCE marked another period of Babylonian grandeur. Nebuchadnezzar's ambitious building projects, including the construction of the Hanging Gardens of Babylon, one of the Seven Wonders of the Ancient World, showcased the city's architectural prowess and artistic achievements.

Babylon's influence extended far beyond its physical boundaries. The city served as a hub for trade and cultural exchange, fostering connections with neighboring regions such as Egypt, Persia, and Assyria. Its strategic position on major trade routes facilitated the flow of goods, ideas, and knowledge, propelling Babylon to become a vibrant cosmopolitan center.

Furthermore, Babylon's intellectual contributions cannot be understated. The Babylonians excelled in various fields, including mathematics, astronomy, and literature. Their mathematical system, based on a sexagesimal numeral system, laid the foundation for modern time measurement and geometry. Astronomical observations carried out in Babylon contributed to the development of early astronomy, with the Babylonians creating intricate star catalogs and tracking celestial phenomena.

The fall of Babylon to the Persian Empire in the 6th century BCE marked a significant turning point in its history. However, its cultural and intellectual legacy endured, as subsequent empires recognized the city's importance and sought to integrate its traditions and knowledge into their own.

Through its remarkable urban planning, architectural achievements, legal system, trade networks, and intellectual pursuits, ancient Babylon emerged as a prominent center of civilization. Its historical significance lies not only in its physical remains but also in the enduring impact it had on subsequent cultures and societies. Exploring the history of ancient Babylon allows us to gain insights into the origins of human civilization, the complexities of governance, and the diverse intellectual pursuits that shaped our world.

Examples, Problems, and Exercises:

Analyze the Hammurabi Code and discuss its historical significance in shaping Babylonian society and its lasting impact on legal systems.

Investigate the architectural features of the Hanging Gardens of Babylon and explore their symbolic significance within the context of Babylonian culture.

Examine Babylonian trade routes and discuss their impact on cultural exchange, economic development, and the diffusion of ideas in the ancient Near East.

Engage in a group discussion on the mathematical contributions of the Babylonians, such as their numeral system and its influence on modern mathematics.

Research Babylonian astronomical observations and their role in understanding celestial phenomena, and present a case study on a significant discovery made by Babylonian astronomers.

Overview of Babylonian Culture and Society

The society of ancient Babylon was structured hierarchically, with distinct social classes that played a crucial role in shaping the cultural fabric of the civilization. At the top of the social order were the ruling elite, consisting of the king, nobility, and high-ranking officials. They held significant political power and often claimed divine authority, as they were believed to be chosen by the gods to govern.

Below the ruling elite were the free citizens, who formed the majority of the population. Free citizens encompassed various professions, including farmers, artisans, merchants, and scribes. They engaged in agricultural and commercial activities, contributing to the economic prosperity of Babylon. While their social status was lower than the ruling elite, they enjoyed certain rights and participated in local governance through councils and assemblies.

Slavery was prevalent in Babylonian society, with slaves considered the lowest social class. Slavery primarily arose from captives of war or as a result of indebtedness. Slaves performed various tasks, ranging from domestic chores to labor-intensive work on construction projects or in agricultural fields. Despite their low social status, some slaves managed to acquire wealth and even obtain their freedom.

Babylonian Religious System

Religion held a central position in Babylonian culture, permeating all aspects of daily life. The Babylonians worshipped a pantheon of deities, each associated with different aspects of life and natural forces. The most prominent deities included Marduk, the chief god of Babylon, Ishtar, the goddess of love and war, and Ea, the god of wisdom and magic.

Rituals and ceremonies played a vital role in Babylonian religious practices. The temples, considered the dwelling places of the gods, served as centers of worship and community gathering. These magnificent structures were attended by priests, who acted as intermediaries between the human realm and the divine. Priests performed intricate rituals, offered sacrifices, and recited prayers to ensure the favor and protection of the gods.

Divination, a practice deeply rooted in Babylonian culture, aimed to interpret signs and omens as a means of understanding the will of the gods and predicting the future. Various methods of divination were employed, such as examining the movements of celestial bodies, interpreting dreams, or analyzing the patterns in animal entrails. These practices allowed the Babylonians to seek guidance and make informed decisions in both personal and political matters.

Art, Literature, and Education

Babylonian culture thrived in the realms of art, literature, and education. The Babylonians excelled in craftsmanship, producing intricate sculptures, jewelry, and pottery. They also developed advanced techniques in mural painting and employed vibrant colors to decorate the walls of temples and palaces.

Literature held a prominent place in Babylonian society, with epic tales, myths, and hymns being composed and preserved on clay tablets. The Epic of Gilgamesh, one of the oldest surviving works of literature, is an epic poem that explores themes of mortality, friendship, and the search for immortality.

Education was highly valued in Babylonian society, with schools established to educate future scribes and officials. The curriculum encompassed subjects such as reading, writing, mathematics, and legal codes. The Babylonians made significant advancements in the field of mathematics, developing the concept of a place-value numeral system and solving complex mathematical problems.

Examples, Problems, and Exercises:

Explore the role of women in Babylonian society, analyzing both the restrictions they faced and the opportunities available to them.

Investigate the role of the king in Babylonian society and discuss how the concept of divine kingship influenced political and religious power structures.

Examine a specific Babylonian religious ritual or ceremony, discussing its symbolic significance and its role in maintaining social cohesion.

Research a Babylonian literary work other than the Epic of Gilgamesh and analyze its themes and cultural significance.

Engage in a group discussion on the role of education in Babylonian society, comparing it to the educational systems of other ancient civilizations and evaluating its impact on social mobility.

By gaining an understanding of the intricate social hierarchy, religious practices, and cultural achievements of ancient Babylon, we can appreciate the multifaceted nature of this remarkable civilization and its profound influence on mystical traditions that emerged within its boundaries.

Influence of Ancient Babylon on Mystical Traditions

The influence of Ancient Babylon on mystical traditions can be observed through its rich repertoire of magical practices. The Babylonians believed in the existence of supernatural forces and sought to harness their powers through various rituals and incantations. Magical practices in Babylon encompassed a wide range of activities, including the invocation of deities, the use of spells and charms, and the utilization of symbolic objects.

Magical rituals often involved the recitation of spells and incantations, which were believed to possess inherent power and the ability to influence the spiritual realm. These incantations were inscribed on clay tablets or written on other materials, demonstrating the importance placed on preserving and transmitting mystical knowledge. By reciting these spells, practitioners sought to connect with divine entities and request their assistance in achieving desired outcomes.

Symbolic objects, such as amulets and talismans, played a significant role in Babylonian magical practices. These objects were imbued with specific qualities or energies and were believed to provide protection, enhance personal power, or attract desired influences. For example, the Eye of Horus amulet was worn for protection against evil forces, while the Tree of Life symbol represented fertility and abundance.

Divination in Ancient Babylon

Divination, the practice of seeking insights into the future or the divine will, held a prominent place in Babylonian society. Divinatory practices allowed individuals to gain guidance and make informed decisions in various aspects of life, including personal matters, governance, and warfare. Babylonians employed diverse methods of divination, each with its own unique techniques and symbolism.

One prevalent form of divination in Babylon was astrology, which involved the observation and interpretation of celestial phenomena. The Babylonians meticulously tracked the movements of celestial bodies, such as the sun, moon, planets, and stars, and believed that these cosmic events held significant meaning and influence over human affairs. By analyzing celestial omens and their correlations with earthly events, astrologers provided predictions and advice.

Another common form of divination in Babylon was hepatoscopy, the examination of animal livers to interpret signs and omens. The Babylonians believed that the liver, as a vital organ, served as a conduit between the spiritual and physical realms. By analyzing the shape, color, and texture of animal livers, diviners sought to unveil insights into future events or divine intentions.

Herbalism and Healing in Babylon

Herbalism held a crucial place in Babylonian society, intertwining with mystical traditions and healing practices. The Babylonians possessed extensive knowledge of medicinal plants and their properties, utilizing them to treat various ailments and promote well-being. The practice of herbalism in Babylon involved the identification, preparation, and application of plants for medicinal purposes.

The Babylonians believed that the natural world held inherent healing properties, and the utilization of medicinal plants was a means of tapping into these forces. Herbal remedies were prepared through various methods, such as infusions, poultices, or ointments, depending on the desired outcome. Some common medicinal plants used by the Babylonians included myrrh, frankincense, juniper, and cypress.

Healing practices in Babylon encompassed not only physical ailments but also spiritual and emotional well-being. It was believed that illness could be caused by spiritual imbalance or malevolent influences, and healers employed rituals, prayers, and incantations to restore harmony and aid in the healing process. Herbal remedies were often integrated into these rituals to enhance their efficacy.

Shamanism and Spirituality in Ancient Babylon

Shamanism, a spiritual practice rooted in communication with spirits and the ability to journey into other realms, also found expression in Ancient Babylon. Babylonian shamans, known as ashipu or kalu, played a significant role in the spiritual and healing practices of the society. These individuals were believed to possess the ability to connect with spirits and act as intermediaries between the human and spiritual realms.

Babylonian shamans engaged in various rituals and techniques to induce altered states of consciousness, facilitating their communication with spirits. Drumming, chanting, and rhythmic movements were employed to enter trance-like states, enabling the shamans to embark on spiritual journeys and receive guidance or healing knowledge from the spirit world.

Shamanic practices in Babylon were not limited to healing; they encompassed broader spiritual and religious dimensions as well. Shamans were involved in divinatory practices, performed rituals to honor deities, and participated in communal ceremonies. Their role extended beyond individual healing, contributing to the overall spiritual well-being and harmony of the community.

Examples, Problems, and Exercises:

Research a specific Babylonian magical spell or incantation, translate it, and discuss its intended purpose and symbolism.

Compare and contrast Babylonian divinatory practices, such as astrology and hepatoscopy, with divination methods employed in other ancient civilizations.

Explore the use of specific medicinal plants in Babylonian herbalism, discussing their properties, preparation methods, and associated healing practices.

Investigate the role of shamans in Babylonian society, examining their rituals, techniques, and societal significance.

Engage in a group discussion on the integration of mystical traditions, such as witchcraft, divination, herbalism, shamanism, and ecospirituality, in modern spiritual practices, drawing upon the influence of Ancient Babylon.

By studying the influence of Ancient Babylon on mystical traditions, we gain a profound appreciation for the wisdom, practices, and beliefs that have shaped our understanding of witchcraft, divination, herbalism, shamanism, and ecospirituality. Through the exploration of primary sources, archaeological findings, and scholarly interpretations, we delve into the depths of ancient knowledge and invite critical thinking and discussion into the continued relevance of these mystical traditions in the modern world.

Examples, Problems, and Exercises:

Analyze a Babylonian cuneiform tablet containing magical spells and discuss their potential purposes and efficacy.

Problem: You have come across a cuneiform tablet from ancient Babylon that contains a series of magical spells. Using your knowledge of Babylonian magical practices, analyze the spells and discuss their potential purposes and effectiveness. Consider the specific symbols, incantations, and ritual instructions present on the tablet.

Exercise: Write a brief essay outlining your analysis of the cuneiform tablet. Include an examination of the symbols used, the linguistic elements of the spells, and your interpretation of their intended purposes. Support your analysis with references to relevant scholarly research on Babylonian magical practices.

Research the role of divination in Babylonian society and present a case study on a specific divination method used during that time.

Problem: Select a divination method used in Ancient Babylon, such as astrology, hepatoscopy, or the interpretation of dreams, and research its role and significance within Babylonian society. Create a case study highlighting the process, techniques, and cultural context of this specific divination method.

Exercise: Develop a presentation or written report that explores the chosen divination method in detail. Discuss its historical development, the tools or rituals involved, and the beliefs and cultural significance associated with it. Use primary and secondary sources to support your findings and provide examples of how this divination method was utilized in ancient Babylon.

Investigate the use of specific herbs in Babylonian herbalism and their associated symbolic meanings.

Problem: Select two herbs commonly used in Babylonian herbalism, such as myrrh, frankincense, juniper, or cypress, and explore their properties, uses, and symbolic meanings within the context of Babylonian culture. Analyze how these herbs were incorporated into healing practices and rituals.

Exercise: Write a comparative essay or create a visual presentation that delves into the properties and uses of the selected herbs in Babylonian herbalism. Discuss their medicinal qualities, spiritual or symbolic associations, and any documented rituals or applications related to these herbs. Include references to primary sources and scholarly works on Babylonian medicine and herbalism.

Examine a narrative or mythological account from Babylonian literature that involves a shamanic journey and discuss its significance within the context of shamanism.

Problem: Select a narrative or mythological account from Babylonian literature that portrays a shamanic journey or interaction with spirits. Analyze the narrative's themes, symbols, and cultural context, and discuss its significance in understanding Babylonian shamanism and its spiritual practices.

Exercise: Write a critical analysis of the selected narrative or mythological account, focusing on its portrayal of shamanic practices and beliefs in Ancient Babylon. Interpret the symbolism, narrative structure, and character development within the context of Babylonian shamanism. Discuss how this account contributes to our understanding of the role of shamans and their connection to the spirit world in Babylonian society.

Engage in a group discussion on the ecological principles found in Babylonian texts and their relevance to contemporary ecospiritual practices.

Problem: Organize a group discussion on the ecological principles reflected in Babylonian texts, such as hymns, prayers, or agricultural treatises, and explore their potential relevance to modern ecospiritual practices. Identify specific passages or concepts that highlight the Babylonians' understanding of the natural world and their relationship with it.

Exercise: In your group discussion, explore the ecological principles evident in Babylonian texts and their implications for contemporary ecospiritual practices. Analyze passages or concepts that emphasize concepts such as harmony with nature, reverence for the environment, or sustainable agricultural practices. Engage in a critical dialogue on how these principles can inform and inspire modern approaches to ecospirituality.

By engaging in these examples, problems, and exercises, students will deepen their understanding of mystical traditions in Ancient Babylon and develop critical thinking skills necessary for analyzing primary sources, interpreting cultural contexts, and making connections between ancient practices and contemporary spiritual frameworks.

Unveiling the Secrets of Witchcraft, Divination, Herbalism, and Magic
Part 1

Chapter 2: Witchcraft in Ancient Babylon

Within the rich tapestry of ancient Mesopotamia, the practice of witchcraft holds a significant place. In this chapter, we delve into the enigmatic world of witchcraft in Ancient Babylon, exploring its historical development, beliefs, rituals, and the roles of witches within the society. By examining primary sources, archaeological findings, and scholarly interpretations, we aim to provide a comprehensive understanding of the complexities and nuances surrounding witchcraft in this ancient civilization.

Historical Development of Witchcraft in Ancient Babylon

The origins of witchcraft in Ancient Babylon can be traced back to the earliest periods of Mesopotamian civilization. It evolved alongside the complex religious and magical practices that permeated Babylonian society. Witchcraft in Babylon was not limited to the stereotype of malevolent spell-casters; it encompassed a broad spectrum of practices and beliefs, including healing, divination, protection, and fertility rites.

Problem: Analyze the historical development of witchcraft in Ancient Babylon and identify key factors that contributed to its growth and cultural significance.

Exercise: Write a reflective essay outlining the historical development of witchcraft in Ancient Babylon. Discuss the social, religious, and cultural factors that influenced the practice of witchcraft, including the role of deities, societal beliefs, and interactions with other mystical traditions. Support your arguments with evidence from primary sources and scholarly research.

Beliefs and Concepts in Babylonian Witchcraft

The belief system underlying Babylonian witchcraft was deeply rooted in animistic and polytheistic traditions. Witches were believed to possess a unique connection with the divine and supernatural realms, often acting as intermediaries between humans and the gods. They were thought to harness the powers of various deities and spirits to bring about desired outcomes, such as protection, healing, or the casting of spells.

Problem: Examine the core beliefs and concepts in Babylonian witchcraft and discuss their implications for the role and practices of witches.

Exercise: Create a concept map or diagram illustrating the interconnected beliefs and concepts in Babylonian witchcraft. Include key elements such as the role of deities, the concept of sympathetic magic, the use of charms and amulets, and the relationship between witches and spirits. Reflect on the implications of these beliefs for the role and practices of witches in Ancient Babylon.

Rituals and Practices of Babylonian Witches

The rituals and practices of Babylonian witches were diverse and multifaceted. They involved the use of spells, incantations, divination methods, and symbolic objects. Witches performed ceremonies and rituals in sacred spaces, such as temples or private sanctuaries, often accompanied by the burning of incense, the offering of libations, and the chanting of prayers. These rituals aimed to invoke the aid of deities, manipulate natural forces, or communicate with the spirit realm.

Problem: Explore the rituals and practices of Babylonian witches and their significance within the context of ancient Mesopotamian culture.

Exercise: Choose one specific ritual or practice of Babylonian witches, such as the casting of spells, the use of divination tools, or the creation of magical objects. Research and document the steps involved in this ritual, the purpose it served, and its cultural significance. Present your findings in a creative format, such as a visual presentation or a step-by-step guide.

Witchcraft and Social Dynamics in Ancient Babylon

The practice of witchcraft in Ancient Babylon was intertwined with social dynamics and power structures. Witches held a unique position in society, occupying roles as healers, advisors, and protectors. However, they also faced scrutiny and suspicion, as their powers were seen as potentially dangerous or malevolent. The relationship between witches and the broader community varied, with instances of collaboration, reverence, fear, and even persecution.

Problem: Analyze the social dynamics surrounding witchcraft in Ancient Babylon and discuss the complexities of the relationship between witches and the broader community.

Exercise: Conduct a mock debate or panel discussion on the topic: "The Role and Perception of Witches in Ancient Babylonian Society." Divide the class into groups representing different perspectives, such as religious leaders, common citizens, witches themselves, and skeptics. Each group should present arguments based on historical evidence and engage in critical dialogue to understand the diverse viewpoints on this subject.

In conclusion, this chapter provides a comprehensive exploration of witchcraft in Ancient Babylon, delving into its historical development, beliefs, rituals, and social dynamics. Through the study of primary sources, archaeological findings, and scholarly research, students will develop a nuanced understanding of the complexities and significance of witchcraft within the context of ancient Mesopotamia. The accompanying examples, problems, and exercises aim to foster critical thinking, encourage deep engagement with the subject matter, and facilitate discussions that broaden perspectives and challenge assumptions.

Understanding the Concept of Witchcraft

Witchcraft, a concept shrouded in mystery and intrigue, held significant meaning and relevance in the ancient civilization of Babylon. To comprehend the intricacies of witchcraft in Babylon, it is essential to delve into its conceptual framework, examining its definitions, cultural significance, and various interpretations within the historical and social context. In this section, we will explore the multifaceted nature of witchcraft in Ancient Babylon, drawing upon a range of scholarly sources, primary texts, and archaeological evidence.

Defining Witchcraft in Ancient Babylon

Defining witchcraft in the context of Ancient Babylon requires a comprehensive examination of its multifaceted nature. The concept of witchcraft encompassed a wide range of practices and beliefs, making it a complex and elusive subject for scholars. Different perspectives offer valuable insights into the diverse dimensions of witchcraft in Ancient Babylon, shedding light on its practical, spiritual, and religious aspects.

✧   Practical Witchcraft:

One approach to defining witchcraft in Ancient Babylon focuses on its practical aspects. It perceives witchcraft as the manipulation of supernatural forces for practical purposes, such as healing, protection, or divination. Witches in Babylon were believed to possess specialized knowledge and skills to interact with the supernatural realm. Through the use of spells, incantations, and ritual practices, they sought to influence the course of events and bring about desired outcomes. Practical witchcraft aimed to address everyday concerns and fulfill the needs of individuals and communities.

✧   Spiritual and Religious Witchcraft:

Another perspective views witchcraft as a spiritual and religious practice deeply embedded in the Babylonian belief system. Witches were considered intermediaries between humans and the divine, possessing the ability to commune with deities and spirits. They invoked specific gods and goddesses, employed magical rituals, and channeled their powers to accomplish spiritual goals. This aspect of witchcraft involved the performance of religious rites, the recitation of sacred texts, and the utilization of symbolic objects. Spiritual witchcraft served as a means of connecting with the sacred, seeking divine guidance, and accessing spiritual realms.

Witchcraft and the Supernatural World

Witchcraft in Ancient Babylon was intricately linked to the supernatural world, where witches drew their powers and influence. To comprehend the nature of witchcraft, it is crucial to understand its relationship with the supernatural realm.

✧ Invocation of Deities:

Central to Babylonian witchcraft were the rituals and practices involving the invocation of deities. Witches understood the power and influence that the gods and goddesses held over different aspects of life, and they sought to establish a connection with these divine beings. Through the act of invocation, witches aimed to gain the favor and assistance of specific deities who were associated with their desired outcomes.

Each deity in the Babylonian pantheon had their own domain of influence, such as Ishtar, the goddess of love and fertility, or Marduk, the god of protection and victory. Witches would carefully select the appropriate deity based on their intentions and needs. They believed that by invoking these deities, they could tap into their divine attributes and channel their energies towards their desired outcomes.

The invocation of deities was not a mere verbal request but rather a ritualistic practice accompanied by various ceremonial elements. Witches would create sacred spaces, often within their homes or designated places of worship, where they could connect with the divine realm. They would prepare altars adorned with symbols, offerings, and sacred objects associated with the deity they sought to invoke.

Rituals and offerings played a vital role in the invocation process. Witches would perform specific gestures, recite incantations, and offer sacrifices to honor and appease the deities. These offerings could include food, drink, flowers, or other items that held symbolic value to the deity in question. The act of offering was seen as a gesture of devotion and a means to establish a reciprocal relationship with the gods.

Prayers were an essential component of the invocation process as well. Witches would recite prayers, often composed in poetic or rhythmic forms, expressing their intentions, seeking blessings, and demonstrating their devotion to the deity. These prayers served as a means of communication, expressing the witches' desires and establishing a spiritual connection with the divine.

By invoking deities and engaging in these rituals, witches believed they could harness the power of the gods and goddesses to influence the natural and supernatural realms. They sought divine assistance in matters such as love, fertility, protection, healing, or guidance. The invocation of deities was seen as a way to align themselves with the cosmic forces and tap into the vast wisdom and powers of the divine realm.

It is important to note that Babylonian witchcraft was deeply intertwined with the religious beliefs and practices of the time. The invocation of deities was not considered separate from the broader Babylonian religious framework but rather an integral part of it. Witches, as practitioners of witchcraft, played a unique role as intermediaries between the mortal realm and the divine realm, seeking to bridge the gap and gain favor from the gods through their invocations and rituals.

✧   Magical Spells and Incantations:

Witchcraft in Babylon encompassed the art of casting magical spells and reciting potent incantations. Witches believed that these mystical utterances held immense power, capable of influencing the fabric of reality and accessing the forces of the natural and supernatural realms. Through the skillful use of specific words, formulas, and gestures, witches sought to activate the transformative energies contained within the spells.

The recitation of spells and incantations was a deliberate and ritualistic practice. Witches would carefully choose the appropriate spell for their intended purpose, considering the desired outcome and the specific deities or spirits they wished to invoke. These spells were often passed down through generations, carried within the oral traditions and written texts of Babylonian witchcraft.

The words and phrases within the spells were carefully crafted, using symbolic language and poetic structures to amplify their potency. The chosen words were believed to possess inherent power, carrying vibrations and resonances that harmonized with the intended magical effects. Witches understood the significance of sound and the spoken word, recognizing that through vocalization, they could manifest their intentions into reality.

In addition to the verbal components, witches incorporated gestures and actions to enhance the effectiveness of their spells. They would perform specific hand movements, body postures, or dance-like rituals, synchronizing their physical expressions with the spoken words. These gestures served as conduits for channeling the energy of the spell and directing it towards the desired outcome.

Symbolic objects, such as amulets, talismans, or magical tools, played a crucial role in Babylonian witchcraft. Witches would often incorporate these objects into their spellcasting, considering them as sources of concentrated power and protective energies. Amulets and talismans, inscribed with symbols or engraved with specific words, were believed to amplify the effects of the spells and offer additional layers of protection or guidance.

The recitation of spells and incantations was not limited to a private practice. Witches would often perform their rituals in sacred spaces, such as temples or outdoor sanctuaries, where they could connect with the spiritual energies of the natural world. They understood the importance of creating an atmosphere conducive to their magical work, surrounded by the elements, sacred symbols, and the presence of supportive spirits or deities.

Witchcraft in Babylon viewed spells and incantations as a means of accessing and manipulating the unseen forces that governed existence. Witches sought to harmonize with these forces, tapping into their transformative potential to achieve desired outcomes, such as healing, protection, love, or prosperity. Through the careful selection and skilled recitation of spells, they aimed to bring about positive changes in the lives of individuals or the community.

It is important to note that Babylonian witchcraft was deeply rooted in the cultural and religious beliefs of the time. The use of magical spells and incantations was not seen as separate from the broader Babylonian worldview but rather an integral part of it. Witches, as practitioners of witchcraft, were considered guardians of esoteric knowledge and agents of change, utilizing their skills to navigate the realms of the visible and invisible and effect transformation in accordance with their intentions.

✦　Cultural Perceptions of Witchcraft

The definition and understanding of witchcraft in Ancient Babylon varied within the society, reflecting the diverse cultural perceptions and beliefs held by different segments of the population. The interpretation of witchcraft was influenced by various factors such as regional customs, religious practices, social hierarchies, and individual perspectives.

Within Babylonian society, there were multiple ways in which witchcraft was understood and conceptualized. Some viewed witchcraft as a revered and essential practice, with witches being regarded as highly skilled individuals who possessed specialized knowledge and abilities to commune with the supernatural realms. These witches were seen as intermediaries between humans and the divine, capable of harnessing magical forces for the benefit of individuals or the community. They were respected for their wisdom and spiritual insight, and their services were sought after for various purposes such as healing, protection, and divination.

On the other hand, there were segments of Babylonian society that held a more negative perception of witchcraft. They saw witches as practitioners of dark arts, engaging in malevolent activities and using magic for harmful or selfish purposes. In these contexts, witches were often associated with curses, hexes, or the manipulation of negative energies. Such perceptions were influenced by cultural fears, superstitions, and societal anxieties about the potential misuse of supernatural powers.

The understanding of witchcraft in Ancient Babylon was also shaped by religious beliefs and practices. Babylonians had a complex pantheon of gods and goddesses, and their religious rituals and ceremonies played a significant role in the societal perception of witchcraft. In some cases, witchcraft was viewed as an extension of religious practices, with witches being seen as individuals who possessed a special connection to specific deities or spirits. They were believed to work in harmony with these divine beings, using their magical abilities to carry out the will of the gods or to seek their favor.

Furthermore, social hierarchies and power dynamics influenced the perception of witchcraft in Babylonian society. The role of witches often intersected with other social roles such as priestesses, healers, or diviners. The societal significance of witchcraft could vary based on the status and influence of the individuals practicing it. In some cases, witches held positions of power and were respected members of the community, while in other instances they might be viewed with suspicion or even face persecution if their practices challenged established authority or societal norms.

It is important to recognize that the understanding of witchcraft in Ancient Babylon was not a monolithic concept. It encompassed a range of beliefs, attitudes, and practices that varied across different cultural, religious, and social contexts. The significance of witchcraft was shaped by the diverse perspectives and experiences of the people within Babylonian society, and these varied understandings contributed to the complex and multifaceted nature of witchcraft in the ancient world.

✧   Social Roles and Identity:

Within Babylonian society, witches held distinct social roles and were recognized for their specialized knowledge and skills. They occupied a unique position, often regarded as powerful individuals who possessed the ability to commune with supernatural forces and manipulate magical energies. Their expertise in witchcraft set them apart from the general populace and granted them a certain level of respect and influence.

Witches in Ancient Babylon were often seen as repositories of wisdom, possessing deep knowledge of mystical practices, herbal remedies, divination techniques, and rituals. They were believed to have a profound understanding of the natural and supernatural realms, enabling them to tap into hidden forces and work with them for various purposes. This expertise allowed them to fulfill important societal roles such as healers, diviners, or advisors, providing guidance and assistance to individuals and the community as a whole.

In many instances, witches were revered for their abilities and held in high regard. Their services were sought after for matters such as fertility, love, protection, or resolving conflicts. People turned to witches for spiritual guidance, seeking their insights into personal matters, navigating challenges, and gaining a deeper understanding of the divine will. In this context, witches played an essential role in maintaining the well-being and spiritual harmony of Babylonian society.

However, despite their respected positions, witches in Babylonian society were not universally accepted or understood. Societal perceptions of witches varied, and some individuals regarded them with suspicion, fear, or even hostility. This could be due to the potential misuse of magical powers, fears of malevolent witchcraft, or a general unease about individuals who held esoteric knowledge and abilities beyond the ordinary. These perceptions might have been influenced by cultural superstitions, rivalries, or the desire to maintain social control.

The ambiguity surrounding the social roles and identities of witches contributed to the diverse interpretations of witchcraft in Ancient Babylon. Different individuals held contrasting views, ranging from reverence and appreciation to skepticism and caution. The specific cultural, religious, and social context in which witches operated influenced how they were perceived and the roles they played within the broader societal framework.

Overall, the social roles and identities of witches in Babylonian society were multifaceted, reflecting both admiration and suspicion. The respected and powerful status of witches was accompanied by societal variations in perceptions, contributing to the complex and diverse understanding of witchcraft in Ancient Babylon.

✧   Witchcraft and Gender:

Gender indeed played a significant role in the perception of witchcraft in Babylonian society. The majority of individuals practicing witchcraft were women, and their involvement in mystical practices contributed to the association between women and the spiritual realm. This association was rooted in societal notions and stereotypes that portrayed women as inherently more attuned to the supernatural, intuitive, and mystical aspects of life.

The cultural beliefs and religious traditions of Ancient Babylon contributed to the gendered perception of witchcraft. The Babylonian pantheon included powerful goddesses associated with fertility, love, and magic, such as Ishtar and Ninhursag. The presence of these revered female deities reinforced the idea that women possessed a natural affinity for mystical powers and divination.

Furthermore, the Babylonian society was patriarchal, with men holding dominant positions in various aspects of life. The association between women and witchcraft can be seen as a way to both acknowledge and confine their spiritual influence within prescribed boundaries. By portraying women as witches, society recognized their connection to the supernatural realm while simultaneously positioning them as separate and potentially dangerous entities. This duality allowed for the expression of female spirituality within certain limits while maintaining established gender hierarchies.

However, it is important to note that not all women were considered witches, and not all individuals practicing witchcraft were women. Men could also engage in magical practices and be recognized as witches or sorcerers. While the majority of practitioners were women, there were instances of men involved in witchcraft, particularly in roles such as diviners or priests who performed magical rituals. The relationship between witchcraft and gender was complex, influenced by cultural, religious, and social factors, and not solely determined by biological sex.

The perception of witchcraft in relation to gender varied across different social strata within Babylonian society. The views of the ruling elite, religious authorities, and common people might have differed regarding the role and significance of witches and their gendered associations. It is crucial to consider the specific cultural and historical context when examining the connection between witchcraft and gender in Ancient Babylon, as beliefs and interpretations evolved over time.

In summary, gender played a significant role in the perception of witchcraft in Babylonian society. The association between women and mystical practices was rooted in societal stereotypes and cultural beliefs. However, the relationship between witchcraft and gender was complex and influenced by various factors. Not all women were considered witches, and men could also engage in magical practices. Understanding the nuances of the gendered perception of witchcraft in Ancient Babylon requires considering the cultural, religious, and social dynamics of the time.

Examples, Problems, and Exercises:

Analyze a Babylonian magical spell and discuss its intended purpose and the symbolism embedded within it.

Compare and contrast the practical and spiritual aspects of witchcraft in Ancient Babylon, providing examples to illustrate each perspective.

Research the social perception of witchcraft in Ancient Babylon and present a case study highlighting the divergent views within the society.

Engage in a group discussion on the role of gender in Babylonian witchcraft, exploring the societal implications and potential reasons for the association between witchcraft and women.

By engaging with the multifaceted nature of witchcraft in Ancient Babylon, students will gain a nuanced understanding of this mystical tradition and its cultural significance. Through critical analysis, comparisons, and discussions, students will develop a comprehensive grasp of the diverse perspectives surrounding the definition and practice of witchcraft in this ancient civilization.

Problem: Analyze different scholarly definitions of witchcraft in Ancient Babylon and evaluate their strengths and limitations.

Exercise: Write a comparative essay critically assessing the different scholarly definitions of witchcraft in Ancient Babylon. Analyze the strengths and limitations of each definition and discuss the implications for our understanding of this mystical tradition. Support your arguments with references to primary texts and scholarly works.

Cultural Significance of Witchcraft in Ancient Babylon

Witchcraft held immense cultural significance in the ancient city of Babylon, influencing various aspects of society, religion, and everyday life. It played a pivotal role in religious rituals, healing practices, divination, and the maintenance of social order. The Babylonians believed that witches possessed special connections to deities and spirits, allowing them to influence both the natural and supernatural realms. Witches were regarded as intermediaries between humans and the divine, capable of communing with spirits, casting spells, and providing guidance to individuals and communities.

✧   Religious Rituals and Beliefs:

Witchcraft held a central and revered position within the religious rituals and beliefs of the Babylonians. Witches were regarded as intermediaries between the human and divine realms, possessing unique abilities to communicate with and channel the powers of the gods. Their role in religious practices was crucial, as they played an active and vital part in performing rituals, offering sacrifices, and seeking divine guidance.

In Babylonian society, the presence of witches in religious ceremonies underscored their special connection and favor with the gods. They were seen as individuals who possessed the knowledge and skills to effectively interact with the spiritual realm. Through their rituals and incantations, witches sought to establish a direct line of communication with the deities, requesting their intervention and blessings on behalf of the community.

Witches were often involved in various religious activities, including the performance of sacred rites and the offering of sacrifices. Their expertise and understanding of the intricate rituals ensured that the offerings made to the gods were conducted appropriately, maximizing their effectiveness and ensuring the divine response. This active involvement in religious ceremonies reinforced the belief that witches had the ability to influence the course of events through their connection to the divine.

Furthermore, witches were sought after for their ability to seek guidance and divine insight. Individuals and communities turned to them in times of uncertainty or when facing challenges, seeking their counsel and assistance. Through their unique connection with the gods, witches were believed to possess the ability to interpret signs, omens, and dreams, offering guidance and predictions about future events. This gave them a significant role in shaping the decisions and actions of individuals and communities, aligning them with the will of the gods.

The recognition of witches as important figures within the religious context of Ancient Babylon contributed to their elevated status and influence. Their role as mediators between humans and the gods bestowed upon them a position of authority and respect within the community. They were seen as indispensable in establishing and maintaining a harmonious relationship between mortals and the divine, ensuring the spiritual well-being of the society.

In summary, witchcraft occupied a central position in the religious rituals and beliefs of the Babylonians. Witches were viewed as intermediaries who could communicate with and channel the powers of the gods. Their active participation in religious ceremonies, offering sacrifices, and seeking divine guidance reinforced their special connection with the divine. Their role as mediators and advisors allowed them to shape the religious practices and spiritual well-being of the Babylonian society.

✦   Healing and Herbalism:

Witches in Ancient Babylon held a special place in the realm of healing practices and herbalism. They were esteemed for their extensive knowledge of medicinal herbs and their skill in administering remedies for physical ailments. The Babylonian witches' profound understanding of the properties and uses of various plants allowed them to harness the healing power of nature, offering solace and relief to those in need.

The practice of herbalism was deeply intertwined with the realm of magic and spirituality. Babylonian witches recognized that the medicinal properties of plants were not solely derived from their physical attributes but also from the metaphysical forces they represented. They believed that plants possessed inherent spiritual energies that could be tapped into and utilized for healing purposes.

Through their profound knowledge of herbs, Babylonian witches were able to diagnose ailments, prepare remedies, and administer treatments tailored to specific conditions. They understood the intricate properties of different plants and their effects on the body, allowing them to prescribe effective treatments for a wide range of illnesses and injuries. Whether it was a soothing salve for a skin ailment, a poultice for a sprained joint, or a potion to alleviate digestive issues, witches possessed the expertise to create and administer the appropriate herbal remedies.

The practice of herbalism by Babylonian witches was not limited to the physical realm alone. They believed that the power of plants extended beyond their material form and encompassed spiritual aspects as well. Witches incorporated magical rituals, incantations, and spells into their healing methods, recognizing that the mind and spirit played a crucial role in the process of restoring health.

In their healing practices, witches would often combine the physical application of herbal remedies with the recitation of incantations and invocations. They believed that these mystical utterances enhanced the potency of the herbs, amplifying their healing properties and directing their energies towards the desired outcome. By infusing their healing rituals with magical elements, witches sought to address not only the physical symptoms but also the underlying spiritual and energetic imbalances contributing to the illness.

The integration of magic and herbalism by Babylonian witches was a testament to their comprehensive approach to healing. They recognized that physical ailments were often intertwined with spiritual and energetic imbalances, and sought to address all aspects of well-being. Through their practice, they not only provided physical relief but also offered a holistic approach to healing, promoting balance and harmony in the lives of those they served.

In summary, witches in Ancient Babylon were highly revered for their expertise in healing practices and herbalism. Their profound knowledge of medicinal herbs and their ability to administer remedies for physical ailments made them valued members of the community. By intertwining magic and spirituality with the practice of herbalism, witches recognized the inherent spiritual energies of plants and harnessed them to promote healing and restore well-being. Their holistic approach to healing addressed not only the physical symptoms but also the underlying spiritual and energetic imbalances, offering a comprehensive path to health and wholeness.

✧   Divination and Prophetic Insight:

Divination, the practice of seeking knowledge and insights about the future or divine intentions, played a vital role in Babylonian society, and witches were highly esteemed as skilled practitioners in this art. The Babylonians recognized the inherent wisdom and divinatory abilities possessed by witches, and they turned to them for guidance and prophetic insights.

Witches in Ancient Babylon employed a wide array of divinatory techniques and methods to access the spiritual realm and gain insights into the mysteries of the future. One of the prominent divinatory practices among witches was the interpretation of omens. They closely observed signs and occurrences in the natural world, such as the flight patterns of birds, the behavior of animals, or the appearance of unusual phenomena, believing that these events held symbolic messages from the gods. By interpreting these omens, witches could provide individuals with valuable guidance and predictions about important life events or upcoming situations.

Another significant divinatory method utilized by Babylonian witches was the reading of celestial signs. They closely observed the movements and positions of celestial bodies, including the sun, moon, planets, and stars, as they believed these heavenly phenomena conveyed divine messages and influences on human affairs. Through careful observation and interpretation of celestial patterns and alignments, witches could offer prophetic insights about the destiny of individuals, the outcomes of certain events, and even the overall social and political landscape.

Rituals were an integral part of divination practices among Babylonian witches. They conducted ceremonies, made offerings, and engaged in specific rituals to establish a connection with the gods and seek their guidance. These rituals were designed to create a sacred space and foster a spiritual atmosphere in which witches could commune with the divine realm. By invoking the deities associated with divination and performing the necessary rituals, witches believed they could receive direct insights and messages from the gods, offering profound wisdom and guidance to those who sought their counsel.

Divinatory tools were also employed by witches in Babylon to enhance their abilities to access the spiritual realm and interpret the messages received. These tools could include items such as divination boards, crystal balls, oracles, or symbolic objects used in specific rituals. By utilizing these tools, witches sought to deepen their connection with the divine and amplify their divinatory insights.

The Babylonians placed great trust and value in the predictions and counsel provided by witches. The divinatory abilities of witches were regarded as sources of wisdom and guidance, aiding individuals in making important decisions, navigating through life challenges, and preparing for future events. The knowledge and prophetic insights offered by witches were seen as invaluable resources that could illuminate the path ahead and bring clarity to uncertain situations.

In conclusion, divination held significant importance in Babylonian society, and witches were revered as skilled practitioners of this art. Through their divinatory techniques, such as interpreting omens, reading celestial signs, and conducting rituals, witches offered prophetic insights and guidance to individuals seeking knowledge about their personal lives, important decisions, or forthcoming events. The Babylonians placed great trust in the divinatory abilities of witches, considering their predictions as valuable sources of wisdom that could illuminate the path forward in an uncertain world.

✧   Social Order and Mediation:

Witches played a vital role in maintaining social order and resolving conflicts within Babylonian society. Their position as intermediaries between the human and divine realms granted them unique influence and authority. Babylonian witches were sought after for their ability to mediate disputes, offer spiritual guidance, and provide resolutions for interpersonal conflicts. Their involvement in social matters demonstrated the cultural significance attributed to their wisdom, judgment, and perceived ability to access higher realms of knowledge.

By understanding the cultural significance of witchcraft in Ancient Babylon, we gain insight into the pivotal role witches played in the society. The integration of witchcraft into religious rituals, healing practices, divination methods, and social dynamics highlights the profound impact they had on various aspects of Babylonian life. Exploring the cultural significance of witchcraft enhances our appreciation for the complexity of ancient belief systems and societal structures, fostering a deeper understanding of the historical and cultural context in which witchcraft thrived in Ancient Babylon.

Problem: Analyze the cultural significance of witchcraft in Ancient Babylon and its implications for religious practices, healing traditions, and social order. Provide examples from primary sources, such as religious texts, medical treatises, and legal documents, to support your analysis.

Exercise: Conduct a comparative study of the cultural significance of witchcraft in Ancient Babylon and another ancient civilization, such as Ancient Egypt or Ancient Greece. Compare and contrast the roles and perceptions of witches in these societies, examining their influence on religious beliefs, healing practices, and social dynamics. Analyze the cultural factors that contributed to the similarities or differences observed.

Engaging with the cultural significance of witchcraft in Ancient Babylon allows us to appreciate the profound impact that witchcraft had on the society and the multifaceted roles witches played. Through critical analysis and comparative studies, we deepen our understanding of the rich tapestry of ancient mystical practices and their cultural contexts, fostering a holistic comprehension of the historical significance of witchcraft.

Problem: Analyze the cultural significance of witchcraft in Ancient Babylon and discuss its impact on religious, social, and individual practices.

Exercise: Prepare a presentation exploring the cultural significance of witchcraft in Ancient Babylon. Identify key cultural practices, rituals, and beliefs associated with witchcraft, and discuss their implications for religious ceremonies, social dynamics, and personal spirituality. Utilize primary sources and archaeological evidence to support your analysis.

Witchcraft as a Contested Concept in Ancient Babylon

Witchcraft in Ancient Babylon was not a uniform concept, but rather a subject of intense debate and disagreement among different segments of society. The varying opinions and beliefs regarding the nature and practice of witchcraft gave rise to conflicting narratives and diverse perspectives. This contestation reflected the complex dynamics of Babylonian society, where different groups held contrasting views on the role and significance of witches.

One perspective that emerged within Babylonian society was the reverential view of witches as powerful individuals with access to supernatural forces. These individuals were often regarded as wise and knowledgeable, possessing the ability to communicate with deities and spirits. In this interpretation, witches were seen as intermediaries between the human realm and the divine, capable of harnessing magical powers for the benefit of individuals and communities. They were sought after for their healing abilities, divinatory skills, and spiritual guidance.

However, alongside this reverence, there existed a contrasting perspective that viewed witchcraft with suspicion and fear. Some members of Babylonian society associated witchcraft with malevolence, dark forces, and harmful intentions. Witches were seen as capable of inflicting harm, casting malicious spells, and manipulating supernatural powers for personal gain or to cause misfortune. This negative perception of witches stemmed from the belief that their practices could disrupt social order, threaten the well-being of individuals, and challenge the authority of established religious institutions.

The contestation of witchcraft's nature and impact extended beyond mere disagreements about the existence of witches or their abilities. It had implications for societal norms, legal systems, and religious practices. The tensions surrounding witchcraft prompted the development of laws and regulations aimed at controlling and punishing those suspected of practicing harmful magic. These laws reflected the anxieties of those who believed that witchcraft posed a threat to social harmony and stability.

Moreover, the conflicting perspectives on witchcraft led to the emergence of diverse narratives within Babylonian literature and mythology. Stories and myths featuring witches often portrayed them as complex characters, capable of both benevolent and malevolent actions. These narratives served to explore the intricate relationship between witches, society, and the divine, offering different interpretations and moral lessons.

Problem: Analyze the contestation of witchcraft in Ancient Babylon and discuss its implications for social dynamics and religious institutions.

Exercise: Write a research paper analyzing the contestation of witchcraft in Ancient Babylon. Investigate the primary sources, including legal texts, religious texts, and mythological narratives, to understand the various viewpoints held within the society. Discuss the implications of this contestation for social dynamics and religious institutions. Evaluate how different perspectives on witchcraft influenced the formulation of laws and the role of religious authorities in controlling or accommodating magical practices.

By understanding the contestation surrounding witchcraft in Ancient Babylon, students can gain insight into the complexities of belief systems, societal dynamics, and power structures within this ancient civilization. This exploration encourages critical thinking, allowing students to recognize the diversity of perspectives and challenge preconceived notions about witchcraft in Ancient Babylon.

Problem: Explore the contested nature of witchcraft in Ancient Babylon and analyze the different viewpoints held by various segments of the society.

Exercise: Conduct a group discussion on the contested nature of witchcraft in Ancient Babylon. Divide the class into smaller groups, assigning each group a specific perspective, such as religious leaders, common citizens, skeptics, or practitioners of other mystical traditions. Engage in a dialogue that explores the different viewpoints, allowing each group to present arguments, counterarguments, and supporting evidence based on historical sources and scholarly research.

In conclusion, understanding the concept of witchcraft in Ancient Babylon requires a comprehensive exploration of its definitions, cultural significance, and contested nature. By examining primary sources, archaeological findings, and scholarly interpretations, students can gain a nuanced understanding of this mystical tradition within its historical and social context. The accompanying examples, problems, and exercises aim to foster critical thinking, encourage deep engagement with the subject matter, and facilitate discussions that broaden perspectives and challenge assumptions.

Babylonian Witchcraft Practices and Beliefs

Babylonian witchcraft encompassed a rich tapestry of practices and beliefs that were integral to the religious and spiritual fabric of ancient Babylonian society. This section delves into the core elements of Babylonian witchcraft, providing an in-depth analysis of its rituals, spells, and magical techniques.

✧   Rituals and Ceremonies:

Rituals were an integral and central aspect of Babylonian witchcraft practices, serving as powerful tools for establishing connections with the supernatural realm and harnessing magical powers. Witches performed elaborate ceremonies that involved a range of elements, including the invocation of deities, the use of symbolic objects, and the recitation of spells and incantations.

The invocation of deities was a fundamental component of Babylonian witchcraft rituals. Witches called upon specific gods and goddesses associated with different aspects of life, such as fertility, love, protection, or wisdom. By invoking these deities, witches sought their favor and assistance in fulfilling their intentions. This act of invocation was accompanied by prayers, offerings, and rituals to create a sacred space and establish a direct connection with the divine realm.

Symbolic objects played a significant role in Babylonian witchcraft rituals. These objects, such as amulets, talismans, or sacred tools, were believed to possess inherent magical properties or serve as conduits for spiritual energies. Witches incorporated these objects into their rituals, either by wearing them, placing them on altars, or using them in specific ceremonial actions. The symbolic objects acted as focal points for concentration and served to amplify the intentions and energies of the witches during the ritual.

Spells and incantations were essential components of Babylonian witchcraft rituals. Witches used specific words, formulas, and gestures to activate and direct magical energies towards their intended purposes. The recitation of spells and incantations was believed to invoke supernatural forces, enabling witches to manipulate the natural and supernatural realms. These mystical utterances were often accompanied by rhythmic chants, rhythmic movements, or the use of sacred objects, further enhancing their potency.

Babylonian witchcraft rituals encompassed a wide range of purposes and intentions. Purification ceremonies were performed to cleanse individuals or spaces of negative energies or spiritual impurities. Divinatory rituals were conducted to seek guidance and insights into the future, employing various divinatory tools and techniques, such as the interpretation of omens or the reading of celestial signs. Rites for healing and protection aimed to restore health, ward off malevolent spirits, or safeguard individuals from harm.

The performance of rituals in Babylonian witchcraft served multiple functions. They were a means of establishing connections with the supernatural realm and seeking the assistance of deities. Rituals also provided a framework for witches to channel and direct their magical powers towards specific intentions or outcomes. Through the elaborate ceremonial practices, witches sought to tap into the vast reservoirs of cosmic energy and spiritual forces, harnessing them to manifest their desires and bring about desired changes in the natural and supernatural realms.

In conclusion, rituals held a central place in Babylonian witchcraft practices. These rituals involved the invocation of deities, the use of symbolic objects, and the recitation of spells and incantations. They served as powerful tools for establishing connections with the supernatural realm, seeking divine assistance, and harnessing magical powers. Babylonian witches performed various rituals, such as purification ceremonies, divinatory rituals, and rites for healing and protection, each serving a specific purpose within the broader framework of witchcraft.

✧   Spellcasting and Incantations:

Babylonian witches were highly skilled in the art of spellcasting and the recitation of powerful incantations. They believed that specific words, formulas, and gestures held profound magical significance, capable of invoking supernatural forces and bringing about the desired outcomes. Spellcasting was a meticulous practice, and Babylonian witches invested considerable time and effort in crafting spells that were tailored to address specific intentions or purposes.

The spells used by Babylonian witches were diverse and covered a wide range of areas, including love, fertility, protection, healing, and prosperity. Each spell was carefully constructed with precise wording and ritualistic actions to maximize its effectiveness. The belief was that by uttering the correct words and performing the associated gestures, the inherent power within the spells would be unleashed, initiating the desired changes in the natural and supernatural realms.

Babylonian magical texts, such as the "Maqlû" series, were invaluable resources for witches seeking to expand their repertoire of spells and incantations. These texts contained a wealth of knowledge and provided detailed instructions on the performance of various rituals and the recitation of specific incantations. They served as guidebooks for witches, offering them a vast array of spells and incantations to choose from based on their specific needs and intentions.

The spells and incantations in Babylonian witchcraft were not merely a collection of random words or actions. They were imbued with deep symbolism and carried spiritual significance. The words used in the spells were often archaic or in a special language, believed to possess inherent power and connect with divine forces. The formulas were structured in a rhythmic and repetitive manner, creating a mesmerizing effect that heightened the potency of the incantations.

The gestures and actions accompanying the recitation of spells were equally crucial. Witches would perform specific movements, such as waving their hands, touching certain parts of their bodies, or manipulating symbolic objects, to align their physical energy with the spiritual forces they were invoking. These gestures served as physical manifestations of intent and were believed to amplify the power of the spellcasting process.

Babylonian witches employed spells and incantations as dynamic tools of transformation. They held the belief that by accessing the supernatural through these ritualistic practices, they could influence the course of events, overcome obstacles, and bring about positive changes in their lives and the lives of those they served. The precise recitation of spells, combined with the performance of ritualistic actions, served as a conduit for channeling and directing the cosmic energies and spiritual forces necessary for manifesting the intended outcomes.

In summary, Babylonian witches possessed a profound understanding of spellcasting and the recitation of powerful incantations. They believed in the efficacy of specific words, formulas, and gestures to invoke supernatural forces and manifest desired outcomes. Spells were meticulously crafted and tailored to address specific intentions, drawing upon a rich repertoire of spells and incantations found in texts like the "Maqlû" series. Babylonian witches viewed spellcasting as a transformative practice, harnessing the inherent power within spells to shape their lives and the world around them.

✧   Symbolism and Symbolic Objects:

Symbolism held significant importance in Babylonian witchcraft, as witches utilized a variety of symbolic objects to enhance the potency of their magical practices. These objects, including amulets, talismans, and sacred plants, were believed to embody specific qualities, energies, and spiritual essences, infusing rituals and spells with deeper layers of meaning and intention.

Amulets were commonly employed by Babylonian witches as powerful symbols of protection and guidance. These small objects, often made of precious metals or gemstones, were believed to possess inherent spiritual properties that could ward off evil and bring good fortune. Amulets were carefully crafted and inscribed with mystical symbols or words of power, believed to activate their protective qualities. Wearing or carrying these amulets during rituals or daily life was thought to provide a constant connection to the spiritual realm and ensure the support and favor of the gods.

Talismans, similar to amulets, held symbolic significance in Babylonian witchcraft. These objects were specifically created or charged with magical energy to attract or manifest desired outcomes. Talismans could take various forms, such as engraved stones, engraved metal plates, or intricate symbols drawn on specific materials. Each talisman was selected or designed with intention, representing the desired qualities or intentions the witch sought to bring forth. By incorporating talismans into their magical practices, witches believed they could harness and amplify specific energies and intentions, directing them towards their desired goals.

Sacred plants and herbs were also integral to Babylonian witchcraft, as they carried potent symbolic associations and spiritual properties. Different plants were believed to possess unique qualities and powers, such as healing, protection, purification, or divination. Babylonian witches carefully selected and prepared these plants, incorporating them into their rituals, spells, and potions. The use of specific herbs symbolized the desired outcome or intention, and their inclusion added an extra layer of symbolism and effectiveness to the magical practices.

The symbolic objects used in Babylonian witchcraft served as tangible representations of deeper spiritual concepts and energies. They acted as focal points for the witch's intention, providing a physical connection between the mundane and the mystical realms. By utilizing these objects, witches believed they could tap into the inherent power and qualities they symbolized, harnessing them in their magical workings.

Furthermore, the incorporation of symbolism in Babylonian witchcraft allowed for a shared language and understanding among practitioners. Symbols carried cultural and religious significance, reflecting collective beliefs and practices. The use of specific symbols and objects within rituals and spells created a sense of continuity and shared understanding among Babylonian witches, fostering a sense of community and connection with their spiritual heritage.

In conclusion, symbolism played a crucial role in Babylonian witchcraft. Witches employed a range of symbolic objects, such as amulets, talismans, and sacred plants, to enhance the potency of their magical practices. These objects carried specific qualities, energies, and spiritual essences, embodying deeper layers of meaning and intention. The inclusion of symbolism allowed witches to tap into the spiritual realm, manifest desired outcomes, and establish a shared language and understanding within their community.

Beliefs and Worldview in Babylonian Witchcraft

Understanding the beliefs and worldview that underpinned Babylonian witchcraft is essential to grasp the cultural significance and spiritual foundations of this mystical tradition. This section explores the key beliefs and concepts that shaped Babylonian witchcraft.

✧   Connection with Deities and Spirits:

In Babylonian witchcraft, witches held a profound belief in their special connection with deities and spirits. They viewed themselves as intermediaries between the human and divine realms, possessing the ability to communicate with supernatural beings and access their powers and wisdom. This belief in their divine connection formed the basis for the witches' authority and the efficacy of their magical practices.

Babylonian witches believed that their unique spiritual bond allowed them to establish relationships with various deities and spirits. They regarded these supernatural beings as powerful allies and sought their guidance, assistance, and favor. Through rituals, invocations, and offerings, witches aimed to establish and maintain these spiritual alliances, recognizing the reciprocal nature of their relationship with the divine.

The belief in their connection with deities and spirits granted Babylonian witches access to divine knowledge and supernatural powers. They believed that through their rituals, spells, and incantations, they could tap into the energies and abilities of these celestial beings. By invoking specific deities associated with various aspects of life, such as fertility, love, or protection, witches sought their aid in fulfilling their intentions and desires.

The witches' connection with the divine also provided them with a source of guidance and insight. They turned to the gods for answers to important questions, seeking divinatory insights into the future or advice on personal matters. Divination techniques, such as interpreting omens, reading celestial signs, or conducting rituals, were employed to receive messages from the divine realm. The witches' belief in their ability to communicate with the supernatural realm allowed them to act as conduits for divine knowledge and to provide prophetic insights and counsel to those seeking guidance.

The special connection between Babylonian witches and the supernatural realm reinforced their authority within the community. They were regarded as individuals with privileged access to divine wisdom and powers, and their role as intermediaries between humans and deities bestowed upon them a position of respect and influence. The efficacy of their magical practices and the belief in their divine connection solidified their reputation as skilled practitioners and spiritual leaders.

Moreover, the belief in their connection with deities and spirits instilled a sense of purpose and responsibility within Babylonian witches. They recognized the importance of maintaining ethical conduct, as their actions not only affected individuals but also had repercussions in the divine realm. Witches understood that their role as intermediaries carried both privileges and obligations, requiring them to act with integrity, respect, and reverence for the sacredness of their craft.

In summary, Babylonian witches firmly believed in their special connection with deities and spirits. They saw themselves as intermediaries between the human and divine realms, capable of communicating with supernatural beings and accessing their powers and wisdom. This belief formed the foundation of their authority, efficacy in magical practices, and their role as spiritual guides. Through rituals, invocations, and offerings, witches sought divine guidance, invoked deities for assistance, and established spiritual alliances, recognizing the reciprocal nature of their relationship with the divine.

✧   Cosmic Order and Harmony:

Babylonian witchcraft operated within the understanding of a broader cosmic order and harmony. Witches perceived the universe as a vast and interconnected web of forces and energies, where humans, deities, and natural elements were intricately linked. Within this cosmic framework, maintaining balance and harmony was of utmost importance, and Babylonian witches played a vital role in upholding this cosmic order through their magical practices.

Witches recognized that disruptions in the cosmic balance could lead to various challenges, such as illness, misfortune, or disharmony within individuals and the community. Their aim was to rectify these disruptions and restore equilibrium by working in alignment with the cosmic forces. Witches believed that by harmonizing with the natural rhythms and energies of the universe, they could bring about positive changes and alleviate imbalances.

Spells and rituals formed an essential part of Babylonian witchcraft, serving as tools to restore cosmic harmony. These magical practices were meticulously crafted and performed with the intent of aligning individuals with the cosmic order and reestablishing their connection to the divine. Through invocations, gestures, and the recitation of spells, witches sought to activate the underlying forces that governed the universe.

Babylonian witches understood that their actions within the magical realm had a direct impact on the cosmic balance. They approached their craft with a deep sense of responsibility, recognizing that their role as mediators between humans and the divine required them to work in harmony with the natural and supernatural forces. By aligning themselves with the cosmic order, witches aimed to bring about positive transformations, not only for individuals but also for the greater cosmic framework.

Moreover, Babylonian witches viewed the natural elements as manifestations of the divine and integral parts of the cosmic order. They recognized the sacredness and power inherent in the earth, water, air, and fire, and incorporated these elements into their rituals and spells. By engaging with the natural world, witches sought to tap into its inherent energies and align themselves with the primal forces that governed the cosmos.

The belief in the interconnectedness of all beings and elements within the cosmic order also influenced the ethical dimension of Babylonian witchcraft. Witches understood that their actions had consequences not only for individuals but for the entire fabric of the universe. They practiced their craft with a deep reverence for the interconnectedness of all things, emphasizing the importance of acting responsibly, ethically, and in harmony with the cosmic balance.

In summary, Babylonian witchcraft operated within the framework of a broader cosmic order and harmony. Witches perceived the universe as an interconnected web of forces and energies, where humans, deities, and natural elements were intricately linked. They recognized the significance of maintaining balance and harmony within this cosmic framework and utilized spells and rituals to restore equilibrium and align individuals with the cosmic order. By working in harmony with the natural and supernatural forces, Babylonian witches sought to bring about positive transformations and uphold the sacred balance of the universe.

✧   Ethics and Responsibility:

Babylonian witches adhered to a set of ethical principles that guided their actions and underscored the responsibility that came with their craft. While their practices involved manipulating supernatural forces and harnessing magical powers, witches understood the need to wield their abilities responsibly, ethically, and in service of the greater good. They recognized that their actions had the potential to create significant impacts on individuals and the community, and they held themselves accountable for the consequences of their practices.

One of the key ethical principles upheld by Babylonian witches was the pursuit of the greater good. They recognized that their magical abilities granted them a certain level of influence and power, which they were expected to use in ways that benefited individuals and society as a whole. Witches understood that their role as mediators between humans and the divine required them to act with wisdom, compassion, and fairness, considering the well-being of others in their decisions and actions.

Babylonian witches also placed importance on considering the consequences of their magical practices. They understood that their actions had ripple effects that extended beyond immediate results. They carefully assessed the potential impacts of their spells, rituals, and incantations, taking into account the long-term implications for individuals and the community. Witches recognized the interconnectedness of all beings and elements within the cosmic order, and they aimed to ensure that their actions aligned with the greater balance and harmony of the universe.

Integrity and honesty were valued virtues in the ethical framework of Babylonian witchcraft. Witches were expected to conduct themselves with integrity, upholding truthfulness and sincerity in their interactions and practices. They recognized the importance of maintaining trust and credibility within their communities, and they approached their craft with a commitment to authenticity and transparency.

Babylonian witches also demonstrated respect for the autonomy and free will of individuals. They understood that while their magical abilities allowed them to influence certain outcomes, they should not impose their will upon others or manipulate their choices. Instead, they aimed to empower individuals with knowledge, guidance, and support, allowing them to make informed decisions and exercise their own agency.

Furthermore, Babylonian witches recognized the sacredness of life and the inherent value of all beings. They treated others with kindness, empathy, and compassion, embracing a sense of interconnectedness and fostering harmonious relationships within the community. They sought to uplift and support individuals, providing guidance, healing, and protection when needed.

In summary, Babylonian witches adhered to a set of ethical principles that guided their actions and underscored the responsibility that came with their craft. They recognized the need to wield their powers responsibly, ethically, and in service of the greater good. By considering the consequences of their actions, acting with integrity, respecting the autonomy of individuals, and demonstrating compassion and empathy, Babylonian witches aimed to uphold the highest ethical standards in their practices.

Examples, Problems, and Exercises:

Analyze a Babylonian ritual for healing and protection, identifying its key components and explaining their symbolic significance.

Research a specific Babylonian spell from the "Maqlû" series and discuss its purpose, incantations used, and the cultural context in which it was employed.

Engage in a group discussion on the ethical considerations in Babylonian witchcraft, examining the potential conflicts between personal desires and the greater good.

Create a hypothetical Babylonian ritual for a specific intention, incorporating symbolic objects and the recitation of incantations.

By immersing themselves in the practices and beliefs of Babylonian witchcraft, students will develop a comprehensive understanding of this ancient mystical tradition. Through analysis, research, and critical thinking exercises, they will gain insights into the rituals, spells, and worldview that shaped Babylonian witchcraft practices, fostering a deeper appreciation for its cultural significance and spiritual foundations.

Role of Witches in Babylonian Society

In the vibrant tapestry of ancient Babylonian society, witches occupied a unique and influential role. This section explores the multifaceted aspects of the witches' presence, shedding light on their social, religious, and cultural significance.

✧　　Social Perception and Status:

Witches in Babylonian society occupied a unique and multifaceted position, evoking a complex mix of reverence, fear, and curiosity among the populace. The perception of witches varied greatly across different social strata and was shaped by a range of factors, including their reputation, skills, and the specific role they played within the community.

For many individuals, witches were regarded with reverence and awe. Their perceived special connections to deities and supernatural forces elevated their status in society. Witches were seen as powerful figures who possessed knowledge and skills beyond the ordinary, allowing them to tap into hidden realms and manipulate cosmic energies. They were sought after for their ability to communicate with deities, provide spiritual guidance, and harness magical forces for the benefit of individuals and the community. As mediators between humans and the divine, witches held a unique position of influence and were often regarded as wise and respected figures.

However, alongside reverence, witches also evoked fear and suspicion in some segments of Babylonian society. The association of witchcraft with mystical practices and supernatural powers sometimes gave rise to concerns about potential malevolence or the misuse of magical abilities. Some individuals believed that witches had the capacity to inflict harm, manipulate fate, or invoke dark forces. These fears were often fueled by misconceptions, superstitions, and occasional instances of misuse of power by individuals claiming to be witches.

The perception of witches was not uniform across all social groups. Their status and reputation varied depending on factors such as their skills, knowledge, and the specific role they played within the community. Those who demonstrated a strong command over magical practices and were renowned for their wisdom and beneficial contributions often enjoyed a higher standing and greater respect. In contrast, individuals with questionable intentions or whose actions were seen as harmful or manipulative were likely to be viewed with suspicion or even ostracized.

The curiosity surrounding witches also played a significant role in the perception of their societal role. Their mysterious abilities and the enigmatic nature of their practices fueled intrigue and fascination among many individuals. The desire to understand the workings of the supernatural world and to seek guidance or assistance from witches contributed to their continued relevance and presence within Babylonian society.

In conclusion, witches in Babylonian society were regarded with a complex mix of reverence, fear, and curiosity. While some individuals held them in high esteem for their perceived connections to deities and supernatural forces, others approached them with suspicion and apprehension. The perception of witches varied across different social strata and was influenced by factors such as reputation, skills, and the specific role they played within the community.

✧   Religious and Spiritual Function:

Witches held an integral and revered place within the religious and spiritual landscape of ancient Babylon. As intermediaries between humans and the divine, they played a crucial role in facilitating communication with deities and spirits, bridging the gap between the mortal and supernatural realms. Their unique abilities and deep understanding of mystical practices made them sought after for their expertise in invoking supernatural forces, performing rituals, and providing spiritual guidance.

One of the primary functions of witches was to invoke and communicate with deities and spirits on behalf of individuals and the community. They possessed the knowledge and skills necessary to navigate the complexities of the supernatural realm, allowing them to establish connections with divine beings. Through various ritualistic practices, witches sought to establish a direct line of communication with the gods, seeking their guidance, blessings, and intervention in the lives of individuals or the affairs of the community.

The ability to perform rituals was a significant aspect of a witch's role. They conducted elaborate ceremonies, often accompanied by the recitation of spells, incantations, and the use of symbolic objects. These rituals were designed to invoke and channel the powers of the supernatural realm for specific purposes, such as fertility, protection, healing, or prosperity. Witches possessed the knowledge of sacred rites, invocations, and offerings that were believed to elicit a response from the divine forces and influence the desired outcomes.

In addition to their role as facilitators of communication, witches were revered for their spiritual guidance and wisdom. They offered counsel and advice to individuals seeking answers or solutions to personal or communal issues. Witches possessed profound understanding of the mystical and spiritual aspects of life, allowing them to navigate complex situations and provide insights into the workings of the supernatural realm. Their guidance was highly valued, as it was believed to be grounded in the profound knowledge and connection they had with the divine.

The services provided by witches were not limited to individual needs but extended to the betterment of the community as a whole. They were called upon to perform rituals for the benefit of society, such as ensuring favorable harvests, averting disasters, or seeking divine protection. Their presence and involvement in communal religious ceremonies and festivals reinforced the belief in their unique connection to the gods and their ability to influence the spiritual and physical well-being of the community.

In conclusion, witches held an integral place within Babylonian religious and spiritual practices. They served as intermediaries between humans and the divine, facilitating communication with deities and spirits. With their ability to invoke supernatural forces, perform rituals, and provide spiritual guidance, witches played a vital role in harnessing the powers of the supernatural realm for the betterment of individuals and the community. Their knowledge, skills, and connection to the divine were revered and sought after, making them central figures in the religious and spiritual fabric of ancient Babylon.

✦ Magical Practices and Services:

Babylonian witches possessed a vast repertoire of magical skills and offered a wide range of services to the society. Their expertise spanned different aspects of life, catering to the diverse needs of individuals and the community as a whole. Through their abilities in crafting and casting spells, divination, and performing rituals, witches became indispensable figures for those seeking solutions to their personal and societal concerns.

One of the essential services provided by witches was healing. Drawing upon their knowledge of medicinal herbs, incantations, and supernatural forces, they offered remedies and treatments for physical ailments. Babylonian witches possessed a deep understanding of the properties and uses of various plants, using them to restore health and well-being. By combining their knowledge of herbalism with magical rituals and incantations, they aimed to bring about healing on both the physical and spiritual levels.

Protection was another crucial area where witches excelled. They were sought after for their ability to ward off malevolent forces and provide safeguarding against harm. Through the use of amulets, talismans, and protective rituals, witches created a shield of spiritual defense for individuals and their households. Their expertise in protective magic offered reassurance and a sense of security to those who sought their services.

Divination played a significant role in the repertoire of Babylonian witches. Utilizing various divinatory tools and methods, such as reading omens, interpreting celestial signs, or consulting oracles, they provided prophetic insights and guidance into the future. Individuals turned to witches for knowledge about important decisions, impending events, or personal matters. By tapping into the supernatural realm, witches offered glimpses into the unseen, enabling individuals to make informed choices and navigate their lives with greater clarity.

Love spells and fertility rites were among the services sought from Babylonian witches. Whether it was attracting a desired partner, enhancing existing relationships, or seeking assistance in matters of conception and childbirth, witches were believed to possess the ability to influence matters of the heart and fertility. Through their magical practices, incantations, and rituals, they aimed to evoke and enhance the forces of love and fertility, providing individuals with hope and the prospect of fulfilling their desires.

Witches were consulted for both practical and spiritual needs, addressing a wide range of concerns within Babylonian society. Their expertise in influencing the natural and supernatural realms made them invaluable figures for individuals seeking assistance. By utilizing their knowledge and skills in spellcraft, divination, and ritual, witches offered a unique blend of practical and mystical solutions, catering to the multifaceted needs of their clientele.

In conclusion, Babylonian witches offered a wide range of magical services to society, encompassing areas such as healing, protection, divination, love spells, and fertility rites. Their expertise in crafting and casting spells, divining the future, and performing rituals made them highly sought after for both practical and spiritual matters. By tapping into the forces of the supernatural realm, witches provided individuals with solutions and guidance, addressing their personal and societal concerns. Their services played a crucial role in the fabric of Babylonian society, providing a means to navigate life's challenges and harness the powers of the unseen.

Witchcraft and Social Dynamics

Understanding the role of witches in Babylonian society necessitates examining their impact on social dynamics and power structures. This section delves into the social implications of witchcraft and the relationships between witches and other members of the community.

✧   Community Integration and Support:

Within Babylonian communities, witches held a unique position and enjoyed a certain level of integration and acceptance. They were regarded as sources of wisdom, guidance, and assistance, and their presence played a vital role in maintaining social cohesion and well-being. The abilities and services of witches were valued by the community, as they provided a sense of stability, security, and a connection to the supernatural realm.

One of the primary roles of witches was that of healers. Through their knowledge of medicinal herbs, spiritual practices, and magical rituals, they offered remedies and treatments for various physical and spiritual ailments. Their expertise in healing not only addressed the physical well-being of individuals but also provided emotional and spiritual comfort. By offering their services, witches became pillars of support, instilling faith in the restorative powers of the supernatural and providing solace to those facing health challenges.

Witches also played a crucial role in protection within their communities. Individuals sought their assistance in safeguarding themselves and their households from malevolent forces and negative energies. Through the use of amulets, talismans, and protective rituals, witches created a shield of spiritual defense, instilling a sense of security and well-being. Their presence and services reassured community members, fostering a sense of trust and reliance on the supernatural guardianship provided by witches.

Resolving conflicts and disputes was another area where witches contributed to the social cohesion of Babylonian communities. Their abilities to communicate with deities and channel divine wisdom allowed them to identify underlying causes of discord and propose solutions in alignment with the greater good. As impartial mediators, witches played a crucial role in restoring harmony and facilitating peaceful resolutions. Their guidance and interventions helped mend relationships, maintain social order, and ensure the overall well-being of the community.

The integration of witches within their communities was also fueled by the faith individuals placed in their abilities. People sought the assistance of witches in times of need, knowing that they possessed unique insights, skills, and connections to the supernatural realm. Witches were trusted as sources of wisdom and guidance, and their advice was sought for important decisions, personal matters, and even spiritual dilemmas. Their ability to tap into the forces beyond the physical realm provided individuals with a sense of hope, direction, and clarity in navigating life's challenges.

Overall, witches in Babylonian society played an integral role in maintaining social cohesion and offering support to their communities. Their position as sources of wisdom, guidance, and assistance allowed them to become trusted figures, revered for their abilities to heal, protect, and resolve conflicts. By bridging the gap between the human and supernatural realms, witches provided a sense of stability, security, and solace to individuals and the community as a whole. Their presence and services were instrumental in fostering faith in the supernatural, promoting a sense of unity, and ensuring the well-being of Babylonian society.

✧   Gender Dynamics and Empowerment:

The role of witches in Babylonian society held significant implications for gender dynamics, as it provided a distinct space for women to exercise agency, acquire knowledge, and exert influence. In a patriarchal society where women often faced limitations and societal expectations, witchcraft offered a unique avenue for women to transcend these boundaries and assert their power.

It is important to note that while the majority of witches were women, not all women were considered witches, and not all witches were women. Nevertheless, the association of witchcraft with women was prevalent in Babylonian society, and it contributed to the perception of women's inherent connection to the spiritual and supernatural realms.

Witchcraft provided women with a means to challenge traditional gender roles and participate in social and religious spheres on their own terms. Within the context of witchcraft, women gained access to knowledge and practices that were typically denied to them in other areas of society. They acquired specialized skills in spellcasting, divination, healing, and ritual performance, which bestowed them with a unique authority and influence.

The power and authority of witches stemmed from their ability to communicate with deities, invoke supernatural forces, and perform magical rituals. This spiritual connection granted them a level of autonomy and independence not afforded to many women in Babylonian society. By harnessing the forces of the supernatural, witches transcended societal expectations and assumed a role that was revered and respected.

The involvement of women in witchcraft challenged the established gender dynamics and provided them with a platform to shape their own narratives. Through their practice of witchcraft, women gained recognition for their knowledge, wisdom, and abilities. They emerged as leaders and experts in their communities, offering guidance, healing, and spiritual support.

Furthermore, the authority of witches extended beyond their immediate communities. They often served as advisors to rulers and played significant roles in religious ceremonies and rituals. Their involvement in these domains allowed them to exert influence and make their voices heard in spaces traditionally dominated by men.

While the empowerment and agency experienced by witches were notable, it is essential to recognize that the societal perception of witchcraft was complex and multifaceted. Some individuals viewed witches with reverence and respect for their unique powers, while others held them in suspicion or fear, associating their practices with malevolence and dark forces. The perception of witches varied across different social strata, and the specific reputation, skills, and role of the witch within the community influenced how they were regarded.

In summary, the role of witches in Babylonian society intersected with gender dynamics, providing women with a distinct avenue to exercise agency, acquire knowledge, and exert influence. By participating in witchcraft, women challenged traditional gender roles and gained access to a sphere of power and authority rooted in their connection to the spiritual and supernatural realms. This allowed them to transcend societal limitations and contribute to the social and religious fabric of Babylonian society.

Examples, Problems, and Exercises:

Research and discuss the role of witches in specific Babylonian religious rituals, highlighting the significance of their presence and the functions they performed.

Analyze a mythological account or narrative involving witches in Babylonian literature, exploring their portrayal and the insights it provides into their societal role.

Engage in a group discussion on the potential conflicts and tensions that may have arisen between witches and other members of Babylonian society, considering differing perspectives and social hierarchies.

Create a role-play scenario where students assume the roles of different members of Babylonian society, exploring their interactions with witches and the implications for power dynamics and social relationships.

By examining the role of witches in Babylonian society, students will gain a nuanced understanding of the complex dynamics between witches and the community. Through analysis, research, and engaging exercises, they will explore the social, religious, and gender dimensions of witchcraft, fostering critical thinking and a deeper appreciation for the diverse roles witches played in ancient Babylonian society.

Examples of Babylonian Witchcraft Rituals and Spells

✧　The Ritual of Healing:

In Babylonian society, witches were highly sought after for their expertise in healing. One example of a witchcraft ritual for healing involved the use of incantations, herbal remedies, and ritualistic gestures. The witch would invoke specific deities associated with healing, such as Ea or Marduk, and recite spells to cleanse the body of ailments and restore health. The ritual often incorporated the burning of aromatic herbs and the use of sacred objects to enhance the effectiveness of the healing process.

To perform a healing ritual influenced by Babylonian witchcraft, you will need the following items:

A quiet and comfortable space: Find a calm and peaceful area where you can focus your energy and engage in the ritual undisturbed.

Incense or aromatic herbs: Select fragrant herbs or incense known for their healing properties, such as lavender, eucalyptus, or rosemary. These will be used for their aromatic qualities and symbolic significance.

Sacred objects: Choose objects that hold personal meaning or symbolism for you, such as crystals, stones, or amulets, to enhance the ritual's sacredness and provide a connection to the spiritual realm.

Candle(s): Select a candle that represents healing energy, such as a blue or green candle. This will serve as a focal point during the ritual.

A written invocation or prayer: Prepare a heartfelt invocation or prayer that expresses your intention for healing and calls upon the assistance of specific healing deities or energies. Adapt this invocation to your personal beliefs and the deities or energies you resonate with.

Optional: Additional tools and materials, such as a small bowl of water, feathers, or a healing symbol that holds personal significance.

Once you have gathered the necessary items, follow these steps:

Begin by cleansing the space: Light the incense or herbs and walk around the area, allowing the fragrant smoke to purify the space energetically. Visualize any stagnant or negative energy being dispelled and replaced with pure, healing energy.

Set up your altar: Arrange your sacred objects, candle(s), and any additional items on a small table or altar in front of you. Create a sacred space that feels sacred and conducive to your healing intention.

Center yourself: Take a few deep breaths, grounding yourself in the present moment. Allow any distractions or tension to fade away as you focus your attention on the healing ritual.

Light the candle(s): As you light the candle, visualize the flame as a source of healing energy, radiating warmth and light.

Invoke the healing deities or energies: Recite your written invocation or prayer, calling upon the specific healing deities or energies you resonate with. Speak from the heart, expressing your intention for healing and seeking their guidance and assistance.

Engage in ritualistic gestures: Incorporate ritualistic gestures, such as gently waving your hands over the sacred objects or passing them through the incense smoke, to infuse them with your intentions and connect with the healing energy present.

State your healing affirmations: Speak affirmations or healing statements aloud, affirming your desire for health and well-being. Use positive language and visualize yourself being bathed in healing light or experiencing a state of vibrant health.

Meditate and visualize: Close your eyes and enter a meditative state. Visualize yourself surrounded by healing energy, experiencing a profound sense of well-being and restoration. See any ailments or imbalances being cleansed and transformed into health and vitality.

Express gratitude and conclude the ritual: Express gratitude to the healing deities or energies, acknowledging their presence and assistance. Thank them for their guidance and support throughout the ritual. Blow out the candle(s) to signify the conclusion of the ritual.

Remember, this adapted ritual draws inspiration from Babylonian witchcraft practices and is intended for personal healing purposes.

✧   The Spell of Protection:

Babylonian witches were known for their ability to provide protection against malevolent forces and ward off evil spirits. One commonly used spell of protection involved the creation of amulets or talismans infused with magical symbols and inscriptions. These objects were believed to possess the power to repel negative energies and provide a shield of safety. The witch would recite incantations and perform rituals to imbue the amulet with protective energies, ensuring the well-being and security of the individual seeking protection.

To perform a protection spell influenced by Babylonian witchcraft, you will need the following items:

A quiet and comfortable space: Find a serene location where you can focus your energy and perform the ritual without interruptions.

Amulet or talisman: Choose a protective object that holds personal significance to you, such as a pendant, stone, or symbol. Select an item that resonates with the intention of protection and acts as a physical representation of your shield against negative energies.

Symbols or inscriptions: Research symbols and inscriptions associated with protection in Babylonian culture or other traditions that resonate with you. Consider using sigils, runes, or sacred geometries that hold protective qualities. You can draw or inscribe these symbols on your amulet or have them ready for visualization.

Candle(s): Select a candle that represents protection, such as a white or black candle. This will serve as a focal point during the spell.

Written incantation or prayer: Prepare a written incantation or prayer that affirms your intention for protection and invokes the assistance of specific protective deities or energies. Adapt the incantation or prayer to your personal beliefs and the deities or energies you feel a connection to.

Optional: Additional tools and materials, such as sacred herbs or oils for purification, a small bowl of salt or protective crystals, or a piece of fabric to wrap your amulet.

Once you have gathered the necessary items, follow these steps:

Cleanse the space: Begin by purifying the space. Light the candle(s) and pass the amulet through the flame or hold it over the smoke of cleansing herbs, envisioning any negative or harmful energies being dispelled.

Set up your altar: Arrange your candle(s), amulet, and any additional tools on a small table or altar. Create a sacred space that feels appropriate for your protection spell.

Center yourself: Take a few moments to calm your mind and focus your intention. Take deep breaths and visualize a sphere of protective light surrounding you.

Light the candle(s): As you light the candle(s), visualize the flame as a source of divine protection, casting a warm and radiant shield around you.

Invoke protective deities or energies: Recite your written incantation or prayer, calling upon the specific protective deities or energies you resonate with. Speak with confidence and conviction, expressing your desire for strong and effective protection.

Empower the amulet: Hold the amulet in your hands, focusing your attention on its significance as a protective object. Visualize it radiating with a bright, impenetrable light. You may choose to recite the incantation or prayer again, directing the energy into the amulet.

Visualize the shield of protection: Close your eyes and envision a powerful shield of energy surrounding you. See it as a barrier that repels negative influences and keeps you safe. Visualize the amulet acting as a focal point, amplifying and extending the protective energy.

Affirm your protection: State affirmations aloud that affirm your intention for protection. Use positive language and visualize yourself moving through life shielded from harm and negativity. Express gratitude for the protection that surrounds you.

Conclude the ritual: Express gratitude to the protective deities or energies, acknowledging their presence and assistance. Thank them for their support and the shield of protection they have provided. Blow out the candle(s) to signify the conclusion of the ritual.

✧   The Divination Ritual:

Divination was a prominent practice in Babylonian witchcraft, aiming to gain insights into the future or understand divine intentions. One example of a divination ritual involved the use of a specific divination tool, such as a clay tablet inscribed with symbols or a set of engraved bones or stones. The witch would concentrate her focus, invoke the assistance of a deity associated with divination, and cast or interpret the symbols on the chosen medium. Through the interpretation of these symbols, the witch would reveal hidden knowledge and provide guidance to individuals seeking answers or making important decisions.

Divination tool: Choose a divination tool that resonates with you. This could be a deck of tarot cards, a set of runes, a scrying mirror or bowl, or any other tool commonly used for divination. Select a tool that you feel a connection to and that aligns with your personal beliefs.

Sacred space: Find a quiet and comfortable space where you can focus your energy and perform the ritual without interruptions. Set up a small altar or designated area where you can place your divination tool and create a sacred atmosphere.

Candle(s): Select a candle(s) that represents divination and intuition, such as a purple or white candle. This will serve as a focal point during the ritual and provide a calming ambiance.

Written invocation or prayer: Prepare a written invocation or prayer that calls upon the assistance of a deity or higher power associated with divination. Adapt the invocation or prayer to your personal beliefs and the specific deity or energy you wish to invoke.

Optional: Additional tools, such as a cloth to lay out your divination tool, crystals or herbs known for their divinatory properties, or a journal to record your insights and interpretations.

Once you have gathered the necessary items, follow these steps:

Cleanse the space: Begin by purifying the space. Light the candle(s) and use cleansing herbs or incense to cleanse the area. Pass your divination tool through the smoke or hold it above the flame, envisioning any negative or stagnant energies being cleared away.

Set up your altar: Arrange your candle(s), divination tool, and any additional tools on your altar or sacred space. Create an atmosphere that feels conducive to divination and introspection.

Center yourself: Take a few moments to ground yourself and quiet your mind. Take deep breaths, allowing yourself to enter a state of calm focus.

Invoke the divine: Recite your written invocation or prayer, calling upon the deity or higher power associated with divination. Request their guidance, wisdom, and insight as you embark on the divination ritual.

Connect with your divination tool: Hold your divination tool in your hands, feeling its energy and connecting with its symbolism. Set your intention to receive clear and accurate messages during the divination process. You may choose to recite the invocation or prayer again, directing your focus towards the divination tool.

Perform the divination: Follow the specific method of divination associated with your chosen tool. This could involve shuffling and drawing cards, casting runes or stones, scrying into a mirror or bowl, or any other divinatory practice you have chosen. Focus your attention, ask your question or seek guidance, and interpret the symbols or messages that come forth.

Record your insights: Keep a journal nearby to record your divination results, insights, and interpretations. This will allow you to reflect on the messages received and track any patterns or developments over time.

Express gratitude: Once you have completed the divination, express gratitude to the deity or higher power you invoked for their guidance and assistance. Thank them for the messages and insights received. Blow out the candle(s) to signify the conclusion of the ritual.

Chapter 3: Divination in Ancient Babylon

Divination, the practice of seeking knowledge of the future or understanding divine will, held significant importance in the ancient civilization of Babylon. From the observation of celestial bodies to the interpretation of symbols and signs, the Babylonians developed intricate methods and systems to gain insights into the unknown. This chapter delves into the fascinating realm of divination in ancient Babylon, exploring its cultural significance, prevalent methods, and the role of diviners in Babylonian society.

Chapter Overview:

The Cultural Significance of Divination

 ✧   The Divinatory Tradition in Babylonian Society

Divination played a central role in the religious, social, and political fabric of Babylonian society.

It was viewed as a means of connecting with the gods, seeking their guidance, and aligning human actions with divine will.

Divination provided a sense of reassurance, stability, and direction in the face of uncertainty and the unpredictability of life.

 ■   The Divine Realm and Human Destiny

The Babylonians believed that the gods held the power to shape human destiny.

Divination served as a bridge between the divine realm and mortal existence, allowing individuals to gain insight into their future and make informed decisions.

The belief in predetermined fate, influenced by divine forces, underscored the significance of divination in shaping personal and collective actions.

Methods and Practices of Divination

 ✧   Celestial Divination: The Observation of Celestial Phenomena

Babylonian astronomers meticulously observed celestial bodies, including the sun, moon, planets, and stars, to discern messages from the gods.

The movements, positions, and interactions of celestial bodies were interpreted as signs of divine intent and held clues about future events.

Astrological systems, such as omen lists and celestial calendars, were developed to aid in the interpretation of celestial phenomena.

✦　　Augury and Omens: Reading Signs in the Natural World

The Babylonians placed great importance on signs and omens observed in the natural world.

Diviners closely observed animal behavior, weather patterns, and various natural phenomena to interpret messages from the gods.

A comprehensive system of omen interpretation, encompassing thousands of recorded signs, enabled diviners to provide insights into the future based on these observations.

✦　　Divinatory Rituals and Oracle Consultation

Divination rituals were conducted by skilled diviners, who employed specific rituals and techniques to invoke the gods' presence and receive guidance.

Oracle consultation involved seeking divine responses through direct communication with deities or their representatives, such as priests or priestesses.

These rituals often included the use of sacred objects, incantations, and offerings to establish a spiritual connection and receive divine messages.

The Role of Diviners in Babylonian Society

✦　　The Expertise of Diviners

Diviners were highly respected members of Babylonian society, esteemed for their specialized knowledge and skills.

They possessed extensive training and experience in various divination techniques, ensuring accuracy and reliability in their readings.

Diviners served as intermediaries between the divine and human realms, providing counsel, predictions, and guidance to individuals, communities, and even rulers.

✦　　Divination in Decision-Making and Governance

Divination played a crucial role in important decision-making processes, both on a personal and societal level.

Rulers sought divinatory guidance before engaging in military campaigns, initiating construction projects, or making significant policy decisions.

Divination offered legitimacy to rulers' actions, as they could claim divine sanction for their choices based on the insights provided by diviners.

Conclusion:

The study of divination in ancient Babylon offers a captivating glimpse into the cultural and spiritual practices of this ancient civilization. From celestial observations to the interpretation of omens, divination was deeply ingrained in the fabric of Babylonian society. The methods and rituals employed by diviners allowed individuals to seek guidance, gain insight, and navigate the complexities of life. In the following chapters, we will explore specific divination practices in greater detail, enabling a comprehensive understanding of the rich and diverse world of Babylonian divination.

Examples, Problems, and Exercises:

Example: Read and interpret a Babylonian omen from a translated text, discussing its potential implications and significance.

Problem: Analyze the impact of divination on decision-making in Babylonian society, highlighting specific examples from historical records.

Exercise: Create a personal divination ritual inspired by Babylonian practices, incorporating symbols, gestures, and invocations to seek guidance for a specific question or situation. Reflect on your experience and compare it to historical divination methods.

The Importance of Divination in Babylonian Culture

Divination, the practice of seeking knowledge of the future or understanding divine will, held profound significance in the ancient civilization of Babylon. Rooted in their rich religious and spiritual beliefs, divination permeated various aspects of Babylonian culture, influencing social, political, and personal spheres. In this chapter, we delve into the importance of divination in Babylonian culture, exploring its role in shaping their worldview, maintaining societal order, and establishing connections with the divine.

Divination as a Tool for Understanding the Gods' Will

✧   The Babylonian Cosmology and Divine Order

In order to fully grasp the significance of divination in Babylonian culture, it is essential to delve into their cosmological beliefs and the divine order that governed their worldview. Babylonians envisioned a complex cosmology where gods and goddesses played pivotal roles in shaping the natural and supernatural realms. Through divination, individuals sought to understand the will and intentions of these deities, enabling them to align their actions with the larger divine plan.

According to Babylonian cosmology, the universe was comprised of multiple interconnected layers. At the center of this cosmic structure was Babylon itself, considered the earthly dwelling place of the gods. Surrounding the city were the heavens, which housed the celestial deities responsible for various celestial phenomena, such as the movement of the stars, the changing seasons, and the celestial omens. Below the earth, an underworld known as the "netherworld" existed, where the spirits of the deceased resided.

Babylonians believed that each aspect of the natural world, such as the rivers, mountains, and forests, was under the dominion of a specific deity or goddess. For instance, Enlil, the god of wind and storms, governed the skies and controlled the elements, while Ea, the god of wisdom, presided over the waters. This divine hierarchy extended to every facet of existence, ensuring order and balance in the universe.

Divination played a crucial role in the Babylonian understanding of the divine order. Through divinatory practices, individuals sought to gain insights into the will and intentions of the gods, allowing them to navigate their lives in accordance with the divine plan. Babylonians believed that the gods communicated their desires and intentions through various signs and omens, which could be interpreted through the practice of divination.

The Babylonians utilized a diverse range of divination methods to discern the messages of the gods. These methods included observing the movements of celestial bodies, such as the position of the stars and planets, as well as interpreting the behavior of animals, such as birds or sacrificial animals. Additionally, they also relied on intricate rituals and the interpretation of symbols and dreams.

By consulting diviners, individuals sought guidance and advice on matters such as marriage, childbirth, illness, and warfare. Divination allowed them to understand the divine will and make decisions that were in alignment with the larger cosmic order. It was believed that by adhering to the divine plan, individuals could ensure their well-being and success in life.

In conclusion, the Babylonian cosmology and divine order provided the foundation for their beliefs and practices surrounding divination. The complex hierarchy of gods and goddesses that governed the various realms of existence was believed to be accessible through divination. By understanding the will of the gods, individuals could align their actions and choices with the larger cosmic plan. Divination served as a means to seek guidance and navigate life in harmony with the divine order, offering a profound sense of purpose and connection to the gods.

Examples, Problems, and Exercises:

Example: Analyze a Babylonian divination tablet that depicts celestial omens, discussing its significance in relation to the Babylonian cosmology and divine order.

Problem: Compare and contrast the Babylonian cosmology with the cosmologies of other ancient civilizations, such as the Egyptian or Greek cosmologies, highlighting the unique features of each system and their implications for divination practices.

Exercise: Create a visual representation, such as a diagram or illustration, that depicts the Babylonian cosmology and the hierarchy of gods and goddesses. Explain the significance of each deity and their role in maintaining the divine order.

✦ Communication with the Divine Realm

One of the primary functions of divination in ancient Babylonian culture was to establish a means of communication between mortals and the gods. Divination served as a channel through which individuals sought answers, guidance, and blessings from the divine realm. By engaging in divinatory practices, Babylonians believed they could gain profound insights into their own lives, predict significant events, and effectively navigate the challenges they encountered.

In Babylonian society, the gods were considered the ultimate authorities and arbiters of human fate. They held immense power and wisdom, and their influence extended over all aspects of life. However, direct communication with the gods was not easily accessible to ordinary individuals. Divination, therefore, played a crucial role in bridging the gap between mortals and the divine, providing a means for humans to connect with the gods and seek their guidance.

Through divination, individuals believed they could access the knowledge and intentions of the gods. Divinatory practices aimed to interpret the signs and symbols believed to be sent by the deities, enabling mortals to gain insight into the divine plan. By understanding the messages conveyed through these signs, individuals could align their actions and decisions with the divine will, thus ensuring their well-being and success.

Babylonians employed a variety of divinatory methods to communicate with the divine realm. These methods included celestial divination, where the movements and positions of celestial bodies were observed to determine their significance; extispicy, which involved examining the entrails of sacrificed animals to interpret omens; and the interpretation of dreams, where visions during sleep were considered divine messages. Additionally, diviners specialized in specific divination techniques and acted as intermediaries between the mortal and divine realms, providing interpretations and guidance to those seeking divine insight.

By engaging in divination, individuals sought answers to their most pressing questions and concerns. They sought to understand the gods' desires and intentions, predict future events, receive advice on important decisions, and seek divine intervention in times of crisis. Divination provided a sense of security and empowerment, as it allowed mortals to actively participate in the unfolding of their destinies and seek divine favor.

Furthermore, divination rituals often involved making offerings, reciting prayers, and performing specific actions to invoke the gods' presence and establish a sacred atmosphere conducive to communication. These rituals were designed to show reverence and respect to the deities, creating a connection and fostering a reciprocal relationship between humans and the divine.

In conclusion, divination in ancient Babylon served as a vital means of communication with the divine realm. Through divinatory practices, individuals sought answers, guidance, and blessings from the gods. By interpreting signs, symbols, and omens, mortals gained insight into the divine plan and aligned their actions with the will of the gods. Divination provided a sense of connection and empowerment, allowing individuals to actively participate in shaping their lives and seeking divine intervention when needed.

Examples, Problems, and Exercises:

Example: Analyze a specific divinatory text from ancient Babylon, such as an extispicy report or a celestial omens tablet, discussing its role in facilitating communication with the divine realm.

Problem: Compare and contrast the methods of communication with the divine realm in ancient Babylon with those in other ancient civilizations, such as ancient Egypt or Greece, highlighting the similarities and differences in their approaches.

Exercise: Engage in a divination practice inspired by ancient Babylonian techniques, such as casting lots, scrying, or interpreting dream symbols. Reflect on your experience and discuss how it enhanced your understanding of communication with the divine realm.

Divination and Personal Decision-Making

✧   Divination as a Source of Guidance

Divination played a crucial role in the lives of the Babylonians, serving as a trusted source of guidance when making important decisions. Individuals sought divination to gain insights and clarity regarding various aspects of their lives, such as relationships, health, and career paths. By consulting the divine through divination, Babylonians believed they could make informed choices and select the most favorable courses of action.

In Babylonian society, life was filled with uncertainties, and individuals faced numerous challenges and dilemmas. Whether it was choosing a suitable partner for marriage, deciding on a career path, or seeking solutions to personal or societal issues, divination offered a means to navigate these complexities. Divinatory practices provided a glimpse into the hidden forces and influences at play, allowing individuals to access information beyond their immediate perception and rational understanding.

When seeking guidance through divination, Babylonians approached the process with reverence and respect. They recognized that the insights gained were not mere coincidence or chance but were messages from the divine realm. Divination rituals were often performed with the assistance of skilled diviners who possessed deep knowledge and expertise in interpreting signs and symbols.

Through divination, individuals received guidance that helped them make informed decisions. For example, in matters of relationships, divination could offer insight into compatibility, potential challenges, and long-term prospects. This knowledge empowered individuals to choose partners wisely and build harmonious relationships. In the realm of health, divination could provide indications of potential illnesses or offer guidance on preventive measures and suitable remedies. Divination also guided individuals in career choices, helping them identify fields of work where their talents and passions would flourish.

One common divination method in Babylonian culture was the interpretation of celestial omens. Observing the movements and positions of celestial bodies, such as the moon, sun, and planets, allowed Babylonians to discern patterns and interpret their significance. These celestial signs were believed to hold profound meaning and were consulted to gain guidance and understanding.

Divination rituals were often accompanied by specific prayers, offerings, and ritualistic gestures. By engaging in these practices, individuals created a sacred atmosphere conducive to receiving divine guidance. The process of divination itself was seen as a dialogue with the gods, wherein individuals presented their questions and concerns, seeking answers and advice. The insights received through divination provided a sense of direction and confidence, guiding individuals towards the most favorable paths and outcomes.

Examples, Problems, and Exercises:

Example: Analyze a specific divinatory text from ancient Babylon, focusing on how it provided guidance and influenced decision-making in a particular context, such as marriage or career choices.

Problem: Explore the ethical implications of relying on divination as a source of guidance. Discuss potential drawbacks and limitations of divination and consider alternative approaches to decision-making.

Exercise: Engage in a divination practice, such as using a tarot deck, casting runes, or interpreting dream symbols. Reflect on the guidance received and how it influenced your decision-making process. Discuss the role of intuition and rationality in divination-based decision-making.

✧ Divination and Personal Accountability

In Babylonian culture, the concept of personal accountability was deeply ingrained in their worldview. They believed that individual choices, actions, and behaviors played a significant role in shaping one's destiny. Divination, as a tool for seeking guidance and insight, served not only as a means to gain foresight into future events but also as a reminder of personal accountability in the face of those events.

The Babylonians understood that divination was not a means to control or manipulate fate but rather a way to navigate the complex web of cause and effect. They recognized that while certain events may be influenced by external factors or divine will, personal decisions and actions could greatly impact the outcomes. Divination allowed individuals to assess the potential consequences of their choices, enabling them to take responsibility for shaping their own fate.

By engaging in divination practices, Babylonians actively sought to understand the possible outcomes of their actions. They sought insights from the divine realm to gauge the repercussions of their decisions and adjust their course of action accordingly. Divination provided a valuable opportunity for individuals to reflect on the alignment of their intentions and behaviors with their desired outcomes.

The divinatory process itself prompted individuals to consider the ethical and moral implications of their actions. It encouraged them to think critically about the potential consequences that their choices could have on themselves and others. Divination acted as a moral compass, reminding individuals of the interconnectedness of their lives and the responsibility they held in shaping their own destiny.

Babylonians recognized that divination was not a substitute for personal agency and responsibility but rather a tool to support informed decision-making. It encouraged individuals to reflect on their own motivations, intentions, and values before taking action. The insights gained through divination were meant to guide individuals towards choices that aligned with their higher purpose and contributed to their overall well-being and the well-being of the community.

The practice of divination also fostered a sense of humility and acceptance of the limitations of human knowledge. It served as a reminder that despite one's best efforts to foresee the future, there would always be unknown factors and unexpected circumstances. Divination encouraged individuals to approach life with openness and adaptability, recognizing that personal accountability also meant being responsive and flexible in the face of unforeseen events.

Examples, Problems, and Exercises:

Example: Explore a specific divinatory text or practice in Babylonian culture that emphasizes personal accountability. Analyze how the guidance provided in the context of this practice encourages individuals to take responsibility for their choices and actions.

Problem: Discuss the potential challenges in balancing personal accountability and the recognition of external factors in shaping one's destiny. How can divination help individuals navigate this balance?

Exercise: Reflect on a recent decision or action you have taken. Use divination (e.g., tarot cards, a pendulum, or scrying) to gain insights into the potential outcomes and consequences of your choice. Consider how this exercise influences your sense of personal accountability and your willingness to take responsibility for shaping your own destiny.

Divination and Societal Order

✧   Divination in the Political Realm

Divination played a significant role in the political sphere of ancient Babylon. Rulers and leaders turned to divination as a means to seek guidance and validation for their decisions regarding matters of state, including war, governance, and alliances. The practice of divination in the political realm added an element of legitimacy to the rulers' actions, as they could claim divine approval based on the insights received from the gods.

In Babylonian society, the rulers were regarded as intermediaries between the divine and the mortal realms. They were believed to have a special connection with the gods, granting them access to divine wisdom and guidance. As such, it was expected that rulers would consult with diviners and engage in divinatory practices before making important political decisions.

One common form of political divination in Babylon was the interpretation of celestial omens. Babylonians observed the movements of celestial bodies, such as the positions of the stars, planets, and comets, as well as atmospheric phenomena like thunder and lightning. These celestial events were believed to carry messages from the gods, indicating their favor or disapproval of certain actions or events.

Babylonian rulers would consult with skilled diviners who were well-versed in the interpretation of celestial omens. These diviners would carefully analyze the patterns and alignments of celestial phenomena and provide guidance on the political course of action that would be most favorable. By heeding the insights gained through divination, rulers sought to align their decisions with the will of the gods and ensure divine support for their political endeavors.

The consultation of divination in the political realm also served as a means to mitigate risks and anticipate potential challenges. By seeking divine guidance, rulers aimed to foresee potential outcomes and make informed choices that would lead to successful outcomes. Divination offered a glimpse into the possible consequences of political actions, enabling rulers to adjust their strategies and policies accordingly.

Moreover, the use of divination in political decision-making helped to reinforce the rulers' authority and establish their legitimacy in the eyes of the people. By claiming divine approval and support for their actions, rulers could assert their right to govern and solidify their position as the rightful leaders of the realm. The insights gained through divination were seen as a validation of their rule, strengthening their political authority and ensuring the loyalty of their subjects.

However, it is important to note that the interpretation of divinatory messages was not always straightforward. Different diviners might offer varying interpretations of celestial omens or other divination methods, leading to conflicting advice. This created space for political manipulation and the potential for rulers to selectively choose interpretations that aligned with their own agendas. Thus, while divination added legitimacy to rulers' decisions, it was not immune to political influence and manipulation.

Examples, Problems, and Exercises:

Example: Explore a specific historical event in ancient Babylon where the consultation of divination had a significant impact on political decision-making. Analyze the role of divination in shaping the outcome of that event and its implications for the rulers' legitimacy.

Problem: Discuss the potential ethical dilemmas that may arise when rulers heavily rely on divination for political decision-making. How can the interpretation of divinatory messages be influenced by personal biases or political agendas?

Exercise: Imagine you are a ruler in ancient Babylon facing a critical political decision. Engage in a divination practice, such as consulting the positions of the stars or using a divinatory tool, to gain insights into the potential outcomes of different courses of action. Reflect on how this exercise influences your decision-making process and your understanding of the role of divination in political governance.

✧   Divination and Social Cohesion

In ancient Babylonian society, divination served as a powerful tool for maintaining social cohesion and resolving conflicts. The practice of seeking divine guidance through divination allowed individuals and communities to find resolutions that aligned with the will of the gods, fostering a sense of collective purpose and unity.

One of the key ways in which divination contributed to social cohesion was by providing a shared framework of beliefs and values. The Babylonians believed that the gods played an active role in human affairs and that their will could be discerned through divination. This shared belief system created a sense of common understanding and purpose among the members of society, as they all recognized the importance of seeking divine guidance in decision-making.

When conflicts or disagreements arose within the community, divination offered a means to reach resolutions that were perceived as fair and just. By turning to the gods for guidance, individuals and communities could transcend personal biases and preferences and instead prioritize the divine will. Divination helped to shift the focus from individual interests to the greater good of the community, promoting cooperation and cooperation and fostering a sense of social harmony.

One example of how divination contributed to social cohesion was through its role in mediating disputes. When conflicts arose between individuals or groups, they could seek the assistance of diviners to help resolve the issue. The diviners would employ various divination methods, such as casting lots, interpreting dreams, or consulting oracles, to gain insights into the underlying causes of the conflict and propose potential solutions. By considering the divine guidance received through divination, the parties involved could find a resolution that was perceived as just and acceptable to all.

Divination also played a role in maintaining social order by providing a means of addressing grievances and ensuring accountability. In cases where individuals committed offenses or violated social norms, divination could be used to determine the appropriate actions or punishments. By consulting the gods, the community could ascertain the divine judgment and implement measures that were believed to be in line with the gods' will. This helped to prevent vigilante justice and promote a sense of fairness and justice within the society.

Furthermore, the act of seeking divine guidance through divination fostered a sense of collective responsibility and unity. It encouraged individuals to consider the well-being of the community as a whole and make decisions that were in the best interest of all. The belief that the gods' will was accessible through divination created a shared sense of purpose and a commitment to working together for the greater good.

However, it is important to note that divination was not always a perfect solution and could still be subject to human interpretation and biases. Different diviners might offer varying interpretations of the divine messages, leading to potential disagreements and challenges in reaching consensus. Additionally, the selective use of divination by those in positions of power could be used to manipulate or justify certain actions, potentially undermining the ideals of social cohesion and justice.

Examples, Problems, and Exercises:

Example: Explore a historical case in ancient Babylon where the practice of divination played a pivotal role in resolving a significant conflict within the community. Analyze how the consultation of divine guidance through divination contributed to social cohesion and the restoration of harmony.

Problem: Discuss the potential challenges and limitations of using divination as a means of conflict resolution in a society. How can personal biases or the interpretation of divinatory messages impact the fairness and effectiveness of the process?

Exercise: Imagine you are part of a community in ancient Babylon facing a divisive issue. Engage in a simulated divination practice, such as casting lots or consulting an oracle, to seek divine guidance for resolving the conflict. Reflect on how this exercise influences your perception of the issue and your willingness to work towards a collective resolution.

Conclusion:

Divination held a central position in Babylonian culture, shaping their worldview, decision-making processes, and interactions with the divine. The Babylonians firmly believed in the power of divination to provide insights, guidance, and a sense of order in an often unpredictable world. As we explore the various forms of divination practiced in ancient Babylon, we will gain a deeper appreciation for its profound influence on their society and the enduring legacy of their divinatory traditions.

Examples, Problems, and Exercises:

Example: Analyze a Babylonian divination text, discussing its cultural context, purpose, and methods used to gain insights.

Problem: Compare and contrast the role of divination in Babylonian culture with divination practices in other ancient civilizations, such as ancient Egypt or ancient Greece.

Exercise: Design a divination ceremony inspired by Babylonian practices, incorporating elements of ritual, symbolism, and the invocation of deities. Reflect on your experience and discuss the potential meanings and implications of the insights gained.

Divination Methods and Techniques

Divination, the practice of seeking divine guidance to gain insight into the unknown or the future, encompasses a wide array of methods and techniques. In ancient Babylon, various divination methods were employed, each offering a unique approach to connecting with the gods and receiving their messages. Let us explore some of the prominent divination methods and techniques used in Babylonian society.

✧   Astrology:

Astrology, a divination method deeply rooted in ancient Babylonian culture, holds a prominent place in the study of cosmic influences on human affairs. In Babylonian society, skilled astrologers closely observed and interpreted the movements and positions of celestial bodies, attributing profound meaning to their configurations. This chapter will delve into the intricate world of astrology, exploring its principles, techniques, and the significance it held in ancient Babylonian society.

Historical Context:

To understand the origins of astrology, it is essential to explore the rich historical context of ancient Babylon. Dating back to the 2nd millennium BCE, the Babylonians were pioneers in developing a systematic approach to celestial observation and interpretation. Through their meticulous observations of the heavens, they identified patterns and established a comprehensive system of astrology that would later influence numerous cultures and civilizations.

Foundations of Astrology:

A. Celestial Bodies and Their Significance:

The Babylonians regarded celestial bodies as powerful entities with significant influence over human existence. They observed the movements and positions of these celestial bodies and developed a comprehensive understanding of their symbolic meanings and effects on individuals and society as a whole.

The Sun:

The sun, in Babylonian astrology, occupied a position of immense importance and symbolized various aspects related to vitality, life force, and leadership. It was considered a powerful celestial body that represented the divine spark within individuals and held significant influence over their lives.

In Babylonian cosmology, the sun was associated with the source of life and illumination. It was revered as a symbol of warmth, light, and energy, essential for the growth and sustenance of all living beings. The sun's presence in the sky was perceived as a daily reminder of the divine order and the cyclical nature of life.

Within the framework of astrology, the position of the sun in an individual's birth chart was a key factor in determining their core essence, ego, and overall character. It was believed to reflect the fundamental qualities and characteristics that defined a person's identity and sense of self.

The sun represented an individual's drive for self-expression, creativity, and the pursuit of personal goals. It symbolized their inner fire and the motivation to shine and make their mark in the world. The placement of the sun in a person's astrological chart provided insights into their natural talents, strengths, and areas where they could exercise leadership and influence.

In Babylonian astrology, the sun was associated with attributes such as confidence, vitality, ambition, and a strong sense of purpose. It represented the energy and life force that fueled one's actions and aspirations. The sun's position in relation to other celestial bodies in the chart also influenced how these qualities were expressed and channeled.

Individuals born under a strong sun influence were believed to possess a natural radiance, charisma, and an inherent ability to lead. They were seen as having the potential to exert influence and inspire others. The sun's placement in different zodiac signs further shaped the expression of these qualities, adding unique flavors and characteristics to an individual's personality.

The Babylonians recognized the importance of honoring and aligning with the energy of the sun. Rituals and ceremonies were conducted to pay homage to this celestial body and seek its blessings. By harnessing the energy of the sun, individuals could tap into their inner vitality, express their true selves, and embrace their life's purpose.

In summary, the sun held immense importance in Babylonian astrology, representing vitality, life force, and leadership. It symbolized the divine spark within individuals and played a central role in determining their core essence, ego, and overall character. The sun's position in an astrological chart provided insights into a person's drive for self-expression, creativity, and pursuit of personal goals. Understanding and aligning with the energy of the sun allowed individuals to embrace their unique qualities and make a meaningful impact in their lives and the world around them.

The Moon:

In Babylonian astrology, the moon held a crucial position, symbolizing emotions, intuition, and the subconscious mind. It was regarded as a celestial body that governed the inner emotional landscape of individuals, influencing their moods, instincts, and instinctual reactions to the world.

The moon's association with emotions stemmed from its cyclical nature, reflecting the waxing and waning phases that mirrored the ebb and flow of human feelings. Babylonians recognized the moon as a potent force that influenced the ebb and flow of emotions within individuals. Its gravitational pull was believed to have a profound impact on the tides of human emotions.

The moon's position in an astrological chart provided valuable insights into a person's emotional nature. It revealed their innate sensitivities, nurturing instincts, and receptivity to the world around them. Those with a strong moon influence were thought to possess heightened emotional awareness, empathy, and an intuitive understanding of others.

The moon was also associated with the subconscious mind, representing the realm of dreams, intuition, and the hidden depths of the psyche. It symbolized the inner world of thoughts, feelings, and memories that shape an individual's psychological landscape.

The moon's placement in an astrological chart offered clues about a person's unconscious patterns, emotional needs, and intuitive abilities.

In Babylonian culture, the moon was deeply connected to the feminine principle and was associated with nurturing and fertility. It represented the maternal qualities of care, compassion, and the instinct to protect and nourish. The moon's influence was seen as embodying the qualities of motherhood, highlighting the importance of emotional bonding, family, and community.

The Babylonians recognized the significance of honoring the moon's energy and the cyclical rhythms it represented. They conducted rituals and ceremonies to align with the lunar cycles, seeking to harmonize their emotional well-being and tap into the intuitive wisdom offered by the moon. These practices aimed to enhance emotional balance, promote self-reflection, and deepen the connection with the subconscious mind.

In summary, the moon held a crucial role in Babylonian astrology, symbolizing emotions, intuition, and the subconscious mind. It governed the inner emotional landscape, influencing moods, instincts, and instinctual reactions. The moon's position in an astrological chart provided insights into a person's emotional nature, nurturing instincts, and receptivity to the world. It also represented the feminine principle and the nurturing aspect of life. Understanding and aligning with the moon's energy allowed individuals to embrace their emotional depths, cultivate intuition, and foster a sense of emotional balance and connection with the world around them.

The Planets:

The Babylonians recognized several planets, including Mercury, Venus, Mars, Jupiter, and Saturn, each associated with distinct qualities and energies. These planets were named after their corresponding deities, and their positions in the sky held great significance.

Mercury: In Babylonian astrology, Mercury held significant symbolism, representing communication, intellect, and the exchange of ideas. It was associated with the realm of the mind and played a vital role in shaping an individual's mental abilities, thought processes, and communication style.

Mercury's association with communication stemmed from its role as the messenger of the gods in Babylonian mythology. It was believed to facilitate the flow of information, ideas, and knowledge between the human realm and the divine realm. Babylonians recognized the importance of effective communication in all aspects of life, from personal relationships to business transactions and governance.

The position of Mercury in an astrological chart provided valuable insights into a person's mental abilities and intellectual inclinations. It revealed their capacity for learning, reasoning, and problem-solving. A strong influence of Mercury suggested a sharp intellect, quick thinking, and a natural curiosity to explore new ideas and concepts.

Mercury also influenced one's communication style, indicating how individuals express their thoughts and ideas to others. It represented linguistic skills, persuasive abilities, and adaptability in conveying messages. The position of Mercury in an astrological chart revealed whether an individual possessed a more analytical and precise communication style or a more imaginative and expressive approach.

Babylonians recognized the importance of effective communication in various aspects of life, including trade, diplomacy, and education. They understood that clear and articulate communication was essential for fostering understanding, building relationships, and exchanging knowledge.

Mercury's influence extended beyond verbal communication to other forms of expression, including writing, teaching, and storytelling. It encompassed the ability to convey ideas through written words, engage in meaningful discussions, and impart knowledge to others.

In Babylonian society, Mercury's energy was considered essential for successful endeavors in fields such as law, commerce, and education. The alignment with Mercury's energy was believed to enhance one's intellectual capacities, improve communication skills, and facilitate the exchange of ideas.

Understanding the influence of Mercury in an astrological chart allowed individuals to harness its energy effectively. They could cultivate their intellectual abilities, refine their communication skills, and adapt their thought processes to different situations. By aligning with Mercury's energy, individuals sought to enhance their capacity for effective communication, foster intellectual growth, and engage in meaningful exchanges of ideas.

In summary, Mercury held significant symbolism in Babylonian astrology, representing communication, intellect, and the exchange of ideas. Its position in an astrological chart provided insights into a person's mental abilities, thought processes, and communication style. Understanding and aligning with Mercury's energy allowed individuals to cultivate their intellectual capacities, refine their communication skills, and engage in meaningful exchanges of ideas.

Venus: In Babylonian astrology, Venus held profound significance as it symbolized love, beauty, harmony, and relationships. It represented the qualities and experiences associated with romance, sensuality, aesthetics, and social connections. Venus's placement in an astrological chart provided valuable insights into an individual's approach to love, their aesthetic preferences, and their interactions within social settings.

As the planet of love, Venus played a central role in Babylonian understanding of romantic relationships and emotional connections. It governed the expression of affection, attraction, and desire. The position of Venus in an astrological chart revealed the individual's romantic inclinations, their capacity for emotional intimacy, and their style of expressing love and affection.

Venus also represented beauty and aesthetics, influencing an individual's sense of taste, appreciation for art, and attraction to physical beauty. It encompassed an individual's preferences for harmonious and visually appealing environments. The placement of Venus in an astrological chart shed light on an individual's aesthetic sensibilities, their artistic inclinations, and their appreciation for beauty in all its forms.

Additionally, Venus influenced an individual's social interactions and ability to establish harmonious relationships. It governed their ability to attract and maintain friendships, alliances, and partnerships. The position of Venus in an astrological chart provided insights into an individual's social grace, diplomatic skills, and their inclination towards cooperation and compromise in relationships.

Babylonians recognized the importance of harmonious relationships and the role of love in maintaining social cohesion. Venus's influence extended beyond personal relationships to encompass the broader social fabric of the community. It reflected the ideals of fairness, cooperation, and balance within social interactions.

The alignment with Venus's energy was considered favorable for cultivating fulfilling relationships, fostering emotional connections, and appreciating the beauty in the world. Babylonians sought to embrace the qualities associated with Venus to create harmonious and loving environments within their personal lives and society at large.

Understanding the influence of Venus in an astrological chart allowed individuals to navigate their love lives, cultivate their aesthetic preferences, and enhance their social interactions. By aligning with Venus's energy, individuals sought to nurture their relationships, enhance their sense of beauty and aesthetics, and foster harmony within their social circles.

In summary, Venus represented love, beauty, harmony, and relationships in Babylonian astrology. Its placement in an astrological chart provided insights into an individual's approach to love, their aesthetic preferences, and their interactions within social settings. Aligning with Venus's energy allowed individuals to cultivate fulfilling relationships, appreciate beauty in all its forms, and create harmonious social connections.

Mars: In Babylonian astrology, Mars held great significance as it symbolized energy, action, and assertion. It represented the driving force within individuals, their capacity for initiative, and their ability to take decisive action in pursuit of their goals. Mars's placement in an astrological chart provided valuable insights into a person's assertiveness, ambition, and approach to challenges.

As the planet of energy, Mars represented the dynamic and active aspects of an individual's personality. It signified their stamina, physical strength, and the assertive qualities needed to overcome obstacles and achieve their desires. The position of Mars in an astrological chart indicated the individual's level of motivation, their capacity for taking risks, and their ability to persevere in the face of challenges.

Mars also governed ambition and the drive for success. It reflected an individual's competitive nature and their willingness to put forth the effort necessary to achieve their goals. The placement of Mars in an astrological chart revealed the person's desire for achievement, their need for recognition, and their approach to asserting themselves in various areas of life.

Furthermore, Mars represented the ability to take decisive action and make bold choices. It reflected an individual's courage, determination, and willingness to confront challenges head-on. The position of Mars in an astrological chart shed light on the person's assertiveness, their ability to make quick decisions, and their inclination to take the lead in various situations.

In Babylonian society, Mars's energy was regarded as vital for progress, success, and overcoming obstacles. The alignment with Mars's energy allowed individuals to tap into their inner strength, assert themselves effectively, and channel their energy towards constructive endeavors. Babylonians valued the qualities associated with Mars, such as courage, initiative, and a strong work ethic, as they believed these qualities were essential for personal growth and societal advancement.

Understanding the influence of Mars in an astrological chart provided individuals with insights into their drive, ambition, and approach to taking action. By aligning with Mars's energy, individuals sought to harness their assertiveness, cultivate a strong work ethic, and pursue their goals with determination. They recognized the importance of channeling their energy and taking decisive action to achieve their desired outcomes.

In summary, Mars symbolized energy, action, and assertion in Babylonian astrology. Its position in an astrological chart provided insights into an individual's drive, ambition, and ability to take decisive action. Aligning with Mars's energy allowed individuals to tap into their inner strength, assert themselves effectively, and channel their energy towards constructive endeavors. By embodying the qualities associated with Mars, individuals aimed to achieve their goals, overcome obstacles, and make significant progress in their lives.

Jupiter: In Babylonian astrology, Jupiter held significant meaning as the planet of expansion, growth, and wisdom. It represented the expansive and abundant qualities within individuals and reflected their potential for success, prosperity, and personal growth. The placement of Jupiter in an astrological chart provided valuable insights into a person's aspirations, beliefs, and capacity for wisdom.

Jupiter symbolized expansion on both a material and spiritual level. It represented opportunities, abundance, and the potential for growth in various aspects of life, including career, finances, knowledge, and personal development. The position of Jupiter in an astrological chart indicated the individual's capacity to attract favorable circumstances, experience growth, and manifest their aspirations.

Furthermore, Jupiter represented wisdom and higher knowledge. It reflected an individual's capacity for understanding, learning, and seeking truth. Jupiter's placement in an astrological chart shed light on the person's philosophical inclinations, their curiosity about the world, and their desire to broaden their horizons through education and exploration.

Jupiter also governed beliefs, optimism, and the ability to see the bigger picture. It represented the person's capacity for faith, optimism, and the ability to maintain a positive outlook even in challenging times. The position of Jupiter in an astrological chart revealed the individual's belief systems, their values, and their capacity to find meaning and purpose in life.

In Babylonian society, Jupiter's energy was highly regarded as it represented the potential for growth, success, and wisdom. Aligning with Jupiter's energy allowed individuals to tap into their expansive qualities, embrace opportunities, and experience abundance in various areas of life. Babylonians believed that cultivating a positive mindset, maintaining faith, and seeking higher knowledge were essential for personal and spiritual growth.

Understanding the influence of Jupiter in an astrological chart provided individuals with insights into their potential for expansion, success, and wisdom. By aligning with Jupiter's energy, individuals sought to embrace opportunities, broaden their horizons, and pursue personal growth and fulfillment. They recognized the importance of cultivating optimism, maintaining a positive outlook, and seeking knowledge to navigate life's challenges and achieve their goals.

In summary, Jupiter represented expansion, growth, and wisdom in Babylonian astrology. Its placement in an astrological chart provided insights into an individual's potential for success, abundance, and personal growth. Aligning with Jupiter's energy allowed individuals to embrace opportunities, cultivate wisdom, and experience abundance in various aspects of life. By embodying the qualities associated with Jupiter, individuals aimed to expand their horizons, manifest their aspirations, and lead a fulfilling and meaningful life.

Saturn: In Babylonian astrology, Saturn held significant symbolism as the planet associated with discipline, responsibility, and life lessons. It represented the areas of life where individuals faced challenges, limitations, and the need for personal growth through perseverance and hard work. The placement of Saturn in an astrological chart provided valuable insights into the individual's capacity for self-discipline, resilience, and the lessons they needed to learn in their journey.

Saturn symbolized the principle of structure and order. It represented the areas of life that required a strong sense of responsibility, commitment, and discipline. Its placement in an astrological chart revealed the areas where individuals would encounter obstacles, delays, and limitations. It highlighted the need for patience, hard work, and perseverance to overcome these challenges and achieve long-term success.

Saturn's influence also extended to the realm of personal growth and maturity. It represented the lessons and experiences that individuals needed to learn in order to develop wisdom, resilience, and inner strength. The position of Saturn in an astrological chart indicated the specific life areas where individuals would undergo transformative experiences and face tests of character. These experiences often involved facing one's fears, taking on responsibilities, and learning important life lessons that contributed to personal growth and maturation.

Additionally, Saturn symbolized the concept of time and the cyclical nature of life. It represented the passage of time, the cycles of growth and decay, and the inevitability of change. Saturn's placement in an astrological chart highlighted the areas where individuals would experience significant transitions, challenges, and the need for adaptation. It emphasized the importance of embracing change, accepting responsibilities, and learning from past experiences in order to build a solid foundation for the future.

In Babylonian society, Saturn's energy was regarded as an important aspect of personal and spiritual development. Its influence reminded individuals of the need for self-discipline, responsibility, and the willingness to face challenges head-on. Saturn's lessons were seen as valuable opportunities for growth and transformation, providing individuals with the chance to develop resilience, inner strength, and a deeper understanding of themselves and the world around them.

Understanding the influence of Saturn in an astrological chart allowed individuals to gain insights into the areas of life where they would encounter challenges, limitations, and the need for personal growth. By embracing Saturn's energy, individuals aimed to develop discipline, take on responsibilities, and persevere through difficult times. They recognized the importance of learning life lessons, cultivating patience, and building a solid foundation for long-term success and personal fulfillment.

In summary, Saturn represented discipline, responsibility, and life lessons in Babylonian astrology. Its placement in an astrological chart revealed the areas where individuals would encounter challenges, limitations, and the need for personal growth. Embracing Saturn's energy involved developing self-discipline, accepting responsibilities, and persevering through difficult times. By learning the lessons associated with Saturn, individuals aimed to cultivate resilience, inner strength, and a solid foundation for personal and spiritual development.

The Stars:

In Babylonian astrology, the significance of stars as celestial bodies extended beyond their mere visual beauty. Each star was believed to possess its own unique meaning and influence, contributing to the complex tapestry of human destinies. The position and alignment of specific stars in relation to planets and other celestial bodies were considered crucial in understanding and interpreting an individual's character, potential, and life path.

Certain stars were associated with favorable outcomes and good fortune. Their presence in an astrological chart indicated potential blessings, opportunities, and positive experiences in the corresponding areas of life. These stars were seen as beneficial and were often associated with prosperity, success, and harmony.

On the other hand, some stars were linked to challenges and obstacles. Their influence in an astrological chart suggested areas of life where individuals might face difficulties, setbacks, or limitations. These stars represented the need for perseverance, self-reflection, and personal growth in order to overcome obstacles and achieve desired outcomes.

Additionally, specific stars were associated with different areas of life, such as love, career, health, and relationships. Their alignment in an astrological chart provided insights into the corresponding aspects of an individual's life. For example, a star associated with love might indicate romantic relationships and emotional connections, while a star linked to career could signify professional pursuits and achievements.

The Babylonians believed that the celestial bodies, including stars, planets, and other astronomical phenomena, were archetypal forces that influenced human experiences. These celestial energies were seen as interconnected with the natural and supernatural realms, shaping the course of individual lives. By analyzing the positions and interactions of these celestial bodies, Babylonian astrologers sought to gain a deeper understanding of the cosmic forces at play and their impact on human destinies.

The study of stars and their meanings in Babylonian astrology allowed individuals to gain guidance and insights into various aspects of their lives. By consulting astrologers, individuals could navigate challenges, make informed decisions, and align their actions with the cosmic energies associated with specific stars. This alignment was believed to bring about harmony, fulfillment, and a deeper connection to the greater cosmic order.

Overall, stars held significant importance in Babylonian astrology, representing powerful archetypal forces that shaped human experiences. Their individual meanings and influences were considered integral in understanding an individual's character, potential, and life path. By studying the positions and alignments of stars in relation to other celestial bodies, Babylonian astrologers provided guidance and interpretation, assisting individuals in navigating life's challenges, making informed choices, and aligning with the cosmic energies at play.

B. Astrological Houses:

The Babylonian astrological tradition encompassed the concept of dividing the sky into twelve distinct sections, known as houses. Each house represented a specific area of life and held significant meaning in the interpretation of an individual's astrological chart. The positions of celestial bodies within these houses were meticulously calculated and analyzed to gain insights into various aspects of a person's life.

The First House - House of Self:

In Babylonian astrology, the first house, commonly referred to as the Ascendant, held great significance as it represented an individual's self-image, physical appearance, and overall personality. This house played a pivotal role in shaping how individuals presented themselves to the world and reflected their unique approach to life.

The first house served as a window through which others perceived an individual, as it symbolized the outer persona and the mask one wore in social interactions. It reflected the way individuals projected themselves to others, their behavior, and the impression they made on those around them. The qualities associated with the first house influenced the individual's style, demeanor, and overall presence.

Additionally, the first house was closely linked to an individual's physical appearance and body. It represented their physical attributes, features, and the way they presented themselves visually. This included factors such as height, weight, facial features, and overall body structure. The energies of the first house influenced how individuals presented themselves physically and the image they conveyed to others.

Beyond the physical aspect, the first house played a crucial role in defining an individual's personality. It represented the core essence of their being and encapsulated their fundamental traits, characteristics, and temperament. The energies associated with the first house influenced one's sense of self, self-confidence, and the overall expression of their individuality.

Moreover, the first house also held insights into an individual's approach to life. It revealed their personal goals, aspirations, and their inherent nature in navigating the world. The energies of this house influenced how individuals approached challenges, interacted with others, and pursued their ambitions. It represented the driving force behind their actions and the lens through which they viewed the world.

By analyzing the position and aspects of planets within the first house, Babylonian astrologers gained valuable insights into an individual's self-perception, physical appearance, and overall personality. This information was essential in understanding how individuals presented themselves to the world and how they approached various aspects of life.

Understanding the dynamics of the first house allowed individuals to develop a deeper self-awareness and make conscious choices in aligning their actions and behaviors with their authentic selves. It provided them with insights into their strengths, weaknesses, and the areas in which personal growth and development were needed.

In Babylonian astrology, the first house represented the individual's self-image, physical appearance, and overall personality, acting as a foundational pillar for understanding one's unique expression and approach to life. By delving into the energies and influences associated with the first house, individuals could gain a deeper understanding of themselves and navigate their personal journey with greater self-awareness and authenticity.

The Second House - House of Finances and Values:

In Babylonian astrology, the second house held significant meaning as it was closely associated with personal finances, material possessions, and self-worth. This house provided insights into an individual's attitudes towards money, their values related to wealth, and their overall ability to accumulate financial resources.

The second house represented the practical aspects of life, particularly in terms of finances and material well-being. It reflected an individual's financial situation, including their income, savings, investments, and overall financial stability. The energies associated with the second house influenced how individuals earned, managed, and utilized their financial resources.

Beyond the external aspects of money, the second house also shed light on an individual's inner values and beliefs related to wealth and material possessions. It represented the individual's relationship with money, their understanding of abundance, and their sense of self-worth in relation to their financial status. The energies of the second house influenced how individuals approached financial matters, their ability to attract wealth, and their overall financial success.

Moreover, the second house played a role in revealing an individual's priorities and what they considered valuable in life. It reflected their personal values and the things they deemed important in terms of material possessions and resources. The energies associated with the second house influenced an individual's desires and motivations for accumulating wealth and material comforts.

Additionally, the second house provided insights into an individual's ability to manage and utilize their financial resources effectively. It reflected their attitudes towards saving, budgeting, and making wise financial decisions. The energies of this house influenced an individual's capacity to build financial security, make sound investments, and create a stable foundation for their material well-being.

By analyzing the position and aspects of planets within the second house, Babylonian astrologers gained valuable insights into an individual's financial potential, attitudes towards money, and overall relationship with material possessions. This information was essential in understanding how individuals approached their financial goals, their ability to manifest abundance, and their overall sense of self-worth.

Understanding the dynamics of the second house allowed individuals to develop a greater awareness of their financial patterns and behaviors. It provided them with insights into their beliefs about money, their values related to wealth, and any potential blockages or challenges they might face in achieving financial success. This knowledge empowered individuals to make conscious choices, set realistic financial goals, and align their actions with their desired financial outcomes.

In Babylonian astrology, the second house represented personal finances, material possessions, and self-worth, providing individuals with a deeper understanding of their financial potential and attitudes towards money. By delving into the energies and influences associated with the second house, individuals could gain insights into their financial patterns, make informed decisions, and work towards creating a solid foundation of financial stability and abundance in their lives.

The Third House - House of Communication and Learning:

In Babylonian astrology, the third house held significant influence over communication, intellectual pursuits, and short-distance travel. It provided valuable insights into an individual's style of communication, their learning abilities, and their relationships with siblings and neighbors.

The third house represented the realm of communication, encompassing both verbal and written expression. It reflected an individual's communication style, including how they articulate their thoughts, ideas, and opinions. The energies associated with the third house influenced the individual's ability to convey information effectively, engage in meaningful dialogue, and express themselves clearly.

Moreover, the third house shed light on an individual's learning abilities and intellectual pursuits. It represented their capacity for intellectual curiosity, their preferred modes of learning, and their aptitude for acquiring knowledge. The energies of the third house influenced how individuals processed information, engaged in intellectual endeavors, and expanded their mental capacities.

Additionally, the third house played a role in revealing an individual's relationships with siblings and neighbors. It reflected the dynamics within these close social connections, including the level of communication, cooperation, and understanding. The energies associated with the third house influenced the quality of these relationships, the ease of communication with siblings and neighbors, and the potential for collaboration and support.

Furthermore, the third house was associated with short-distance travel. It represented local travel, daily commuting, and the exploration of nearby surroundings. The energies of this house influenced an individual's inclination and experiences related to short trips, local outings, and interactions with their immediate environment.

By analyzing the position and aspects of planets within the third house, Babylonian astrologers gained valuable insights into an individual's communication abilities, intellectual pursuits, and relationships with siblings and neighbors. This information was essential in understanding how individuals expressed themselves, engaged in intellectual pursuits, and nurtured their close social connections.

Understanding the dynamics of the third house allowed individuals to develop a greater awareness of their communication patterns, learning styles, and interactions with siblings and neighbors. It provided them with insights into their strengths and areas of improvement in terms of communication, their intellectual interests and pursuits, and the potential for harmonious relationships with those in their immediate social circles.

Moreover, the third house highlighted the importance of effective communication and the role it played in facilitating understanding, building connections, and fostering intellectual growth. By consciously working with the energies of the third house, individuals could enhance their communication skills, cultivate their intellectual curiosity, and foster harmonious relationships with siblings and neighbors.

In Babylonian astrology, the third house governed communication, intellectual pursuits, and short-distance travel, providing individuals with a deeper understanding of their communication style, learning abilities, and relationships with close social connections. By delving into the energies and influences associated with the third house, individuals could gain insights into their communication patterns, engage in fulfilling intellectual pursuits, and nurture meaningful relationships with their siblings and neighbors.

The Fourth House - House of Home and Family:

In Babylonian astrology, the fourth house held significant symbolism, representing the home, family, and ancestral roots. It provided valuable insights into an individual's emotional foundation, family dynamics, and connection to their heritage.

The fourth house is often referred to as the "House of Home" because it signifies the physical dwelling where an individual feels most rooted and secure. It represents one's private space, personal sanctuary, and the foundation from which they navigate the world. The energies associated with the fourth house influence an individual's sense of emotional security, comfort, and stability within their own home environment.

Moreover, the fourth house sheds light on family dynamics and the role of family in shaping an individual's life. It reflects the influence of one's parents, siblings, and other family members on their emotional well-being, values, and sense of belonging.

The energies of the fourth house reveal the ancestral heritage, traditions, and cultural influences that contribute to an individual's identity and sense of rootedness.

The fourth house also encompasses the concept of "inner emotional foundation." It represents an individual's emotional core, their deep-seated needs for emotional security, and their sense of belonging within their family and broader ancestral lineage. The energies associated with this house influence an individual's emotional well-being, their ability to establish a nurturing and supportive home environment, and their capacity to foster emotional connections with their loved ones.

Furthermore, the fourth house highlights an individual's connection to their heritage and ancestral roots. It reflects the influences of past generations, cultural traditions, and the collective wisdom that has been passed down through the family lineage. The energies of the fourth house provide insights into the individual's affinity for their cultural heritage, their desire to maintain family traditions, and their connection to the ancestral lineage.

By analyzing the position and aspects of planets within the fourth house, Babylonian astrologers gained valuable insights into an individual's emotional well-being, family dynamics, and connection to their ancestral roots. This information was essential in understanding an individual's need for emotional security, their relationship with family members, and the influence of their cultural heritage on their sense of identity.

Understanding the dynamics of the fourth house allowed individuals to create a nurturing and supportive home environment, cultivate healthy family relationships, and honor their ancestral lineage. It provided them with insights into their emotional needs, the importance of family bonds, and the significance of their cultural heritage.

Moreover, the fourth house highlighted the importance of creating a sense of emotional security and belonging within the home environment. By consciously working with the energies of the fourth house, individuals could cultivate a nurturing space that supports their emotional well-being and fosters harmonious relationships with their family members.

In Babylonian astrology, the fourth house represents the home, family, and ancestral roots, providing individuals with a deeper understanding of their emotional foundation, family dynamics, and connection to their heritage. By delving into the energies and influences associated with the fourth house, individuals can gain insights into their need for emotional security, cultivate harmonious family relationships, and honor their ancestral lineage.

The Fifth House - House of Creativity and Pleasure:

In Babylonian astrology, the fifth house holds significant symbolism, representing creativity, self-expression, romance, and personal enjoyment. It provides insights into an individual's artistic inclinations, love affairs, and experiences of joy and entertainment.

The fifth house is often referred to as the "House of Pleasure" because it governs the areas of life associated with personal enjoyment, self-expression, and the pursuit of creative endeavors. It reflects the individual's capacity for creativity, their artistic inclinations, and their ability to express themselves authentically.

Creativity is a central theme of the fifth house, encompassing various forms of self-expression such as art, music, dance, writing, and theater. The energies associated with this house inspire individuals to tap into their innate talents and share their unique gifts with the world. It represents the joy and fulfillment that arise from creative self-expression and the ability to manifest one's artistic vision.

Additionally, the fifth house is closely linked to romantic relationships and love affairs. It reflects an individual's approach to romance, their desire for affection and intimacy, and their capacity to experience joy and pleasure through romantic connections. The energies of the fifth house influence one's romantic pursuits, highlighting their love style, preferences, and their ability to express love and affection.

The fifth house is also associated with children and the experience of parenthood. It signifies the potential for fertility, childbirth, and the joy that comes from nurturing and raising children. The energies of the fifth house reveal an individual's attitudes towards parenting, their creative approach to raising children, and the impact of children on their personal fulfillment and happiness.

Moreover, the fifth house reflects the individual's relationship with leisure, entertainment, and recreational activities. It represents their capacity to find joy and pleasure in hobbies, recreational pursuits, and leisurely endeavors. The energies associated with this house encourage individuals to engage in activities that bring them happiness, enjoyment, and a sense of playfulness.

By analyzing the position and aspects of planets within the fifth house, Babylonian astrologers gained valuable insights into an individual's creative potential, romantic inclinations, and capacity for joy and personal fulfillment. This information was essential in understanding how individuals could tap into their creativity, foster fulfilling romantic relationships, and cultivate a sense of joy and pleasure in their lives.

Understanding the dynamics of the fifth house allowed individuals to explore their creative passions, engage in activities that bring them joy, and experience fulfilling romantic connections. It provided them with insights into their unique gifts and talents, their approach to love and romance, and the importance of incorporating leisure and playfulness into their lives.

Moreover, the fifth house highlighted the significance of self-expression and embracing one's authentic creative voice. By consciously working with the energies of the fifth house, individuals could tap into their creative potential, express themselves authentically, and cultivate a sense of joy and pleasure in their everyday experiences.

In Babylonian astrology, the fifth house represents creativity, self-expression, romance, and personal enjoyment. By delving into the energies and influences associated with the fifth house, individuals can gain insights into their creative potential, cultivate fulfilling romantic relationships, and embrace a sense of joy and pleasure in their lives. It encourages individuals to express themselves authentically, explore their artistic inclinations, and find fulfillment through the pursuit of their passions.

The Sixth House - House of Health and Service:

In Babylonian astrology, the sixth house is an essential part of the astrological chart, representing health, daily routines, and work. It provides valuable insights into an individual's approach to wellness, their work ethic, and their commitment to service or helping others.

The sixth house governs matters related to physical and mental well-being, highlighting the importance of maintaining a healthy lifestyle and taking care of one's body and mind. It reflects an individual's attitudes towards health, their habits, and their overall well-being practices. The energies of the sixth house encourage individuals to establish regular routines, prioritize self-care, and adopt healthy habits that contribute to their overall vitality.

Within the realm of work, the sixth house represents the individual's approach to their job, their work ethic, and their daily responsibilities. It reflects their attitude towards work, their dedication, and their willingness to contribute their skills and efforts in their chosen profession. The energies of the sixth house motivate individuals to strive for excellence, maintain discipline, and be conscientious in fulfilling their work-related duties.

Moreover, the sixth house is associated with service, indicating an individual's inclination towards helping others and making a meaningful contribution to their community or society. It reflects their capacity for empathy, compassion, and their desire to assist those in need. The energies of the sixth house inspire individuals to engage in acts of service, volunteer work, or professions that involve caring for others.

The sixth house also governs daily routines and habits. It represents the rituals, systems, and structures that individuals incorporate into their everyday lives to enhance productivity, efficiency, and well-being. This can include aspects such as organization, time management, and the establishment of healthy lifestyle practices. The energies of the sixth house encourage individuals to create harmonious and balanced daily routines that support their overall goals and well-being.

By examining the planets and aspects within the sixth house, Babylonian astrologers gained insights into an individual's approach to health, work, and service. This information was instrumental in understanding how individuals could optimize their well-being, improve their work performance, and find fulfillment through service to others.

Understanding the dynamics of the sixth house allowed individuals to establish healthy habits, prioritize self-care, and maintain a strong work ethic. It highlighted the importance of finding meaningful work that aligns with one's values and contributes to personal fulfillment. The energies associated with the sixth house also encouraged individuals to engage in acts of service and contribute to the well-being of others, fostering a sense of purpose and fulfillment in their lives.

In Babylonian astrology, the sixth house plays a significant role in understanding an individual's approach to health, daily routines, and work. By delving into the energies and influences associated with the sixth house, individuals can gain insights into their work ethic, commitment to wellness, and inclination towards service. It encourages individuals to establish healthy habits, maintain a disciplined approach to work, and find fulfillment through meaningful service to others.

The Seventh House - House of Relationships:

In Babylonian astrology, the seventh house holds great significance as it governs partnerships, both personal and professional. It represents marriage, business partnerships, and significant relationships, offering insights into an individual's approach to collaboration, cooperation, and the pursuit of harmonious connections.

The seventh house is primarily associated with romantic relationships and marriage. It reveals how an individual engages in intimate partnerships and the qualities they seek in a life partner. It reflects their desires for companionship, love, and commitment. The energies of the seventh house encourage individuals to seek balance, harmony, and mutual understanding in their relationships. It highlights the importance of compromise, cooperation, and shared values as essential elements for a successful partnership.

In addition to personal relationships, the seventh house also governs professional partnerships and collaborations. It reveals an individual's attitude towards teamwork, their ability to work effectively with others, and their inclination towards establishing mutually beneficial alliances. The energies of the seventh house encourage individuals to cultivate diplomacy, negotiation skills, and the ability to form harmonious working relationships. It signifies the importance of cooperation and collaboration in achieving professional success.

The seventh house not only signifies the qualities an individual seeks in a partner but also reflects their own qualities as a partner. It provides insights into how one approaches relationships, their capacity for compromise, and their ability to maintain balance and harmony within partnerships. It prompts individuals to consider the needs and perspectives of their partners, fostering mutual respect and understanding.

Moreover, the seventh house plays a role in revealing the dynamics of significant relationships beyond romantic and professional partnerships. It includes relationships with close friends, family members, and even adversaries. It provides insights into the nature of these relationships, the lessons they offer, and the potential for growth and harmony.

By examining the planets and aspects within the seventh house, Babylonian astrologers gained valuable information about an individual's approach to partnerships, the qualities they seek in a partner, and their capacity for cooperation and collaboration. This knowledge allowed individuals to understand their relationship patterns, work towards establishing healthy and balanced partnerships, and foster greater harmony and understanding in their connections with others.

Understanding the dynamics of the seventh house empowers individuals to cultivate healthy and fulfilling relationships in both personal and professional spheres. It encourages them to seek partnerships that align with their values, foster mutual growth, and contribute to their overall well-being. The energies associated with the seventh house inspire individuals to prioritize cooperation, compromise, and the pursuit of harmonious connections.

In Babylonian astrology, the seventh house serves as a guide for individuals seeking to establish meaningful partnerships. By delving into the energies and influences associated with the seventh house, individuals can gain insights into their approach to relationships, the qualities they seek in a partner, and their capacity for collaboration. It encourages individuals to foster balance, cooperation, and harmony in their connections with others, leading to more fulfilling and successful partnerships.

The Eighth House - House of Transformation:

In Babylonian astrology, the eighth house holds significant meaning as it represents transformation, shared resources, and intimacy. It delves into the depths of human experience, reflecting experiences of deep emotional bonds, inheritances, and matters related to life, death, and regeneration.

The eighth house is associated with transformation and the process of personal growth and evolution. It symbolizes the profound changes and transformations that individuals undergo throughout their lives. This includes psychological, emotional, and spiritual transformations that often result from intense experiences or significant life events. The energies of the eighth house prompt individuals to confront their fears, explore their inner depths, and undergo profound personal change.

Shared resources, including finances, investments, and inheritances, are also governed by the eighth house. It reflects an individual's approach to managing and sharing material wealth with others. This includes joint ventures, business partnerships, and financial agreements such as loans, debts, and inheritances. The eighth house signifies the importance of trust, transparency, and the responsible management of shared resources.

In matters of intimacy, the eighth house reveals an individual's approach to deep emotional connections and intimate relationships. It represents the experiences of trust, vulnerability, and bonding that occur in relationships. The energies of the eighth house encourage individuals to explore the depths of their emotional being, embrace emotional intimacy, and forge transformative connections with others.

The eighth house is also associated with matters related to life, death, and regeneration. It reflects the individual's relationship with mortality, their beliefs about the cycle of life and death, and their attitudes towards transformation and rebirth. This includes experiences related to grief, loss, and letting go, as well as the exploration of spiritual and metaphysical realms.

The energies of the eighth house prompt individuals to confront the shadow aspects of their personality and delve into their subconscious mind. It encourages self-reflection, introspection, and the exploration of the mysteries of life. The eighth house invites individuals to embrace the process of letting go, releasing what no longer serves them, and embracing new beginnings.

By examining the planets and aspects within the eighth house, Babylonian astrologers gained valuable insights into an individual's experiences of transformation, their approach to shared resources and intimacy, and their relationship with life, death, and regeneration. This knowledge allowed individuals to navigate the depths of their emotions, embrace personal growth, and cultivate meaningful connections with others.

Understanding the dynamics of the eighth house empowers individuals to navigate transformative experiences, manage shared resources responsibly, and embrace the depths of emotional intimacy. It encourages individuals to explore their subconscious mind, confront their fears, and embrace the process of personal growth and evolution. The energies associated with the eighth house inspire individuals to embrace the cycles of life, release what no longer serves them, and embrace transformation and rebirth.

In Babylonian astrology, the eighth house serves as a guide for individuals seeking personal growth, deep emotional connections, and a balanced approach to shared resources. By delving into the energies and influences associated with the eighth house, individuals can gain insights into their transformative journey, their approach to managing shared resources, and their capacity for emotional intimacy. It encourages individuals to embrace change, let go of what no longer serves them, and forge meaningful connections that contribute to their personal and spiritual evolution.

The Ninth House - House of Higher Learning and Travel:

In Babylonian astrology, the ninth house holds significant meaning as it governs higher education, philosophy, spirituality, and long-distance travel. It represents an individual's beliefs, quest for knowledge, and connection to broader perspectives.

The ninth house is associated with higher education and represents the pursuit of intellectual growth and expansion of knowledge. It reflects an individual's interest in subjects such as philosophy, religion, law, and spirituality. The energies of the ninth house inspire individuals to explore and develop their beliefs, seeking wisdom and understanding through formal education, self-study, or spiritual practices.

Philosophy and spirituality are key domains governed by the ninth house. It represents an individual's quest for meaning, their worldview, and their personal philosophy of life. The ninth house prompts individuals to contemplate the deeper questions about existence, purpose, and the nature of reality. It encourages the exploration of different spiritual and philosophical traditions, seeking to expand one's understanding and cultivate a broader perspective.

The ninth house also signifies long-distance travel, both physically and intellectually. It represents the desire to venture beyond one's immediate surroundings and expand horizons. This includes physical travel to distant lands, as well as the exploration of different cultures, languages, and belief systems. The energies of the ninth house inspire individuals to seek new experiences, broaden their understanding of the world, and embrace diverse perspectives.

In matters of higher education, the ninth house reflects an individual's approach to learning and the pursuit of knowledge. It signifies the desire for intellectual growth, the development of expertise, and the expansion of one's educational horizons. This includes formal education at universities, specialized training, or the pursuit of advanced degrees. The ninth house represents the ability to synthesize information, develop a comprehensive understanding of complex subjects, and apply knowledge to broader contexts.

The energies of the ninth house encourage individuals to explore different belief systems, spiritual practices, and philosophical frameworks. It prompts individuals to question and challenge their existing beliefs, seeking personal truth and spiritual enlightenment. The ninth house represents the integration of knowledge and spirituality, allowing individuals to develop a holistic understanding of themselves and the world around them.

By examining the planets and aspects within the ninth house, Babylonian astrologers gained valuable insights into an individual's quest for knowledge, their belief systems, and their connection to higher truths. This knowledge allowed individuals to navigate their educational pursuits, cultivate a personal philosophy, and embark on spiritual journeys aligned with their true nature.

Understanding the dynamics of the ninth house empowers individuals to embrace lifelong learning, expand their perspectives, and cultivate a sense of spiritual connection. It encourages individuals to explore different cultures and belief systems, broadening their understanding of the world and fostering tolerance and acceptance. The energies associated with the ninth house inspire individuals to seek higher truths, question existing paradigms, and embark on transformative intellectual and spiritual journeys.

In Babylonian astrology, the ninth house serves as a guide for individuals seeking intellectual growth, spiritual enlightenment, and a broader understanding of the world. By delving into the energies and influences associated with the ninth house, individuals can gain insights into their educational pursuits, their belief systems, and their spiritual journey. It encourages individuals to embrace intellectual curiosity, explore diverse perspectives, and seek wisdom and enlightenment in their quest for personal and spiritual growth.

The Tenth House - House of Career and Public Life:

In Babylonian astrology, the tenth house holds significant meaning as it is associated with career, social status, and public reputation. It represents an individual's professional ambitions, achievements, and the public image they project.

The tenth house is often referred to as the "Midheaven" and represents the highest point in the sky at the time of an individual's birth. It holds a prominent position in the astrological chart and signifies the individual's aspirations and achievements in their chosen career path.

One of the primary focuses of the tenth house is career and professional life. It reflects an individual's ambitions, goals, and their drive to succeed in their chosen vocation. The energies of the tenth house inspire individuals to work hard, pursue excellence, and make a meaningful impact in their respective fields. It represents the individual's vocational path, the role they play in society, and their professional contributions.

The tenth house also symbolizes social status and recognition. It reflects how an individual is perceived by others, their reputation, and the level of respect they command in their community or professional sphere. The energies of the tenth house encourage individuals to cultivate a positive public image, display leadership qualities, and strive for success in their chosen field.

In addition to career and social status, the tenth house also influences an individual's sense of purpose and their contribution to society. It represents the individual's calling, their unique gifts and talents, and how they utilize them to make a meaningful impact. The energies of the tenth house inspire individuals to align their career choices with their true passions and values, allowing them to find fulfillment and purpose in their work.

The tenth house is closely tied to ambition and the pursuit of worldly success. It represents the desire for recognition, achievement, and professional advancement. Individuals with strong emphasis on the tenth house often possess a strong work ethic, determination, and the drive to climb the ladder of success in their careers.

The position of planets within the tenth house provides valuable insights into an individual's career trajectory and their potential for professional success. For example, a well-aspected planet in the tenth house may indicate a person who excels in their chosen field, attains leadership positions, and enjoys recognition for their accomplishments. Conversely, challenging aspects may suggest obstacles or a need for perseverance and strategic planning in career pursuits.

Understanding the dynamics of the tenth house empowers individuals to make informed decisions regarding their career choices, set goals for professional development, and cultivate a positive public image. It encourages individuals to align their actions with their professional aspirations and to seek opportunities that allow them to express their unique talents and make a significant impact in their respective fields.

In Babylonian astrology, the tenth house plays a vital role in understanding an individual's career path, social status, and public reputation. By exploring the energies associated with the tenth house, individuals can gain insights into their vocational calling, their drive for success, and the impact they have on the world around them. It encourages individuals to pursue fulfilling careers, strive for excellence, and make a positive contribution to society through their professional endeavors.

The Eleventh House - House of Hopes and Dreams:

In Babylonian astrology, the eleventh house holds significant meaning as it governs friendships, social networks, and aspirations. It represents an individual's involvement in groups, communities, and their vision for the future.

The eleventh house is often referred to as the house of "Friends" and reflects the individual's social life, networks, and connections with others. It represents the friendships and associations that play a significant role in shaping one's life and experiences. This house emphasizes the importance of social interaction, collaboration, and the support received from like-minded individuals.

One of the primary focuses of the eleventh house is friendships and social relationships. It reflects the type of friends and acquaintances an individual attracts and the role they play in the person's life. The eleventh house signifies the individual's ability to connect with others, form meaningful friendships, and build supportive networks. It represents the collective energy and camaraderie shared among like-minded individuals who come together for a common purpose.

The eleventh house also represents social groups, organizations, and communities to which an individual belongs. It reflects their involvement in clubs, professional associations, charitable organizations, or any other group that shares their interests or values. The energies of the eleventh house inspire individuals to actively participate in social activities, contribute to their communities, and find a sense of belonging among their peers.

In addition to friendships and social networks, the eleventh house is associated with aspirations and the vision for the future. It reflects an individual's long-term goals, dreams, and the ideals they strive to achieve. The eleventh house encourages individuals to explore their aspirations, pursue their passions, and align themselves with causes that resonate with their values.

The eleventh house signifies the collective endeavors and achievements that individuals can accomplish through collaboration and cooperation. It represents the individual's ability to work harmoniously with others, share resources, and support each other in the pursuit of common goals. It reflects the impact that group efforts can have in creating positive change and shaping a better future.

The position of planets within the eleventh house provides valuable insights into an individual's social life, the quality of their friendships, and their involvement in groups and communities. For example, a well-aspected planet in the eleventh house may indicate a person who enjoys a wide network of friends, actively participates in social activities, and is well-connected to influential circles. Challenging aspects, on the other hand, may suggest difficulties in forming or maintaining friendships, or a need to overcome obstacles in group settings.

Understanding the dynamics of the eleventh house empowers individuals to cultivate meaningful friendships, expand their social networks, and contribute to the betterment of their communities. It encourages individuals to seek out like-minded individuals who share their goals and aspirations, and to actively engage in activities that align with their vision for the future.

In Babylonian astrology, the eleventh house plays a vital role in understanding an individual's friendships, social networks, and aspirations. By exploring the energies associated with the eleventh house, individuals can gain insights into the importance of social connections, the power of collective endeavors, and the role they can play in shaping a better future. It encourages individuals to actively engage in social activities, seek out supportive communities, and contribute their unique talents and perspectives to collective endeavors.

The Twelfth House - House of Spirituality and Subconscious:

In Babylonian astrology, the twelfth house holds profound significance as it represents spirituality, the subconscious mind, and hidden matters. It reflects an individual's inner world, their connection to the divine, and the exploration of subconscious patterns and spirituality.

The twelfth house is often referred to as the house of "Hidden Things" or the "House of the Unconscious." It signifies the deeper layers of the psyche, the realm of the subconscious mind, and the spiritual dimensions of an individual's life. This house brings attention to what lies beneath the surface, the hidden aspects of oneself, and the mysteries that can be uncovered through self-exploration.

One of the primary focuses of the twelfth house is spirituality. It represents an individual's spiritual path, their connection to the divine, and the pursuit of transcendence. The twelfth house encourages individuals to explore their inner world, seek meaning beyond the material realm, and develop a connection with higher realms of consciousness. It represents the capacity for spiritual growth, inner transformation, and the exploration of mystical and metaphysical realms.

The twelfth house also represents the subconscious mind, dreams, and the realm of the unconscious. It reflects the hidden aspects of the self, including deeply ingrained patterns, fears, and desires that may influence behavior and experiences. The twelfth house encourages individuals to delve into their subconscious, bring awareness to unconscious patterns, and engage in introspection and self-reflection. By understanding the workings of the subconscious mind, individuals can uncover hidden motivations, heal emotional wounds, and cultivate self-awareness.

Additionally, the twelfth house governs hidden matters and secrets. It signifies aspects of life that are kept private or concealed from others. This house relates to solitude, seclusion, and the need for introspective retreat. It encourages individuals to find solace in solitude, engage in introspection, and honor the need for privacy and inner reflection.

The twelfth house also brings attention to matters related to confinement, institutions, and self-sabotaging patterns. It represents the need for release, surrender, and the transcendence of limitations. This house encourages individuals to confront their fears, break free from self-imposed restrictions, and embark on a journey of personal liberation and spiritual growth.

The placement of planets within the twelfth house provides valuable insights into an individual's spiritual inclinations, hidden talents, and areas of personal growth. For example, a well-aspected planet in the twelfth house may indicate a person with a strong intuitive and spiritual nature, while challenging aspects could suggest the need to address subconscious patterns or navigate spiritual challenges.

Understanding the dynamics of the twelfth house empowers individuals to explore their spiritual path, uncover hidden aspects of the self, and connect with the divine. It encourages individuals to engage in practices such as meditation, dream analysis, and self-reflection to deepen their understanding of themselves and their connection to the larger cosmos.

In Babylonian astrology, the twelfth house plays a vital role in understanding an individual's spirituality, the exploration of the subconscious mind, and the uncovering of hidden aspects of the self. By exploring the energies associated with the twelfth house, individuals can gain insights into their spiritual journey, engage in self-reflection, and embark on a path of self-discovery and personal transformation. It encourages individuals to honor the mysteries of the inner world, embrace the depths of their being, and connect with the divine within and beyond themselves.

Understanding the positions of celestial bodies within these houses allows astrologers to provide insights into specific areas of life. By interpreting the interactions and influences between the planets and the houses, astrologers can gain a comprehensive understanding of an individual's strengths, challenges, potentials, and life circumstances. The houses form an integral part of astrological readings, offering a detailed and holistic perspective on an individual's life journey.

C. Astrological Charts and Interpretation:

Babylonian astrologers constructed astrological charts, known as horoscopes, to map the positions of celestial bodies at the time of an individual's birth or a significant event. These charts served as a fundamental tool for interpreting the cosmic influences upon a person's life. Let's delve into the process of constructing astrological charts and the interpretation methods employed by Babylonian astrologers:

Construction of Astrological Charts:

To create an astrological chart in Babylonian astrology, precise astronomical observations were crucial. Babylonian astrologers recorded the exact positions of celestial bodies, such as the sun, moon, planets, and stars, at a specific moment in time, whether it was the birth of an individual or the occurrence of a significant event. This recording of positions was typically done using instruments like the astrolabe or quadrant, which aided in measuring the angles and distances between celestial bodies.

Observations were made by aligning these instruments with specific reference points on Earth, such as the horizon and the celestial equator. The horizon provided a frame of reference for the ascendant (rising sign) in the astrological chart, while the celestial equator helped establish the position of celestial bodies in relation to Earth's equator.

By meticulously recording the positions of the celestial bodies in relation to these reference points, Babylonian astrologers could create a visual representation known as an astrological chart or horoscope. This chart depicted the positions of the celestial bodies in the zodiacal signs and the specific houses of the astrological system. It served as a symbolic map of the heavens at the moment of the observation.

The astrological chart provided a snapshot of the cosmic energies and influences present at the time of the observation. Babylonian astrologers believed that the positions of celestial bodies at the moment of an event or a person's birth could reveal insights into their character, potentials, and life circumstances. By interpreting the interactions and relationships between the celestial bodies within the chart, astrologers could provide guidance and predictions about various aspects of a person's life, including personality traits, career, relationships, and major life events.

Overall, the process of creating an astrological chart in Babylonian astrology involved precise astronomical observations and the mapping of celestial positions in relation to Earth's reference points, resulting in a visual representation that formed the foundation for astrological analysis and interpretation.

Interpretation of Astrological Charts:

Once the astrological chart was constructed, Babylonian astrologers meticulously interpreted the positions, aspects, and relationships between the celestial bodies to gain insights into various aspects of an individual's life. Here are some key elements considered in the interpretation:

Planetary Positions: In Babylonian astrology, the positions of celestial bodies within the astrological chart were carefully examined to discern their influence on different areas of life. Each celestial body was associated with specific qualities, energies, and archetypal influences that shaped an individual's character, experiences, and potentials.

For instance, the placement of the sun in the chart held great significance. The sun represented the core essence of an individual, their ego, and their overall character. It symbolized their vitality, life force, and self-expression. Its placement in a specific zodiac sign and house within the chart provided insights into the individual's personality traits, motivations, and their approach to life. The sun's position in the chart indicated the area of life where the person was likely to shine and exert their influence.

Similarly, the moon's placement in the chart revealed important information about an individual's emotional nature and inner needs. The moon represented the realm of emotions, instincts, and the subconscious mind. Its position in a zodiac sign and house reflected the individual's emotional responses, nurturing instincts, and receptivity to the world around them. The moon's influence in the chart shed light on how a person sought emotional security, expressed their feelings, and connected with others on an emotional level.

In addition to the sun and moon, other celestial bodies like Mercury, Venus, Mars, Jupiter, and Saturn also played significant roles in shaping different aspects of an individual's life. Each of these planets represented specific energies and qualities that influenced areas such as communication, love, passion, expansion, discipline, responsibility, and more. Their positions in the chart provided valuable insights into an individual's mental abilities, approach to relationships, drive for success, and lessons to be learned.

By analyzing the positions of these celestial bodies within the astrological chart, Babylonian astrologers could offer a comprehensive understanding of an individual's strengths, challenges, potentials, and life circumstances. The interactions and relationships between the celestial bodies were carefully examined to gain deeper insights into the dynamics and influences at play in different areas of the person's life. This allowed for a more nuanced interpretation and provided guidance on how to navigate challenges, make informed decisions, and align with the cosmic energies at work.

Ultimately, the examination of the positions of celestial bodies within the astrological chart formed the basis of Babylonian astrology, enabling astrologers to provide detailed and holistic perspectives on an individual's life journey and the various factors that shape their experiences.

Aspects: In Babylonian astrology, astrologers delved deeper into the dynamics between celestial bodies by analyzing the geometric relationships, known as aspects, that formed between them within the astrological chart. Aspects provided valuable insights into the harmonious or challenging interactions between planets, further shaping an individual's personality traits, strengths, and areas of potential difficulty.

Conjunctions were one of the most significant aspects. They occurred when two celestial bodies were in close proximity to each other, occupying the same zodiac sign or closely aligned within a few degrees. Conjunctions indicated a strong blending and fusion of energies between the planets involved. Depending on the nature of the planets involved, conjunctions could enhance and intensify their combined qualities, creating a potent and focused energy. This could manifest as heightened abilities, concentrated drive, or the potential for significant achievements in the areas represented by those planets.

Oppositions, on the other hand, occurred when two celestial bodies were approximately 180 degrees apart from each other. Oppositions represented a tension or conflict between the energies of the planets involved. This aspect often highlighted areas of inner struggle or external challenges in the individual's life. However, it also presented an opportunity for growth, as the opposition called for finding a balance between the opposing forces and integrating their energies constructively.

Trines were considered harmonious aspects and occurred when two celestial bodies were approximately 120 degrees apart from each other. Trines indicated a flow of energy and ease of expression between the planets involved. This aspect represented areas of natural talent, opportunities, and positive circumstances in the individual's life. Trines were seen as supportive influences that facilitated the manifestation of the planets' energies in a harmonious and productive manner.

There were also other aspects, such as squares, sextiles, and quincunxes, each with its own unique qualities and influences. Squares, for example, occurred when two celestial bodies were approximately 90 degrees apart and represented tension, challenges, and opportunities for growth. Sextiles, occurring at approximately 60 degrees apart, indicated opportunities for cooperation, growth, and creative expression. Quincunxes, with an approximate angle of 150 degrees, reflected adjustments and subtle shifts required for balancing energies.

By studying these aspects within the astrological chart, Babylonian astrologers gained a deeper understanding of the interplay between the celestial bodies and how they influenced the individual's life. The aspects revealed the nuances of the relationships between planets, shaping the individual's personality, strengths, and areas of potential difficulty. They provided astrologers with valuable information to guide individuals in harnessing their potentials, navigating challenges, and aligning with the cosmic energies in a harmonious and constructive way.

In summary, the analysis of aspects within the astrological chart allowed Babylonian astrologers to uncover the intricate interconnections between celestial bodies. By understanding the harmonious and challenging interactions between planets through aspects, astrologers provided valuable insights into an individual's personality traits, strengths, and areas of potential difficulty, enabling them to offer guidance for personal growth, self-awareness, and navigating life's challenges.

House Placement: In Babylonian astrology, the positioning of celestial bodies within the twelve astrological houses held significant importance in the interpretation of an individual's chart. Each house represented a specific area of life, and the placement of planets within these houses provided valuable insights into the individual's experiences, opportunities, and challenges in those particular domains.

The astrological houses represent different facets of human existence, creating a framework through which astrologers analyze and understand various aspects of a person's life journey. Each house has its own unique significance and is associated with specific themes, which are influenced by the celestial bodies residing within them.

For example, the first house, also known as the Ascendant, represents the individual's self-image, physical appearance, and overall personality. It signifies how one presents themselves to the world and reflects their approach to life. Planets positioned in the first house can reveal important aspects of the individual's character, temperament, and outward expression.

By examining the positioning of celestial bodies within these twelve astrological houses, Babylonian astrologers gained a comprehensive understanding of an individual's strengths, challenges, potentials, and life circumstances. This holistic approach allowed astrologers to provide detailed insights into specific areas of life, guiding individuals in their personal growth, decision-making, and alignment with the cosmic energies at play. The interaction between planets and houses formed a rich tapestry of information that enhanced the astrological reading, offering a nuanced understanding of an individual's life journey and the various forces shaping their experiences.

Planetary Relationships: Babylonian astrologers recognized that the relationships between different planets within an astrological chart held significant meaning and contributed to the overall interpretation of an individual's life circumstances and interpersonal dynamics. These relationships, known as planetary aspects, were believed to create specific energetic dynamics that influenced various areas of life.

One of the most notable planetary aspects is the conjunction, which occurs when two or more planets are positioned closely together in the chart. A conjunction signifies a blending of energies, intensifying the influence of the involved planets. It creates a powerful synergy that can manifest in different ways depending on the planets involved. For example, a conjunction between Mars and Venus might indicate a passionate and harmonious expression of love and desire, while a conjunction between Saturn and Pluto could suggest a transformative and intense period of personal growth.

Another important aspect is the opposition, which occurs when two planets are positioned directly across from each other in the chart. An opposition signifies a polarity or tension between the energies represented by the involved planets. It often reflects a need to find balance or integration between opposing forces. For instance, an opposition between the sun and the moon might indicate a conflict between one's individuality and emotional needs, requiring a conscious effort to reconcile these aspects of oneself.

Trines and sextiles are considered harmonious aspects in which planets are positioned at approximately 120 and 60 degrees apart, respectively. These aspects indicate ease, flow, and opportunities for positive interactions between the involved planets. Trines and sextiles often symbolize areas of natural talents, creativity, and fortunate circumstances. For example, a trine between Mercury and Uranus might suggest a natural aptitude for innovative thinking and intellectual pursuits.

On the other hand, squares and quincunxes are considered challenging aspects that create tension and friction between planets. Squares occur when two planets are positioned at approximately 90 degrees apart, while quincunxes occur at around 150 degrees apart. These aspects often represent areas of internal conflict, obstacles, and lessons to be learned. They may highlight areas of personal growth and the need to overcome challenges. For instance, a square between Mars and Saturn could indicate a struggle to find a balance between assertiveness and discipline.

By analyzing these planetary aspects within the chart, Babylonian astrologers gained deeper insights into the energetic dynamics at play in an individual's life. They could identify areas of harmony, tension, growth, and challenge, providing a more nuanced understanding of the individual's personality, relationships, and life circumstances. The interactions between planets through aspects added layers of complexity to the astrological interpretation, allowing astrologers to paint a more detailed picture of the individual's unique journey.

Fixed Stars: In Babylonian astrology, fixed stars held a significant place in the interpretation of an astrological chart. Fixed stars were specific stars that appeared to maintain a relatively fixed position in the night sky, in contrast to the wandering planets. These stars were believed to possess their own unique qualities and influences that could enhance or modify the effects of the planets they interacted with.

The position of fixed stars in relation to the celestial bodies within the chart added an additional layer of interpretation and significance. Babylonian astrologers meticulously observed and recorded the positions of these fixed stars, noting their proximity to planets and other important points in the chart, such as the Ascendant or Midheaven. This information provided astrologers with valuable insights into the specific qualities and influences associated with each fixed star.

Each fixed star was associated with its own set of meanings, mythological associations, and qualities. For example, the star Regulus, also known as the "Heart of the Lion," was associated with themes of leadership, ambition, and creativity. Its alignment with a planet in the chart could amplify these qualities, indicating a strong drive for success and recognition.

The effects of fixed stars were often interpreted in conjunction with the planets they interacted with. The influence of a fixed star could modify or enhance the qualities of a planet, adding depth and nuance to its interpretation. For example, if a planet was closely aligned with a fixed star known for its positive qualities, it could signify a favorable or fortunate influence in the individual's life. On the other hand, alignment with a fixed star associated with challenges or difficulties might indicate areas of struggle or obstacles to overcome.

The interpretations of fixed stars in Babylonian astrology were based on both astronomical observations and ancient mythological associations. The lore and symbolism surrounding these stars were passed down through generations, contributing to a rich tapestry of astrological knowledge. Babylonian astrologers carefully studied the positions and alignments of fixed stars, utilizing their insights to provide a more nuanced understanding of an individual's life circumstances, personality traits, and potential.

By considering the influence of fixed stars alongside the planets within an astrological chart, Babylonian astrologers gained a deeper understanding of the intricate web of cosmic influences that shaped an individual's life. The unique qualities and mythological associations of fixed stars added an extra layer of interpretation, allowing for a more comprehensive and nuanced astrological reading.

Interpretive Principles:

The interpretation of astrological charts was guided by a set of principles and symbolic associations established by Babylonian astrologers. These principles included recognizing the significance of celestial bodies, understanding the meanings of aspects and house placements, and considering the broader cultural and mythological context associated with specific planets and stars.

The interpretation of astrological charts aimed to provide insights into an individual's personality traits, potentials, challenges, and life circumstances. It allowed individuals to gain a deeper understanding of themselves, their relationships, and their life paths. Babylonian astrologers provided guidance based on the cosmic influences revealed in the chart, enabling individuals to make informed decisions and navigate their lives with greater self-awareness.

It is important to note that the interpretation of astrological charts is a complex and nuanced process that requires deep knowledge and expertise. Babylonian astrologers dedicated years to studying and refining their skills in order to provide accurate and insightful readings based on the positions and relationships of celestial bodies within astrological charts.

Cultural Significance:

A. The Royal Court and Ruling Class:

Astrology held a prominent role within the royal court and among the ruling elite in ancient Babylon. The Babylonian rulers recognized the profound influence of celestial forces on human affairs and considered astrology as a valuable tool for decision-making and governance. Let us explore the significance of astrology within the royal court and its impact on the ruling class:

Guidance for State Affairs:

Babylonian rulers held a deep belief in the power of astrology and its ability to provide guidance from the divine realm. They recognized that celestial alignments and the timing of significant events played a crucial role in the outcome of their endeavors. As a result, they heavily relied on the expertise of astrologers to make important decisions regarding state affairs.

Astrologers in ancient Babylon were considered highly skilled and knowledgeable individuals who possessed the ability to interpret the celestial movements and their impact on human affairs. They carefully observed and recorded the positions of planets, stars, and other celestial bodies, using sophisticated instruments like astrolabes and quadrants to track their movements. By analyzing these celestial patterns and alignments, astrologers could provide valuable insights into the auspicious timings and favorable conditions for various activities.

When it came to matters of great significance, such as initiating military campaigns, establishing new cities, or conducting important ceremonies, Babylonian rulers sought the counsel of astrologers. These astrologers would study the celestial configurations and advise the rulers on the most opportune moments to commence these activities. They would consider factors such as the positions of planets and stars, the alignment of constellations, and the overall cosmic energies present at a given time.

The Babylonian rulers believed that by aligning their actions with the cosmic forces, they could ensure success and gain the favor of the gods. They understood that the celestial bodies were seen as embodiments of the divine, and their movements and interactions were believed to reflect the will of the gods. By heeding the guidance of astrologers, rulers aimed to harmonize their intentions and actions with the cosmic order, seeking divine approval and support for their endeavors.

Astrologers played a crucial role in advising Babylonian rulers on matters of statecraft, helping them navigate the complexities of decision-making in alignment with the cosmic forces. Their insights and predictions were highly valued, and their counsel carried significant weight in shaping the course of events. Rulers understood that by consulting astrologers and considering the auspicious timings and celestial alignments, they could increase their chances of success and mitigate potential risks.

The reliance on astrologers by Babylonian rulers was not merely a matter of personal belief or superstition. It was deeply rooted in the cultural and religious context of the time, where the connection between the celestial and earthly realms was seen as a fundamental aspect of life. The rulers recognized the importance of cosmic harmony and the need to align their actions with the divine order, as they believed it had a direct impact on the prosperity and well-being of their kingdom.

In conclusion, Babylonian rulers placed great trust in the expertise of astrologers to seek guidance and make crucial decisions pertaining to state affairs. Astrologers provided insights into celestial alignments and auspicious timings, enabling rulers to align their actions with the cosmic forces and seek divine approval. Their counsel played a significant role in shaping the course of events and ensuring the success of important endeavors.

Determining Auspicious Dates:

Astrology held immense significance in the Babylonian royal court when it came to selecting auspicious dates for important events and ceremonies. Babylonian astrologers meticulously analyzed the positions and interactions of celestial bodies to identify favorable cosmic alignments that were believed to bring blessings, good fortune, and success to these occasions.

The Babylonian rulers understood that the cosmic energies at specific times could greatly influence the outcome and impact of important events. They recognized that by selecting auspicious dates aligned with favorable celestial configurations, they could enhance the significance of the occasion, legitimize their authority, and ensure the success of the event or ceremony.

Babylonian astrologers, well-versed in the intricate knowledge of celestial movements, carefully observed the positions of planets, stars, and other celestial bodies. They studied their alignments, such as planetary conjunctions, favorable aspects, or the absence of challenging aspects, to determine the most propitious moments for various activities within the royal court.

For example, coronations, royal weddings, or the birth of an heir were pivotal events that required careful consideration of the cosmic influences. The astrologers would analyze the astrological chart for the specific date and time proposed for the event. They would examine the positioning of celestial bodies, paying close attention to planets like the sun, moon, and significant stars. They would also consider the astrological houses and aspects to understand the potential impact on the individuals involved and the overall success of the occasion.

By selecting an auspicious date aligned with favorable celestial alignments, the rulers believed they could harness the supportive cosmic energies, attracting blessings and ensuring the success of the event. It was believed that these cosmic alignments would not only enhance the ruler's authority and prestige but also contribute to the overall harmony and prosperity of the kingdom.

The importance of astrology in determining auspicious dates extended beyond the royal court to various ceremonies and public events within Babylonian society. From religious festivals to agricultural rituals and military campaigns, the guidance of astrologers played a significant role in selecting the most favorable times to initiate these activities. The astrologers' expertise and insights were sought to ensure the alignment of human actions with the divine cosmic order.

The belief in the power of astrology to shape the outcome of important events and ceremonies was deeply ingrained in Babylonian culture and religious practices. The rulers and the people alike placed great trust in the wisdom of astrologers, recognizing that the cosmic forces were intimately connected to their everyday lives and the well-being of the kingdom.

In summary, astrology held a critical role in determining auspicious dates for important events and ceremonies within the Babylonian royal court. The careful examination of celestial positions and interactions by astrologers enabled the identification of favorable cosmic alignments that were believed to bring blessings, good fortune, and success to these occasions. The selection of auspicious dates enhanced the significance of the events, further legitimizing the ruler's authority and ensuring the overall prosperity of the kingdom.

Establishing Alliances:

Astrology played a significant role in the formation of alliances and diplomatic relations in ancient Babylon. The Babylonian rulers recognized the potential impact of celestial configurations on the compatibility and success of alliances, and they sought the guidance of astrologers to assess these factors.

When considering potential alliances with other kingdoms or city-states, Babylonian rulers consulted astrologers to examine the astrological charts of both parties. The astrologers analyzed the positions of celestial bodies, the aspects between them, and the overall cosmic dynamics to determine the compatibility and potential benefits of the alliance.

By comparing the astrological charts of the two entities, the astrologers could gain insights into the harmonious or challenging aspects of their cosmic influences. They looked for alignments that indicated mutual support, shared goals, and compatible energies. These alignments were believed to foster cooperation, strengthen the bond between the kingdoms, and ensure the success of collaborative endeavors.

For example, if the astrologers identified favorable aspects, such as harmonious planetary conjunctions or trines, between the celestial bodies representing the ruling entities, it was considered a positive indication of compatibility and alignment of interests. This was seen as an auspicious cosmic configuration that would promote mutual understanding, harmony, and success in diplomatic and political matters.

Conversely, if the astrologers observed challenging aspects, such as planetary squares or oppositions, between the celestial bodies of the two entities, it was seen as a potential source of conflict or discord. These alignments would raise caution and require careful consideration before proceeding with the alliance.

The Babylonian rulers understood that by aligning their kingdom with another entity that had favorable celestial influences, they could potentially benefit from the positive energies associated with that alliance. They believed that the cosmic forces at play could create a favorable environment for cooperation, mutual growth, and shared prosperity.

Astrology, therefore, served as a valuable tool in the diplomatic arena, enabling the rulers to assess the potential compatibility and success of alliances based on celestial configurations. By considering the cosmic influences, the rulers could make informed decisions and strategically align their kingdom with those believed to have favorable celestial connections.

The utilization of astrology in the formation of alliances and diplomatic relations was not limited to Babylonian rulers. Other ancient civilizations also recognized the importance of celestial influences and consulted astrologers to assess compatibility and ensure the success of alliances.

In summary, astrology played a crucial role in the formation of alliances and diplomatic relations in ancient Babylon. Rulers sought the guidance of astrologers to assess the compatibility and potential benefits of alliances based on celestial configurations. By aligning their kingdom with entities believed to have favorable celestial influences, the rulers aimed to strengthen the alliances and ensure mutual benefits. Astrology provided a framework for evaluating compatibility and making informed decisions in the realm of diplomacy and international relations.

Legitimacy and Divine Approval:

In ancient Babylon, the perceived alignment of cosmic forces with the ruler's decisions and actions played a significant role in adding legitimacy and divine approval to their authority. The belief in the connection between celestial influences and earthly rulership was deeply ingrained in the Babylonian culture and worldview.

The Babylonian rulers understood that their actions and decisions had far-reaching consequences, not only for their kingdom but also in the cosmic realm. They believed that by aligning their rule with the celestial influences, they were demonstrating their adherence to the cosmic order and harmonizing their actions with the divine will.

By consulting astrologers and seeking guidance based on celestial configurations, the rulers aimed to ensure that their decisions were in harmony with the cosmic forces. This alignment was seen as a sign of divine favor and approval, as it implied that the ruler was in tune with the higher powers that governed the universe.

The belief in the connection between celestial forces and earthly rulership served to reinforce the ruler's position and justify their decisions in the eyes of the people. It provided a framework for understanding the ruler's authority as being rooted in something greater than mere human governance.

When the ruler could demonstrate that their actions were in alignment with the cosmic influences, it added a sense of legitimacy to their rule. It conveyed the idea that the ruler's authority was sanctioned by the gods and that their decisions were guided by higher wisdom.

This perception of divine approval enhanced the ruler's prestige and authority among the populace. The people believed that the ruler's alignment with the cosmic forces would bring about favorable outcomes, protect the kingdom from harm, and ensure the prosperity and well-being of the people.

The belief in the connection between celestial forces and rulership also fostered a sense of cosmic order and stability within the society. It provided a framework for understanding the larger purpose and meaning behind the ruler's actions and decisions. This belief system helped to maintain social cohesion and reinforce the hierarchical structure of Babylonian society.

Furthermore, the perceived alignment with cosmic forces allowed the rulers to present themselves as rightful and ordained leaders. They could assert that their rule was not based solely on human power or political maneuvering but was sanctioned by the divine realm.

In summary, the perceived alignment of cosmic forces with the ruler's decisions and actions added legitimacy and divine approval to their authority in ancient Babylon. By demonstrating their adherence to the cosmic order and aligning their rule with the celestial influences, the rulers presented themselves as rightful and ordained leaders. This belief in the connection between celestial forces and earthly rulership reinforced the ruler's position and justified their decisions in the eyes of the people. It provided a sense of stability, order, and divine purpose within the society, strengthening the ruler's authority and fostering a belief in the cosmic significance of their rule.

Propagating Power and Authority:

The rulers' patronage of astrology and their close association with astrologers played a crucial role in solidifying their power and authority within Babylonian society. By aligning themselves with the practice of astrology, the rulers demonstrated their access to privileged knowledge and their ability to harness the cosmic forces for the benefit of the kingdom.

Astrology held immense significance in Babylonian culture, with its practitioners being regarded as highly skilled and knowledgeable individuals. Astrologers were seen as intermediaries between the celestial and earthly realms, capable of interpreting the messages of the stars and providing guidance based on their observations and calculations.

By cultivating a close relationship with astrologers, the rulers showcased their connection to this esoteric field of study. They presented themselves as individuals who had insight into the workings of the universe and could use that knowledge to make informed decisions that would shape the destiny of their kingdom.

The rulers' patronage of astrology also elevated their status within society. It highlighted their ability to access specialized knowledge that was not readily available to the general populace. This association with astrology served to set them apart from ordinary individuals and further solidify their position as leaders who possessed unique insight and wisdom.

Moreover, the rulers' close relationship with astrologers allowed them to utilize the cosmic forces as a tool for governance. They sought the guidance of astrologers to make important decisions, such as determining auspicious timings for significant events, assessing potential alliances, or initiating military campaigns. This reliance on astrology implied that the rulers' actions were not solely based on personal ambition or political calculations but were in harmony with the larger cosmic order.

The rulers' patronage of astrology also had a practical aspect. Astrologers' knowledge and calculations could be utilized to enhance the kingdom's prospects for success and prosperity. By consulting astrologers, the rulers aimed to align their actions with favorable celestial influences, thus increasing the likelihood of positive outcomes for their rule and the well-being of the kingdom.

In the eyes of the people, the rulers' association with astrology provided reassurance and confidence. It created a sense that the rulers were guided by higher powers and had access to wisdom that surpassed ordinary human capabilities. This association added an air of mystique and authority to the rulers' persona, contributing to their overall image as powerful and enlightened leaders.

By patronizing astrology and maintaining a close relationship with astrologers, the rulers were able to establish themselves as central figures in the cosmic narrative of their kingdom. Their alignment with the celestial forces and their ability to harness the wisdom of astrology reinforced their power, authority, and divine mandate in the eyes of their subjects.

In conclusion, the rulers' patronage of astrology and their association with astrologers played a vital role in solidifying their power and authority within Babylonian society. Their close relationship with astrology showcased their access to privileged knowledge and their ability to harness the cosmic forces for the benefit of the kingdom. This association elevated their status, consolidated their rule, and created a sense of confidence and legitimacy among the people.

Influence on Court Culture:

The significance of astrology within the royal court of ancient Babylon extended far beyond its practical applications in decision-making. It was deeply ingrained in the court culture and had a profound influence on various aspects of Babylonian society. Astrology shaped religious practices, architectural design, and artistic expressions, emphasizing the belief in the interconnectedness of the celestial and earthly realms.

Religious rituals and practices were intricately tied to astrology within the royal court. Temples and sacred spaces were often constructed and oriented in alignment with celestial events, such as the solstices or equinoxes. These celestial alignments were believed to enhance the spiritual connection between the rulers, the gods, and the people. The timing of festivals and rituals was also carefully determined based on astrological considerations. Astrologers would identify auspicious dates and times for religious ceremonies, ensuring that they were conducted in harmony with the cosmic energies and aligning the intentions of the rulers with divine forces.

Astrology also influenced the architectural design of the royal court. Buildings and structures were often constructed with astrological symbolism in mind. For example, the positioning of windows, doorways, and other architectural elements may have been influenced by the alignment of celestial bodies. These design choices not only served aesthetic purposes but were also believed to create a harmonious and auspicious environment in accordance with astrological principles.

Artistic expressions within the royal court were also influenced by astrology. Artists often depicted celestial motifs and symbols in their artworks, reflecting the belief in the celestial influences on earthly affairs. Paintings, sculptures, and other forms of artistic representations showcased celestial bodies, zodiac signs, and mythological figures associated with astrology. These artworks not only celebrated the rulers' connection to the cosmic forces but also served as a visual reminder of the larger cosmic order and the ruler's place within it.

Furthermore, astrology within the royal court fostered a sense of spirituality and cosmic awareness. The rulers and the ruling class embraced the belief that their actions and decisions were interconnected with the celestial realm. This understanding influenced their worldview and their perception of themselves as both earthly leaders and participants in a larger cosmic narrative. By aligning their rule with the celestial influences, they sought to ensure the prosperity, success, and divine approval of their kingdom.

In conclusion, astrology held immense significance within the royal court of ancient Babylon, going beyond practical decision-making. It permeated the court culture, shaping religious practices, architectural design, and artistic expressions. Astrology influenced the timing of festivals and rituals, the construction of sacred spaces, and the artistic depictions within the royal court. It emphasized the belief in the interconnectedness of the celestial and earthly realms, strengthening the spiritual connection between the rulers, the gods, and the people. Astrology played a fundamental role in shaping the cultural and religious fabric of the royal court and left a lasting impact on Babylonian society as a whole.

B. Personal Guidance and Self-Knowledge:

In ancient Babylonian society, astrology served as a powerful tool for individuals seeking personal guidance and self-knowledge. It provided a framework for understanding oneself and one's place in the universe. Let's delve deeper into how astrology offered insights into personal characteristics, relationships, and life paths:

Personality Traits and Characteristics:

The Babylonians held a strong belief in the influence of celestial bodies on human lives, particularly at the time of birth. They believed that the positions of the sun, moon, and planets at the moment of an individual's birth held profound significance and played a crucial role in shaping their personality, traits, and inclinations. Astrologers meticulously analyzed these celestial placements within the astrological chart to provide insights into an individual's unique nature.

The sun, as the central celestial body in the chart, represented the core essence and individuality of a person. Its position indicated their fundamental character, ego, and sense of self. The sun's placement in specific zodiac signs and houses revealed key aspects of an individual's temperament, strengths, and weaknesses. For example, a person with the sun in a fire sign might exhibit a passionate and outgoing nature, while someone with the sun in an earth sign might possess practicality and groundedness.

The moon, representing emotions and instincts, held equal importance in the Babylonian astrological system. Its placement in the chart shed light on an individual's emotional landscape, nurturing instincts, and intuitive reactions. The moon's sign and house placement revealed one's emotional needs, responses to different situations, and attunement to the world around them. For instance, a person with the moon in a water sign might be highly empathetic and sensitive, while someone with the moon in an air sign might prioritize intellectual understanding over emotional expression.

Beyond the sun and moon, the positions of other planets in the astrological chart provided additional layers of insight into an individual's personality and inclinations. Each planet represented specific energies and archetypal qualities that influenced different areas of life. For example, Mercury symbolized communication and intellect, Venus represented love and aesthetics, Mars signified action and assertion, Jupiter denoted expansion and wisdom, and Saturn represented discipline and life lessons. The zodiac sign and house placements of these planets contributed to an understanding of an individual's mental abilities, approach to love and relationships, drive for achievement, potential for growth, and areas of personal challenge.

By delving into these astrological influences, individuals gained a deeper understanding of themselves and their unique qualities. Astrology provided a framework for self-reflection, self-acceptance, and personal growth. It allowed individuals to recognize and embrace their strengths, navigate their weaknesses, and align with their natural inclinations. Furthermore, astrology offered insights into the dynamics between different planetary placements, revealing patterns of interaction and potential areas of harmony or challenge within an individual's life.

In Babylonian society, astrology served as a tool for self-awareness and self-empowerment. By understanding their astrological influences, individuals could harness their inherent strengths and work on areas of improvement. It provided a language to discuss and explore human nature, fostering a sense of connection with the cosmic order. Through astrology, the Babylonians sought to gain a deeper understanding of themselves and the world around them, ultimately enhancing their personal growth, relationships, and overall well-being.

Relationship Dynamics:

Astrology has long been utilized as a valuable tool for understanding and navigating relationships in Babylonian society and beyond. Astrologers examined the astrological compatibility between individuals, analyzing the interplay of their birth charts to gain insights into the dynamics of their relationships.

In romantic relationships, astrology provided valuable guidance on compatibility and potential challenges. By comparing the sun signs, moon signs, and other planetary placements of both partners, astrologers could assess the level of harmony and understanding between them. For example, a compatible sun sign pairing could indicate shared values and overall compatibility, while contrasting moon signs might suggest differing emotional needs that require understanding and compromise. Astrologers also considered aspects between Venus (representing love and romance) and Mars (symbolizing passion and desire) to gauge the potential for chemistry and attraction.

In familial relationships, astrology shed light on the dynamics and interactions within the family unit. Birth charts of family members were analyzed to uncover potential areas of similarity or conflict. Understanding the astrological influences at play could help family members navigate differences in temperament, communication styles, and emotional needs. For instance, knowing that a family member has a strong emphasis on fire signs might suggest a more energetic and assertive nature, while an emphasis on earth signs might indicate practicality and stability.

Astrology also played a role in understanding social relationships and friendships. By comparing birth charts, individuals could gain insights into their shared interests, common values, and areas of connection. For example, if two individuals had compatible placements in the house of communication, they might find it easier to connect intellectually and enjoy engaging conversations. By understanding the astrological influences at play, individuals could navigate their social interactions with more empathy, understanding potential areas of friction and finding common ground.

Astrology not only provided insights into potential challenges within relationships but also offered guidance on how to cultivate harmonious connections. Astrologers would identify areas of compatibility and strengths between individuals, highlighting the potential for mutual understanding, support, and growth. By recognizing and working with these harmonious aspects, individuals could nurture healthier and more fulfilling relationships.

Moreover, astrology offered a language and framework for discussing and understanding relationship dynamics. It provided individuals with a deeper awareness of their own and others' unique qualities, needs, and communication styles. This understanding fostered empathy, compassion, and better communication, as individuals could appreciate the differences and similarities that astrological influences bring to their relationships.

In summary, astrology served as a valuable tool for understanding and navigating relationships. By examining astrological compatibility and understanding the astrological influences at play, individuals gained insights into potential challenges, areas of harmony, and opportunities for growth within their relationships. Astrology provided a framework for communication, empathy, and understanding, enhancing the quality of connections and fostering more fulfilling relationships in Babylonian society.

Life Path and Potential Challenges:

Astrology has long been regarded as a powerful tool for gaining insights into an individual's life path and the potential challenges they may face. By analyzing the astrological chart, astrologers could identify significant planetary aspects and alignments that hold significance in shaping an individual's journey.

The astrological chart, also known as the natal chart or birth chart, is a snapshot of the positions of the celestial bodies at the moment of an individual's birth. It provides a unique blueprint that outlines the potential energies and influences that will shape their life experiences. By studying the planetary placements, aspects, and houses within the chart, astrologers can uncover valuable information about an individual's life path, talents, challenges, and areas of growth.

Significant planetary aspects and alignments within the chart offer insights into the potential challenges an individual may encounter. For example, a challenging aspect between Saturn and the Moon could indicate a need for emotional maturity and a potential struggle with emotional security. Awareness of such challenges empowers individuals to proactively address and navigate them with resilience and self-awareness.

Additionally, astrologers can identify supportive aspects and alignments that indicate areas of strength and potential opportunities for growth. These aspects can highlight innate talents, favorable circumstances, and favorable alignments of cosmic energies that individuals can tap into to enhance their life path. For instance, a harmonious aspect between Jupiter and the Sun might indicate a natural inclination towards personal growth, success, and expansion in one's chosen path.

By gaining insights into the potential challenges and opportunities indicated in the astrological chart, individuals can make informed decisions and align themselves with the cosmic influences that are at play in their lives. Astrology empowers individuals to proactively prepare for challenges, make strategic choices, and seize opportunities that are in harmony with their cosmic influences.

Astrology also provides individuals with a sense of purpose and direction. By understanding the unique qualities and inclinations suggested by the astrological chart, individuals can gain a deeper understanding of their life's purpose and the areas of life where they are likely to find fulfillment and growth. This knowledge helps individuals make conscious choices that align with their inherent potentials, fostering a sense of fulfillment and meaning in their journey.

It is important to note that while astrology provides valuable insights and guidance, it does not determine an individual's destiny or negate the importance of personal agency and free will. Rather, it offers a framework for self-reflection, self-awareness, and understanding the energies at play in one's life. With this understanding, individuals can navigate their life path with greater clarity, purpose, and alignment with their cosmic influences.

In conclusion, astrology offers individuals a sense of their life path and potential challenges they may encounter along the way. By analyzing the astrological chart, astrologers provide insights into significant planetary aspects and alignments that shape an individual's journey. This knowledge enables individuals to prepare for and navigate potential obstacles, make informed decisions, and pursue opportunities that align with their cosmic influences. Astrology empowers individuals to live more consciously and purposefully, embracing their unique potentials and embracing the journey of self-discovery and growth.

Self-Awareness and Decision Making:

Astrology serves as a powerful tool for fostering self-awareness and facilitating personal growth. By delving into the insights provided by astrology, individuals gain a deeper understanding of their unique qualities, tendencies, and potentials. This heightened self-awareness enables individuals to make more informed decisions and choices that align with their true nature and cosmic influences.

Astrology offers a language and framework for understanding oneself on a profound level. Through the analysis of the astrological chart, individuals can identify their strengths, weaknesses, and potential challenges. For example, a person with a strong Mars placement may possess great energy and assertiveness but may need to work on channeling this energy constructively rather than becoming overly aggressive. By recognizing these tendencies, individuals can consciously leverage their strengths while actively addressing areas that require improvement.

The insights provided by astrology help individuals navigate their life journey with a greater sense of purpose and direction. Astrology sheds light on an individual's inclinations, passions, and purpose, offering a deeper understanding of what drives them and what brings them fulfillment. For instance, a person with a prominent placement of Venus may find great joy and satisfaction in pursuing creative endeavors or nurturing loving relationships. By aligning their actions with these inclinations, individuals can lead more fulfilling and authentic lives.

Astrology also acts as a guide for personal growth and development. By understanding the potential challenges indicated in the astrological chart, individuals can actively work on those areas to overcome obstacles and grow as individuals. For instance, if the chart suggests a tendency towards perfectionism and self-criticism due to a challenging aspect between Mercury and Saturn, the individual can consciously cultivate self-compassion and strive for a healthier balance between self-improvement and self-acceptance.

Furthermore, astrology offers individuals validation and affirmation of their unique qualities and experiences. It provides a context for understanding the reasons behind certain patterns, preferences, and life events. This validation can be empowering and liberating, as individuals realize that they are not alone in their experiences and that their cosmic influences are part of a larger cosmic tapestry.

Ultimately, astrology serves as a tool for personal empowerment. It empowers individuals to embrace their true selves, make choices aligned with their authentic nature, and actively work on personal growth and development. By recognizing their strengths, weaknesses, and potential challenges, individuals can navigate their life paths with greater self-awareness, purpose, and fulfillment. Astrology offers a profound opportunity for individuals to embrace their cosmic influences and embark on a journey of self-discovery, self-acceptance, and personal transformation.

Navigating Life's Complexities:

Indeed, life can be a complex and unpredictable journey, filled with various challenges and uncertainties. In such a context, astrology serves as a guiding light, offering individuals a sense of direction and purpose. By delving into their astrological influences, individuals gain a unique perspective that helps them navigate the intricacies of life with greater understanding and clarity.

Astrology provides a lens through which individuals can view their experiences and circumstances. It offers insights into the cosmic energies at play during specific periods of their lives, allowing them to make sense of the challenges and opportunities they encounter. For example, during a period characterized by a challenging aspect between Saturn and Uranus, an individual may experience a clash between the need for stability and the desire for change and innovation. Understanding this cosmic dynamic provides valuable insight into the underlying forces influencing their experiences and assists in making informed decisions.

By understanding their astrological influences, individuals gain a deeper sense of purpose and meaning in their lives. Astrology unveils the unique qualities, talents, and potentials that individuals possess, shedding light on their life path and soul's journey. It helps individuals identify their passions, strengths, and areas of personal growth, enabling them to align their actions with their cosmic influences. This alignment brings a sense of fulfillment and satisfaction as individuals pursue paths that resonate with their authentic selves.

Astrology also provides individuals with a broader perspective on life's challenges and uncertainties. By recognizing that certain periods may be more conducive to introspection, growth, or change, individuals can navigate these phases with greater acceptance and resilience. They understand that challenges are part of their personal evolution and that even the most difficult circumstances can hold valuable lessons and opportunities for growth.

Moreover, astrology offers individuals a sense of reassurance and comfort during times of uncertainty. It reminds them that they are part of a larger cosmic web, interconnected with the rhythms and cycles of the universe. In moments of doubt or confusion, astrology can provide a sense of validation and guidance, reassuring individuals that their experiences are not arbitrary but have purpose and meaning within the greater cosmic order.

Astrology encourages individuals to embrace their free will while acknowledging the cosmic influences that shape their lives. It empowers them to make conscious choices that align with their unique cosmic blueprint, rather than feeling like passive recipients of fate. Individuals can actively engage with their astrological influences, making informed decisions and taking proactive steps towards personal growth, relationships, career paths, and overall well-being.

In summary, astrology offers individuals a valuable tool for navigating life's complexities. By understanding their astrological influences, individuals gain a deeper sense of purpose, meaning, and direction. It provides a lens through which they can view their experiences, offering insights and perspectives that guide decision-making and foster personal growth. Astrology empowers individuals to embrace their unique cosmic influences, make informed choices, and approach life's challenges with resilience and a deeper sense of understanding.

Cultivating Self-Reflection and Growth:

Astrology has always encouraged individuals to engage in self-reflection and personal growth. By examining their astrological chart and considering the insights provided by astrologers, individuals are prompted to delve deeper into their own patterns, behaviors, and choices. This introspective process allows for personal growth and self-improvement, as individuals gain a deeper understanding of themselves and their potential.

Astrology serves as a catalyst for self-reflection by offering individuals a language and framework to explore their inner world. By examining the placements of celestial bodies and the aspects within their astrological chart, individuals can uncover patterns and themes that shape their lives. For example, they may recognize recurring challenges or recurring strengths that provide insight into their personal growth journey.

Through astrology, individuals gain a greater awareness of their strengths, weaknesses, and areas for personal development. They become more attuned to their unique qualities, talents, and aspirations, which allows them to make conscious choices aligned with their authentic selves. By understanding their astrological influences, individuals can identify areas of growth and work towards self-improvement. For instance, if their chart reveals a challenging aspect related to communication, they may focus on developing effective communication skills and overcoming barriers in expressing themselves.

Astrology also fosters self-acceptance and self-compassion. By recognizing that their astrological influences shape certain aspects of their personality and life circumstances, individuals can embrace and accept themselves more fully. They understand that they are part of a larger cosmic tapestry and that their individual journey is meaningful within the broader context of the universe.

Furthermore, astrology encourages individuals to take responsibility for their actions and choices. It highlights the interplay between free will and cosmic influences, emphasizing that while individuals have agency in shaping their lives, they are also subject to the energetic currents of the universe. This awareness prompts individuals to make conscious decisions and consider the potential outcomes and consequences of their choices.

In conclusion, astrology serves as a valuable tool for personal growth and self-knowledge. It prompts individuals to engage in self-reflection, recognize their patterns and potentials, and make informed choices aligned with their cosmic influences. Astrology fosters self-awareness, self-acceptance, and self-compassion, empowering individuals to navigate life's challenges and embrace their unique journey of personal growth.

C. Cultural and Religious Practices:

Astrology played a significant role in Babylonian religious and cultural practices. Temples and sacred spaces were aligned with celestial events and dedicated to specific deities associated with celestial bodies. Festivals and rituals were often timed according to astrological considerations, allowing the harnessing of cosmic energies for spiritual connection and communal celebration.

Legacy and Influence:

The Babylonian astrological system laid the foundation for subsequent astrological traditions that emerged across different cultures and time periods. Its influence can be seen in Hellenistic astrology, which flourished during the Greco-Roman period, as well as in Islamic astrology and medieval European astrology. The basic principles and concepts developed by the Babylonians continue to shape astrological practices and interpretations to this day.

➢   Constructing Astrological Charts:

A. The Natal Chart:

The natal chart, also referred to as a birth chart or horoscope, is a fundamental tool in Babylonian astrology. It is a graphical representation of the positions of celestial bodies at the precise time and location of an individual's birth. The natal chart is believed to imprint individuals with distinct characteristics and predispositions that shape their lives. Let's explore the components and significance of the natal chart in more detail:

Gathering Birth Information:

Constructing a natal chart in astrology requires accurate birth information, as it forms the foundation for interpreting the celestial influences on an individual's life. The three key components needed are the date, time, and location of an individual's birth.

The date of birth provides the starting point for calculating the positions of the celestial bodies at the time of birth. Each day corresponds to a specific alignment of the planets, stars, and other celestial bodies. This information is essential for accurately mapping the positions of the sun, moon, planets, and other significant celestial bodies within the natal chart.

The time of birth is a crucial factor in constructing an accurate natal chart. The positions of celestial bodies are constantly in motion, and even a difference of a few minutes can lead to significant variations in the chart. The birth time determines the exact moment when the individual takes their first breath and enters the world. This moment marks the initiation of their unique journey, and the positions of celestial bodies at that precise instant are believed to shape their personality traits, potentials, and life experiences. Accurate birth time allows astrologers to pinpoint the exact positions of celestial bodies and determine their specific influences on an individual's life.

The location of birth is another crucial element in constructing a natal chart. The latitude and longitude of the birthplace are necessary to accurately calculate the angles and houses within the chart. The positions of the celestial bodies are observed and recorded based on specific reference points, such as the horizon and the celestial equator. The location of birth provides the necessary coordinates to determine these reference points and accurately place the celestial bodies within the chart.

It's important to note that an accurate birth chart requires precise and reliable birth information. In some cases, individuals may not have access to their exact birth time, which can introduce some uncertainties in the chart's interpretation. In such situations, astrologers may use alternative methods, such as rectification techniques, to approximate the birth time and construct a more accurate chart.

In conclusion, constructing a natal chart in astrology requires accurate birth information, including the date, time, and location of an individual's birth. The precise moment of birth is crucial because the positions of celestial bodies constantly shift, and even a slight difference in birth time can lead to significant variations in the natal chart's interpretation. Accurate birth information forms the basis for understanding an individual's unique cosmic influences and provides insights into their personality traits, potentials, and life experiences.

Mapping the Celestial Bodies:

Once the accurate birth information is gathered, Babylonian astrologers used it to map the positions of celestial bodies onto the natal chart. The natal chart is a graphical representation of the positions of celestial bodies at the exact moment of an individual's birth. It serves as a snapshot of the cosmic energies influencing the individual's life.

The most commonly included celestial bodies in the natal chart are the sun, moon, and planets. The sun represents the core essence of an individual, their vitality, and their sense of self. Its position in the zodiac sign and degree indicates the individual's basic character traits, ego expression, and overall life purpose.

The moon symbolizes emotions, instincts, and the inner emotional world. Its position in the natal chart reveals an individual's emotional nature, needs, and responses to the world around them. The moon's zodiac sign and degree provide insights into the individual's emotional patterns, nurturing tendencies, and subconscious influences.

The planets, including Mercury, Venus, Mars, Jupiter, Saturn, Uranus, Neptune, and Pluto, each represent specific energies and areas of life. The position of each planet in the natal chart signifies different aspects of the individual's personality, inclinations, and life experiences. For example, Mercury is associated with communication and intellect, Venus with love and relationships, Mars with passion and assertiveness, and so on. The zodiac sign and degree of each planet in the chart provide further details about how these energies manifest in the individual's life.

In addition to the sun, moon, and planets, Babylonian astrologers sometimes considered significant asteroids or fixed stars in the natal chart. Asteroids such as Chiron, Ceres, Juno, and Vesta, among others, may provide additional insights into specific areas of life, such as healing, nurturing, partnership, and devotion. Fixed stars, which are specific stars believed to maintain a fixed position in the sky, were also occasionally considered for their symbolic significance and potential influences on an individual's life.

The positions of celestial bodies in the natal chart are identified by their zodiacal sign and degree. The zodiac consists of twelve signs, each associated with specific qualities and characteristics. The degree of a celestial body's position within a zodiac sign refines the interpretation and provides additional information about its influence.

By mapping the positions of celestial bodies onto the natal chart and noting the zodiac signs and degrees, Babylonian astrologers gained a comprehensive understanding of an individual's unique cosmic influences. These positions formed the basis for interpreting the individual's personality traits, inclinations, and life experiences, providing valuable insights into their journey through life.

In conclusion, using the gathered birth information, Babylonian astrologers mapped the positions of celestial bodies onto the natal chart. The most commonly included celestial bodies are the sun, moon, and planets, each representing different aspects of the individual's personality and life experiences. The zodiacal sign and degree of each celestial body's position provide further details about their influence. Additional considerations may include significant asteroids or fixed stars. By understanding the positions of these celestial bodies in the natal chart, astrologers gained valuable insights into an individual's unique cosmic influences and could interpret their personality traits, inclinations, and life experiences.

Zodiacal Signs:

The zodiacal signs are the twelve equal divisions along the ecliptic, which is the apparent path that the sun follows across the sky throughout the year. Each zodiacal sign spans 30 degrees of the celestial sphere, forming a complete circle of 360 degrees.

The zodiacal signs are named after the constellations that the sun appears to pass through during its annual journey. These constellations are remnants of ancient star patterns that were observed by early civilizations. Over time, different cultures developed their own systems of dividing the zodiac and assigning meanings to each sign.

Babylonian astrology, which was practiced in ancient Babylon, primarily used the Babylonian zodiac. The Babylonian zodiac slightly differed from the zodiac commonly used in modern Western astrology. While the modern Western zodiac is based on the tropical zodiac, which aligns with the seasons, the Babylonian zodiac was based on the sidereal zodiac, which aligned with the actual positions of the stars at the time.

Each zodiacal sign represents specific qualities, characteristics, and energies associated with the constellation it is named after. These qualities provide a framework for understanding different aspects of human nature and experiences. For example, Aries, the first sign of the zodiac, is associated with assertiveness, individuality, and pioneering spirit, reflecting the energy of the ram. Taurus, the second sign, represents stability, sensuality, and perseverance, akin to the strength and endurance of the bull.

The other signs in the Babylonian zodiac include Gemini, Cancer, Leo, Virgo, Libra, Scorpio, Sagittarius, Capricorn, Aquarius, and Pisces. Each sign has its own unique qualities, strengths, and challenges. These qualities are considered when interpreting an individual's natal chart and understanding how the celestial bodies interact with the energies represented by the signs.

Astrologers analyze the zodiacal signs and their positions in the natal chart to gain insights into an individual's personality traits, preferences, inclinations, and potential life experiences. The interactions between celestial bodies and the zodiacal signs can further refine the interpretation, providing a more nuanced understanding of how these energies manifest in an individual's life.

In conclusion, the zodiacal signs are the twelve equal divisions along the ecliptic, named after the constellations that the sun appears to pass through during its annual journey. Babylonian astrology primarily used the Babylonian zodiac, which differed slightly from the zodiac commonly used today. Each zodiacal sign represents specific qualities, characteristics, and energies associated with the constellation it is named after. These signs provide a framework for understanding different aspects of human nature and experiences, and astrologers consider them when interpreting an individual's natal chart.

Houses:

The natal chart is divided into twelve sections known as houses, each representing different areas of life. The houses are determined by the individual's birth time and location. Each house corresponds to specific aspects of life, such as personality, relationships, career, health, and spirituality. The position of celestial bodies within these houses provides insights into the areas of life they influence.

Aspects and Relationships:

In addition to the positions of celestial bodies within the zodiacal signs, the natal chart also takes into account the angles and relationships formed between these bodies. These relationships, known as aspects, play a crucial role in understanding the dynamics and influences within the chart.

Aspects represent the geometric angles formed between the positions of planets, as well as other celestial bodies such as the sun, moon, and asteroids. These angles are measured in degrees and provide insights into the interactions and connections between these celestial bodies. Astrologers pay close attention to the aspects in a natal chart as they reveal important energetic dynamics and patterns.

Some of the most commonly used aspects include conjunctions, squares, trines, and oppositions. Each aspect carries its own unique meaning and influence:

Conjunction: A conjunction occurs when two celestial bodies are in close proximity to each other, typically within a few degrees. This aspect signifies a merging or blending of energies, intensifying the qualities of the planets involved. It often indicates a strong focus and emphasis on the energies represented by those planets.

Square: A square occurs when two celestial bodies are approximately 90 degrees apart. This aspect signifies a dynamic and potentially challenging relationship between the planets. It can bring about tension, obstacles, and the need for adjustment or growth. However, squares also offer opportunities for growth and transformation by providing the impetus for change and development.

Trine: A trine occurs when two celestial bodies are approximately 120 degrees apart. This aspect represents a harmonious and flowing connection between the planets. It indicates ease, support, and natural talents in the areas of life associated with the planets involved. Trines often indicate a sense of ease and cooperation in expressing the energies represented by the planets.

Opposition: An opposition occurs when two celestial bodies are approximately 180 degrees apart. This aspect signifies a polarizing and potentially conflicting relationship between the planets. It represents a tension between opposing forces, often requiring balance and integration. Oppositions can bring awareness to contrasting energies and the need for finding middle ground or compromise.

These are just a few examples of the various aspects that astrologers consider when analyzing a natal chart. Each aspect adds depth and complexity to the interpretation, revealing the potential harmonies, tensions, and opportunities present within an individual's life. By understanding the aspects between celestial bodies, astrologers gain insights into the patterns of energy and the ways in which these energies interact and influence an individual's personality, experiences, and life path.

In conclusion, aspects in the natal chart represent the geometric angles formed between celestial bodies. Common aspects include conjunctions, squares, trines, and oppositions. Each aspect carries its own meaning and energetic influence, highlighting the connections and interactions between planets and other celestial bodies. These aspects provide valuable insights into the dynamics and patterns of energy within an individual's life, revealing potential harmonies or tensions that shape their experiences and personality traits. Astrologers carefully analyze these aspects to gain a comprehensive understanding of an individual's natal chart and its significance.

Interpretation:

Interpreting the natal chart is a multifaceted process that involves analyzing various elements and their interactions to gain a comprehensive understanding of an individual's personality, challenges, and life path. Astrologers carefully examine the positions of celestial bodies, zodiacal signs, houses, and aspects, taking into account the archetypal qualities associated with each element.

Celestial bodies: The positions of celestial bodies, such as the sun, moon, and planets, provide insights into different facets of an individual's personality and life experiences. Each celestial body is associated with specific archetypal qualities and energies. For example, the sun represents the core identity, ego, and life purpose, while the moon signifies emotions, instincts, and inner needs. The planets each carry their own symbolism and influence, contributing to the overall personality profile.

Zodiacal signs: The zodiacal signs represent specific qualities and characteristics associated with each of the twelve divisions along the ecliptic. Astrologers consider the zodiacal sign in which each celestial body is placed, as it adds depth and nuance to their interpretation. Each zodiac sign possesses distinct traits, elemental qualities, and ruling planets, contributing to the overall personality dynamics of the individual.

Houses: The houses in the natal chart represent different areas of life, such as career, relationships, health, and spirituality. The placement of celestial bodies within these houses provides insights into an individual's experiences and potentials in those specific areas. Astrologers analyze the house placements to understand how the energies of celestial bodies manifest in different aspects of an individual's life.

Aspects: As mentioned earlier, aspects represent the geometric relationships between celestial bodies. Astrologers examine the aspects formed between planets and other celestial bodies to determine how their energies interact and influence one another. The aspects reveal potential harmonies, tensions, and challenges within an individual's chart. For example, a harmonious aspect, such as a trine, indicates a natural flow of energy and ease, while a challenging aspect, like a square or opposition, signifies potential conflicts and areas of growth.

To interpret the natal chart, astrologers consider the interplay between these elements, combining technical knowledge with intuitive insight. They look for patterns, themes, and connections within the chart, identifying strengths, weaknesses, potential challenges, and areas of growth. The interpretation process involves synthesizing the information and weaving a narrative that captures the individual's unique qualities, life path, and potentials.

It's important to note that while the natal chart provides valuable insights, it doesn't determine an individual's fate or restrict their choices. Astrology is a tool for self-awareness and personal growth, offering guidance and understanding, but ultimately individuals have free will and the ability to shape their own lives.

In conclusion, interpreting the natal chart involves analyzing the positions of celestial bodies, zodiacal signs, houses, and aspects to gain insights into an individual's personality traits, potential challenges, and life path. Astrologers consider the archetypal qualities associated with each celestial body, the house placements, and the interplay between different elements. This complex and nuanced process requires both technical knowledge and intuitive insight, allowing astrologers to provide a comprehensive understanding of an individual's natal chart and its significance.

Personalized Insight and Guidance:

The natal chart serves as a personalized roadmap that provides individuals with valuable insight and guidance about themselves and their life journey. It is a snapshot of the cosmic energies and potentials present at the moment of their birth, reflecting their unique qualities, strengths, and challenges.

One of the primary benefits of the natal chart is its ability to reveal an individual's inherent strengths and talents. By examining the positions of celestial bodies and their interactions, astrologers can identify the areas in which individuals are naturally gifted or inclined to excel. For example, the placement of the sun may indicate their core identity and purpose, shedding light on their unique qualities and leadership potential. The positioning of other celestial bodies, such as Venus or Mars, can provide insights into their creative abilities, relationship dynamics, or assertiveness.

The natal chart also highlights potential challenges and areas for growth. Through the analysis of aspects and house placements, astrologers can identify potential obstacles or patterns that individuals may encounter in their lives. These challenges may present opportunities for personal development and self-improvement. By understanding these potential difficulties, individuals can prepare themselves, develop strategies to overcome obstacles, and make choices that are aligned with their cosmic influences.

Furthermore, the natal chart offers individuals a sense of purpose and direction. It reveals their unique life path and potentials, guiding them towards fulfilling their true calling. By understanding the energies imprinted in their chart, individuals gain insight into their motivations, passions, and the experiences that may contribute to their personal growth. This knowledge empowers individuals to make informed decisions, pursue paths aligned with their cosmic influences, and live a life that is in harmony with their authentic selves.

The natal chart provides a holistic view of an individual's personality, potentials, and life journey. It encourages self-reflection, self-awareness, and personal growth. By embracing the insights and guidance offered by the natal chart, individuals can navigate their lives with a deeper sense of purpose, make choices that resonate with their true selves, and cultivate a greater understanding of themselves and their place in the world.

It is important to note that while the natal chart provides valuable insights, individuals still have free will and the ability to shape their own destinies. The natal chart serves as a tool for self-discovery and self-empowerment, offering guidance and understanding, but the choices individuals make and the actions they take ultimately shape their experiences and determine their life path.

In conclusion, the natal chart provides personalized insight and guidance by revealing an individual's strengths, weaknesses, potential challenges, and life purpose. It offers a blueprint of the unique cosmic influences at the moment of their birth, allowing individuals to gain a deeper understanding of themselves, their motivations, and the life experiences they may encounter. Embracing the insights of the natal chart empowers individuals to make informed decisions, navigate challenges, and live a life that is in alignment with their authentic selves.

Evolution and Growth:

The natal chart, while capturing the cosmic energies at the moment of an individual's birth, is not a fixed entity but rather an evolving map that interacts with the ongoing movement of celestial bodies. Transits and progressions are two important techniques used in astrology to understand the dynamic nature of the natal chart and provide forecasts and guidance for individuals as they navigate different stages of life.

Transits refer to the current positions of celestial bodies in relation to an individual's natal chart. These transiting planets continue their journey through the zodiac, forming new aspects and angles with the planets in the natal chart. Astrologers analyze these transits to gain insights into the current energies and influences that individuals are experiencing. Transits can indicate opportunities, challenges, or significant events that may arise in various areas of life. For example, a favorable transit of Jupiter to an individual's natal Venus might signify a period of increased harmony and positive experiences in relationships or creative endeavors.

Progressions, on the other hand, involve the symbolic movement of the natal chart itself over time. Different progression methods, such as secondary progressions or solar arc progressions, advance the positions of the planets in the natal chart at a certain rate. Progressions reflect the internal growth and development of an individual, unveiling new potentials and life themes as time unfolds. For instance, a progressed Sun moving into a new zodiac sign might indicate a shift in an individual's identity and life focus.

Astrologers consider both transits and progressions to provide comprehensive forecasts and guidance for individuals. By examining the ongoing interactions between transiting planets and the natal chart, astrologers can offer insights into the timing of events, opportunities for personal growth, and potential challenges that individuals may face during specific periods. These techniques allow individuals to make informed decisions, prepare for upcoming changes, and navigate their lives with greater awareness and intention.

It is important to note that while transits and progressions provide valuable information, they do not determine an individual's fate or remove their free will. Rather, they offer a framework for understanding the cosmic energies at play and suggest potential themes and influences that individuals may encounter. Ultimately, individuals have the power to make choices and shape their own experiences in response to the guidance provided by astrology.

In conclusion, the natal chart serves as the foundation for astrological analysis, offering personalized insight into an individual's character, potentials, and life path. However, the natal chart is not static and evolves as individuals grow and experience life. Transits and progressions, involving the ongoing movement of celestial bodies, interact with the natal chart, influencing personal development and life events. Astrologers use these techniques to provide forecasts and guidance, helping individuals navigate various stages of life and make informed decisions. The natal chart, along with transits and progressions, offers individuals a framework for self-discovery, personal growth, and guidance throughout their lives.

Example:

To create a Babylonian natal chart, you would need the following information:

Date of Birth: The exact date of birth is crucial for accurate chart construction. The day, month, and year of birth are needed to determine the position of the celestial bodies on that specific date.

Time of Birth: The precise time of birth is important as it determines the alignment of celestial bodies at the moment of your birth. The time should be recorded as accurately as possible, including the hour and minute.

Location of Birth: The birthplace is needed to determine the geographic coordinates (latitude and longitude) of the location. This information is essential for calculating the position of celestial bodies specific to that location.

With these three pieces of information - date, time, and location of birth - an astrologer can construct a Babylonian natal chart for you. The chart will depict the positions of the sun, moon, planets, and other celestial bodies at the moment of your birth, providing insights into your personality traits, potential challenges, and life path based on Babylonian astrological principles.

Date of Birth: March 22, 2003
Time of Birth: 7:49 am
Location of Birth: Latitude 41.4368065248, Longitude -82.2373516711

Sun Sign: Aries
Moon Sign: Taurus
Ascendant (Rising Sign): Leo

Sample Natal Chart:

Sun in Aries in the 1st House
Moon in Taurus in the 2nd House
Mercury in Pisces in the 12th House
Venus in Aquarius in the 11th House
Mars in Capricorn in the 10th House
Jupiter in Leo in the 5th House
Saturn in Gemini in the 3rd House
Uranus in Aquarius in the 11th House
Neptune in Aquarius in the 11th House
Pluto in Sagittarius in the 9th House

Detailed meaning:

Natal Chart for March 22, 2003, 7:49 am, Latitude 41.4368065248, Longitude -82.2373516711:

Sun in Aries in the 1st House:

The Sun represents your core identity and purpose. With the Sun in Aries, you possess strong leadership qualities, a dynamic personality, and a pioneering spirit. You are assertive, confident, and courageous, always ready to take on new challenges and initiate action. Your presence is charismatic, and you have a natural ability to inspire others.

Moon in Taurus in the 2nd House:

The Moon represents your emotional nature and inner needs. With the Moon in Taurus, you seek stability, security, and comfort in your emotional life. You have a strong connection to the material world and value the pleasures and comforts it offers. You are grounded, patient, and reliable, and you approach life with a steady and practical attitude.

Mercury in Pisces in the 12th House:

Mercury represents communication, thinking, and intellectual abilities. With Mercury in Pisces, your mind is intuitive, imaginative, and sensitive. You have a deep understanding of the subconscious mind and are highly perceptive of others' emotions. Your thoughts and communication style may be poetic, dreamy, and empathetic. You may have a natural inclination towards artistic and spiritual pursuits.

Venus in Aquarius in the 11th House:

Venus represents love, beauty, and harmony. With Venus in Aquarius, you have a unique and unconventional approach to relationships. You value independence, friendship, and intellectual connection in your romantic partnerships. You are attracted to people who are intellectually stimulating and share your ideals and progressive values. You may be involved in social causes and have a strong desire for equality and freedom in relationships.

Mars in Capricorn in the 10th House:

Mars represents your energy, drive, and ambition. With Mars in Capricorn, you are determined, disciplined, and focused on achieving your goals. You have a strong work ethic and strive for success and recognition in your career. You are practical, responsible, and willing to put in the necessary effort to climb the ladder of success. You have natural leadership qualities and excel in positions of authority.

Jupiter in Leo in the 5th House:

Jupiter represents expansion, growth, and opportunities. With Jupiter in Leo, you possess a joyful and generous spirit. You have a strong desire for self-expression and creative pursuits. Your enthusiasm and charisma attract abundance and opportunities for personal growth. You may have a love for the arts, entertainment, or working with children. Your optimism and positivity inspire others.

Saturn in Gemini in the 3rd House:

Saturn represents discipline, structure, and responsibility. With Saturn in Gemini, you have a practical and logical mind. You are diligent in your communication and learning, and you have a strong sense of responsibility when it comes to sharing information. You may have a cautious approach to expressing your ideas and may strive for precision and clarity in your communication.

Uranus in Aquarius in the 11th House:

Uranus represents innovation, uniqueness, and change. With Uranus in Aquarius, you are a free thinker and a visionary. You possess progressive ideas and a strong desire for social change and reform. You are drawn to unconventional and alternative approaches and may have a knack for technology or scientific advancements. Your individuality and forward-thinking mindset inspire others.

Neptune in Aquarius in the 11th House:

Neptune represents imagination, spirituality, and compassion. With Neptune in Aquarius, you have a deep concern for the collective and a strong desire to contribute to society. You may be idealistic and visionary, seeking to bring about humanitarian and spiritual advancements. Your intuitive and compassionate nature guides you in connecting with others on a deeper level.

Pluto in Sagittarius in the 9th House:

Pluto represents transformation, power, and regeneration. With Pluto in Sagittarius, you have a deep desire for knowledge, exploration, and personal growth. You are drawn to philosophical and spiritual pursuits and may undergo significant transformations through your beliefs and worldview. You may have a profound desire to understand the meaning of life and to make a positive impact on society.

B. Calculating Planetary Positions:

Babylonian astrologers employed intricate mathematical techniques to accurately determine the positions of celestial bodies in the sky. Through careful astronomical observations, they plotted the positions of the sun, moon, and planets along the zodiac, which is a band of the sky divided into twelve equal segments. Let's delve into the process of calculating planetary positions in more detail:

Astronomical Observations:

Babylonian astrologers were renowned for their meticulous observations of the night sky. They recognized the importance of accurately recording the movements and positions of celestial bodies to understand their influence on human affairs. To achieve this, they would spend countless hours observing and tracking the paths of celestial bodies, making detailed notes and measurements.

Babylonian astrologers often relied on landmarks or specific stars to establish reference points. These reference points helped them determine the positions of celestial bodies relative to known fixed locations in the sky. By observing the regular patterns of celestial bodies and their interactions with these reference points, they were able to establish a system for predicting future positions and movements.

The Babylonian astrologers' observations were typically conducted using simple instruments, such as sighting tubes or plumb lines, which helped them align their gaze accurately. They would carefully note the positions of celestial bodies at specific moments, paying attention to the rising and setting times, as well as their positions in relation to other stars or landmarks.

Over time, these recorded observations formed a vast database of celestial movements and positions. Babylonian astrologers used this wealth of information to develop mathematical models and tables that allowed them to calculate the positions of celestial bodies for any given date and time. These calculations enabled them to create accurate and reliable ephemerides, which served as essential references for their astrological practices.

The meticulous recording of celestial observations by Babylonian astrologers not only provided the foundation for calculating planetary positions but also allowed for the identification of patterns and correlations between celestial events and earthly phenomena. Their commitment to precise observation and recording laid the groundwork for the development of astrological techniques and the refinement of astrological knowledge in ancient Babylon.

Ecliptic and Zodiac:

The Babylonians were astute observers of the celestial phenomena and noticed that the sun, moon, and planets seemed to move along a particular path in the sky. This path, known as the ecliptic, became a fundamental concept in Babylonian astrology.

The ecliptic is the apparent annual path traced by the sun against the background of stars as observed from Earth. It creates a circle around the Earth, seemingly following a specific route. The Babylonians recognized that this path was not perfectly aligned with the celestial equator, which is the projection of Earth's equator onto the celestial sphere.

The ecliptic's inclination relative to the celestial equator is due to the Earth's axial tilt, which causes the sun's apparent position to change throughout the year. The Babylonians divided this path into twelve equal segments, which became known as the zodiacal signs.

Each zodiacal sign corresponds to a 30-degree portion of the ecliptic, starting with Aries and ending with Pisces. The division of the ecliptic into twelve equal parts allowed the Babylonians to associate specific constellations and symbolic meanings with each zodiacal sign. These associations formed the basis for understanding the influence of celestial bodies as they traversed different signs.

The zodiacal signs provided the Babylonian astrologers with a framework for interpreting the positions of celestial bodies in relation to human affairs. The specific qualities and characteristics attributed to each zodiacal sign shaped the astrological understanding of individual personalities, compatibility, and life events.

By dividing the ecliptic into twelve equal segments, the Babylonians established a system that continues to be used in astrology to this day. The zodiacal signs serve as a reference point for understanding the movement and positions of celestial bodies, allowing astrologers to analyze their influences on individuals and events.

The Babylonian recognition of the ecliptic and the division into zodiacal signs marked an important milestone in the development of astrology. It provided a framework for astrologers to understand the relationship between the celestial and terrestrial realms, laying the foundation for the intricate and multifaceted system of astrology that has evolved over thousands of years.

Zodiacal Division:

The Babylonian astrologers developed a system known as the "twelve-fold way" to divide the ecliptic into twelve equal segments, each representing a zodiacal sign. This division allowed them to assign specific zodiacal signs to different portions of the ecliptic, creating a framework for interpreting the positions of celestial bodies within the astrological chart.

The twelve-fold way involved dividing the 360-degree circle of the ecliptic into twelve equal parts, with each part spanning 30 degrees. These divisions corresponded to the twelve zodiacal signs: Aries, Taurus, Gemini, Cancer, Leo, Virgo, Libra, Scorpio, Sagittarius, Capricorn, Aquarius, and Pisces.

Each zodiacal sign was associated with specific qualities, characteristics, and energies that influenced the interpretation of celestial bodies positioned within it. For example, Aries was considered a fiery sign associated with assertiveness, initiative, and independence, while Taurus was associated with stability, practicality, and sensuality.

The division of the ecliptic into twelve equal segments allowed Babylonian astrologers to determine which zodiacal sign a celestial body was positioned in at any given time. This information provided valuable insights into the influences and energies at play in an individual's natal chart or a specific event's astrological analysis.

By assigning zodiacal signs to specific sections of the ecliptic, Babylonian astrologers created a symbolic framework that linked celestial positions with human qualities and experiences. This allowed them to interpret the influences of celestial bodies in a more nuanced and personalized manner.

The zodiacal signs served as reference points for understanding the archetypal qualities associated with different areas of life, personality traits, and compatibility between individuals. The celestial bodies positioned within a particular zodiacal sign were believed to take on the characteristics and energies associated with that sign, shaping the interpretation of an individual's natal chart or the astrological analysis of an event.

The twelve-fold way and the division of the ecliptic into twelve equal segments provided Babylonian astrologers with a systematic approach to understanding the influences of celestial bodies. This system formed the basis for the development of astrological interpretations that continue to be used in modern astrology, allowing individuals to gain deeper insights into their personalities, relationships, and life experiences.

Mathematical Calculations:

Babylonian astrologers were not only keen observers of the night sky but also skilled mathematicians. They developed sophisticated mathematical calculations to determine the precise positions of celestial bodies along the zodiac.

To calculate the positions of celestial bodies, Babylonian astrologers relied on various mathematical techniques, including trigonometry, geometry, and algebra. These calculations were based on the recorded astronomical observations they meticulously gathered over time.

Trigonometry played a crucial role in determining the angular distances and relationships between celestial bodies. By measuring the angles formed by the celestial bodies with respect to reference points, such as stars or landmarks, astrologers could determine their positions along the zodiac. Trigonometric functions, such as sine, cosine, and tangent, allowed them to calculate the celestial bodies' coordinates and movements with remarkable accuracy.

Geometry was also employed to analyze the spatial relationships between celestial bodies and their positions in relation to Earth. Babylonian astrologers used geometric principles to determine the distances, sizes, and shapes of the celestial bodies. By understanding these geometric aspects, they could interpret the significance of the celestial bodies' positions within the natal chart or in relation to specific events.

In addition to trigonometry and geometry, algebraic techniques were used to solve complex mathematical equations and derive mathematical models that could predict the positions of celestial bodies at different times. These algebraic calculations involved variables representing time, angles, and distances, enabling astrologers to project the movements and positions of celestial bodies into the future or retrospectively determine their past positions.

The mathematical calculations performed by Babylonian astrologers required precision, attention to detail, and a deep understanding of mathematical principles. They developed tables, algorithms, and mathematical formulas that facilitated these calculations, allowing for accurate determinations of celestial positions.

By applying their mathematical prowess to the recorded astronomical observations, Babylonian astrologers could deduce the coordinates of celestial bodies along the zodiac. These calculations formed the basis for constructing natal charts, predicting celestial events, and interpreting the influences of celestial bodies on human lives.

The integration of mathematical calculations into Babylonian astrology allowed for a more precise and systematic approach to understanding the celestial influences. It demonstrated the sophistication of their astronomical knowledge and mathematical acumen, highlighting the interplay between observation, calculation, and interpretation in the practice of Babylonian astrology.

Astronomical Tables:

Babylonian astrologers recognized the need for efficient and accurate calculations in their practice, and to achieve this, they compiled extensive astronomical tables.

These tables served as valuable references and tools for astrologers, containing pre-calculated values and formulas that facilitated the determination of planetary positions based on specific dates and locations. The tables incorporated various factors to ensure precision in the calculations.

One crucial factor taken into account was the Earth's axial tilt, which causes the celestial bodies to appear at different heights above the horizon depending on the observer's location. By considering this tilt, the tables provided corrections that allowed astrologers to accurately determine the positions of celestial bodies for specific latitudes and longitudes.

Another important consideration was the apparent motions of the celestial bodies. While the planets and stars appear to move across the sky, their motions are not uniform. Babylonian astrologers carefully observed and recorded the irregularities and deviations in the motions of celestial bodies. The astronomical tables took these deviations into account, incorporating correction factors that enabled astrologers to calculate the precise positions of celestial bodies at specific moments in time.

The astronomical tables also included other relevant data, such as the rising and setting times of celestial bodies, lunar phases, and eclipses. This comprehensive information allowed astrologers to accurately determine celestial positions and events, providing a solid foundation for astrological calculations and interpretations.

The compilation and maintenance of these astronomical tables required meticulous record-keeping and continuous observations. Babylonian astrologers devoted significant time and effort to ensuring the accuracy of the tables, making adjustments and updates as new astronomical data became available.

The availability of these tables greatly facilitated the work of Babylonian astrologers. Instead of performing complex calculations manually for each chart or prediction, astrologers could consult the tables to obtain precise positions and values for celestial bodies, saving time and minimizing the risk of calculation errors.

The use of astronomical tables in Babylonian astrology exemplified the fusion of observation, calculation, and practicality. These tables enhanced the accuracy of astrological calculations, allowing astrologers to provide more precise predictions and interpretations for their clients. They served as indispensable tools that contributed to the advancement and sophistication of Babylonian astrology as a scientific and practical discipline.

Celestial Almanacs:

In Babylonian astrology, celestial almanacs played a vital role in the practice of astrology. These almanacs were comprehensive compilations of calculated positions of celestial bodies for specific times and locations.

The celestial almanacs provided Babylonian astrologers with the essential information needed to construct accurate natal charts, make predictions, and offer astrological interpretations. They contained detailed tables and charts that listed the positions of the sun, moon, and planets in relation to the zodiacal signs and other celestial reference points.

The almanacs were organized in a systematic and user-friendly manner, allowing astrologers to quickly and easily find the relevant positions for a given date and location. These positions were typically presented in terms of degrees, minutes, and zodiacal sign placements.

By consulting the almanacs, astrologers could determine the precise positions of celestial bodies at the time and place of an individual's birth. This information was crucial for constructing accurate natal charts, which formed the basis for astrological interpretations and predictions.

Astrologers would refer to the almanacs to identify the zodiacal sign placements of the sun, moon, and planets for a particular birth date. They would also take into account the positions of other celestial bodies and reference points, such as fixed stars or significant planetary aspects.

The availability of celestial almanacs greatly facilitated the work of Babylonian astrologers. Instead of having to perform extensive calculations each time they needed to construct a natal chart or make predictions, they could consult the almanacs to obtain the accurate positions of celestial bodies for a given time and location.

The use of celestial almanacs not only saved time but also enhanced the accuracy and reliability of Babylonian astrology. Astrologers could confidently rely on the calculated positions provided in the almanacs, knowing that they were based on meticulous observations and mathematical calculations.

Furthermore, the use of celestial almanacs allowed for consistency and standardization in the practice of astrology. Astrologers across different regions and cities could access and use the same almanacs, ensuring a unified approach and interpretation of astrological charts and predictions.

In summary, celestial almanacs were essential tools in Babylonian astrology. They provided Babylonian astrologers with the calculated positions of celestial bodies for specific times and locations, enabling them to construct accurate natal charts, make predictions, and offer astrological interpretations. The use of almanacs enhanced the efficiency, accuracy, and consistency of Babylonian astrology, contributing to its development as a sophisticated and respected system of knowledge.

Continuous Refinement:

The Babylonian astrological tradition was characterized by a continuous quest for refinement and improvement in both mathematical techniques and astronomical observations. Babylonian astrologers recognized the importance of accuracy and reliability in their calculations, and they were dedicated to incorporating new data and adjusting their methods as new astronomical insights emerged.

A key aspect of their approach was the meticulous observation of the night sky. Babylonian astrologers carefully recorded the movements and positions of celestial bodies over time, noting their positions relative to specific reference points, such as stars or landmarks on the horizon. These observations served as the foundation for calculating the precise positions of celestial bodies.

To ensure the accuracy of their calculations, Babylonian astrologers developed sophisticated mathematical techniques. They employed trigonometry, geometry, and algebraic principles to determine the celestial bodies' coordinates along the zodiac. By applying these mathematical principles to the recorded astronomical observations, they could deduce the positions of the sun, moon, and planets with a high degree of precision.

Furthermore, Babylonian astrologers compiled extensive astronomical tables to facilitate calculations and enhance accuracy. These tables contained pre-calculated values and formulas that allowed for the efficient determination of planetary positions based on specific dates and locations. Incorporating factors such as the Earth's axial tilt and the celestial bodies' apparent motions, these tables provided the necessary information to calculate the positions of celestial bodies at any given time.

The use of celestial almanacs was another crucial element in the Babylonian astrological tradition. These almanacs contained the calculated positions of celestial bodies for specific times and locations. Babylonian astrologers consulted these almanacs to construct accurate natal charts, make predictions, and offer astrological interpretations. The availability of these almanacs significantly enhanced the efficiency, accuracy, and consistency of Babylonian astrology.

The Babylonians' commitment to precision and their continuous refinement of mathematical techniques contributed to the development and enduring influence of Babylonian astrology. By striving for accuracy in their calculations and incorporating new astronomical insights, Babylonian astrologers established a foundation of knowledge that has persisted throughout history.

In conclusion, Babylonian astrologers' development of sophisticated mathematical techniques and their meticulous astronomical observations allowed them to calculate the precise positions of celestial bodies. The use of mathematical calculations, astronomical tables, and celestial almanacs formed the basis for constructing natal charts, making predictions, and providing astrological interpretations. The Babylonians' dedication to precision and their continuous refinement of their methods contributed to the advancement and enduring influence of Babylonian astrology as a sophisticated system of knowledge.

C. Interpreting the Natal Chart:

Interpreting a natal chart, also known as a birth chart or horoscope, is a complex process that requires a profound understanding of astrological symbolism and its correlation with human experiences. Babylonian astrologers meticulously analyzed the relationships between celestial bodies, their positions within the zodiac, and their interactions with the astrological houses. By decoding these intricate patterns, they were able to unveil the potential strengths, challenges, and life themes of an individual. Let's explore the key elements involved in interpreting a natal chart:

Celestial Bodies:

The natal chart, also known as the birth chart or horoscope, is a graphical representation of the positions of celestial bodies at the exact moment and location of an individual's birth. It serves as a personalized cosmic map that provides valuable insights into an individual's character, potentials, and life path.

The natal chart includes several key celestial bodies. The most prominent among them is the sun, which represents the core essence, vitality, and conscious self-expression of an individual. It symbolizes one's identity, ego, and the fundamental traits that shape their personality.

The moon, another significant celestial body, reflects the emotional nature, instincts, and subconscious patterns of an individual. It represents their emotional needs, nurturing qualities, and intuitive responses to the world around them. The moon's position in the natal chart offers insights into an individual's emotional landscape and their instinctual reactions.

In addition to the sun and moon, the natal chart incorporates the positions of various planets, including Mercury, Venus, Mars, Jupiter, Saturn, Uranus, Neptune, and Pluto. Each planet carries its own unique symbolism and archetypal energy. For example:

Mercury, the planet of communication and intellect, influences thinking patterns, learning style, and how one expresses themselves verbally.

Venus, the planet of love, beauty, and harmony, represents one's values, relationships, and aesthetic preferences.

Mars, the planet of action and motivation, governs assertiveness, passion, and the drive to achieve goals.

Jupiter, the planet of expansion and growth, signifies opportunities, abundance, and the desire for meaning and purpose in life.

Saturn, the planet of discipline and responsibility, represents limitations, structure, and the lessons an individual needs to learn in order to achieve long-term success.

Uranus, the planet of innovation and change, represents individuality, rebellion, and unconventional thinking.

Neptune, the planet of imagination and spirituality, symbolizes dreams, intuition, and the longing for transcendence.

Pluto, the planet associated with transformation and regeneration, represents profound change, personal power, and the potential for rebirth.

In addition to these celestial bodies, the natal chart may also include other significant points, such as the Ascendant (rising sign) and Midheaven. The Ascendant represents the individual's outward personality, first impressions, and the way they interact with the world. The Midheaven, also known as the Medium Coeli (MC), represents one's aspirations, career path, and public image.

By examining the positions of these celestial bodies in the natal chart, astrologers gain insights into an individual's character, potential challenges, and life path. The unique combination of celestial influences in the natal chart shapes an individual's personality traits, inclinations, and the experiences they are likely to encounter throughout their life journey.

In conclusion, the natal chart is a powerful tool that includes the positions of celestial bodies at the time and location of an individual's birth. It encompasses the sun, moon, planets, and other significant points, each symbolizing distinct qualities, energies, and archetypal influences. By analyzing the natal chart, astrologers can gain valuable insights into an individual's character, potentials, and life path, offering guidance and a deeper understanding of their unique cosmic makeup.

Zodiac Signs:

The zodiac signs play a crucial role in understanding the dynamics of the celestial bodies within the natal chart. Each zodiac sign represents a distinct set of qualities, themes, and energies that influence the expression of the celestial bodies placed within them.

The zodiac consists of twelve equal divisions along the ecliptic, with each division spanning 30 degrees. These divisions are named after the constellations that the sun appears to pass through during its annual journey. The Babylonian astrologers recognized the significance of these zodiacal signs and their association with specific qualities and characteristics.

When a celestial body is placed within a particular zodiac sign in the natal chart, it takes on the characteristics and energies associated with that sign. For example, if the sun is in Aries, the individual may exhibit traits such as courage, assertiveness, and a pioneering spirit. If Venus is in Taurus, the person may have a deep appreciation for beauty, sensuality, and a strong desire for stability in relationships.

The interplay between the celestial bodies and the zodiac signs adds layers of complexity and depth to the interpretation of the natal chart. The celestial bodies bring their archetypal influences, while the zodiac signs provide a framework for expressing those influences in unique ways.

Astrologers consider the qualities of both the celestial bodies and the zodiac signs to gain insights into an individual's personality traits and tendencies. By analyzing the interplay between the two, they can determine how the energies of the celestial bodies manifest within the context of the zodiac sign.

For example, if Mars, the planet of action and assertiveness, is placed in the zodiac sign of Gemini, known for its intellectual curiosity and adaptability, it may indicate a person who is quick-thinking, intellectually driven, and highly communicative in their pursuit of goals. On the other hand, if Mars is in the zodiac sign of Scorpio, known for its intensity, passion, and desire for transformation, it may suggest an individual who possesses deep emotional drive and determination in their actions.

By considering the celestial bodies' placements within specific zodiac signs, astrologers can gain insights into an individual's personality traits, tendencies, and how they express themselves in various areas of life. This understanding helps in providing a more nuanced and accurate interpretation of the natal chart and offers valuable guidance for self-awareness, personal growth, and navigating life's complexities.

In conclusion, the interplay between the celestial bodies and the zodiac signs is a fundamental aspect of astrology. The zodiac signs represent unique qualities and energies, influencing the expression of the celestial bodies placed within them. By analyzing this interplay, astrologers gain insights into an individual's personality traits, tendencies, and the ways in which they manifest their cosmic influences. Understanding the dynamics between the celestial bodies and the zodiac signs adds depth and richness to the interpretation of the natal chart, offering valuable guidance and self-awareness.

➢ Astrological Guidance:

A. Personal Insight and Self-Understanding:

Astrology, particularly through the exploration of natal charts, provided individuals with a profound means of self-reflection and self-understanding. Babylonian astrologers recognized that each individual possessed a unique combination of celestial influences imprinted in their natal chart, and these influences played a significant role in shaping their personality traits, strengths, weaknesses, and potential life paths. Let's delve into the details of how astrology facilitated personal insight and self-understanding:

Unveiling Personality Traits:

The analysis of a natal chart provides individuals with a deeper understanding of their inherent personality traits and characteristics. By examining the positions of celestial bodies and their interactions within the chart, individuals can recognize the qualities and energies associated with each planet and zodiac sign, gaining valuable insights into their unique makeup.

The placement of the sun in a specific zodiac sign is particularly significant as it represents the core essence of an individual's personality. For instance, someone with the sun in Leo tends to possess natural leadership qualities, a strong sense of self-expression, and a vibrant, creative spirit. They may exude confidence, radiate warmth, and seek recognition for their talents and achievements.

On the other hand, the placement of the moon in a specific zodiac sign influences an individual's emotional nature and inner world. For example, someone with the moon in Cancer is likely to be highly empathetic, nurturing, and deeply connected to their emotions. They may have a strong need for security, a caring and protective nature, and a profound sense of loyalty and attachment to family and loved ones.

The natal chart also considers the positions of other celestial bodies, such as Mercury, Venus, Mars, and Jupiter, each representing different facets of an individual's personality. For instance, Mercury governs communication and thinking patterns,

Venus signifies love and relationships, Mars symbolizes assertiveness and drive, and Jupiter represents expansion and growth.

By understanding these personality traits and qualities associated with celestial bodies, individuals can embrace their strengths and leverage them in various areas of life. They can also become aware of areas that may require growth or improvement. This self-awareness enables individuals to make conscious choices and align their actions with their inherent tendencies, fostering personal growth and fulfillment.

Additionally, the natal chart provides a roadmap for individuals to develop their potential. It highlights the areas where their energies are naturally inclined, guiding them towards pursuits that align with their inherent qualities. For example, someone with strong Leo energy might thrive in creative or leadership roles, while someone with a prominent Cancer influence may excel in nurturing professions or roles that involve emotional support.

Understanding the personality traits and tendencies revealed in the natal chart empowers individuals to embrace their authentic selves, make conscious choices, and cultivate self-improvement. It allows them to align their actions and decisions with their natural inclinations, leading to a more fulfilling and purposeful life.

In conclusion, the analysis of a natal chart provides individuals with a deeper understanding of their inherent personality traits. By examining the positions of celestial bodies and their interactions, individuals can recognize the qualities and energies associated with each planet and zodiac sign. This understanding helps individuals embrace their strengths, work on areas of potential growth, and make conscious choices aligned with their authentic selves. The natal chart serves as a valuable tool for self-awareness, personal development, and the cultivation of a fulfilling and purposeful life.

Identifying Strengths and Weaknesses:

Astrology plays a significant role in helping individuals identify their strengths and weaknesses more clearly. By examining the natal chart, individuals can gain insights into areas of life where they naturally excel and those where they may face challenges or obstacles.

The positions of celestial bodies, such as Venus, Mars, Saturn, and others, within the natal chart provide valuable information about an individual's inherent strengths and weaknesses. For example, a strong placement of Venus in the chart often indicates a natural talent for fostering harmonious relationships, artistic expression, and a deep appreciation for beauty and aesthetics. Individuals with such a placement may possess charm, grace, and the ability to create harmony in their interactions with others.

On the other hand, challenging aspects involving Saturn in the chart can present obstacles related to discipline, self-doubt, and self-imposed limitations. Individuals with these aspects may face struggles in areas requiring structure, perseverance, and a sense of responsibility. However, these challenges can also serve as opportunities for personal growth and development, as they encourage individuals to overcome limitations, develop discipline, and build resilience.

By recognizing these strengths and weaknesses through astrology, individuals gain a clearer understanding of their unique qualities and areas where they may need to focus on personal development. This self-awareness allows individuals to make conscious choices that align with their inherent qualities and navigate life more effectively.

For example, someone with a strong Venus placement may choose to pursue careers or hobbies that involve creativity, aesthetics, or working with people in a harmonious and supportive environment. They can leverage their natural talents to foster positive relationships and create beauty in various forms.

Similarly, someone with challenging Saturn aspects may choose to actively work on developing discipline, perseverance, and a sense of responsibility. They can engage in practices that cultivate self-discipline, seek mentors or support systems that provide guidance, and set realistic goals to overcome their self-imposed limitations.

Astrology empowers individuals to embrace their strengths, while also acknowledging and working on their weaknesses. It provides a framework for personal development and encourages individuals to focus on areas that require growth. By leveraging their strengths and addressing their weaknesses, individuals can make conscious choices that align with their inherent qualities, leading to a more authentic and fulfilling life.

In conclusion, astrology enables individuals to identify their strengths and weaknesses more clearly by examining the natal chart. The chart provides insights into areas where individuals naturally excel and those where they may face challenges. This knowledge empowers individuals to focus on personal development and make conscious choices that align with their inherent qualities. Recognizing and working on these strengths and weaknesses through astrology can lead to personal growth, self-improvement, and a more authentic and fulfilling life journey.

Understanding Life Path and Potential:

The examination of a natal chart in astrology offers individuals a glimpse into their potential life paths. Babylonian astrologers believed that the configuration of celestial bodies in the chart could reveal the overarching themes and patterns that individuals were likely to encounter in their lives. By understanding these potential paths, individuals could make informed decisions and actively engage in shaping their future.

The natal chart provides valuable insights into various areas of life, including career, relationships, health, and personal growth. Each astrological house represents a specific life domain, and the positions of celestial bodies within these houses offer indications of the potential experiences and challenges that individuals may encounter in those areas.

For example, a strong emphasis on the tenth house, which governs career and public image, suggests a potential for success and recognition in professional endeavors. Individuals with this emphasis may find themselves driven to achieve ambitious goals, attain leadership positions, and make a significant impact in their chosen field.

On the other hand, a focus on the seventh house, which represents relationships and partnerships, indicates a significant emphasis on forming and maintaining connections with others. Individuals with this emphasis may prioritize collaboration, seek harmonious relationships, and place great importance on finding a compatible partner.

These indications in the natal chart serve as guideposts, helping individuals navigate their life paths with greater awareness and clarity. By understanding the potential themes and patterns highlighted in their chart, individuals can make informed decisions and actively engage in shaping their future.

For instance, someone with a strong emphasis on the tenth house may choose a career path that aligns with their natural talents and ambitions. They may take on leadership roles, seek opportunities for professional growth, and actively work towards achieving their career goals.

Similarly, someone with a focus on the seventh house may prioritize building meaningful relationships, placing value on partnership and collaboration in their personal and professional life. They may seek out opportunities for cooperation, invest time and energy in nurturing their relationships, and make choices that support harmonious connections.

It's important to note that while the natal chart offers insights into potential life paths, it does not determine a predetermined fate. The chart provides individuals with a roadmap that can be used as a tool for self-awareness and decision-making. It offers guidance, but ultimately, individuals have the agency to shape their own lives.

In conclusion, the examination of a natal chart in astrology offers individuals a glimpse into their potential life paths. By understanding the configuration of celestial bodies in the chart and the corresponding astrological houses, individuals gain insights into the overarching themes and patterns likely to influence their lives. This knowledge empowers individuals to make informed decisions and actively engage in shaping their future. Understanding the potential paths indicated in the chart allows individuals to align their choices and actions with their unique cosmic influences, leading to a more purposeful and fulfilling life journey.

Enhancing Self-Awareness:

Astrology provided individuals with a framework for enhanced self-awareness. By delving into their natal charts and studying the various elements and influences, individuals gained a deeper understanding of their unique qualities, preferences, and inclinations. This self-awareness extended beyond surface-level personality traits and encompassed broader aspects of life, such as relationships, career choices, and personal aspirations.

Astrology recognizes that each person is a complex tapestry of energies and potentials, and the natal chart acts as a guide to unraveling these intricate layers. Through the analysis of the celestial bodies, zodiac signs, houses, and aspects within the natal chart, individuals were able to gain insights into their strengths, challenges, and life purpose.

The natal chart provided a mirror for individuals to explore and recognize their authentic selves. By understanding the astrological influences at play, individuals gained clarity about their natural inclinations, talents, and passions. For example, someone with a strong placement of Venus in their chart might feel a deep resonance with artistic expression and find fulfillment in creative endeavors. Recognizing these inherent qualities allowed individuals to embrace and nurture their passions, leading to a more authentic and fulfilling expression of themselves.

Moreover, astrology offered individuals a lens through which to understand their relationships and interactions with others. By examining the compatibility between their chart and the charts of others, individuals gained insights into potential dynamics and challenges in their personal and professional connections. Understanding these dynamics empowered individuals to navigate relationships with greater compassion, empathy, and communication, fostering healthier and more harmonious connections.

Career choices and personal aspirations also found guidance through astrology. By examining the astrological indicators related to career and life purpose, individuals could align their professional pursuits with their inherent strengths and aspirations. For example, someone with a strong emphasis on the ninth house, which represents higher education and travel, might feel a deep calling to explore new cultures, expand their knowledge, and seek careers that involve teaching or traveling. Understanding these astrological influences allowed individuals to make informed decisions about their career paths, leading to a greater sense of fulfillment and alignment with their true calling.

Astrology, therefore, served as a powerful tool for self-reflection, offering individuals a deeper understanding of their unique qualities, preferences, and aspirations. By recognizing and aligning with their authentic selves, individuals were able to make conscious choices that nurtured their personal growth and fulfillment. Astrology provided a framework for enhanced self-awareness, guiding individuals to live more in tune with their true nature and empowering them to create a life that resonated with their deepest values and desires.

In conclusion, astrology provided individuals with a framework for enhanced self-awareness. By exploring their natal charts, individuals gained insights into their unique qualities, preferences, and aspirations. This self-awareness extended beyond personality traits and encompassed broader aspects of life, such as relationships, career choices, and personal aspirations. Understanding their astrological influences allowed individuals to align their actions and decisions with their authentic selves, fostering a sense of fulfillment and personal fulfillment. Astrology served as a powerful tool for self-reflection and personal growth, empowering individuals to live a life that resonated with their true nature and purpose.

Conscious Decision-Making:

Armed with the insights derived from astrology, individuals were empowered to make conscious choices aligned with their inherent qualities and life aspirations. The understanding of their strengths and weaknesses allowed them to approach challenges with resilience and strategize accordingly. Rather than being held back by their limitations, individuals could harness their strengths and leverage them to overcome obstacles and achieve their goals.

By recognizing their natural inclinations and preferences, individuals could identify opportunities that resonated with their authentic selves. Whether it was choosing a career path that aligned with their passions or seeking relationships that complemented their values, astrology provided a valuable tool for decision-making. It allowed individuals to make choices that were in harmony with their inherent qualities and aspirations, leading to a greater sense of fulfillment and personal growth.

Astrology also offered individuals a sense of validation and self-acceptance. By understanding their unique astrological makeup, individuals could embrace their quirks, talents, and challenges as part of their journey. They realized that their experiences were not random but were influenced by celestial energies, providing a broader perspective and a sense of purpose.

Furthermore, astrology provided individuals with guidance during times of uncertainty or major life transitions. When faced with important decisions or life-changing events, individuals could consult their natal charts and seek astrological insights. This allowed them to make more informed choices, consider potential outcomes, and navigate transitions with a deeper understanding of their personal dynamics.

In conclusion, astrology provided individuals with a profound means of self-reflection and self-understanding. By exploring their natal charts and gaining insights into their unique personality traits, strengths, weaknesses, and potential life paths, individuals were empowered to make conscious choices that aligned with their inherent qualities. The deepened self-awareness facilitated by astrology fostered personal growth, self-acceptance, and a more fulfilling engagement with life's journey. Armed with the wisdom of astrology, individuals could navigate challenges, pursue opportunities, and make choices that honored their authentic selves, ultimately leading to a more fulfilling and purposeful life.

B. Predictive Astrology:

Babylonian astrologers utilized astrology as a powerful tool for predicting future events and outcomes. By carefully analyzing the ongoing celestial movements and their alignment with an individual's natal chart, astrologers provided guidance and insights into various aspects of life. Predictive astrology aimed to help individuals navigate important decisions, anticipate potential challenges, and seize opportunities by understanding the cosmic influences at play. Let's delve into the details of predictive astrology:

Celestial Movements and Transits:

Astrologers paid close attention to the movements of celestial bodies, such as the planets and luminaries, as they progressed through the zodiac. These ongoing transits and progressions formed the basis for predictive astrology, which aimed to forecast and understand the potential influences and energies that individuals may encounter throughout their lives.

Transits refer to the current positions of celestial bodies in relation to an individual's natal chart. Astrologers would compare the positions of planets, including slower-moving ones like Jupiter and Saturn, to the positions of planets in the natal chart. The interactions between transiting planets and the planets in the natal chart could reveal important themes and events that may manifest in the individual's life. For example, if a transiting planet formed a conjunction or square aspect with a planet in the natal chart, it could signify a period of intensified energy, opportunities, challenges, or significant life events related to the qualities associated with those planets.

Progressions, on the other hand, involve the symbolic movement of the natal chart over time. Astrologers use various techniques to progress the natal chart, such as secondary progressions or solar arc directions. These techniques assign a specific rate of symbolic movement to the planets and points in the natal chart, reflecting the individual's growth and evolution as they age. By progressing the natal chart, astrologers can assess the shifts and developments that individuals may experience as they progress through different life stages. Progressed aspects and planetary positions offer insights into evolving potentials, changes in priorities, and shifts in consciousness.

The analysis of transits and progressions allows astrologers to make predictions and provide guidance regarding the potential influences and energies that individuals may encounter at different times in their lives. Astrologers can identify periods of growth, challenges, opportunities, or significant life events based on the interaction between transiting and progressing celestial bodies and the natal chart. This information helps individuals understand the timing and dynamics of their experiences, providing them with a broader perspective and empowering them to navigate life's transitions with greater awareness and preparedness.

It is important to note that astrological predictions are not deterministic or set in stone. They offer insights into potential energies and influences, but individuals still possess free will and the ability to make choices that can shape their lives. Astrology serves as a tool for self-reflection, guidance, and understanding, allowing individuals to align their actions and decisions with the prevailing energies and potentials of a given time.

In conclusion, astrologers pay close attention to the ongoing transits and progressions of celestial bodies to provide predictive insights. By comparing the current positions of planets and luminaries to an individual's natal chart, astrologers can assess the potential impact of these celestial movements on different areas of life. Transits and progressions offer valuable guidance and understanding of the timing and themes of personal growth, challenges, and opportunities. Through the analysis of these astrological techniques, individuals can gain insights into the unfolding energies of their lives, empowering them to make informed decisions and navigate their life's journey with greater awareness.

Timing and Cycles:

Predictive astrology, as practiced by Babylonian astrologers, involved a deep understanding of the cyclical nature of celestial phenomena and how they influenced human experiences. These astrologers recognized that certain planetary configurations and transits had specific timing patterns and corresponded to significant life events or shifts in energy.

One example of a significant timing pattern in predictive astrology is the Saturn return. Saturn takes approximately 29.5 years to complete its orbit around the Sun, and when it returns to the same position it occupied at the time of an individual's birth, it marks a significant milestone in their life. The first Saturn return typically occurs around the age of 29-30, and the second Saturn return occurs around the age of 58-60. These periods are often associated with profound personal and professional shifts, as individuals face important life decisions, undergo major life transitions, and reassess their values and goals.

Another planetary cycle that astrologers observed and studied was Jupiter's 12-year cycle. Jupiter takes approximately 12 years to complete its orbit around the Sun. When Jupiter returns to its natal position in an individual's chart, it signifies a period of expansion, growth, and opportunities. It is often associated with favorable circumstances, increased optimism, and the potential for personal and professional advancement. Astrologers would pay attention to Jupiter's transits and progressions to identify periods of abundance, luck, and potential breakthroughs in various areas of life.

In addition to these specific cycles, Babylonian astrologers also studied the overall cyclical patterns of celestial phenomena. They recognized that planetary transits, such as the movement of Mars or Venus through the zodiac, had distinct timing patterns and corresponded to different energetic influences. These patterns helped astrologers predict and understand the timing of events or shifts in a person's life.

By studying these planetary cycles and timing patterns, astrologers gained insights into the timing of major life transitions, events, and opportunities. They could provide individuals with guidance and foresight regarding favorable periods for certain endeavors or challenges they may face during specific phases of their lives. This understanding of timing empowered individuals to make informed decisions, seize opportunities, and navigate transitions more effectively.

It's important to note that while these timing patterns provide valuable insights, astrology does not imply a fixed destiny or predetermined outcomes. The interpretation of these cycles is not deterministic, but rather offers guidance and potential energies that individuals can work with and respond to based on their free will and personal choices.

In conclusion, predictive astrology in Babylonian tradition involved understanding the cyclical nature of celestial phenomena and how they influenced human experiences. Astrologers recognized specific timing patterns, such as the Saturn return and Jupiter's 12-year cycle, which corresponded to major life transitions and shifts in energy. By studying these cycles and observing planetary transits, astrologers provided individuals with insights into the timing of events and opportunities, empowering them to make conscious decisions and navigate their life's journey with greater awareness.

Anticipating Life Circumstances:

Astrologers utilized predictive astrology to anticipate and provide guidance on a wide range of life circumstances and events. By examining the current positions of celestial bodies in relation to an individual's natal chart, astrologers could offer insights and predictions regarding various areas of life, including career, finance, relationships, health, and personal growth.

In the realm of career, astrology provided valuable guidance on potential career advancements and opportunities. Astrologers would analyze the transits and progressions of planets through the houses and signs of the natal chart to identify favorable periods for professional growth, job changes, or entrepreneurial endeavors. For example, if a person's chart indicated a strong alignment between their natal Venus and the current position of Jupiter, it might suggest a favorable time for pursuing creative endeavors or seeking financial rewards in their career.

Financial matters were also a significant area of focus in predictive astrology. Astrologers would analyze the positions of celestial bodies in relation to the second and eighth houses of the natal chart, which govern wealth, assets, and financial resources. They would consider the transits and aspects involving planets such as Jupiter, Venus, and the lunar nodes to assess potential financial opportunities, investments, and financial stability.

Predictive astrology also played a role in relationship matters. Astrologers would examine the positions of Venus, Mars, and the seventh house, which represents partnerships, to provide insights into romantic relationships, marriage prospects, and compatibility with others. They would assess the transits and aspects involving these planets to determine favorable periods for meeting a significant other, deepening existing relationships, or resolving relationship challenges.

Health-related matters were not overlooked in predictive astrology. Astrologers would consider the positions of planets such as Mars, Saturn, and the sixth house, which governs health and well-being. By analyzing the transits and aspects involving these planets, astrologers could provide insights into potential health challenges, preventive measures, and favorable periods for focusing on self-care and well-being.

Personal growth and self-development were important considerations in predictive astrology as well. Astrologers would examine the positions of the outer planets, such as Uranus, Neptune, and Pluto, which represent transformative energies and spiritual growth. They would analyze the transits and progressions of these planets to identify periods of personal transformation, introspection, and opportunities for spiritual or psychological growth.

It's important to note that while astrology can provide guidance and insights, it does not guarantee specific outcomes or events. Astrological predictions offer possibilities and potential energies, which individuals can choose to engage with or navigate in their own unique ways.

In conclusion, predictive astrology encompassed various life circumstances and events. Astrologers utilized the positions of celestial bodies in relation to an individual's natal chart to provide guidance on matters related to career, finance, relationships, health, and personal growth. By analyzing the transits and aspects involving different planets and houses, astrologers offered insights into potential opportunities, challenges, and timing for different aspects of life. This information empowered individuals to make informed decisions, navigate life's ups and downs, and embrace their personal growth journey.

Identifying Challenges and Opportunities:

Predictive astrology sought to assist individuals in anticipating potential challenges and opportunities in their lives. Astrologers closely examined significant planetary aspects to assess the potential obstacles or favorable circumstances that might arise during specific periods.

Aspects are specific angular relationships between celestial bodies in a natal chart or in transit. They indicate how different energies interact and influence one another. Some common aspects include squares (90 degrees), oppositions (180 degrees), trines (120 degrees), and sextiles (60 degrees), among others. Each aspect carries its own distinct energy and can have varying effects on an individual's experiences.

When analyzing predictive astrology, astrologers pay particular attention to challenging aspects such as squares and oppositions. These aspects often represent areas of tension, conflict, or obstacles in one's life. For example, a square aspect between Mars and Saturn might indicate a period of heightened frustration, delays, or challenges in achieving one's goals. This aspect could bring forth a need for patience, discipline, and strategic planning to overcome obstacles.

Conversely, harmonious aspects such as trines and sextiles indicate a flow of energy and potential favorable circumstances. They can signify periods of ease, cooperation, and opportunities. For instance, a trine aspect between Venus and Jupiter might suggest a time of abundance, joy, and positive relationships. This aspect could bring forth opportunities for growth, happiness, and a harmonious social life.

In addition to considering the planetary aspects, astrologers also analyze the specific houses and signs involved in the aspects. This provides further context and helps to refine the interpretation of the potential challenges or opportunities.

It is essential to note that while predictive astrology can offer insights into potential influences and energies, it does not determine specific outcomes. Individuals always maintain their free will and can choose how to navigate and respond to the energies indicated by the aspects. Astrology serves as a tool for self-awareness and guidance, empowering individuals to make informed decisions and take appropriate actions.

In conclusion, predictive astrology aims to help individuals anticipate potential challenges and opportunities in their lives. Astrologers analyze significant planetary aspects, such as squares, oppositions, trines, and sextiles, to assess the potential obstacles or favorable circumstances that may arise during specific periods. Challenging aspects highlight areas of tension or conflict, while harmonious aspects indicate periods of ease and potential growth. By understanding these aspects, individuals can gain valuable insights and make conscious choices to navigate their life experiences.

Decision-Making and Strategic Planning:

Predictive astrology served as a valuable tool for individuals seeking insights to support decision-making and strategic planning. By understanding the potential influences and energies at play during specific periods, individuals could make informed choices aligned with their goals and values.

Astrological guidance allowed individuals to navigate challenges more effectively. By anticipating potential obstacles indicated by challenging aspects or transits, individuals could prepare themselves mentally, emotionally, and practically. They could develop strategies to overcome difficulties, manage conflicts, and find creative solutions. For example, if a challenging aspect suggested a period of heightened work-related stress, individuals could proactively implement self-care practices, time management techniques, or seek support from mentors or coaches.

Predictive astrology also highlighted favorable opportunities. Astrologers examined harmonious aspects or beneficial transits that indicated periods of abundance, growth, and positive developments. This insight allowed individuals to seize these opportunities and make the most of them. For instance, if a harmonious aspect indicated a favorable time for starting a new business venture, individuals could launch their enterprise with confidence, knowing that the cosmic energies were supportive of their endeavors.

Furthermore, predictive astrology played a significant role in assisting individuals with career decisions. By analyzing the planetary positions and aspects, astrologers could provide guidance on optimal timing for career advancements, job changes, or educational pursuits. Individuals could align their actions with cosmic energies and make choices that aligned with their true vocational aspirations. This knowledge empowered individuals to make career decisions with greater clarity, enhancing their chances of success and personal fulfillment.

In personal relationships, predictive astrology offered insights into potential dynamics and compatibility. Individuals could gain an understanding of the timing of romantic encounters, significant relationship milestones, or periods of emotional intensity. This awareness helped individuals navigate their love lives more consciously, fostering healthier connections, and making decisions that were in line with their long-term happiness.

In conclusion, predictive astrology provided individuals with valuable insights to support decision-making and strategic planning. By understanding the potential influences and energies at play during specific periods, individuals could make informed choices aligned with their goals and values. Astrological guidance helped individuals navigate challenges, seize favorable opportunities, and make the most of cosmic alignments in their personal and professional lives. By incorporating astrology into their decision-making processes, individuals were empowered to create lives that were in harmony with their authentic selves and aspirations.

Awareness and Self-Preparation:

Predictive astrology also emphasized the importance of self-preparation. By anticipating potential challenges or shifts in energy, individuals could proactively develop strategies to cope with difficult circumstances or maximize positive opportunities. Astrology served as a tool for self-awareness, enabling individuals to navigate life's ups and downs with resilience, self-reflection, and a deeper understanding of the cosmic forces at work.

In conclusion, predictive astrology played a crucial role in Babylonian society by offering insights and guidance on future events and outcomes. By analyzing ongoing celestial movements and their alignment with an individual's natal chart, astrologers provided valuable information on various life circumstances. Predictive astrology allowed individuals to navigate important decisions, anticipate challenges, and seize opportunities by understanding the cosmic influences at play. This knowledge empowered individuals to make informed choices and approach life with heightened self-awareness and strategic planning.

Examples, Problems, and Exercises:

Example: Analyze the natal chart of a famous Babylonian figure, such as Hammurabi or Nebuchadnezzar II, and interpret the astrological influences on their reign and accomplishments. Discuss how astrology may have shaped their leadership styles and decision-making processes.

Problem: Compare and contrast Babylonian astrology with modern Western astrology, focusing on their similarities and differences in terms of astrological houses, planetary symbolism, and interpretation techniques. Explore how cultural and historical factors influenced the development of each system.

Exercise: Create your own natal chart using a reputable astrology software or online tool. Analyze the positions of the celestial bodies and their alignment with the astrological houses. Reflect on the potential insights gained from the chart and how they relate to your personal experiences and aspirations.

✧   Divinatory Dream Interpretation:

Dreams have long been regarded as a profound source of insight and guidance in Babylonian divination practices. The ancient Babylonians believed that dreams served as a direct communication channel between mortals and the gods, offering glimpses into the future, glimpses into the future, and access to divine wisdom. This chapter delves into the intricacies of divinatory dream interpretation, exploring the methods and principles employed by Babylonian diviners to unravel the hidden meanings embedded within the dream realm.

➢   Understanding the Significance of Dreams:

A. Divine Communication:

Divine communication through dreams held significant importance in Babylonian culture. It was believed that during sleep, individuals entered a realm where they could receive direct messages from the gods. Dreams were considered a sacred and powerful channel through which the gods communicated with mortals, revealing their intentions, foretelling future events, and offering guidance and advice.

In Babylonian society, divination played a crucial role in interpreting dreams and deciphering their divine messages. Skilled diviners, known as "baru," were consulted to interpret dreams and unravel their hidden meanings. These diviners possessed deep knowledge of religious texts, mythologies, and the symbolic language used by the gods in dreams.

Diviners employed various techniques and rituals to access the divine insights contained within dreams. They would often engage in purification rituals, prayer, and the invocation of specific deities associated with dreams and divination. By entering a state of heightened spiritual awareness, diviners sought to establish a connection with the gods and gain clarity in interpreting the dreams.

Dreams were seen as omens and portents, offering glimpses into the future and providing guidance on important matters. Babylonians believed that the gods used dreams to communicate their will and offer counsel to those seeking answers or facing important decisions. For individuals seeking divine guidance, paying attention to dreams and seeking interpretation from skilled diviners was an essential practice.

The interpretations of dreams were highly contextual and specific to the individual and their circumstances. Diviners considered various factors such as the dreamer's social status, occupation, personal experiences, and the cultural and religious symbolism associated with the dream elements. Dreams were analyzed for their symbolic significance, patterns, and connections to the waking world. Diviners drew upon their knowledge of Babylonian myths, religious rituals, and the cultural context to decipher the hidden messages within the dreams.

Dreams were not the only form of divine communication in Babylonian culture. Other methods of divination, such as the interpretation of celestial omens, the examination of animal entrails, or the casting of lots, were also used to seek guidance from the gods. However, dreams held a special place as a direct means of divine communication, providing personal and intimate insights into an individual's life and circumstances.

Overall, in Babylonian culture, dreams were considered a sacred conduit for divine communication. They were believed to carry profound messages from the gods, offering guidance, warnings, and glimpses into the future. Diviners played a vital role in interpreting these dreams, unraveling their symbolic language, and helping individuals navigate the complexities of their lives based on the divine insights received. The practice of divine communication through dreams reflects the deep spiritual connection between the gods and the people of ancient Babylon.

B.Symbolic Language:

Babylonian divinatory dream interpretation was a complex and nuanced process that involved deciphering the symbolic language of dreams. It was believed that dreams contained hidden meanings and metaphors, requiring skilled interpretation to unveil their true significance. Diviners meticulously examined the vivid imagery, events, and emotions experienced within dreams to identify the underlying messages conveyed by the divine.

The interpretation of dreams in Babylonian culture was not a literal analysis of the dream content, but rather an exploration of its symbolic representation. Dreams were seen as a form of divine communication, and the gods communicated their messages through the use of symbols, allegories, and metaphors. Therefore, understanding the symbolic language of dreams was essential in unlocking their true meanings.

Diviners drew upon a rich repertoire of mythological, cultural, and religious symbolism to interpret dreams. They were well-versed in the narratives of the gods and the cosmological beliefs of Babylonian society. This knowledge allowed them to identify the recurring motifs and archetypal symbols present in dreams and connect them to specific deities, celestial bodies, or significant events in mythology.

The process of dream interpretation involved analyzing the various elements present in the dream, such as people, animals, objects, locations, and actions. Diviners paid close attention to the relationships between these elements, as well as the emotions and reactions experienced by the dreamer. Every detail held potential significance and provided clues to the message being conveyed.

Diviners employed a combination of intuition, personal experience, and traditional symbolism to unravel the layers of meaning within a dream. They would consider the cultural and social context of the dreamer, their personal history, and the current events or concerns in their life. This contextual analysis helped diviners relate the dream to the dreamer's specific circumstances and provide more accurate interpretations.

The interpretation of dreams in Babylonian culture was not standardized, as the symbolic language of dreams was highly subjective and open to multiple interpretations. Diviners relied on their expertise, experience, and knowledge of the individual dreamer to offer personalized insights. The same dream could have different meanings for different individuals, depending on their personal associations and cultural background.

Dream interpretation was not limited to the realm of individual experiences but also extended to the interpretation of collective dreams and prophetic dreams that foretold significant events. Babylonians believed that dreams could reveal hidden truths, forewarn of impending dangers, or offer guidance on important decisions. Therefore, the interpretation of dreams had practical implications in various aspects of life, including personal matters, social issues, and political affairs.

Overall, Babylonian divinatory dream interpretation was a skillful art that relied on the decoding of symbolic language within dreams. Diviners used their knowledge of mythology, cultural symbolism, and personal context to uncover the hidden messages and metaphors within dreams. Through this process, they sought to provide individuals with guidance, insight, and a deeper understanding of their own lives and the divine forces at work.

➤ The Role of the Dream Interpreter:

A. Expertise in Symbols and Omens:

Interpreting dreams and omens in Babylonian culture required a deep understanding of symbolic language and the significance attached to various symbols and events. Diviners were experts in decoding the messages embedded within dreams, drawing on their extensive knowledge of the cultural context and the meanings associated with specific symbols.

Babylonian diviners possessed a vast repertoire of symbolic knowledge that encompassed both universal and culturally specific symbols. They were familiar with the symbolic meanings attributed to objects, animals, natural phenomena, celestial bodies, and various events. These symbols were deeply ingrained in Babylonian culture and were believed to carry hidden messages from the divine.

Symbols in dreams were not interpreted in isolation but were understood in relation to the dreamer's personal circumstances and the broader cultural and mythological context. For example, a lion symbolized strength, power, and royal authority, reflecting the qualities associated with the god Marduk, the supreme deity in Babylonian mythology. Diviners considered the presence of a lion in a dream as a sign of favorable outcomes and the support of divine forces.

In addition to understanding individual symbols, diviners also recognized the significance of dream sequences and patterns. They looked for recurring symbols, motifs, or narrative structures that conveyed specific messages. For example, dreams involving journeys or encounters with deities might suggest a need for the dreamer to embark on a new path or seek divine intervention.

Omens, which were signs or events believed to foretell future outcomes, were another important aspect of Babylonian divination. Diviners were skilled in interpreting omens observed in daily life, such as the behavior of animals, the appearance of celestial phenomena, or the patterns of natural events. They recognized that these omens carried messages from the gods and provided guidance on important matters.

The expertise of Babylonian diviners in symbols and omens was cultivated through years of study, observation, and shared knowledge within their community. They learned from the accumulated wisdom of previous generations and were guided by traditional texts and manuals that documented the meanings and interpretations of symbols and omens.

It is important to note that while some symbols and omens had generally agreed-upon meanings, interpretations could vary based on the diviner's personal experience, intuition, and the specific context of the dream or omen. Diviners relied on their expertise to discern the most relevant and accurate interpretation for the individual seeking guidance.

Overall, the expertise of Babylonian diviners in symbols and omens was crucial for the interpretation of dreams and the decoding of hidden messages from the divine. Their extensive knowledge of symbolic language and their understanding of the cultural and mythological context allowed them to unravel the rich tapestry of meaning embedded within dreams and omens.

B. Contextual Understanding:

In Babylonian divination, the recognition of the dreamer's personal circumstances and the contextual factors surrounding the dream was a crucial aspect of accurate interpretation. Diviners understood that dreams were not isolated experiences but were deeply intertwined with the dreamer's waking life, including their social status, occupation, and personal relationships. By taking these factors into account, diviners provided a more comprehensive analysis of the dream's meaning.

The social status of the dreamer was an important consideration in dream interpretation. Babylonian society was hierarchical, with distinct roles and expectations for individuals based on their position within the social structure. Diviners recognized that dreams could reflect the concerns, aspirations, and anxieties specific to different social classes. For example, a dream involving interactions with nobility or references to royal affairs might hold different significance for a member of the ruling elite compared to a commoner.

Occupation also played a significant role in dream interpretation. Babylonian society was diverse, encompassing various professions and trades. Diviners understood that the dreams of a farmer, a merchant, or a priest would be influenced by their respective occupations and the specific challenges and desires associated with them. Dreams related to one's work or specific tasks performed in daily life could provide insights into professional success, financial matters, or the fulfillment of one's occupational responsibilities.

Personal relationships were another essential factor considered by Babylonian diviners. Dreams often contained symbols and scenarios that reflected the dreamer's interactions with family members, friends, or romantic partners. Diviners recognized that the dynamics within these relationships held significant emotional and psychological significance for the dreamer. Dreams involving conflicts, reconciliations, or expressions of affection could reveal underlying tensions or desires within these personal connections.

In addition to personal circumstances, diviners also considered prevalent cultural beliefs and values when interpreting dreams. Babylonian culture was rich with mythology, religious beliefs, and shared symbols that influenced the collective understanding of dreams. Diviners relied on this cultural backdrop to decipher the dream's symbolism and uncover its broader meaning within the cultural and religious framework. Cultural symbols, rituals, and deities often found their way into dreams, providing clues to the dreamer's relationship with the divine and the broader community.

By taking into account the dreamer's personal circumstances and the contextual factors surrounding the dream, Babylonian diviners provided a more nuanced and accurate interpretation. They recognized that dreams were not isolated events but reflections of the dreamer's lived experiences, social roles, and cultural milieu. This holistic approach ensured that the interpretation encompassed the unique concerns and aspirations of the individual, allowing for a deeper understanding of the dream's significance within their life.

➢   Techniques of Divinatory Dream Interpretation:

A. Symbolic Analysis:

In Babylonian divination, the recognition of the dreamer's personal circumstances and the contextual factors surrounding the dream was a crucial aspect of accurate interpretation. Diviners understood that dreams were not isolated experiences but were deeply intertwined with the dreamer's waking life, including their social status, occupation, and personal relationships. By taking these factors into account, diviners provided a more comprehensive analysis of the dream's meaning.

The social status of the dreamer was an important consideration in dream interpretation. Babylonian society was hierarchical, with distinct roles and expectations for individuals based on their position within the social structure. Diviners recognized that dreams could reflect the concerns, aspirations, and anxieties specific to different social classes. For example, a dream involving interactions with nobility or references to royal affairs might hold different significance for a member of the ruling elite compared to a commoner.

Occupation also played a significant role in dream interpretation. Babylonian society was diverse, encompassing various professions and trades. Diviners understood that the dreams of a farmer, a merchant, or a priest would be influenced by their respective occupations and the specific challenges and desires associated with them. Dreams related to one's work or specific tasks performed in daily life could provide insights into professional success, financial matters, or the fulfillment of one's occupational responsibilities.

Personal relationships were another essential factor considered by Babylonian diviners. Dreams often contained symbols and scenarios that reflected the dreamer's interactions with family members, friends, or romantic partners. Diviners recognized that the dynamics within these relationships held significant emotional and psychological significance for the dreamer. Dreams involving conflicts, reconciliations, or expressions of affection could reveal underlying tensions or desires within these personal connections.

In addition to personal circumstances, diviners also considered prevalent cultural beliefs and values when interpreting dreams. Babylonian culture was rich with mythology, religious beliefs, and shared symbols that influenced the collective understanding of dreams. Diviners relied on this cultural backdrop to decipher the dream's symbolism and uncover its broader meaning within the cultural and religious framework. Cultural symbols, rituals, and deities often found their way into dreams, providing clues to the dreamer's relationship with the divine and the broader community.

By taking into account the dreamer's personal circumstances and the contextual factors surrounding the dream, Babylonian diviners provided a more nuanced and accurate interpretation. They recognized that dreams were not isolated events but reflections of the dreamer's lived experiences, social roles, and cultural milieu. This holistic approach ensured that the interpretation encompassed the unique concerns and aspirations of the individual, allowing for a deeper understanding of the dream's significance within their life.

B. Emotional and Sensory Elements:

In Babylonian divination, diviners recognized the importance of not only the symbols but also the emotions and sensory experiences described by the dreamer. They understood that the intensity and nature of emotions, as well as the sensory details, played a significant role in interpreting the dream accurately.

Emotions expressed within a dream held valuable insights into the dreamer's underlying feelings, desires, and concerns. Diviners paid close attention to the emotions experienced by the dreamer, such as fear, joy, anger, or sadness. The intensity and context of these emotions provided clues to the dream's significance. For example, a dream filled with fear and anxiety might suggest unresolved fears or anxieties in the dreamer's waking life. Conversely, a dream characterized by joy and elation could indicate positive experiences or aspirations.

Sensory details described by the dreamer also held symbolic significance. Diviners recognized that the inclusion of sensory experiences, such as sounds, smells, tastes, and colors, added depth and specificity to the dream's message. For example, the sound of thunder or the scent of incense could carry religious or spiritual connotations, while the taste of bitter herbs might symbolize challenges or adversity. Colors mentioned in the dream could be associated with specific emotions or symbolic meanings within Babylonian culture. By analyzing these sensory details, diviners gained further insights into the dreamer's experiences and the hidden messages within the dream.

Diviners understood that emotions and sensory experiences were not isolated elements but were intricately connected to the dream's overall message. The combination of symbols, emotions, and sensory details formed a cohesive narrative that reflected the dreamer's subconscious thoughts, desires, and concerns. By paying close attention to these aspects, diviners were able to provide a more nuanced interpretation that considered the holistic nature of the dream.

It is important to note that Babylonian diviners relied on their knowledge of the cultural and symbolic associations of emotions and sensory experiences. The interpretations were grounded in the specific cultural context of ancient Babylonia, where certain emotions, sensory details, and symbols carried particular meanings. These interpretations were not universal but rather reflected the understanding and beliefs of the Babylonian society at that time.

By incorporating the emotions and sensory experiences described by the dreamer, Babylonian diviners deepened their understanding of the dream's message and provided a more comprehensive interpretation. The careful analysis of these elements added richness and specificity to the overall understanding of the dream, allowing diviners to guide individuals in deciphering the hidden meanings and implications embedded within their dreams.

C. Contextual Associations:

Babylonian diviners recognized the importance of exploring the connections between dreams and the dreamer's waking life experiences. They understood that dreams were not isolated occurrences but were often influenced by the dreamer's current circumstances, concerns, and experiences. By examining the context surrounding the dream, diviners sought to identify any parallels or correlations between the dream and the dreamer's waking life.

Diviners considered the dreamer's personal circumstances, such as their social status, occupation, and personal relationships, as well as the prevalent cultural beliefs and values of the time. They believed that dreams held messages from the divine that were relevant to the dreamer's specific situation. By examining the dreamer's current circumstances, diviners gained insights into the areas of the dreamer's life that required attention or action.

For example, if a dreamer held a prominent position in society, the diviner would consider the dream in light of the dreamer's role and responsibilities. The dream might provide guidance on matters related to leadership, decision-making, or maintaining harmony within the community. Alternatively, if the dreamer was experiencing challenges in personal relationships, the diviner would explore how the dream reflected those challenges and offer advice on resolving conflicts or fostering better communication.

By connecting the dreamer's waking life experiences to the content of the dream, diviners could provide a more tailored and practical interpretation. This approach allowed the diviners to address the dreamer's specific concerns and provide guidance that was directly applicable to their circumstances.

Additionally, the diviners understood that dreams often served as a reflection of the dreamer's subconscious thoughts, desires, and concerns. By examining the context surrounding the dream, such as recent events or ongoing challenges, diviners could uncover the underlying messages and meanings within the dream. They sought to identify any patterns, symbols, or themes that resonated with the dreamer's waking life experiences.

For example, if a dreamer had recently faced a significant loss or encountered obstacles in their career, the diviner would explore how these experiences might be reflected in the dream. The dream might provide insights into the dreamer's emotional state, offer guidance on navigating the challenges, or present opportunities for growth and transformation.

By exploring the connections between dreams and waking life experiences, Babylonian diviners aimed to provide a more comprehensive understanding of the dream's significance. They recognized that dreams were not isolated fragments but were woven into the broader tapestry of the dreamer's life. By considering the dreamer's context and experiences, diviners could offer interpretations that were grounded in the dreamer's reality and provided practical guidance for addressing their concerns and aspirations.

➤   Applying Divinatory Dream Interpretation:

A. Personal Guidance and Decision-Making:

Divinatory dream interpretation played a vital role in providing individuals with personal guidance and direction in Babylonian society. It was believed that dreams served as a direct means of communication from the gods, offering valuable insights and guidance for the dreamer's life journey.

By seeking the interpretation of their dreams, individuals gained access to hidden knowledge and a deeper understanding of their own lives. Divinatory dream interpretation allowed individuals to tap into their subconscious thoughts, desires, and concerns, which may not be readily accessible during waking hours. Dreams provided a window into the inner workings of the mind and offered a unique perspective on one's personal experiences and challenges.

Through divinatory dream interpretation, individuals were able to make informed decisions based on the messages conveyed in their dreams. By understanding the symbols, metaphors, and narratives within their dreams, they gained insights into their own strengths, weaknesses, and potential paths forward. This self-awareness empowered individuals to navigate their lives with greater clarity and purpose.

Dreams often provided glimpses of potential challenges that lay ahead, enabling individuals to anticipate and prepare for obstacles that might arise. Divinatory dream interpretation allowed individuals to uncover hidden meanings and warnings within their dreams, providing valuable guidance for overcoming difficulties or avoiding potential pitfalls.

Moreover, dreams also presented opportunities for growth and transformation. They revealed untapped potentials, hidden talents, and new possibilities. By interpreting the messages of their dreams, individuals could identify avenues for personal development, explore new paths, and seize opportunities that aligned with their deepest aspirations.

The insights gained through divinatory dream interpretation were not limited to specific areas of life. Dreams could provide guidance on various aspects, including personal relationships, career choices, health concerns, and spiritual matters. By understanding the messages conveyed in their dreams, individuals gained a holistic view of their lives and could make decisions that encompassed their overall well-being and fulfillment.

Ultimately, divinatory dream interpretation served as a valuable tool for individuals seeking personal guidance and direction. It enabled them to access a deeper level of self-understanding, make informed decisions, anticipate challenges, and seize opportunities for growth and fulfillment. By harnessing the wisdom embedded within their dreams, individuals were empowered to navigate their life journeys with greater clarity, purpose, and alignment with their own unique paths.

B. Predictive Insights:

In Babylonian culture, dreams were seen as more than just reflections of the dreamer's inner thoughts and desires; they were believed to have the power to reveal glimpses of the future. The Babylonians regarded dreams as a means through which the gods communicated messages and foretold upcoming events.

Diviners proficient in dream interpretation played a crucial role in helping individuals understand the prophetic nature of their dreams. By carefully analyzing the symbols, narratives, and emotions within the dream, diviners sought to uncover the hidden messages about future events that lay within.

Through their expertise in dream interpretation, diviners provided individuals with valuable insights into what lay ahead. This proactive approach to understanding the future allowed individuals to prepare themselves for potential outcomes or challenges that they might face. By having knowledge of what the future may hold, individuals could take proactive steps to mitigate risks, seize opportunities, or make informed decisions.

For example, if a dream indicated a potential conflict or danger, individuals could take precautions or make changes in their plans to avoid potential pitfalls. Conversely, if a dream revealed positive outcomes or opportunities, individuals could plan and take actions to capitalize on them. Divinatory dream interpretation offered individuals a way to be proactive in navigating the uncertain future, empowering them to make choices that aligned with their desired outcomes.

Additionally, divinatory dream interpretation also provided individuals with a sense of reassurance and guidance during times of uncertainty. It offered a comforting belief that the gods were providing insights and guidance about what was to come. By gaining glimpses into the future through dream interpretation, individuals felt more prepared and supported, knowing that they were not navigating the unknown alone.

It is important to note that while dream interpretation provided valuable glimpses into the future, it was not considered an absolute prediction of events. Babylonians understood that the future was not fixed and could be influenced by individual actions and external factors. However, divinatory dream interpretation served as a tool to enhance awareness, preparedness, and decision-making in the face of the unpredictable nature of life.

In summary, the Babylonians believed that dreams had the power to foreshadow future events, and diviners proficient in dream interpretation played a crucial role in deciphering these messages. By providing individuals with glimpses into what lay ahead, dream interpretation allowed them to take a proactive approach in navigating the uncertain future. This understanding of potential outcomes and challenges empowered individuals to make informed decisions, mitigate risks, and seize opportunities for a more favorable future.

Examples, Problems, and Exercises:

Example: Analyze a dream narrative from ancient Babylonian literature, such as the dream of Gilgamesh in the Epic of Gilgamesh. Interpret the symbols, events, and emotions described in the dream, and discuss how the divine messages within the dream impacted the subsequent events in the story.

Problem: Compare and contrast Babylonian dream interpretation with the practices of other ancient cultures, such as Egyptian or Greek. Explore the similarities and differences in the methods, symbols, and beliefs surrounding dream divination.

Exercise: Keep a dream journal for one week, recording your dreams upon waking. Select one dream and apply the principles of Babylonian dream interpretation to analyze its symbols, emotions, and context. Reflect on the potential messages and insights the dream may hold for your personal life and decision-making.

Conclusion:

Divinatory dream interpretation held immense significance in Babylonian culture, serving as a means to communicate with the gods and access divine wisdom. The complex language of dreams required skilled interpreters who could unlock the hidden messages within the symbolic narratives. By understanding the principles and techniques of Babylonian dream interpretation, individuals could gain profound insights, guidance, and warnings from the divine realm, enhancing their understanding of themselves and their place in the world.

✧   Augury:

Augury, a prominent form of divination in ancient Babylon, involved the interpretation of signs and omens found in the natural world. Babylonian diviners recognized the profound influence of nature and believed that the gods communicated their intentions through various natural phenomena. This chapter explores the practice of augury, delving into the methods, observations, and interpretations used by Babylonian diviners to glean insights from the signs and omens found in nature.

✧   Understanding the Significance of Augury:

A. Divine Messages:

In Babylonian culture, the natural world was seen as a profound manifestation of divine presence and intention. The Babylonians believed that the gods communicated their will and intentions through various natural phenomena, such as the behavior of animals, the flight patterns of birds, or the occurrence of unusual weather events. These signs and omens were considered direct messages from the gods, providing guidance and insights into the future.

Diviners, with their deep knowledge of symbolism and omens, played a crucial role in interpreting these natural signs. They carefully observed and interpreted the behaviors and actions of animals, birds, and other elements of nature to discern their hidden meanings. For example, the sighting of a particular animal in an unexpected place or the sudden change in the behavior of a bird was seen as a significant sign.

The interpretation of these natural signs involved considering both the specific behavior or occurrence and its broader cultural and mythological context. Diviners drew upon a rich tradition of knowledge and symbolism associated with different animals, birds, and natural phenomena. They understood the cultural significance attached to certain animals or events, and how they related to specific gods or cosmic forces.

For instance, the sudden appearance of a particular animal might be associated with a particular deity or represent a specific aspect of life, such as fertility, abundance, or protection. The flight patterns of birds could be interpreted as messages of good fortune, warnings of impending danger, or indications of favorable conditions for certain activities.

Diviners also took into account the overall context and the individual's personal circumstances when interpreting these natural signs. Factors such as the time, location, and the dreamer's social status were considered to provide a more accurate analysis. The diviner would integrate their knowledge of the symbolic language of nature with their understanding of the dreamer's situation to offer a comprehensive interpretation.

The belief in the divine communication through natural signs served multiple purposes. Firstly, it fostered a deep sense of connection and reverence for the natural world. The Babylonians saw nature as a sacred realm intricately intertwined with the workings of the gods. Observing and interpreting these signs was a way to participate in the divine order of the universe.

Secondly, the interpretation of natural signs provided individuals with guidance and insights into the future. By recognizing and understanding the messages conveyed through natural phenomena, individuals could gain a better understanding of the divine intentions and align their actions accordingly. It allowed them to make informed decisions, anticipate potential outcomes, and adapt their plans accordingly.

Overall, the Babylonians perceived nature as a divine canvas upon which the gods painted their intentions. The interpretation of natural signs and omens offered a direct means of communication between the gods and humanity. Diviners played a crucial role in deciphering these messages, providing individuals with guidance, insights, and a deeper connection to the divine presence in the world around them.

B. Symbolic Language:

Augury, a form of divination practiced by the Babylonians, involved the interpretation of symbols and omens found in nature. The Babylonian diviners believed that the gods communicated their intentions and provided guidance through various natural phenomena, and deciphering these signs was essential to understanding the divine messages.

In augury, the diviners closely observed the environment, paying particular attention to specific occurrences, sounds, or appearances in nature. They recognized that certain phenomena were associated with specific meanings and carried symbolic significance. For example, the sudden appearance of a particular bird, such as an owl or an eagle, could be seen as an important omen. The sight of certain animals, such as a serpent or a lion, or the occurrence of particular weather patterns, such as a sudden storm or a calm breeze, were also regarded as significant signs.

The diviners had an intricate understanding of the symbolic language embedded in these natural occurrences. They drew upon a wealth of cultural and mythological knowledge to interpret the messages conveyed by these symbols. These symbols were not arbitrary; they were deeply rooted in the beliefs, myths, and religious traditions of Babylonian society.

For example, the appearance of an owl was often associated with wisdom and insight, while an eagle symbolized power and victory. The sighting of a serpent might signify transformation or hidden knowledge, while the presence of a lion could represent strength and royalty. Similarly, thunder was often regarded as a powerful and awe-inspiring phenomenon, carrying messages of divine significance.

Interpreting these symbols required a combination of knowledge, intuition, and experience. Diviners drew upon their extensive understanding of the cultural and mythological context, as well as their own expertise in the symbolic language of nature. They considered the specific circumstances and the broader context in which the signs appeared to provide a comprehensive interpretation.

Furthermore, the interpretation of these symbols was not only dependent on their individual meanings but also on the combination and arrangement of multiple signs. Diviners recognized that the interplay between different omens and their relationships with one another added layers of meaning to the overall message. The diviners would carefully analyze and integrate these various elements to provide a holistic interpretation.

Augury served multiple purposes in Babylonian society. Firstly, it provided individuals with a means to seek divine guidance and understanding of the gods' intentions. By recognizing and interpreting the symbols and omens in nature, people could gain insights into their own lives, make decisions, and take appropriate actions in accordance with the divine will.

Secondly, augury reinforced the belief in a cosmic order and the interconnectedness of the human realm with the divine realm. The occurrence of these signs and omens served as a reminder of the presence and influence of the gods in everyday life. It fostered a sense of awe, reverence, and responsibility towards the natural world.

In conclusion, augury in Babylonian culture relied on the interpretation of symbols and omens found in nature. Diviners recognized the cultural significance of these signs and omens and understood their connection to the divine messages. By deciphering the symbolic language of nature, diviners provided individuals with valuable insights and guidance, enabling them to navigate their lives in harmony with the divine will.

✧   Techniques of Augury:

A. Observing Animal Behavior:

In Babylonian culture, diviners relied on the behavior of animals as a means to discern omens and receive divine messages. They believed that animals, being closely connected to nature, possessed a heightened sensitivity to the spiritual realm and could act as messengers between the gods and humans.

Babylonian diviners carefully observed the behavior of animals, paying attention to their sudden appearances, movements, or sounds. They recognized that certain deviations from the usual behavior or patterns exhibited by animals were believed to be significant indicators of divine messages.

For example, if an animal appeared in an unexpected or unusual location, it was seen as a potential omen. The specific type of animal and its behavior were also important factors to consider. Diviners took note of animals that were rare or held symbolic significance in Babylonian culture, such as lions, serpents, owls, or eagles. The presence of these animals in certain contexts was thought to carry specific messages.

Diviners also paid attention to the sounds made by animals, such as the calls of birds or the howling of wolves. Unusual or repetitive sounds were seen as potential omens, and diviners interpreted these sounds based on their cultural understanding of animal symbolism.

Interpreting the behavior of animals required a deep knowledge of the cultural and mythological significance attached to different species. Diviners drew upon traditional beliefs and stories to understand the messages conveyed through animal behavior. For example, the appearance of a serpent might symbolize transformation or hidden knowledge, while the presence of a lion could signify strength and royalty.

Diviners also considered the context in which the animal appeared. The location, time of day, and the individual's personal circumstances were taken into account to provide a comprehensive interpretation. For instance, if a rare bird landed near someone during an important decision-making process, it could be seen as a positive omen, signaling guidance and support from the gods.

The expertise of the diviners in observing and interpreting animal behavior allowed them to discern messages from the gods and provide guidance to individuals seeking insight or answers to their questions. The interpretation of these animal omens was not limited to a single event or circumstance but often extended to broader aspects of an individual's life, such as relationships, health, or future outcomes.

The belief in the significance of animal behavior as omens was deeply ingrained in Babylonian society. It fostered a sense of connection and interdependence between humans, nature, and the divine. By closely observing and interpreting the behavior of animals, diviners provided individuals with a deeper understanding of their own lives and the messages conveyed by the gods.

In conclusion, Babylonian diviners closely observed the behavior of animals, considering their appearances, movements, and sounds as significant indicators of divine messages. They recognized that animals held a special connection to the spiritual realm and could act as messengers from the gods. By interpreting the behavior of animals, diviners provided individuals with valuable insights and guidance, helping them navigate their lives in alignment with the divine will.

B. Interpreting Bird Flight:

Birds held a special place in Babylonian augury, and their behavior was closely observed and interpreted by diviners as a means to gain insights into future events and divine intentions.

In Babylonian culture, each bird species was believed to carry specific meanings and symbolism. Diviners familiarized themselves with the characteristics and behaviors of various birds, recognizing that their flight patterns, formations, and calls could provide valuable information about the gods' intentions.

When observing birds, diviners paid attention to several factors. The speed of a bird's flight was considered significant, as it was believed to reflect the urgency or swiftness of the forthcoming event. A fast-flying bird might indicate a sudden and impactful occurrence, while a slower or hovering bird might suggest a more gradual change or a period of reflection.

The direction of the bird's flight was also important in interpretation. Different directions were associated with specific meanings. For example, a bird flying towards the east was often seen as a positive sign, symbolizing new beginnings, growth, and prosperity. A bird flying westward might suggest the need for caution or signal potential challenges ahead. Diviners considered the cultural context and prevailing beliefs when assigning meanings to different flight directions.

The formations and patterns created by birds in flight were also significant. Diviners observed if birds flew in a group, forming specific shapes or patterns, as these formations were believed to convey messages from the gods. For example, a V-shaped formation might be associated with victory or unity, while a dispersed or scattered pattern could signify disruption or conflict.

The calls of birds were another crucial element in Babylonian augury. Diviners recognized that each bird species had its own unique sound, and the specific calls made by birds were considered meaningful. Diviners paid attention to the pitch, tone, and repetition of bird calls, interpreting them as indicators of upcoming events or the gods' approval or disapproval.

Interpreting the movements and behaviors of birds required deep knowledge and understanding of Babylonian culture and its associated symbolism. Diviners drew upon traditional beliefs and mythological associations to decode the messages conveyed by birds. The interpretation of bird augury was not based on individual instances but often took into account broader patterns and repeated sightings over time.

By carefully observing and interpreting the flight patterns, formations, and calls of birds, diviners provided individuals with insights into future events and the intentions of the gods. This allowed individuals to prepare for potential outcomes, make informed decisions, or take appropriate actions based on the messages conveyed through bird augury.

Birds, with their ability to traverse the sky and connect the earthly realm with the heavens, held a special significance in Babylonian culture. The interpretation of their movements and behaviors provided a direct means of communication between the gods and humans, enabling individuals to seek guidance, anticipate events, and align their actions with the divine will.

In summary, birds held special significance in Babylonian augury, and diviners carefully observed their flight patterns, formations, and calls to interpret messages about future events and divine intentions. Each bird species was associated with specific meanings, and their movements were believed to reveal the gods' intentions. By interpreting the speed, direction, and interactions of birds, diviners provided valuable insights into the future and guidance for individuals seeking to navigate their lives in harmony with the divine.

C. Analyzing Weather Phenomena:

Unusual weather events played a crucial role in Babylonian divination, as they were seen as powerful omens carrying messages from the gods. Babylonian diviners closely observed and interpreted these atmospheric phenomena to gain insights into the future and guide individuals in their actions.

In Babylonian culture, storms, lightning, and celestial alignments were considered as direct manifestations of divine power and intervention. These extraordinary weather occurrences were believed to be orchestrated by the gods to communicate their intentions or to signal significant events.

When interpreting unusual weather events, diviners paid attention to several factors. The timing of the event was considered significant, as it was believed to indicate the gods' timing and alignment with specific actions or events. For example, if a storm occurred before a military campaign, it might be interpreted as a warning or a sign of divine approval for the forthcoming battle. The diviners would consider the relationship between the timing of the event and the individual's circumstances to provide accurate guidance.

The intensity and duration of the weather event also held meaning. A severe storm or a particularly intense lightning strike might be seen as a potent omen, suggesting a major event or a critical decision. Diviners interpreted the intensity of the weather event in relation to the individual's situation, offering insights into the significance or impact of the forthcoming event.

Furthermore, celestial alignments, such as the conjunction or opposition of planets, were closely observed and interpreted by Babylonian diviners. They believed that these alignments reflected the cosmic harmony and the gods' influence on earthly affairs. Diviners analyzed the positions of celestial bodies in relation to an individual's birth chart or the specific circumstances at hand to decipher the messages conveyed by these celestial events. For instance, a favorable alignment might indicate a period of opportunity or success, while a challenging alignment could signal a time of adversity or caution.

Diviners relied on their extensive knowledge of celestial phenomena and their correlations with historical events and cultural beliefs to interpret the significance of unusual weather events. They combined their understanding of meteorological patterns with astrological principles to provide comprehensive analyses and guidance.

The interpretation of unusual weather events was not limited to individual instances but often involved recognizing patterns and correlations over time. Diviners sought to identify recurring weather phenomena and their association with specific outcomes or actions. This allowed them to provide individuals with informed guidance and help them navigate their lives in accordance with the divine will.

By recognizing the importance of unusual weather events and interpreting their timing, intensity, and duration, Babylonian diviners provided individuals with insights into the future and guidance for their actions. Understanding the correlation between atmospheric phenomena and the gods' messages allowed individuals to prepare for significant events, make informed decisions, or take necessary precautions.

In summary, unusual weather events such as storms, lightning, and celestial alignments were regarded as significant omens in Babylonian culture. Diviners recognized the correlation between these atmospheric phenomena and the gods' messages, interpreting their timing, intensity, and duration to provide insights into future outcomes or actions individuals should take. By closely observing and interpreting these unusual weather events, diviners helped individuals navigate their lives and align their actions with the divine will.

✧   Applying Augury in Divination:

A. Personal Guidance:

Augury was a sought-after practice in Babylonian culture, as individuals turned to diviners to gain insights and guidance for various personal matters. Diviners would carefully interpret the observed signs and omens in relation to the specific questions or concerns posed by individuals, providing them with valuable information to make informed decisions and navigate their lives.

When seeking augury, individuals would approach diviners with their inquiries or present their specific situations or dilemmas. Diviners would then employ their expertise in interpreting the signs and omens to address the individual's concerns directly.

The process of augury involved observing and analyzing various phenomena, such as the behavior of animals, flight patterns of birds, or unusual weather events. Diviners would interpret these signs and omens in relation to the individual's query or situation, seeking to uncover hidden meanings and insights.

For example, if an individual sought guidance on a potential business venture, diviners might observe the flight patterns of birds and interpret their movements as an indication of success or caution. The appearance of a particular bird species or its behavior during the observation might be associated with positive or negative outcomes. Diviners would take into account the specific circumstances of the individual's venture and provide guidance based on the interpreted signs.

Similarly, if someone had concerns about a personal relationship, diviners would observe the behavior of animals or other natural phenomena to discern messages related to that particular relationship. Unusual interactions or patterns observed in nature might be seen as reflections of the dynamics or potential outcomes of the relationship. Diviners would then interpret these signs in the context of the individual's query, offering insights and guidance for navigating the situation.

The divine messages derived from augury served as a valuable source of guidance, helping individuals make informed decisions, navigate challenges, and seize opportunities. By seeking augury, individuals aimed to gain a deeper understanding of their circumstances and potential outcomes, ultimately empowering themselves to make choices aligned with their goals and desires.

Augury provided individuals with a proactive approach to addressing personal matters. Rather than relying solely on their own perceptions and experiences, individuals sought the wisdom and insights derived from the interpretation of signs and omens. This external perspective provided a broader understanding of their situation, allowing them to consider factors beyond their immediate knowledge.

By incorporating the divine messages derived from augury into their decision-making process, individuals could navigate their lives with a sense of clarity and purpose. Augury served as a guiding light, helping individuals anticipate challenges, recognize opportunities, and align their actions with the cosmic forces believed to influence their lives.

In summary, individuals sought augury to gain insights and guidance for personal matters. Diviners interpreted observed signs and omens in relation to specific questions or concerns, providing individuals with valuable information to make informed decisions and navigate their lives. The divine messages derived from augury helped individuals address their queries, navigate challenges, and seize opportunities, offering them a proactive approach to personal decision-making.

B. Predicting Events:

Augury played a crucial role in Babylonian culture as a means of predicting future events and their outcomes. Diviners were skilled in interpreting the natural signs and omens present in their environment to provide individuals with glimpses into what lay ahead.

Through careful observation and analysis of the natural world, diviners sought to discern the likelihood of success or failure in various endeavors. They recognized that certain phenomena held symbolic meanings and could be interpreted as indicators of future events. By interpreting these signs and omens, diviners could provide individuals with valuable insights to anticipate and prepare for significant events in their lives.

For example, if someone sought augury regarding a potential business venture, diviners might observe the flight patterns of birds, the behavior of animals, or the occurrence of specific weather phenomena. These observations would be interpreted in relation to the individual's query, aiming to gauge the likelihood of success or failure in the venture. The appearance of certain bird species, the behavior of animals, or the occurrence of particular weather events might be seen as positive or negative omens, indicating the outcome of the endeavor.

The insights derived from augury allowed individuals to adopt a proactive approach to their lives. By gaining glimpses into the future, they could make informed decisions, take appropriate actions, and prepare themselves for the potential outcomes. This proactive stance enabled individuals to navigate their lives with greater confidence and preparedness, maximizing their chances of success and minimizing potential setbacks.

Furthermore, augury provided individuals with a sense of control and agency over their own lives. By seeking divinatory guidance, individuals could gain a deeper understanding of the potential events and outcomes they might encounter. This knowledge empowered them to make strategic choices, adjust their plans, or even avoid certain paths altogether.

It is important to note that Babylonian diviners did not provide definitive predictions of the future. Rather, they offered insights based on the interpreted signs and omens, recognizing the inherent uncertainties of life. Augury served as a tool to assess probabilities and likely outcomes, allowing individuals to make informed decisions and take appropriate actions.

In summary, Babylonian diviners utilized augury as a means of predicting future events and their outcomes. By interpreting natural signs and omens, they provided individuals with insights into the likelihood of success or failure in various endeavors. Augury empowered individuals to adopt a proactive approach to anticipate and prepare for significant events in their lives, enabling them to make informed decisions and maximize their chances of success.

✧   Ethical Considerations and Limitations:

A. Ethical Responsibility:

Babylonian diviners recognized the immense responsibility they held in providing accurate and unbiased interpretations to individuals seeking their guidance. They understood that their interpretations could have a profound impact on the lives of those seeking answers, and as such, they approached their role with a strong sense of ethical responsibility.

To ensure the accuracy and integrity of their interpretations, diviners diligently studied and accumulated a wealth of cultural knowledge. They immersed themselves in the symbolic language of dreams, the meanings of natural signs and omens, and the connections between celestial phenomena and human experiences. This deep understanding allowed them to interpret the signs and omens with precision and cultural context.

Diviners also recognized the sacredness of nature and the interconnectedness of all things. They approached their observations and interpretations with reverence and respect, understanding that they were interpreting the messages of the gods communicated through the natural world. This reverence ensured that diviners maintained a sense of humility and awe in the face of the divine, and it guided their interpretations to be in alignment with the broader cosmic order.

Furthermore, diviners strived to provide unbiased interpretations, free from personal biases or preconceived notions. They approached each interpretation with an open mind, recognizing the importance of impartiality in their role as intermediaries between the divine and the individual seeking guidance. Their goal was to offer objective insights that would enable individuals to make their own informed decisions and take responsibility for their actions.

The ethical responsibility of diviners extended beyond the moment of interpretation. They also considered the long-term impact of their guidance on individuals' lives. Diviners understood that their interpretations could influence the choices individuals made and the paths they followed. As such, they endeavored to provide guidance that would lead to the well-being and personal growth of the individuals seeking their counsel.

In summary, Babylonian diviners bore the ethical responsibility of providing accurate and unbiased interpretations. They approached their role with a strong sense of integrity and reverence, grounded in cultural knowledge and respect for the sacredness of nature. Their goal was to offer guidance that was objective, culturally informed, and aligned with the cosmic order, enabling individuals to make informed decisions and navigate their lives with wisdom and responsibility.

B. Interpretation Challenges:

Indeed, augury posed certain challenges for Babylonian diviners due to the inherent nature of interpreting signs and omens. The complexity of the symbols and the subjective nature of their interpretation meant that multiple meanings and potential outcomes could arise from the same sign or omen. Diviners had to navigate these complexities with expertise, cultural knowledge, and careful consideration.

One of the challenges diviners faced was the potential for subjective judgments in interpreting signs and omens. While there were established meanings associated with certain symbols and events, the application of these meanings to specific situations required judgment and discernment. Diviners had to rely on their knowledge, experience, and intuition to make accurate interpretations that aligned with the unique circumstances and questions posed by the individuals seeking guidance.

To address this challenge, diviners relied on their expertise and extensive cultural knowledge. They immersed themselves in the study of symbols, omens, and their associated meanings, allowing them to build a foundation of understanding. Through years of practice and observation, diviners honed their skills in interpreting signs and omens, developing a nuanced understanding of their cultural context and potential implications.

Additionally, diviners recognized the importance of consultation and collaboration with other experienced diviners. When confronted with particularly challenging or ambiguous signs, diviners would seek the input and perspectives of their colleagues. This collaborative approach allowed them to benefit from the collective wisdom and diverse interpretations of their peers, helping to refine their own understanding and arrive at more accurate and comprehensive interpretations.

Furthermore, diviners were mindful of the potential for personal biases and subjective interpretations to influence their readings. They understood the need for objectivity and impartiality in their role as interpreters. By grounding themselves in their cultural knowledge and remaining attuned to the sacredness of their task, diviners sought to minimize the impact of personal biases and deliver interpretations that were as unbiased and objective as possible.

In summary, Babylonian diviners were aware of the challenges inherent in interpreting signs and omens. They navigated these complexities through their expertise, cultural knowledge, and consultation with other experienced diviners. By honing their skills, engaging in collaborative discussions, and remaining mindful of personal biases, diviners sought to provide accurate and comprehensive interpretations that served the individuals seeking their guidance.

Examples, Problems, and Exercises:

Example: Analyze a specific animal behavior or bird flight pattern described in Babylonian texts, such as the Enuma Anu Enlil. Interpret the significance of the observed behavior and explain how diviners might have interpreted it in their augury practice.

Problem: Compare and contrast Babylonian augury with the practices of other ancient cultures, such as Roman or Greek. Explore the similarities and differences in the methods, symbols, and beliefs surrounding natural divination.

Exercise: Spend a day observing and documenting natural signs and omens in your environment. Record animal behavior, bird flight patterns, and weather phenomena. Research the cultural symbolism associated with these observations and interpret their potential meanings using the principles of Babylonian augury.

Conclusion:

Augury, the art of interpreting signs and omens found in nature, played a crucial role in Babylonian divination. By observing and interpreting the behavior of animals, the flight patterns of birds, and unusual weather phenomena, diviners accessed the messages communicated by the gods. Augury provided individuals with valuable insights and guidance for personal decision-making and foresight into future events. Despite the challenges and ethical considerations involved, Babylonian augury demonstrated the profound connection between humanity and the natural world, emphasizing the importance of understanding and interpreting the language of nature.

➢ Cleromancy:

Cleromancy, a divination practice widely employed in ancient Babylon, involved the casting of lots to gain insights into future events or make decisions guided by the divine. In this chapter, we explore the intricacies of cleromancy, examining the methods, significance, and interpretations employed by Babylonian diviners in their quest for knowledge and guidance.

✧   Understanding Cleromancy:

A. Definition and Purpose:

Cleromancy, derived from the Greek words "kleros" meaning "lot" and "manteia" meaning "divination," refers to the process of using lots to access divine insights. Babylonians believed that the casting of lots could reveal the divine will, provide answers to important questions, and guide decision-making.

The process of cleromancy typically involved the following steps: First, the diviner would prepare the lots, which could be small stones, bones, or other marked objects. Each lot would have a distinct symbol or number associated with it. These symbols or numbers held specific meanings and were believed to represent different outcomes or possibilities.

Next, the diviner would cast or draw the lots, often by shaking them in a container or throwing them onto a surface. The lots would then be examined, and their positions or arrangements would be interpreted to determine the divine message.

The interpretation of the lots involved considering various factors such as the symbols or numbers on the lots, their positions in relation to each other, and any patterns or groupings that emerged. Diviners relied on their knowledge of the symbolism and cultural significance attached to each lot to interpret the message conveyed by the arrangement.

Babylonians believed that the casting of lots allowed them to access the divine will and gain insights into important questions or decisions. They regarded cleromancy as a means of seeking divine guidance and ensuring their actions aligned with the intentions of the gods. The practice provided a way to navigate uncertainty and make decisions with a sense of divine approval.

Cleromancy was widely used in Babylonian society, not only for personal matters but also for making important decisions at the societal and political levels. Kings and rulers often sought the counsel of diviners and relied on cleromancy to determine matters of governance, warfare, and other significant events.

Overall, cleromancy was a respected and integral aspect of Babylonian divination. It provided individuals and communities with a means to connect with the divine, seek guidance, and make decisions in alignment with the perceived will of the gods.

B. Lots as Divinatory Tools:

In cleromancy, the lots used for divination were typically small objects that represented different outcomes or answers. These objects could include stones, tokens, marked sticks, or even dice. Each lot was marked or designated in a way that assigned it a specific meaning or significance.

The process of casting the lots was a crucial step in cleromancy. Diviners would often have a controlled method for casting the lots, ensuring that chance or the intervention of the divine played a role in selecting the specific lot. The exact method of casting could vary depending on the diviner's preference or the specific tradition being followed.

For example, diviners might shake a container holding the lots and then pour them out onto a surface, allowing the lots to scatter randomly. Alternatively, they might draw the lots one by one from a container without looking, relying on a sense of divine guidance to select each lot.

The resulting configuration or arrangement of the lots was then carefully examined and interpreted. Diviners paid close attention to the relative positions, groupings, or patterns formed by the lots. These visual cues were believed to hold significant meaning and were considered the divinely guided message.

Interpreting the arrangement of the lots required knowledge of the symbolism associated with each lot and the cultural context in which the divination was being conducted. Diviners would consider factors such as the individual meanings of the lots, their proximity to one another, their order of selection, and any symbolic relationships or connections that emerged.

By interpreting the arrangement of the lots, diviners sought to reveal the intended message from the divine. This message could provide answers to specific questions, offer guidance for decision-making, or shed light on the future outcome of a situation.

Cleromancy provided individuals with a sense of divine intervention and allowed them to seek answers beyond their own limited understanding. It was a method of divination that relied on the belief that the divine would guide the selection and arrangement of the lots, providing insights and guidance for important matters.

The practice of cleromancy was prevalent in various ancient cultures, including Babylonian society. It played a significant role in religious and societal decision-making, as well as in personal matters where individuals sought guidance and clarity.

✧   Techniques of Cleromancy:

A. Casting and Interpretation:

Babylonian diviners employed various methods of casting lots, tailoring their approach to the specific question or concern at hand. These different techniques allowed for a range of interpretations based on the position, proximity, and orientation of the lots.

One common method involved tossing the lots into the air and allowing them to fall randomly. The lots could be small objects, such as stones or tokens, each marked or designated with a specific meaning. As the lots scattered in the air and landed, the diviner would carefully observe their positions and patterns.

Another approach utilized containers or boards with designated spaces or compartments for the lots to land. The diviner would place the lots in the container or on the board, and through a controlled action, such as shaking or flipping the container, the lots would be distributed into the designated spaces. The resulting arrangement of the lots within these spaces would then be interpreted.

The diviner's interpretation of the lots' positions and arrangements was key to extracting meaning from the divine message. Factors such as the proximity of the lots to one another, the groupings or clusters that formed, and the orientation or alignment of the lots were all considered significant.

For example, if certain lots were clustered closely together, it might suggest a strong connection or relationship between the associated meanings. If the lots were scattered far apart, it could indicate disparate or conflicting influences. The diviner would carefully observe the patterns that emerged and consider the symbolism associated with each lot to derive insights.

The interpretation of the lots' positions and arrangements required deep knowledge of the cultural symbolism and the divinatory tradition being followed. Diviners relied on their expertise and intuition to discern the intended message from the divine.

By interpreting the cast lots, Babylonian diviners sought to reveal insights, guidance, or answers to the questions or concerns brought before them. The divine message hidden within the arrangement of the lots was believed to provide a glimpse into the will of the gods and offer direction for decision-making or future outcomes.

Casting lots in Babylonian divination was a revered and respected method of seeking divine guidance. It provided a tangible and visual representation of the divine message, allowing individuals to connect with the unseen and gain clarity on important matters of their lives.

The practice of casting lots was not limited to Babylonian culture but was prevalent in various ancient civilizations. It demonstrated the belief that the divine could influence the random distribution and arrangement of objects, and that through interpretation, profound insights could be obtained.

B. Markings and Symbols:

In cleromancy, the lots used by Babylonian diviners were often marked with symbols, letters, or numbers that held specific meanings. These markings allowed the diviner to associate each lot with a particular outcome, answer, or message.

The diviner possessed a comprehensive understanding of the symbolic language and cultural significance associated with the markings on the lots. This knowledge enabled them to interpret the messages conveyed by the arrangement and patterns formed by the lots.

For example, certain symbols on the lots might represent different aspects of life, such as love, wealth, health, or success. Letters or numbers could be linked to specific people, places, or concepts. The diviner would have a deep familiarity with the meanings assigned to each symbol, letter, or number.

During the casting of lots, the diviner would carefully observe the resulting patterns and arrangements. The positions, relationships, and interactions between the lots were essential for accurate interpretation.

The diviner would examine the proximity of the lots to one another, noting if they were clustered together or spread apart. The groupings and combinations of specific symbols, letters, or numbers within the arrangement of the lots were also significant. The diviner would consider the predetermined meanings associated with each symbol and the potential connections or contrasts between them.

For instance, if certain symbols or letters appeared in close proximity or formed a distinct pattern, it could indicate a strong relationship or connection between the associated meanings. On the other hand, if the lots were scattered randomly or if conflicting symbols appeared in close proximity, it could suggest conflicting influences or potential challenges.

The diviner's expertise in interpreting the patterns formed by the lots allowed them to extract meaning from the divine message. Their comprehensive knowledge of the symbols, letters, or numbers provided a framework for understanding the specific guidance or answers sought by the individual.

Accuracy in interpreting the lots' arrangement and their relation to the predetermined meanings was crucial for providing reliable guidance. Diviners had to exercise their discernment, intuition, and understanding of the symbolic language to ensure accurate and insightful interpretations.

The practice of cleromancy with marked lots provided individuals with a tangible and visually accessible method of seeking divine guidance. It allowed them to receive specific messages and insights based on the arrangement and patterns of the lots, providing clarity and direction in their decision-making processes or in understanding future outcomes.

The use of marked lots in cleromancy was a sacred practice in Babylonian culture, reflecting the belief that the divine could communicate through the random distribution and arrangement of objects. The diviner's ability to decipher the messages hidden within the lots played a vital role in connecting individuals with the divine and offering guidance and answers to their questions or concerns.

✧   Applying Cleromancy in Divination:

A. Decision-Making:

Cleromancy, with its use of lots to access divine insights, provided individuals with a valuable tool for seeking divine guidance when facing important decisions. The practice allowed individuals to gain insight into the potential outcomes associated with different choices or courses of action.

By casting lots, individuals engaged in a process that went beyond mere chance or personal bias. The belief in divine intervention meant that the arrangement and selection of the lots were influenced by higher forces. This added an element of sacredness and reverence to the practice, as individuals sought to align their decisions with the will of the gods.

When faced with a significant decision, individuals would consult a diviner who was skilled in the art of cleromancy. The diviner would guide the individual through the process, ensuring that the lots were cast in a controlled manner to allow the divine intervention to determine the selected lot.

The arrangement and patterns formed by the lots provided individuals with insights into the potential outcomes associated with their choices. It was believed that the divine message, conveyed through the positioning and interaction of the lots, revealed the will of the gods and the likely consequences of each decision.

The diviner's role was crucial in interpreting the divine message encoded within the arrangement of the lots. Drawing upon their extensive knowledge of the symbolic language and cultural significance associated with the markings on the lots, the diviner would provide an analysis of the patterns and their corresponding meanings.

The insights gained through cleromancy empowered individuals to make informed decisions. By understanding the potential outcomes of different choices, individuals could align their actions with the will of the gods and increase the likelihood of favorable results. This gave them a sense of confidence and assurance as they navigated important aspects of their lives.

Cleromancy also provided a sense of responsibility and accountability. Individuals understood that they were seeking divine guidance and that their decisions should be aligned with the messages conveyed through the lots. It was believed that by honoring the divine will, individuals would increase their chances of success and avoid potential pitfalls.

The practice of cleromancy reflected a deep-rooted belief in the interconnectedness between the divine realm and human actions. By engaging in the process, individuals acknowledged their reliance on the gods' guidance and wisdom in making significant decisions.

Furthermore, cleromancy offered individuals a sense of reassurance and a way to mitigate uncertainty. Facing important choices can often be daunting, with the fear of making the wrong decision. Cleromancy provided individuals with a tangible method of seeking divine intervention and accessing insights that went beyond their own limited understanding.

In conclusion, cleromancy served as a means for individuals to seek divine guidance and align their decisions with the will of the gods. By casting lots and interpreting their arrangement, individuals gained insight into potential outcomes and could make informed choices. This practice offered a sense of connection to the divine realm, reassurance in decision-making, and increased the likelihood of favorable outcomes in important endeavors.

B. Predicting Future Events:

In addition to providing guidance for decision-making, Babylonian diviners also employed cleromancy as a means of predicting future events. By interpreting the configuration of the lots, diviners could glean insights into the potential unfolding of events, enabling individuals to prepare for and navigate upcoming circumstances.

The practice of using lots for divination allowed diviners to tap into the wisdom of the gods and access knowledge beyond the realm of ordinary human understanding. The divine intervention believed to be present in cleromancy provided a unique insight into the workings of fate and the potential outcomes of future events.

When individuals sought the services of a diviner to gain insight into future events, the diviner would guide them through the process of casting lots. The lots, marked with symbols, letters, or numbers, would be arranged or cast in a controlled manner, allowing the divine forces to influence the selection and arrangement of the lots.

The diviner's expertise lay in their ability to interpret the patterns, positions, and interactions of the lots. They possessed a deep understanding of the symbolic language associated with the markings on the lots and the cultural significance attached to them. Through this knowledge, they could decipher the divine messages encoded within the arrangement of the lots.

By analyzing the arrangement and patterns formed by the lots, diviners could gain insights into the potential unfolding of future events. Certain arrangements might suggest favorable outcomes, while others might indicate challenges or obstacles. Diviners considered the position, proximity, and orientation of the lots to extract meaning and provide predictions.

These insights into future events allowed individuals to adopt a proactive approach to their lives. By understanding what lay ahead, individuals could better prepare themselves, make informed decisions, and adapt their plans accordingly. Cleromancy offered a way to anticipate and navigate the ever-changing tides of destiny.

The proactive nature of cleromancy in predicting future events provided individuals with a sense of empowerment and a means to take control of their lives. It allowed them to approach future challenges with a greater understanding of what to expect and to make necessary adjustments to their actions or plans.

Moreover, the insights gained through cleromancy allowed individuals to minimize potential risks and seize opportunities. By being aware of upcoming circumstances, individuals could strategize, mitigate potential challenges, and capitalize on favorable conditions.

However, it's important to note that while cleromancy provided glimpses into the potential future, it was not considered an absolute certainty. The interpretation of the lots was subject to the divine will and the inherent uncertainties of life. Babylonians understood that human actions, choices, and external factors could influence the course of events, and the diviner's role was to provide guidance based on the available information.

In conclusion, Babylonian diviners utilized cleromancy not only for decision-making but also for predicting future events. By interpreting the configuration of the lots, diviners gained insights into the potential unfolding of events, allowing individuals to prepare for and navigate upcoming circumstances. Cleromancy offered a proactive approach to anticipate and adapt to the ever-changing tides of destiny, empowering individuals to make informed decisions and seize opportunities while minimizing risks.

✧　　Ethical Considerations and Limitations:

A. Interpretive Responsibility:

Babylonian diviners recognized the immense responsibility that came with interpreting the lots in cleromancy. They understood that their interpretations held the potential to shape individuals' beliefs, decisions, and actions, and could have profound effects on their lives. Therefore, they upheld the highest ethical standards and approached their divinatory practices with honesty, integrity, and a deep understanding of their cultural context.

Integrity was of utmost importance to Babylonian diviners. They strived to provide accurate and unbiased interpretations, free from personal biases or preconceived notions. Diviners recognized that their role was to serve as intermediaries between the divine realm and individuals seeking guidance. As such, they took their responsibilities seriously and made every effort to deliver their interpretations with utmost honesty and authenticity.

To ensure accurate interpretations, diviners relied on their extensive knowledge of symbols, cultural beliefs, and the traditions associated with cleromancy. They dedicated years of study and practice to become well-versed in the symbolic language of the lots and the cultural significance attached to them. This expertise allowed them to interpret the lots with precision and provide individuals with meaningful insights.

Diviners understood that their interpretations should not be swayed by personal agendas or outside influences. They approached their divinatory practices with a sense of detachment and impartiality, focusing solely on the messages conveyed by the lots. This commitment to objectivity ensured that their interpretations were grounded in the divine will and the inherent symbolism of the lots.

Cultural knowledge was also vital for Babylonian diviners. They possessed a deep understanding of the cultural beliefs, traditions, and societal context in which their divinatory practices were embedded. This knowledge allowed them to provide interpretations that were culturally relevant and resonant with the individuals seeking guidance. Diviners took into account the specific cultural circumstances of the individuals and the broader cultural framework within which the lots were interpreted.

Babylonian diviners also recognized the sacredness of their craft. They approached their divinatory practices with reverence, acknowledging the profound connection between the divine realm and the earthly realm. Diviners understood that their interpretations were not solely based on their own abilities, but were a result of the divine intervention and guidance. They respected and honored the spiritual nature of their work, creating a sacred space for divination and maintaining a sense of humility in their role as conduits of divine messages.

By upholding these principles of honesty, integrity, cultural knowledge, and reverence, Babylonian diviners ensured that their interpretations carried weight and meaning. Individuals seeking guidance could place their trust in the diviners' expertise, knowing that the interpretations provided were grounded in ethical practices and a deep understanding of the divinatory arts.

In conclusion, Babylonian diviners bore the ethical responsibility of interpreting the lots accurately and impartially. They approached their divinatory practices with honesty, integrity, and a deep understanding of their cultural context. By upholding these principles, diviners maintained the sacredness of their craft, provided meaningful guidance to individuals, and fostered a sense of trust in their divinatory abilities.

B. Limitations and Subjectivity:

While cleromancy was a revered divinatory method in Babylonian culture, it was not without its limitations and challenges. Babylonian diviners recognized the potential for ambiguity and subjective interpretations that could arise from the arrangement of the lots. They understood that the divine messages conveyed through the lots could sometimes be open to multiple meanings or require careful analysis to unveil their true significance.

Diviners acknowledged that their expertise played a crucial role in mitigating these challenges. Through years of study, practice, and firsthand experience, diviners developed a deep understanding of the symbolic language of the lots and the cultural context in which they operated. Their expertise allowed them to navigate the complexities of the lots' arrangement and interpret their messages with greater accuracy.

Additionally, diviners recognized the value of collaboration and consultation with other experienced diviners. They understood that different diviners might bring unique perspectives, insights, and interpretations to the table. By engaging in discussions and seeking advice from their peers, diviners could broaden their understanding of the lots' symbolism and enhance their interpretations. This collaborative approach helped them refine their interpretations and reduce the potential for subjective biases.

Meticulous analysis of the context and specific question posed by the individual seeking guidance was another strategy employed by Babylonian diviners to address the challenges of subjective interpretations. They understood that the meaning of the lots could vary depending on the circumstances surrounding the question or concern. Diviners carefully considered the personal, social, and cultural context in which the question arose, as well as the specific details provided by the individual. By incorporating these factors into their analysis, diviners aimed to arrive at interpretations that were tailored to the unique situation at hand.

Babylonian diviners also recognized that divination, including cleromancy, involved a level of uncertainty. They understood that the lots were a means of divine communication, but their interpretation still required human judgment. Diviners approached their divinatory practices with humility, acknowledging that their interpretations were subject to the limitations of human understanding. They strived to maintain an open mind and avoid overconfidence, recognizing that the true meaning of the lots might not always be immediately apparent.

In conclusion, Babylonian diviners were aware of the inherent limitations and subjective interpretations that could arise in cleromancy. They employed various strategies to address these challenges, including their expertise, consultation with other experienced diviners, and careful analysis of the context and specific question. By embracing these approaches, diviners aimed to provide interpretations that were as accurate and meaningful as possible, while acknowledging the inherent uncertainties and complexities of divinatory practices.

Examples, Problems, and Exercises:

Example: Describe the process of casting lots in a specific Babylonian divination text, such as the Enuma Anu Enlil. Analyze the interpretation of the resulting arrangement of lots and explain the messages conveyed by the divination.

Problem: Compare and contrast Babylonian cleromancy with similar divinatory practices in other ancient cultures, such as the casting of runes in Norse mythology or the use of the I Ching in Chinese divination. Highlight the similarities and differences in techniques, symbolism, and cultural significance.

Exercise: Create your own set of divinatory lots using small objects, such as stones or tokens. Develop a symbol system and assign meanings to each lot. Practice casting the lots and interpreting the resulting configurations. Reflect on the experience and consider the potential insights gained through cleromancy.

Conclusion:

Cleromancy, the divination practice of casting lots, offered Babylonians a powerful tool to communicate with the divine and gain insights into the future. Through careful casting and interpretation of the lots, diviners navigated decisions, predicted events, and sought guidance from the gods. While cleromancy carried limitations and required ethical considerations, its significance in Babylonian divination cannot be understated. By embracing cleromancy, individuals connected with the unseen forces that shaped their lives, striving to align their actions with the divine will.

➢ Extispicy:

Extispicy, an ancient Babylonian divination practice, involved the interpretation of animal entrails to gain insights into future events, divine intentions, and the will of the gods. In this chapter, we delve into the intricacies of extispicy, examining its historical context, methods, symbolic interpretations, and cultural significance within the realm of Babylonian divination.

✦ Understanding Extispicy:

A. Definition and Significance:

Extispicy was a significant divinatory practice in Babylonian culture, involving the examination and interpretation of the entrails of sacrificial animals. The word "exta" refers to the internal organs, particularly the liver, lungs, and gall bladder, which were carefully observed for signs and messages from the gods. The diviners, known as haruspicators, believed that the gods communicated their intentions and provided guidance through the patterns, shapes, and conditions of these entrails.

The practice of extispicy was considered sacred and held great importance in Babylonian religious and political life. It was believed that by studying the entrails, diviners could gain insight into the divine realm and discern the will of the gods. The sacrificial animal, typically a sheep, goat, or pig, was carefully selected and prepared for the ritual. The animal was cleansed, then offered in a prescribed manner to the gods, with prayers and invocations accompanying the act.

Once the sacrificial animal was slain, the diviner would meticulously examine the entrails, paying close attention to their appearance, texture, color, and any anomalies or abnormalities. Different regions of the entrails held specific significance. The liver, for example, was considered the primary organ for divination and was divided into various sections, each associated with different aspects of life and divinatory meanings.

The haruspicator would interpret the patterns, shapes, and conditions observed in the entrails, seeking to discern the messages and guidance from the gods. Certain features, such as the presence or absence of certain lobes, the appearance of blood vessels, or the formation of nodules, were considered important indicators. The diviner would analyze the entrails holistically and compare the observed features with a body of knowledge passed down through generations.

Extispicy served as a means for individuals and rulers to make informed decisions based on the will of the gods. The interpretations derived from extispicy influenced various aspects of Babylonian life, including matters of state, warfare, agriculture, personal affairs, and even divination itself. The insights gained through extispicy guided individuals and rulers in their decision-making processes, allowing them to align their actions with the desires and intentions of the gods.

It's important to note that extispicy was a complex and nuanced practice that required extensive knowledge, experience, and expertise. Haruspicators underwent rigorous training and were highly respected individuals within Babylonian society. They possessed deep understanding of the symbolic language of the entrails, as well as the cultural and religious context in which the practice was conducted.

In conclusion, extispicy was a divinatory practice in Babylonian culture that involved the meticulous examination and interpretation of the entrails of sacrificial animals. It served as a means to gain insight into the divine realm and make informed decisions based on the will of the gods. The patterns, shapes, and conditions of the entrails were carefully analyzed by diviners to discern the messages and guidance from the gods. Extispicy held great significance in Babylonian religious and political life, influencing various aspects of decision-making and providing a means to connect with the divine.

B. Cultural Context:

Extispicy held a prominent and influential position in Babylonian society, permeating various aspects of religious, political, and personal life. It served as a crucial link between the mortal realm and the divine, providing individuals with a means to connect with the gods, seek guidance, and understand their desires.

Kings, as the political and religious leaders of Babylonian society, often relied on the insights gained from extispicy to make important decisions. The interpretation of entrails was believed to reveal the will of the gods regarding matters of state, warfare, governance, and the overall welfare of the kingdom. Kings would consult skilled extispicy diviners to gain clarity on complex political situations, strategize military campaigns, or seek advice on matters affecting the kingdom's prosperity and stability.

Priests, as the custodians of religious rituals and practices, also held a close association with extispicy. They would perform the sacred rituals and oversee the sacrificial offerings, ensuring the correct procedures were followed to communicate with the gods. Priests possessed deep knowledge of the religious traditions, symbolism, and prayers associated with extispicy. Their expertise allowed them to conduct the rituals with reverence and interpret the entrails accurately, providing guidance to both the ruling class and ordinary individuals.

Ordinary individuals, too, sought the counsel of skilled extispicy diviners to navigate the complexities of their personal lives. They would approach diviners with questions and concerns related to their health, family, relationships, career, or any other aspect of their existence. By examining the entrails, diviners could offer insights, advice, and potential remedies to individuals seeking divine guidance. People believed that by aligning their actions with the will of the gods, they could lead more fulfilling and prosperous lives.

Extispicy, as a divinatory practice, offered a sense of reassurance and comfort in times of uncertainty. It provided a means to understand the divine desires and navigate the intricacies of human existence in harmony with the gods. It was believed that through extispicy, individuals could seek answers to their pressing questions, find guidance during challenging situations, and gain a deeper understanding of their role within the cosmic order.

The practice of extispicy was deeply ingrained in Babylonian culture, and skilled diviners were highly regarded within society. They were seen as intermediaries between the mortal realm and the divine realm, possessing the ability to interpret the messages and desires of the gods. Diviners were entrusted with the ethical responsibility of providing accurate and unbiased interpretations, and their role carried significant influence in shaping individual decisions, societal affairs, and the overall religious fabric of Babylonian civilization.

In summary, extispicy held a significant position in Babylonian society, intertwining religious, political, and personal spheres. Kings, priests, and ordinary individuals sought the guidance of skilled diviners to understand the divine desires, seek guidance in times of uncertainty, and navigate the complexities of human existence in harmony with the gods. Extispicy provided a connection to the divine realm, offering insights, advice, and a sense of purpose within the cosmic order.

✧   Techniques of Extispicy:

A. Animal Selection and Sacrifice:

In the practice of extispicy, specific animals were carefully selected as sacrificial offerings to establish a sacred connection with the divine realm. Sheep, goats, and cattle were among the animals commonly chosen for this purpose. These animals held symbolic significance and were considered suitable conduits for communicating with the gods.

Before the sacrificial act, great care was taken to ensure the purity of the animals. They were selected based on specific criteria, such as their physical condition, health, and absence of any defects or blemishes. The animals were considered representatives of the community or individuals seeking divination, embodying their hopes, concerns, and desires.

The sacrificial process itself was conducted with meticulous attention to detail, reflecting the deep reverence and importance placed on accurate divination. Ritualistic practices were followed to prepare the animals, including purification ceremonies, prayers, and invocations. The diviners and priests involved in the process adhered to strict protocols, ensuring the correct procedures were followed to maintain the sanctity of the ritual.

Once the animals were prepared, the sacrificial act took place in a designated sacred space, such as a temple or an outdoor altar. Skilled priests and diviners conducted the rituals, invoking the presence of the gods and seeking their guidance. The animals were offered to the gods through a specific sacrificial method, often involving the slitting of their throats or the extraction of the entrails.

After the sacrificial act, the focus shifted to the examination and interpretation of the entrails, which formed the core of the extispicy practice. The diviners carefully observed the patterns, shapes, colors, textures, and overall condition of the entrails, seeking divine messages within these intricate details. Each aspect of the entrails was believed to hold symbolic significance and carry messages from the gods.

The diviners, possessing extensive knowledge of symbolism and cultural beliefs, interpreted the entrails based on established associations and their own expertise. They considered factors such as the position, shape, color, and other unique characteristics of the entrails to decipher the intended messages. The diviners understood that the gods communicated their desires, warnings, or guidance through the patterns observed in the entrails.

The process of sacrificial offerings and the meticulous examination of the entrails in extispicy emphasized the belief in the sacredness of the act and the connection between the physical and divine realms. It reflected the profound reverence and respect that Babylonians held for the gods and their desires. The accurate performance of the rituals and the skilled interpretation of the entrails were regarded as crucial for obtaining reliable insights and guidance from the gods.

In summary, specific animals such as sheep, goats, and cattle were chosen for the practice of extispicy. The sacrificial process involved meticulous attention to the animals' purity and the precise methods and rituals used in the act. The examination and interpretation of the entrails formed the core of the divinatory practice, reflecting the deep reverence for the divine and the importance of accurate divination. The sacrificial act and the subsequent examination of the entrails were seen as a means to establish a sacred connection with the gods and gain insights into their desires and guidance.

B. Examination and Interpretation:

In the practice of extispicy, diviners meticulously examined the entrails of the sacrificed animals, paying close attention to various factors that held symbolic significance. These factors included the color, texture, size, placement, and any anomalies or irregularities observed within the entrails. Each aspect of the entrails was believed to carry a message from the divine realm, and skilled diviners possessed a deep understanding of the symbolism associated with these characteristics.

The color of the entrails played a crucial role in interpretation. Certain colors were considered auspicious or inauspicious, indicating different outcomes or divine messages. For example, a vibrant and healthy color might signify prosperity, while a discolored or abnormal color could indicate potential difficulties or warnings.

The texture of the entrails was another important aspect considered by diviners. Smooth and intact textures were often associated with positive outcomes, while rough or damaged textures might suggest challenges or unfavorable circumstances. Diviners carefully observed the textures to discern the intended messages from the gods.

The size of the entrails also carried symbolic meaning. Differences in size, such as enlargement or reduction, were interpreted as indicators of significance. Larger entrails might signify abundance, power, or important events, while smaller entrails might imply scarcity, weakness, or lesser significance.

The placement of the entrails within the sacrificial animal's body was carefully examined as well. The location of specific organs or portions of the entrails held particular significance and was believed to convey different messages. Diviners analyzed the positions of the entrails in relation to each other and to the body as a whole to extract meaning.

Anomalies or irregularities observed in the entrails were regarded as significant indicators. Diviners paid attention to any abnormalities, such as cysts, growths, or unusual formations, which were believed to carry specific messages from the gods. These anomalies were carefully considered in the overall interpretation of the entrails.

Experienced diviners possessed a deep understanding of the symbolism associated with these various factors. They had extensive knowledge of established patterns and cultural beliefs that guided the interpretation process. Through years of training and observation, diviners acquired the ability to discern the divine messages embedded within the entrails.

The interpretations of the entrails were not based on individual diviners' subjective opinions but were grounded in a shared cultural understanding. Diviners followed established guidelines, traditions, and symbols passed down through generations. They relied on this accumulated knowledge to ensure accurate and consistent interpretations.

By carefully analyzing the color, texture, size, placement, and anomalies within the entrails, diviners could extract messages from the divine realm. The combination of these factors, along with the diviners' expertise and cultural knowledge, allowed them to provide insights, guidance, and predictions based on the divine messages revealed through the entrails.

In summary, diviners engaged in a meticulous examination of the entrails of the sacrificial animals, considering various factors such as color, texture, size, placement, and anomalies. Each aspect of the entrails held symbolic significance, and diviners possessed a deep understanding of these symbols based on established patterns and cultural knowledge. The interpretations of the entrails were not subjective but grounded in shared cultural understanding and were aimed at extracting messages from the divine realm.

✧　　Symbolic Interpretations and Divinatory Messages:

A. Organs and Entrails:

In the practice of extispicy, different organs and parts of the entrails held specific meanings and carried symbolic value. Among these, the liver held great importance as the primary organ for divination in Babylonian extispicy.

The liver was considered a vital organ associated with life force and vitality. It was believed to be the seat of the soul and a conduit for divine messages. The examination of the liver provided valuable insights into the divine will and guidance.

Within the liver, specific features and characteristics were carefully observed and analyzed by diviners. These features included the presence of the gallbladder, the lobes of the liver, and the appearance of veins.

The presence or absence of the gallbladder within the liver played a significant role in interpretation. The gallbladder was associated with bile, and its presence or absence was believed to indicate different divine messages. The gallbladder could be seen as a sign of blessing or favor from the gods, while its absence might signify potential challenges or warnings.

The lobes of the liver were also examined for their shape, size, and overall condition. Diviners paid attention to any irregularities or asymmetries in the lobes, as they were believed to carry specific meanings. For example, a well-formed and healthy lobe might indicate prosperity or success, while an abnormal or damaged lobe might suggest difficulties or obstacles.

The appearance of veins within the liver was another important factor considered in divination. Diviners observed the patterns and characteristics of the veins, such as their color, size, and arrangement. The veins were believed to contain the life force and energy flowing within the liver, and their appearance provided further insights into the divine messages. The presence of vibrant and well-defined veins might be seen as a positive omen, while weak or disrupted veins could suggest potential challenges.

Diviners possessed a comprehensive understanding of the symbolic meanings associated with these specific features within the liver. Through their training and experience, they developed the ability to interpret the divine messages conveyed through these characteristics.

It is important to note that the liver was not the only organ examined in extispicy. Other organs, such as the lungs, heart, and kidneys, also carried their own symbolic value and contributed to the overall interpretation. Diviners considered the condition, shape, and features of these organs to extract additional insights from the divine realm.

By carefully examining the liver and other organs within the entrails, diviners sought to interpret the divine messages and gain guidance from the gods. The presence or absence of the gallbladder, the condition of the lobes, and the appearance of veins within the liver were among the factors that influenced the divinatory message. Diviners' expertise and cultural knowledge allowed them to decode the symbolic meanings and provide individuals with valuable insights into their lives and decision-making.

In summary, within the practice of extispicy, the liver held great importance as the primary organ for divination. Specific features such as the presence of the gallbladder, the lobes of the liver, and the appearance of veins were carefully examined and held symbolic value. Diviners' interpretation of these features influenced the overall divinatory message and provided individuals with guidance from the gods.

B. Patterns and Shapes:

In the practice of extispicy, the configuration, arrangement, and patterns formed by the entrails of the sacrificial animals played a vital role in the interpretation of the divine messages. Diviners closely observed and analyzed the shapes, lines, marks, and connections between different parts of the entrails to extract meaning and insights.

The patterns formed by the entrails were believed to be a direct reflection of the divine will and the cosmic order. Diviners understood that the gods communicated their intentions and guidance through these intricate arrangements.

Diviners paid attention to the overall configuration of the entrails, examining how they were positioned and laid out. They observed the way different organs were placed in relation to one another and the overall harmony or dissonance within the arrangement. The spatial relationships between the organs and their alignment held symbolic significance, providing clues about the divine message.

Furthermore, diviners analyzed the shapes and forms within the entrails. They observed the curves, angles, and contours of the organs, as well as any distinctive markings or patterns. These shapes and marks were believed to convey specific meanings and insights into future events or personal circumstances.

Lines and connections between different parts of the entrails were also meticulously examined. Diviners looked for the presence of lines, whether straight, curved, or intersecting, and interpreted their significance. These lines were seen as pathways of communication between the divine realm and the earthly realm, providing a glimpse into the interconnectedness of the cosmic order.

Marks or unusual features found within the entrails were regarded as significant indicators. Diviners paid attention to any irregularities, spots, discolorations, or unusual textures, as they were believed to carry specific messages and omens. These marks were interpreted in relation to their position within the entrails and their association with other organs.

The interpretation of the configuration, arrangement, and patterns formed by the entrails required extensive knowledge, experience, and cultural understanding. Diviners had a deep understanding of the symbolic meanings associated with different shapes, lines, marks, and connections. Through their expertise, they could decipher the messages conveyed by the entrails and provide individuals with insights into their future, personal circumstances, and the broader cosmic order.

It is important to note that the interpretation of the entrails was not done in isolation. Diviners considered various factors, such as the specific question or concern posed by the individual, the context of the ritual, and the prevailing cultural beliefs and practices. All these elements were taken into account to ensure a comprehensive and accurate interpretation of the divine messages.

In summary, the configuration, arrangement, and patterns formed by the entrails played a crucial role in the practice of extispicy. Diviners carefully observed and interpreted the shapes, lines, marks, and connections within the entrails to extract meaning and divine insights. These patterns were seen as a direct reflection of the divine will and provided guidance regarding future events, personal circumstances, and the overall cosmic order. Diviners' expertise and cultural knowledge allowed them to derive meaningful interpretations from the entrails, offering individuals a deeper understanding of their lives and the divine forces at play.

✧   Application and Ethical Considerations:

A. Decision-Making and Guidance:

Extispicy held a significant role in the decision-making processes of the Babylonian society, permeating various aspects of life. The Babylonians firmly believed that by consulting the entrails, individuals could gain insights into the divine will and align their actions and decisions accordingly. This practice enabled them to maximize the potential for success, prosperity, and spiritual growth.

In matters of governance, extispicy played a crucial role in guiding kings and rulers. Kings sought the counsel of skilled diviners to interpret the entrails before making important decisions related to the governance of their kingdom. By seeking divine guidance through extispicy, rulers aimed to ensure that their actions were in harmony with the gods' desires and that their policies would lead to favorable outcomes for their realm.

On a personal level, individuals turned to extispicy for guidance in making important choices. Whether it was a decision related to personal aspirations, career paths, or major life events, consulting the entrails provided individuals with divine insights. By aligning their choices with the divine will, they believed they could increase their chances of success and fulfillment.

Extispicy also played a role in matters of relationships and partnerships. Whether it was seeking a suitable spouse, making decisions regarding marriage or family matters, or managing interpersonal conflicts, individuals consulted the entrails to gain guidance and understanding. By understanding the divine messages, individuals aimed to foster harmonious relationships and navigate challenges with wisdom and insight.

Furthermore, extispicy held importance in matters of health and well-being. Individuals sought divine guidance to understand the underlying causes of illness, to seek remedies, and to make decisions regarding their health. The entrails were believed to hold insights into the individual's physical and spiritual condition, guiding them towards appropriate actions and treatments.

By employing extispicy as a tool for decision-making, individuals aimed to align themselves with the divine will and ensure their actions were in harmony with the cosmic order. It provided a sense of reassurance and confidence in the choices they made, as they believed they were guided by the gods themselves.

The practice of extispicy also fostered a deeper spiritual connection and growth. By regularly engaging in this divinatory practice, individuals cultivated a heightened awareness of the divine presence in their lives. It reinforced their belief in the interconnectedness of the spiritual and earthly realms, and their role in co-creating their destiny with the gods.

In summary, extispicy served as a powerful tool for decision-making in various aspects of life for the Babylonians. Whether in matters of governance, personal choices, relationships, or health, individuals sought guidance through the interpretation of the entrails. By aligning their actions with the divine will, they aimed to maximize their chances of success, prosperity, and spiritual growth. Extispicy provided a profound sense of connection to the gods and a framework for navigating the complexities of life with divine guidance.

B. Ethical Responsibility:

Diviners who practiced extispicy in ancient Babylon held a deep sense of ethical responsibility in their divinatory work. They were aware of the profound impact their interpretations could have on individuals' lives and the overall well-being of the community. As such, they approached their craft with a strong commitment to honesty, integrity, cultural knowledge, and shared ethical standards within the divinatory community.

Accuracy and impartiality were paramount for diviners practicing extispicy. They understood that their interpretations carried weight and could influence important decisions made by individuals, rulers, and communities. Diviners endeavored to provide accurate readings, ensuring that their observations and interpretations of the entrails were grounded in their expertise and deep understanding of the symbolic language inherent in extispicy.

Integrity played a crucial role in the practice of extispicy. Diviners recognized the significance of their role as intermediaries between the divine realm and the human realm. They approached their work with reverence, recognizing that they were conduits for the gods' messages. Diviners held themselves to a high standard of ethical conduct, striving to provide genuine insights and avoiding any form of deception or manipulation in their interpretations.

Cultural knowledge was a fundamental aspect of practicing extispicy ethically. Diviners immersed themselves in the rich cultural traditions, symbolism, and beliefs of the Babylonian society. They understood the intricate meanings associated with different organs, shapes, patterns, and anomalies found in the entrails. Their comprehensive knowledge of the cultural context allowed them to interpret the entrails in a way that resonated with the individuals seeking guidance and aligned with the larger cultural and religious framework.

Diviners who practiced extispicy recognized the importance of shared ethical standards within the divinatory community. They engaged in ongoing learning, discussions, and collaborations with other experienced diviners. By sharing their insights, observations, and interpretations, they ensured a collective approach to ethical divinatory practices. This collaborative environment allowed for checks and balances, reducing the potential for individual biases or subjective interpretations.

The ethical responsibilities of diviners extended beyond the immediate act of divination. They also considered the well-being and welfare of the individuals seeking their guidance. Diviners were mindful of the potential impact their interpretations could have on the emotional, psychological, and spiritual states of those who sought their counsel. They approached their interactions with empathy, compassion, and a genuine desire to help individuals navigate their challenges and make informed decisions.

In summary, diviners practicing extispicy in ancient Babylon embraced a strong sense of ethical responsibility in their divinatory work. They upheld principles of accuracy, impartiality, integrity, cultural knowledge, and shared ethical standards within the divinatory community. By adhering to these principles, diviners aimed to provide individuals with meaningful, reliable, and ethically grounded interpretations that honored the divine messages conveyed through the entrails.

Examples, Problems, and Exercises:

Example: Study a specific extispicy text, such as the "Bārûtu" or "Bārûtu ša Enūma Anu Enlil," and analyze the symbolic interpretations presented within it. Explore how different organs and patterns were interpreted to derive messages and guidance.

Problem: Compare and contrast extispicy with other divination practices, such as astrology or cleromancy, highlighting the unique features, techniques, and cultural contexts of each practice. Discuss the role of divination in Babylonian society and its influence on decision-making.

Exercise: Simulate an extispicy ritual by creating artificial entrails using modeling clay or other materials. Develop a set of symbols and patterns that represent divinatory messages. Practice the interpretation of the simulated entrails and discuss the insights gained from the exercise.

Conclusion:

Extispicy, the art of divination through animal entrails, offered Babylonians a profound connection with the divine realm and a means to seek guidance, make decisions, and align their lives with the will of the gods. Through meticulous examination, symbolic interpretation, and cultural knowledge, diviners unraveled messages from the entrails, empowering individuals with insights into their future and the cosmic order. While extispicy carried ethical considerations and required expertise, its significance in Babylonian divination cannot be understated, demonstrating the deep intertwining of spirituality, divination, and everyday life in ancient Babylon..

Interpretation of Signs and Omens

Throughout history, human beings have sought to unravel the mysteries of the universe and gain insights into the future by interpreting signs and omens. This chapter explores the ancient practice of interpreting signs and omens, drawing examples from various fields such as witchcraft, divination, herbalism, shamanism, ecospirituality, and magic in ancient Babylon. We will delve into the methodologies, symbolism, cultural contexts, and ethical considerations associated with the interpretation of signs and omens.

➢   Understanding Signs and Omens:

A. Definition and Significance:

Signs and omens hold a significant place in divinatory practices and belief systems across different cultures and civilizations. They are perceived as messages from the divine realm, offering guidance, warnings, or insights into both the natural and supernatural worlds. These signs and omens can manifest in a multitude of ways, encompassing various aspects of existence.

Natural phenomena often serve as powerful signs and omens. Unusual weather events, such as storms, lightning, or celestial alignments, are believed to carry symbolic meaning. For example, a sudden change in weather patterns might be interpreted as a sign of impending change or turmoil. Similarly, celestial events like comets, eclipses, or meteor showers are seen as significant omens, potentially foretelling important events or shifts in cosmic energy.

Animal behavior is another avenue through which signs and omens are believed to be conveyed. Animals have long been regarded as messengers from the divine, and their actions are seen as symbolic. Diviners pay close attention to the behavior, movements, or interactions of animals, as they may hold hidden messages. For instance, the sudden appearance of a certain animal or the way it crosses one's path may be interpreted as a sign relating to one's current circumstances or future events.

Dreams have been considered a direct channel of communication between the divine and individuals. They are seen as a realm where messages, guidance, and insights are conveyed. Dreams are rich in symbolism and metaphors, and diviners have developed the skill of deciphering their hidden meanings. By exploring the vivid imagery, events, emotions, and sensory experiences within dreams, diviners can unravel the messages and provide individuals with valuable guidance and foresight.

Unexpected occurrences or synchronicities in daily life are also viewed as signs and omens. These can take the form of meaningful coincidences, repetitive patterns, or serendipitous events that seemingly carry a deeper message. For example, stumbling upon a particular book or encountering a specific person at a crucial moment may be seen as a sign guiding one's path or offering answers to pressing questions.

Interpreting signs and omens requires a deep understanding of their symbolic meaning and cultural context. Diviners possess extensive knowledge of the symbols, metaphors, and archetypes associated with various signs and omens. They draw upon this cultural knowledge and their own expertise to decode the messages embedded within these signs. It is essential to consider the specific cultural beliefs, traditions, and practices within which these signs and omens are interpreted to derive accurate and meaningful insights.

In summary, signs and omens are believed to be messages from the divine realm, offering guidance, warnings, and insights into the natural and supernatural world. They can manifest through natural phenomena, animal behavior, dreams, celestial events, or unexpected occurrences. Interpreting these signs and omens requires a deep understanding of their symbolic meaning and cultural context, enabling diviners to decipher the messages and provide individuals with valuable guidance for navigating their lives.

B. Cultural Context:

The interpretation of signs and omens is a practice that spans across cultures and throughout history. It is a testament to the universal human desire to understand the mysterious forces that shape our lives and to seek guidance from the unseen realms.

In ancient civilizations, such as the Babylonians, Egyptians, Greeks, and Romans, the interpretation of signs and omens held immense cultural and religious significance. These societies believed that the gods or higher powers communicated with mortals through signs and omens, offering insights into the future, providing guidance, or warning of potential dangers. Divination practices, including the interpretation of signs and omens, were an integral part of their religious rituals and societal structures.

Similarly, indigenous cultures around the world have developed their own rich traditions of interpreting signs and omens. These cultures have a deep connection with the natural world and view it as an interconnected web of life. They believe that signs and omens are messages from nature and the spiritual realm, guiding individuals in their daily lives, decision-making, and interactions with the environment. Whether it be the behavior of animals, the movement of clouds, or the rustling of leaves, these signs are seen as direct communications from the divine or ancestral spirits.

In contemporary belief systems, the interpretation of signs and omens continues to play a significant role. Many individuals, regardless of their specific religious or spiritual affiliations, still seek guidance and meaning through signs and omens. This can be seen in practices such as astrology, tarot reading, or other forms of divination, where symbols and signs are used as tools to access deeper insights and make informed decisions.

Interpreting signs and omens serves several purposes in human life. It helps individuals navigate uncertain situations, anticipate challenges, and make decisions aligned with their values and goals. It offers a sense of reassurance and connection to something greater than oneself, fostering a deeper spiritual and cosmic understanding. Additionally, the interpretation of signs and omens cultivates a sense of wonder and awe, reminding us of the vastness and intricacy of the universe.

The interpretation of signs and omens is a dynamic and evolving practice, influenced by cultural beliefs, personal experiences, and individual perspectives. While the specific symbols and methods may differ, the underlying motivation remains the same: to seek meaning, guidance, and a deeper connection with the divine or the unseen forces that shape our lives.

In summary, the interpretation of signs and omens has been practiced in diverse cultures worldwide throughout history. It reflects the human desire to comprehend the unseen forces that shape our lives and to seek guidance from the divine. From ancient civilizations to contemporary belief systems, the interpretation of signs and omens has played a crucial role in guiding human decisions, predicting outcomes, and fostering a deeper connection with the spiritual and cosmic realms.

➢   Methods of Interpretation:

A. Symbolic Associations:

The interpretation of signs and omens relies on understanding their symbolic associations, which can vary across different cultures and belief systems. Symbols hold cultural significance and carry diverse meanings that shape the interpretation of signs and omens. The cultural context in which a symbol is embedded plays a crucial role in determining its interpretation and the messages it conveys.

Symbols can be derived from various sources, including nature, mythology, religious texts, folklore, and collective experiences. These symbols often represent archetypes or universal concepts that resonate with the human psyche. However, their specific meanings and interpretations can differ significantly from one culture to another.

For example, let's consider the symbol of a snake. In some cultures, snakes are associated with wisdom, healing, and transformation, as exemplified by the serpent in ancient Greek mythology, which symbolized renewal and rebirth. In other cultures, snakes may be seen as symbols of danger, deceit, or malevolence, reflecting the biblical depiction of the serpent in the Garden of Eden.

Similarly, the interpretation of celestial events varies across cultures. For instance, a solar eclipse can be seen as a powerful and transformative event in some cultures, representing the convergence of cosmic forces. In contrast, other cultures may view it as a sign of impending doom or upheaval.

Understanding these cultural nuances is essential for accurate interpretation. Diviners and individuals seeking guidance through signs and omens must be familiar with the cultural symbolism and associated meanings within their specific cultural or belief system. They need to consider the collective understanding of symbols within their community and the historical context in which they are situated.

Moreover, personal experiences and individual perspectives can also influence the interpretation of signs and omens. While there may be shared cultural interpretations, individuals may develop their own personal associations with symbols based on their unique experiences and beliefs. Therefore, it is important to strike a balance between cultural knowledge and individual interpretation to arrive at a comprehensive understanding.

In summary, interpreting signs and omens involves deciphering their symbolic associations, which can vary across cultures and belief systems. Symbols carry diverse meanings and are shaped by cultural context, mythology, religious beliefs, and collective experiences. Understanding the cultural nuances and personal associations with symbols is crucial for accurate interpretation. By considering both the shared cultural interpretations and individual perspectives, individuals can gain deeper insights from the signs and omens they encounter, enhancing their ability to navigate life's challenges and make informed decisions.

B. Contextual Analysis:

Context plays a vital role in interpreting signs and omens, as it provides the necessary framework for understanding their significance. The specific circumstances surrounding the occurrence of a sign or omen can greatly influence its interpretation and the message it conveys.

Timing is an important aspect of context. The occurrence of a sign or omen at a particular moment in time can carry specific meaning. For example, if a person is contemplating a significant decision and receives a sign or omen that appears to be aligned with their intentions, it may be interpreted as a positive affirmation or encouragement to proceed. On the other hand, if the sign or omen occurs at a time of uncertainty or doubt, it may serve as a cautionary message, urging individuals to reevaluate their choices or approach the situation with caution.

Location also plays a role in interpreting signs and omens. Certain places or environments may have symbolic associations or cultural significance that inform their interpretation. For instance, encountering a particular bird in a sacred or spiritually significant location may enhance the perceived importance of the omen and amplify its message. Similarly, encountering a sign or omen in a place associated with negative experiences or emotions may influence its interpretation in a different light.

Personal circumstances and individual experiences are another crucial aspect of context. Signs and omens are experienced within the context of an individual's life, and their interpretation is influenced by their unique circumstances, beliefs, and aspirations. For example, if someone is going through a challenging period in their life and receives a sign or omen that appears to offer guidance or support, it may be interpreted as a source of comfort or reassurance specific to their personal situation.

It is important to note that the interpretation of signs and omens in context is not an exact science. It requires a thoughtful and nuanced approach, considering multiple factors and perspectives. Diviners and individuals seeking guidance through signs and omens must take into account the timing, location, and personal circumstances surrounding the occurrence of the sign or omen to derive a comprehensive understanding of its meaning. By considering the contextual elements, individuals can gain deeper insights into the messages being conveyed, enabling them to make more informed decisions and navigate life's complexities with greater clarity.

> Symbolism and Interpretive Systems:

A. Universal Symbols:

Certain symbols do possess universal meanings that transcend cultural and belief system boundaries. These symbols often tap into deep-rooted archetypes and collective human experiences, making them recognizable and meaningful across various cultures. Familiarizing oneself with these universal symbols allows practitioners to draw upon a shared understanding and tap into the collective wisdom associated with them.

One such example is the symbol of a snake. Across cultures, the snake is often associated with transformation and healing. This association stems from the snake's ability to shed its skin and emerge renewed, symbolizing personal growth, rebirth, and the transformative power of change. In many mythologies and spiritual traditions, the snake is seen as a potent symbol of wisdom, vitality, and the life force energy. Whether it is the serpent in ancient Greek mythology or the Kundalini serpent in Hindu and yogic traditions, the snake consistently embodies these transformative qualities.

Another universal symbol is the circle, which represents wholeness and unity. The circle has no beginning or end, symbolizing eternity, completeness, and the cyclical nature of life. It is a symbol of harmony, balance, and the interconnectedness of all things. The circle can be found in various cultural and spiritual contexts, such as the Native American medicine wheel, the yin-yang symbol in Chinese philosophy, and the mandalas in Hinduism and Buddhism. These diverse traditions all recognize the profound symbolism of the circle as a representation of unity and holistic understanding.

By familiarizing themselves with universal symbols, practitioners of sign and omen interpretation can tap into a collective reservoir of knowledge and archetypal associations. These symbols carry a depth of meaning that has been accumulated and refined over generations, making them potent tools for understanding and interpretation. When encountering signs and omens, practitioners can draw upon these universal symbols to deepen their understanding and derive insights that resonate across different cultural and belief systems.

However, it is essential to note that while certain symbols may have universal meanings, their interpretations can still be influenced by cultural and individual contexts. Symbols may carry additional layers of meaning or nuances specific to particular cultures or personal experiences. Therefore, practitioners should approach symbol interpretation with an open mind, considering both the universal meanings and the cultural or individual significance that may shape their interpretation.

By incorporating universal symbols into their practice, practitioners of sign and omen interpretation can access a rich tapestry of symbolic language that transcends cultural boundaries. This allows for a broader and more profound understanding of the messages conveyed by signs and omens, enhancing the depth and accuracy of their interpretations.

B. Cultural Symbolism:

Cultural symbolism plays a significant role in the interpretation of signs and omens, adding depth, specificity, and cultural context to the understanding of these phenomena. Each culture has its unique set of symbols, associations, and interpretations that give meaning to signs and omens within their specific cultural framework.

For example, in ancient Babylon, a lunar eclipse held particular significance and was considered a portent of impending disaster. The Babylonians believed that celestial events, such as an eclipse, were powerful omens sent by the gods. They associated the moon with their deities and considered any disruption or alteration of its usual appearance as a sign of divine displeasure or impending calamity. The cultural symbolism attached to a lunar eclipse in ancient Babylon would have evoked a sense of fear, anxiety, and the need for preparation or appeasement.

Understanding the cultural symbolism associated with specific signs and omens within a particular culture is crucial for accurate interpretation. It allows practitioners to delve deeper into the meaning and significance of these signs within their cultural context. Cultural symbolism provides a framework for interpreting signs and omens in a way that resonates with the beliefs, values, and collective experiences of a specific cultural group.

By recognizing the cultural symbolism surrounding signs and omens, practitioners can gain a more nuanced understanding of the messages conveyed. They can tap into the collective wisdom, mythologies, and belief systems of the culture in question, enabling a more accurate and culturally relevant interpretation. This cultural depth enhances the practitioner's ability to grasp the underlying meanings and implications of signs and omens and to convey their significance to individuals within that cultural context.

Moreover, cultural symbolism allows for a more comprehensive understanding of the social, historical, and religious factors that shape the interpretation of signs and omens within a specific culture. It helps practitioners to appreciate the interplay between cultural beliefs, rituals, and the perceived connections between the natural and supernatural realms. This knowledge enables them to offer insights and guidance that are rooted in the cultural context of the individuals seeking interpretation, fostering a deeper connection and resonance with the symbols and messages encountered.

However, it is important to note that cultural symbolism can evolve over time and may vary even within a single culture or region. Interpretations of signs and omens can be influenced by historical events, changing belief systems, and individual perspectives. Therefore, practitioners should approach the interpretation of signs and omens with sensitivity, taking into account both the cultural symbolism and the specific circumstances and personal experiences of the individuals involved.

In summary, cultural symbolism adds depth and specificity to the interpretation of signs and omens. It provides a framework for understanding the meanings and implications of these phenomena within a particular cultural context, enhancing the accuracy, relevance, and resonance of the interpretations. By recognizing and honoring cultural symbolism, practitioners can offer valuable insights and guidance that align with the beliefs, values, and experiences of the individuals seeking interpretation.

> ➢   Ethical Considerations and Critical Thinking:

A. Objectivity and Bias:

Interpreting signs and omens necessitates practitioners to approach the process with objectivity and open-mindedness. It involves setting aside personal biases and subjective preferences to ensure that the interpretations remain true to the symbolism and cultural context involved.

Objectivity is crucial in the interpretation of signs and omens because personal biases can cloud judgment and lead to misinterpretation. Practitioners must strive to maintain a neutral perspective, free from preconceived notions or personal desires that may influence their understanding of the signs and omens. They should approach each interpretation with a willingness to explore various possibilities and consider multiple perspectives, allowing the symbolism and cultural context to guide their understanding.

Open-mindedness is equally important in the interpretation of signs and omens. It entails being receptive to different interpretations and being willing to expand one's understanding beyond familiar or conventional meanings. By cultivating an open mind, practitioners can explore the depths of symbolism, cultural nuances, and diverse perspectives associated with signs and omens. This approach allows for a richer and more comprehensive interpretation, embracing the complexity and diversity of symbolic systems across cultures.

To ensure objectivity and open-mindedness, practitioners can adopt several strategies. First, they can engage in ongoing self-reflection and self-awareness to recognize their own biases and assumptions. By acknowledging these biases, practitioners can actively work to minimize their influence on the interpretation process.

Second, practitioners can continually educate themselves about different cultural traditions, belief systems, and symbolic meanings. This includes studying the history, mythology, and cultural practices associated with signs and omens in various cultures. By expanding their knowledge, practitioners can develop a broader perspective and a deeper understanding of the diverse ways in which signs and omens are interpreted.

Third, practitioners can seek feedback and consultation from other experienced practitioners or scholars within the field. Engaging in discussions, sharing insights, and considering alternative viewpoints can help challenge and refine interpretations, fostering a collaborative and growth-oriented approach to the interpretation of signs and omens.

Lastly, practitioners can maintain a sense of humility and reverence toward the divinatory process. Recognizing the limitations of human understanding and the vastness of the divine realm encourages practitioners to approach their interpretations with humility and respect. This mindset allows for a greater openness to receiving and interpreting the messages embedded within signs and omens without imposing personal biases or predetermined outcomes.

By approaching the interpretation of signs and omens with objectivity and open-mindedness, practitioners can uphold the integrity and authenticity of their divinatory practices. They can ensure that the interpretations are grounded in the symbolism and cultural context, offering individuals seeking guidance a more accurate and meaningful understanding of the signs and omens they encounter.

B. Critical Thinking and Analysis:

Practitioners of sign and omen interpretation must engage in critical thinking and analysis to avoid superficial or overly simplistic interpretations. By employing these skills, they can delve deeper into the symbolism and uncover the layers of meaning inherent in the signs and omens they encounter.

Critical thinking involves evaluating multiple factors and considering various perspectives to arrive at a well-rounded interpretation. Practitioners must examine the context in which the sign or omen appears, taking into account the specific circumstances, timing, and location. They need to explore the potential connections between the observed sign or omen and the question or situation at hand. By considering the broader context, practitioners can better understand the relevance and significance of the sign or omen in relation to the individual seeking guidance.

Analyzing alternative explanations is another essential aspect of critical thinking in sign and omen interpretation. Practitioners should be open to exploring various possibilities and considering multiple interpretations. This involves examining different symbolic associations, cultural beliefs, and historical contexts to expand the range of potential meanings. By considering alternative explanations, practitioners can avoid narrow or biased interpretations and ensure a more comprehensive understanding of the signs and omens.

Researching cultural beliefs and historical contexts is crucial for practitioners to gain a deeper understanding of the specific symbolism attached to signs and omens within a particular culture or tradition. This involves studying the mythology, folklore, and religious practices associated with the signs and omens. By familiarizing themselves with the cultural and historical background, practitioners can better grasp the nuances and depth of meaning embedded in the signs and omens. This research helps practitioners avoid generalizations or misconceptions, allowing for more accurate and culturally sensitive interpretations.

Engaging in critical thinking and analysis not only enables practitioners to avoid superficial interpretations but also enhances the overall quality of their divinatory practice. By employing these skills, practitioners can offer individuals seeking guidance a more nuanced and insightful interpretation of the signs and omens they encounter. They can provide a deeper understanding of the underlying symbolism and help individuals navigate their lives with greater clarity and wisdom.

Examples, Problems, and Exercises:

Example: Analyze a specific sign or omen from different cultural perspectives, such as the appearance of a rainbow, and explore the varying interpretations and significance attributed to it across different belief systems.

Problem: Discuss the ethical considerations involved in interpreting signs and omens, addressing potential issues such as manipulation, self-fulfilling prophecies, and misinterpretation. Explore strategies for maintaining ethical practices within the field of sign and omen interpretation.

Exercise: Choose a natural phenomenon, such as a thunderstorm or a rare celestial event, and create a comprehensive interpretation guide based on its symbolism and cultural associations. Engage in group discussions to compare and contrast interpretations, encouraging critical thinking and reflection.

Conclusion:

Interpreting signs and omens is an ancient and universal practice that allows individuals to tap into the wisdom of the divine realm and gain insights into the unfolding of their lives. By understanding the symbolism, cultural contexts, and ethical considerations associated with signs and omens, practitioners can navigate the complexities of interpretation and offer valuable guidance. This chapter has provided a comprehensive overview of the interpretation of signs and omens, drawing upon examples from various fields and encouraging students to engage in critical thinking, problem-solving, and cross-cultural analysis.

Role of Diviners in Ancient Babylon

In the ancient civilization of Babylon, diviners held a prominent position as intermediaries between the human and divine realms. This chapter explores the multifaceted role of diviners in Babylonian society, examining their functions, responsibilities, methods, and cultural significance. By examining examples from fields such as witchcraft, divination, herbalism, shamanism, ecospirituality, and magic in ancient Babylon, we gain a comprehensive understanding of the vital role diviners played in facilitating communication with the divine.

➢   Functions of Diviners:

A. Prophecy and Future Prediction:

In ancient Babylon, diviners held a significant role in society as individuals who possessed the ability to tap into the wisdom of the gods and offer insights into the future. They utilized a variety of divinatory practices to provide glimpses into upcoming events, potential outcomes, and divine intentions.

One prominent divinatory practice in Babylon was astrology. Diviners studied the positions and movements of celestial bodies, such as the stars, planets, and the moon, to discern their influence on human affairs. By analyzing the celestial configurations at the time of a person's birth or during significant events, astrologers could offer predictions and guidance. They believed that the alignment of celestial bodies reflected the gods' intentions and could reveal important information about an individual's destiny or the outcome of specific endeavors.

Dream interpretation was another crucial divinatory practice in Babylon. Diviners recognized dreams as a means through which the gods communicated with mortals. Individuals sought the expertise of diviners to understand the messages conveyed in their dreams. Diviners would carefully analyze the symbols, imagery, and emotions within the dream, drawing upon their knowledge of the cultural and symbolic meanings associated with various dream elements. By deciphering the divine messages hidden within dreams, diviners provided individuals with insights into their own lives, enabling them to make informed decisions, anticipate challenges, and seize opportunities.

Omen reading was yet another widely practiced divinatory method in Babylon. Diviners closely observed natural phenomena, animal behavior, and unexpected occurrences to discern signs and omens. These signs were believed to carry messages from the gods, offering guidance and insights into the future. Diviners studied the behavior of animals, such as birds or domesticated animals, the occurrence of unusual weather events, or celestial phenomena like eclipses or comets. By interpreting these signs and omens, diviners could provide individuals and communities with valuable information about what lay ahead, enabling them to prepare for potential outcomes or avoid potential pitfalls.

The role of diviners in Babylon went beyond simply predicting the future. They served as guides and advisors, helping individuals and communities make informed decisions and navigate the uncertainties of life. Their divinatory practices offered a proactive approach to understanding the divine will and aligning human actions with the intentions of the gods. Diviners' insights and guidance were highly valued, as they provided individuals with a sense of direction, clarity, and empowerment in the face of an uncertain future.

Overall, diviners in Babylon played a crucial role in providing glimpses into the future through various divinatory practices. Their ability to access the wisdom of the gods and interpret signs and omens allowed them to guide individuals and communities in making informed decisions, anticipating challenges, and preparing for what lay ahead. Their expertise and divinatory skills provided a valuable source of guidance and reassurance in the complex tapestry of Babylonian society.

B. Problem-Solving and Conflict Resolution:

In addition to their role in providing glimpses into the future, diviners in Babylon played a crucial role in resolving disputes, conflicts, and challenges within the society. Their unique ability to interpret signs and omens allowed them to delve deeper into the underlying causes of discord and offer solutions in alignment with divine guidance.

When conflicts arose, whether between individuals, families, or even larger social groups, diviners were often sought as impartial mediators. They possessed the wisdom and insight to uncover the root causes of the conflict and understand the underlying dynamics at play. Through their divinatory practices, diviners could discern the messages from the gods related to the dispute, shedding light on the factors contributing to the disharmony.

Diviners would carefully analyze the signs and omens, considering the symbolic meaning and cultural context associated with the observed phenomena. They would also take into account the specific circumstances surrounding the conflict, such as the individuals involved, their motivations, and the broader societal context. By combining their divinatory skills with their understanding of human nature and societal dynamics, diviners could provide a comprehensive perspective on the situation.

Based on their interpretations, diviners would offer advice and guidance on how to address the conflict and restore harmony. Their recommendations were rooted in the divine wisdom they accessed through their divinatory practices. Diviners would suggest actions, compromises, or rituals that would bring individuals or groups back into alignment with the will of the gods, thus facilitating reconciliation and resolution.

The impartiality of diviners was paramount in their role as mediators. They approached conflicts without personal biases or vested interests, focusing solely on the divine guidance and the greater good of the community. Their ability to view the situation from a broader perspective, influenced by the gods' messages, allowed them to offer solutions that went beyond personal grievances and addressed the underlying spiritual and societal aspects of the conflict.

By resolving disputes and restoring harmony, diviners played a crucial role in maintaining social cohesion and stability within Babylonian society. Their interventions helped prevent further escalation of conflicts, promoted understanding between parties, and fostered a sense of unity. The reliance on diviners as mediators also instilled trust in the divine wisdom and reinforced the belief that seeking divine guidance was a necessary and effective means of resolving challenges.

Overall, diviners in Babylon were not only fortune-tellers and advisors but also skilled mediators who played a vital role in resolving disputes, conflicts, and challenges. Their ability to interpret signs and omens, combined with their impartiality and understanding of divine guidance, allowed them to identify the underlying causes of discord and offer solutions that restored harmony and social cohesion.

C. Rituals and Offerings:

Diviners in Babylon held a significant responsibility for conducting rituals and offering sacrifices as part of their divine practices. These ceremonies and offerings were essential for establishing and maintaining a strong connection between mortals and deities, fostering a sense of spiritual harmony within the community.

Diviners were regarded as intermediaries between the mortal realm and the divine realm. They understood the importance of honoring and appeasing the gods through rituals and sacrifices to ensure their favor and blessings. These rituals were seen as a means of establishing a harmonious relationship between humans and the divine, acknowledging the gods' power and seeking their guidance, protection, and benevolence.

The rituals performed by diviners varied in their nature and purpose, depending on the specific needs and intentions of the individuals or the community. They involved intricate ceremonial practices, precise incantations, and symbolic actions designed to invoke the presence of the gods and communicate with them. Diviners meticulously followed established protocols and traditions, ensuring that the rituals were conducted with the utmost respect and reverence.

One important aspect of these rituals was the offering of sacrifices. Diviners would carefully select the appropriate animals, grains, or other symbolic offerings to present to the gods. The choice of offerings was based on cultural and religious beliefs, as well as the specific intentions and desires of the individuals or the community. The sacrifices were seen as acts of devotion and gratitude, demonstrating the willingness to give something of value to the gods as an expression of reverence and faith.

Through these rituals and sacrifices, diviners sought to establish a profound spiritual connection between the mortal realm and the divine realm. They believed that by following the prescribed rituals and making sincere offerings, they could communicate their needs, express their gratitude, and seek divine intervention in various aspects of life.

The rituals conducted by diviners were not only performed on behalf of individuals but also on behalf of the community as a whole. In times of crisis, such as natural disasters, epidemics, or social unrest, diviners played a vital role in leading communal rituals and sacrifices to appease the gods and restore balance and harmony. These collective ceremonies were seen as essential for the well-being and prosperity of the entire community.

The responsibility of conducting rituals and offering sacrifices was taken seriously by diviners. They understood the importance of adhering to the established rituals, maintaining the sacredness of the ceremonies, and ensuring that the offerings were presented with sincerity and devotion. The diviners' expertise in performing these rituals, combined with their deep knowledge of the gods' desires and expectations, allowed them to act as mediators and facilitators in the relationship between humans and the divine.

In summary, diviners in Babylon held the responsibility of conducting rituals and offering sacrifices to appease the gods. These rituals were performed to establish and strengthen the connection between mortals and deities, seeking blessings, protection, and divine favor. Through meticulous ceremonial practices and sincere offerings, diviners aimed to foster spiritual harmony and maintain a sacred bond with the divine realm.

➢ Methods of Divination:

A. Astrology:

Astrology played a fundamental role in Babylonian divination, with diviners observing and interpreting the movements and positions of celestial bodies to gain insights into human affairs. They believed that the celestial realm held profound influence over the destiny and character of individuals, as well as the broader social and political landscape.

Babylonian diviners meticulously studied the night sky, charting the paths and positions of celestial bodies such as the Sun, Moon, planets, and stars. They observed the cyclical patterns and alignments of these celestial objects, recognizing their correlation with events and experiences in the mortal realm. Based on these observations, they constructed astrological charts, known as horoscopes, which served as a key tool in their divinatory practice.

The construction of an astrological chart involved mapping out the positions of celestial bodies at the specific time and location of a person's birth or an important event. Diviners used specialized astronomical instruments and mathematical calculations to determine the precise positions of the planets and other celestial objects. These charts provided a snapshot of the cosmic energies at play during that particular moment and served as a foundation for astrological interpretations.

Babylonian diviners believed that each celestial body held specific symbolic meanings and exerted a unique influence on human affairs. For example, the Sun was associated with vitality, leadership, and creativity, while the Moon represented emotions, intuition, and the ebb and flow of life. Planets such as Mars, Venus, and Jupiter were also assigned specific qualities and influences, each contributing to the overall astrological picture.

By analyzing the planetary positions and their interactions, diviners could offer valuable insights into various aspects of an individual's life. Astrology was used to provide guidance on matters such as personal traits, relationships, career paths, and potential challenges and opportunities. Diviners interpreted the astrological chart by considering the relationships between the celestial bodies, their positions in specific zodiac signs, and the houses in the chart, which represented different areas of life.

Astrology was not limited to individual horoscopes. Babylonian diviners also used it to assess the broader social and political landscape. They recognized the influence of celestial configurations on events such as the rise and fall of empires, the outcomes of battles, and the prosperity or challenges faced by a society. Astrological forecasts were sought after by rulers, who relied on them for strategic decision-making and governance.

It is important to note that Babylonian astrology was not divorced from religious and spiritual beliefs. Diviners viewed the movements of celestial bodies as a reflection of the gods' will and intentions. They believed that the gods communicated their messages and guidance through the celestial realm, and astrology provided a means to decipher these divine messages.

The practice of astrology required deep knowledge of astronomical principles, mathematical calculations, and the symbolic associations of celestial bodies. Babylonian diviners dedicated years to studying and honing their astrological expertise, ensuring the accuracy and reliability of their interpretations. They passed down this knowledge through generations, forming a rich astrological tradition that influenced later civilizations.

In summary, astrology was a fundamental divination method used by Babylonian diviners. They observed the movements and positions of celestial bodies, constructed astrological charts, and interpreted their significance and influence on human affairs. Astrology provided valuable insights into the destiny and character of individuals, as well as the broader social and political landscape. By understanding the celestial energies, Babylonian diviners guided individuals and societies in making informed decisions and navigating their lives in harmony with the cosmic forces.

B. Omen Interpretation:

In addition to astrology and other divination practices, Babylonian diviners closely observed signs and omens in the natural world. They recognized that the gods communicated with mortals through various events and phenomena, and these signs and omens carried significant meaning and implications.

Babylonian diviners carefully observed the behavior of animals, as they believed it held valuable insight into the divine will. For example, the flight patterns of birds, the behavior of domesticated animals, or the sudden appearance of certain creatures were considered significant omens. They believed that unusual animal behavior signaled a shift in the natural order, foretelling events or changes in the human realm.

Weather patterns and atmospheric conditions were also closely monitored by Babylonian diviners. They believed that the gods' influence extended to the weather, and specific weather phenomena were considered powerful omens. Unusual cloud formations, changes in wind direction, or sudden shifts in temperature were interpreted as messages from the gods, providing guidance or forewarning of important events.

Other natural phenomena, such as celestial events, eclipses, earthquakes, or unusual celestial alignments, were also regarded as signs and omens. Babylonian diviners observed the movements of celestial bodies and their interactions, interpreting them as indicators of divine will. For example, a solar or lunar eclipse was seen as a significant omen, potentially signaling the occurrence of significant events or changes in the near future.

Interpreting signs and omens required a deep understanding of cultural symbolism and the context in which they occurred. Babylonian diviners possessed extensive knowledge of the symbolic associations of various animals, weather patterns, and natural phenomena. They recognized that the interpretation of a sign or omen was not based solely on its occurrence but also on its specific characteristics, timing, and relation to the broader context.

The interpretations of signs and omens were not standardized but were influenced by the diviner's experience, cultural knowledge, and intuition. Babylonian diviners consulted ancient texts, maintained records of past omens and their outcomes, and often worked in collaboration with other experienced diviners to ensure accurate and comprehensive interpretations.

The ultimate goal of interpreting signs and omens was to understand the divine intentions and gain guidance for human actions and decisions. Babylonian diviners believed that the gods communicated through these signs, offering insights into the future, forewarning of potential dangers, or indicating favorable conditions. By interpreting signs and omens, diviners helped individuals and communities align their actions with the divine will, maximizing the potential for favorable outcomes and avoiding potential pitfalls.

In conclusion, Babylonian diviners closely observed signs and omens in the natural world as an integral part of their divinatory practices. They interpreted animal behavior, weather patterns, celestial events, and other natural phenomena to decipher the messages conveyed by the gods. These signs and omens were regarded as guidance from the divine realm, providing valuable insights and influencing human actions and decisions. By carefully interpreting these signs, Babylonian diviners played a crucial role in guiding individuals and communities in their pursuit of prosperity, harmony, and spiritual connection with the gods.

C. Dream Analysis:

Dream interpretation held a significant place in Babylonian divination practices. The Babylonians believed that dreams were a means through which the divine realm communicated with mortals, offering insights into future events, personal matters, and the desires of the gods.

Diviners in Babylon possessed a deep understanding of the symbolic language of dreams and the connections between dream elements and the divine. They recognized that dreams were not merely random sequences of images but held hidden messages and meanings that required careful interpretation.

When individuals sought the guidance of a diviner, they would recount their dreams in detail, describing the symbols, events, emotions, and any other notable aspects of the dream. Diviners listened attentively, recognizing that each element within the dream had symbolic significance.

Interpreting dreams involved a combination of cultural knowledge, personal intuition, and the diviner's expertise. Diviners had an extensive repertoire of dream symbols and their associated meanings, accumulated through generations of divinatory practice. They were familiar with common symbols and their various interpretations, but they also understood that individual experiences and cultural context played a role in shaping the specific meanings of dream symbols.

Diviners considered not only the symbols within the dream but also the emotions and feelings experienced by the dreamer. The emotional tone of the dream and the dreamer's reaction to the events were taken into account during the interpretation process. Diviners recognized that emotions could provide additional insights into the dream's message and its implications for the dreamer's waking life.

Dream interpretation in Babylon was not a one-size-fits-all approach. Diviners understood the importance of personal context and individual experiences. They considered the dreamer's personal circumstances, concerns, and aspirations, as well as the broader cultural and societal influences that shaped their dreams.

In some cases, diviners would consult ancient texts or records of dream interpretations to enhance their understanding of specific symbols or recurring themes in dreams. This accumulated wisdom and shared knowledge within the divinatory community helped ensure accurate and comprehensive interpretations.

The ultimate goal of dream interpretation was to uncover the hidden messages and insights from the divine realm. Diviners provided individuals with guidance, warnings, or advice based on the interpretation of their dreams. They helped individuals understand the potential outcomes of certain actions, navigate challenges, or make informed decisions that were in alignment with the divine will.

Dream interpretation also served as a means of self-reflection and personal growth. By delving into the symbolism and messages within their dreams, individuals gained a deeper understanding of their own thoughts, desires, and fears. It provided an opportunity for introspection and self-discovery, empowering individuals to make positive changes in their lives.

In conclusion, dream interpretation held a significant role in Babylonian divination practices. Diviners in Babylon analyzed the symbols, events, and emotions within dreams to reveal their hidden messages. By understanding the language of dreams and their connection to the divine, diviners provided individuals with valuable guidance and insights into future events, personal matters, and the desires of the gods. Dream interpretation allowed individuals to make informed decisions, navigate challenges, and embark on a path of personal growth and spiritual connection.

➢   Cultural Significance and Ethical Considerations:

A. Cultural Significance:

Diviners held a position of immense cultural significance in Babylonian society. They were not only fortune-tellers but also served as custodians of traditions, rituals, and spiritual beliefs that formed the foundation of Babylonian culture.

Diviners were highly respected and revered for their wisdom, knowledge, and their ability to communicate with the divine realm. They were seen as intermediaries between the mortal world and the gods, possessing a unique connection to the supernatural forces that governed human existence. This connection gave them insights and guidance that ordinary individuals did not have access to.

The role of diviners extended far beyond individual divinatory consultations. They played an integral part in the fabric of society, contributing to the preservation and transmission of religious and cultural practices. Diviners were responsible for upholding the rituals and ceremonies that ensured the maintenance of spiritual harmony and cosmic order.

Their expertise in divinatory methods such as astrology, extispicy, dream interpretation, and omen reading made them valuable resources for the community. People sought their counsel in times of uncertainty, decision-making, or when facing challenges and conflicts. Diviners provided guidance and advice based on their deep understanding of the gods' will and the intricate workings of the divine realm.

Through their divinatory practices, diviners helped individuals and communities make sense of the world around them. They offered insights into the future, potential outcomes of actions, and the implications of certain events. Diviners aided in the navigation of personal lives, governance, societal matters, and even military campaigns, offering advice that was believed to be divinely inspired.

Diviners also played a crucial role in maintaining social order and spiritual balance. Their presence and involvement in religious ceremonies, rituals, and sacrifices reinforced the connection between mortals and deities. By conducting these sacred acts, diviners ensured the favor of the gods and the well-being of the community as a whole.

The wisdom and knowledge possessed by diviners were considered sacred and were passed down through generations. They were often part of a divinatory community or priesthood, where knowledge and teachings were shared and preserved. This collective knowledge ensured the continuity and integrity of divinatory practices, preventing the loss of ancient wisdom and cultural traditions.

In Babylonian society, diviners were seen as custodians of the divine wisdom that guided human affairs. Their presence and expertise provided a sense of security, comfort, and guidance to the people. They were instrumental in upholding the cultural fabric, preserving religious beliefs, and fostering a deeper connection between mortals and the divine.

In conclusion, diviners held immense cultural significance in Babylonian society. Their role extended beyond fortune-telling, as they were entrusted with preserving traditions, rituals, and spiritual beliefs. Diviners were revered for their wisdom, knowledge, and connection to the divine, and their presence was integral to maintaining social order, spiritual balance, and the transmission of cultural heritage.

B. Ethical Considerations:

The practice of divination in Babylon carried ethical responsibilities for diviners, emphasizing the need for integrity, honesty, and respect for the sacredness of their role. Diviners were aware of the profound impact their interpretations could have on individuals and communities, and they approached their work with a sense of ethical responsibility.

Integrity was a fundamental principle for diviners. They understood the significance of their role as intermediaries between the mortal realm and the divine. Diviners were committed to conducting themselves with honesty and transparency, ensuring that their interpretations were based on genuine insights and their knowledge of divinatory methods. They recognized the trust placed in them by those seeking guidance and strived to provide accurate and meaningful interpretations.

Respect for the sacredness of their role was paramount. Diviners recognized that their practice involved engaging with supernatural forces and divine messages. They treated their divinatory tools, rituals, and symbols with reverence, acknowledging their connection to the gods and the spiritual realm. Diviners conducted themselves in a manner that demonstrated respect for the divine forces they invoked and the cultural traditions they upheld.

Diviners were mindful of the potential impact of their interpretations. They understood that their words could shape decisions, actions, and the lives of individuals and communities. This awareness instilled a sense of responsibility to act in the best interest of those seeking guidance. Diviners strove to provide balanced and objective interpretations, avoiding personal biases and subjective influences. They took into account the cultural context, personal circumstances, and the specific question or concern at hand to offer insights that were relevant and meaningful.

Ethical decision-making was a guiding principle for diviners. They recognized the importance of considering the well-being and welfare of those who sought their counsel. Diviners aimed to provide guidance that would empower individuals and communities to make informed decisions and navigate challenges with wisdom and clarity. They refrained from exploiting their position or manipulating interpretations for personal gain, recognizing that their role was to serve as channels for divine insights rather than to impose their own desires or agendas.

Moreover, diviners often sought to foster the well-being of those who sought their guidance. They recognized that divination was not solely about predicting the future, but also about providing support, reassurance, and guidance in times of uncertainty or difficulty. Diviners approached their practice with empathy and compassion, creating a safe space for individuals to share their concerns and seek solace in the divine messages received.

In conclusion, the practice of divination in Babylon carried ethical responsibilities for diviners. They conducted themselves with integrity, honesty, and respect for the sacredness of their role. Diviners were mindful of the potential impact of their interpretations on individuals and communities, emphasizing ethical decision-making and the well-being of those seeking their guidance. Their commitment to these ethical principles ensured that the practice of divination remained a trusted and valued aspect of Babylonian society.

Critical Thinking Exercises:

Exercise 1: Evaluating the Role of Diviners in Ancient Babylon

In small groups, critically analyze the role of diviners in Babylonian society. Consider their significance in decision-making, conflict resolution, and spiritual guidance. Discuss the potential impact of divination practices on individual lives and the broader community. Share examples from historical texts and artifacts to support your arguments. Reflect on the cultural, social, and political implications of diviners' role in ancient Babylon.

Exercise 2: Ethical Dilemmas in Divination

Engage in a class-wide discussion on the ethical challenges faced by diviners in ancient Babylon. Identify conflicting interests that diviners might have encountered, such as personal biases, pressures from powerful individuals, or the potential for abuse of power. Explore strategies diviners could have employed to navigate these ethical dilemmas while maintaining their integrity and serving the best interests of the community. Consider the cultural and historical context of Babylonian society when proposing solutions.

Exercise 3: Comparative Analysis of Divination Methods

In pairs or small groups, compare and contrast different divination methods practiced in ancient Babylon, such as dream analysis, omen reading, or astrology. Investigate the cultural significance, underlying principles, and specific techniques associated with each method. Discuss the strengths and limitations of each approach in providing guidance, predicting future events, and fostering spiritual connections. Reflect on how the choice of divination method might have varied depending on the context, individual preferences, and cultural beliefs within Babylonian society.

Conclusion:

The diviners of ancient Babylon played a crucial role as intermediaries between the human and divine realms. Through their prophecies, problem-solving skills, and rituals, they facilitated communication with the gods, providing guidance, resolution, and spiritual connection. By understanding their functions, methods, cultural significance, and ethical considerations, students gain a comprehensive appreciation for the pivotal role diviners played in Babylonian society.

Chapter 4: Herbalism in Ancient Babylon

Welcome to Chapter 4 of our New Age Studies course, where we will explore the captivating realm of herbalism in Ancient Babylon. Herbalism, an age-old practice involving the use of plants for medicinal and spiritual purposes, has long played a significant role in alternative healing and holistic wellness. In this chapter, we will dive into the historical context, fundamental principles, and practical applications of herbalism within the context of Ancient Babylon. Through this exploration, we will gain profound insights into the ancient wisdom that continues to shape our understanding of herbal remedies today.

Throughout this chapter, we will embark on a captivating journey through time, unraveling the beliefs and practices of Babylonian herbalism. Our exploration will encompass the core principles that underpinned Babylonian herbalism, the significance of plants within their cosmology, and the methods employed by Babylonian healers to harness the healing properties of nature. From the identification and classification of medicinal plants to the intricate techniques involved in preparing and administering herbal remedies, we will delve into the extensive knowledge and practices that formed the foundation of Babylonian herbalism.

To provide a comprehensive understanding of herbalism in Ancient Babylon, we will draw upon a diverse range of sources, including ancient texts, archaeological findings, and historical accounts. Additionally, we will examine the influence of neighboring cultures on Babylonian herbal practices, acknowledging the interconnectedness and knowledge exchange that characterized the ancient world.

In line with our commitment to fostering critical thinking and analysis, we will present counterarguments and dissenting opinions, offering a balanced and objective examination of the subject matter. By engaging with diverse perspectives, we aim to cultivate an open-minded approach among our students, empowering them to develop their own well-informed opinions.

Throughout this chapter, you will encounter a variety of examples, problems, and exercises carefully designed to stimulate critical thinking and encourage active student engagement. By applying the knowledge gained to real-world scenarios, you will deepen your understanding and cultivate the necessary skills to navigate the complexities of herbalism, both in ancient and contemporary contexts.

By the conclusion of this chapter, you will have acquired a solid foundation in the principles and practices of herbalism in Ancient Babylon. Equipped with this knowledge, you will be able to analyze and evaluate the historical significance of Babylonian herbalism, recognize its contributions to modern herbal traditions, and critically reflect on the intersections between ancient wisdom and present-day approaches to holistic healing.

So, let us embark on this enlightening journey through the annals of time as we unravel the rich tapestry of Babylonian herbalism and its enduring legacy in our modern world. Through the exploration of this ancient art, we open ourselves to the wisdom of the past, deepening our understanding of the healing powers of nature and our profound connection to the world around us. Get ready to embark on this captivating expedition into the realm of Babylonian herbalism!

The Significance of Herbalism in Babylonian Society

In this chapter, we embark on a captivating journey into the intriguing world of herbalism in ancient Babylon. We will delve into the profound significance of herbalism within the tapestry of Babylonian society, shedding light on its cultural, spiritual, and medicinal implications.

Understanding the role of herbalism in ancient civilizations allows us to appreciate the deep connection between humans and the natural world. By examining the historical context and practices of Babylonian herbalism, we gain valuable insights into the profound impact of herbs and plants on the lives of the Babylonian people. Through this exploration, we unlock the wisdom of the past, revealing the intricate relationship between humans and the healing powers of nature.

Throughout this chapter, we will engage in a thorough and in-depth analysis of the significance of herbalism in Babylonian society. We will investigate the historical and cultural context in which herbalism thrived, exploring its roots within the vibrant civilization of ancient Babylon. By considering a wide range of sources, including ancient texts, archaeological findings, and historical accounts, we will paint a comprehensive picture of the cultural and spiritual significance of herbalism during this remarkable era.

Our journey will encompass various aspects of Babylonian herbalism, including its profound influence on medicinal and healing traditions. We will explore the methods employed by Babylonian healers to harness the therapeutic properties of plants, unveiling their intricate knowledge of identification, harvesting, and preparation of medicinal herbs. We will also investigate the pivotal role of herbalists and healers within Babylonian society, illuminating their sacred duties and their contribution to the well-being of their community.

Furthermore, we will delve into the cosmological significance of plants in Babylonian culture. By understanding the symbolism and spiritual importance attributed to plants, we will uncover the profound connections between celestial bodies, plants, and their healing properties. Through this exploration, we gain insight into the holistic worldview of the Babylonians, recognizing the interconnectedness of the natural world and the divine.

In line with our commitment to critical thinking, we will present counterarguments and dissenting opinions, fostering a balanced and objective examination of the subject matter. This encourages students to engage in thoughtful analysis, developing their own informed perspectives and fostering intellectual growth.

To facilitate an interactive learning experience, this chapter will feature examples, problems, and exercises that illustrate key topics and engage students in critical thinking and discussion. By applying the knowledge gained to real-world scenarios, students will deepen their understanding and cultivate their analytical skills.

By the conclusion of this chapter, students will have gained a profound appreciation for the significance of herbalism in Babylonian society. They will recognize the cultural, spiritual, and medicinal contributions of herbalism, and understand its lasting legacy in contemporary herbal traditions. This knowledge will empower students to critically reflect on the intersections between ancient wisdom and present-day approaches to holistic healing.

So let us embark on this enlightening journey through the annals of time, as we unravel the profound significance of herbalism in Babylonian society. Through the exploration of this ancient art, we open ourselves to the wisdom of the past, deepening our understanding of the healing powers of nature and our connection to the world around us.

Historical and Cultural Context

To truly understand the significance of herbalism in Babylonian society, we must immerse ourselves in the rich historical and cultural context in which it thrived. The Babylonian civilization, situated in the fertile lands of Mesopotamia, encompassed a vast period of time spanning several millennia, from the early third millennium BCE to the sixth century BCE. During this period, Babylonians developed a sophisticated and complex society characterized by advancements in various fields, including science, literature, law, and spirituality.

Herbalism held a prominent place within the fabric of Babylonian culture, as plants were revered for their medicinal, spiritual, and symbolic qualities. The

Babylonians believed that the natural world was imbued with divine power, and plants served as conduits for this sacred energy. They recognized that the earth provided an abundance of healing resources and that the proper use of plants could restore balance and harmony to the body, mind, and spirit.

The practice of herbalism in Babylonian society was deeply intertwined with their religious and cosmological beliefs. The Babylonians attributed specific qualities and associations to various plants, often based on their appearance, fragrance, taste, and medicinal properties. They believed that the gods had bestowed upon certain plants the ability to heal and protect, and they incorporated these plants into their religious rituals, ceremonies, and offerings.

The cultural significance of herbalism extended beyond the realm of medicine and spirituality. The Babylonians regarded the study and practice of herbalism as a revered and specialized discipline. Herbalists, known as ashipu or asu, dedicated their lives to the mastery of medicinal plants and the art of healing. They possessed intricate knowledge of the properties and uses of a wide range of plants, and their expertise was sought after by both common people and the ruling elite.

Herbalism in Babylonian society also played a vital role in daily life and socio-economic activities. Plants and their products were utilized in various industries, such as perfumery, cosmetics, and culinary arts. Babylonian merchants traded in aromatic plants, spices, and herbal preparations, establishing a flourishing commerce that connected them with distant lands. The availability and diversity of medicinal plants contributed to the well-being and quality of life of the Babylonian people.

To better comprehend the historical and cultural context of herbalism in Babylonian society, it is essential to explore the significant texts and sources that have survived from this era. The ancient clay tablets, such as the famous "Medical Diagnostic Handbook" and the "Pharmacopoeia," provide valuable insights into the knowledge and practices of Babylonian herbalists. These texts detail the identification, preparation, and administration of herbal remedies, as well as the rituals and incantations associated with their use.

Furthermore, the influence of neighboring cultures, such as the Sumerians and Assyrians, cannot be overlooked when examining the historical context of Babylonian herbalism. The exchange of knowledge, trade, and cultural interactions with these civilizations undoubtedly influenced the development and refinement of herbal practices in Babylonian society.

It is important to note that while the Babylonians held a deep reverence for the healing properties of plants, their understanding of herbalism was not devoid of superstition and magical beliefs. Incantations, rituals, and symbolic actions were often incorporated into the healing process, reflecting the magical worldview prevalent in ancient societies. Nevertheless, this does not diminish the immense contributions of Babylonian herbalists in advancing the understanding and application of herbal remedies.

By critically analyzing the historical and cultural context of herbalism in Babylonian society, we gain a comprehensive understanding of its significance. We recognize that herbalism was deeply ingrained in every aspect of life, from religious ceremonies to everyday healing practices and economic endeavors. The wisdom and knowledge passed down by Babylonian herbalists continue to shape our understanding

Medicinal and Healing Traditions

Within the intricate tapestry of Babylonian society, the practice of herbalism played a pivotal role in the realms of medicine and healing. The ancient Babylonians held a deep understanding of the medicinal properties of plants and utilized them to treat a wide range of ailments and promote overall well-being. By delving into the medicinal and healing traditions of Babylonian herbalism, we gain valuable insights into their approaches to healthcare and their profound contributions to the field of natural medicine.

The Babylonians believed that illnesses and diseases were often caused by imbalances within the body, and the use of medicinal plants was seen as a means to restore harmony and facilitate the body's innate healing abilities. Herbal remedies were prepared using various parts of plants, such as leaves, stems, roots, and flowers, which were carefully selected based on their specific therapeutic properties.

One notable aspect of Babylonian herbalism was its emphasis on a holistic approach to healing. The Babylonians recognized the interconnectedness of the physical, mental, and spiritual aspects of human existence, and their medicinal practices reflected this understanding. Herbal remedies were not solely focused on addressing physical symptoms but also took into account the emotional and spiritual well-being of the individual.

To administer herbal treatments, Babylonian herbalists employed a range of techniques. They utilized various methods of preparation, including decoctions, infusions, poultices, and ointments, each tailored to the specific needs of the patient and the nature of the ailment. Additionally, incantations and rituals were often incorporated into the healing process, reflecting the belief that spiritual elements could enhance the effectiveness of herbal remedies.

The Babylonians possessed a vast pharmacopoeia of medicinal plants, with extensive knowledge of their therapeutic properties. They classified plants based on their attributes, such as cooling or warming effects, and their ability to stimulate or calm the body. For instance, plants such as licorice and fennel were known for their digestive properties, while thyme and myrrh were valued for their antiseptic and antimicrobial qualities.

Babylonian herbalists were skilled observers of nature, and they drew upon their observations to understand the healing potential of different plants. They recognized that certain plants possessed distinct characteristics that indicated their medicinal properties. For example, plants with a bitter taste were often associated with their ability to stimulate digestion and alleviate digestive disorders.

The use of herbal remedies extended beyond physical ailments and encompassed psychological and emotional well-being. Babylonian herbalists recognized the connection between the mind and the body, and they utilized specific plants to address mental and emotional imbalances. For instance, chamomile was often used to promote relaxation and alleviate anxiety, while rosemary was believed to enhance cognitive function and memory.

The knowledge and practices of Babylonian herbalism were documented in ancient texts, such as the "Medical Diagnostic Handbook" and the "Pharmacopoeia." These texts provided detailed instructions on the identification, preparation, and administration of herbal remedies, along with guidance on the appropriate times and conditions for their use.

However, it is important to note that Babylonian herbalism was not without its limitations and challenges. The ancient Babylonians, like other ancient civilizations, lacked the advanced scientific understanding and tools available to modern medicine. Their practices were rooted in a worldview that incorporated both empirical observations and mystical beliefs. While their herbal remedies undoubtedly provided relief for many ailments, their understanding of the underlying mechanisms of diseases was limited.

In conclusion, the medicinal and healing traditions of Babylonian herbalism were deeply ingrained in the fabric of Babylonian society. The holistic approach to healthcare, the meticulous classification of plants, and the utilization of spiritual elements reflect the profound contributions of Babylonian herbalists to the field of natural medicine. By studying their practices and understanding the historical context in which they thrived, we can gain a deeper appreciation for the wisdom and knowledge they imparted and recognize the enduring relevance of their healing traditions.

Examples:

Consider the following scenario: A Babylonian herbalist is presented with a patient suffering from digestive issues. How would the herbalist approach the treatment using their knowledge of medicinal plants? List the plants they might select and explain their therapeutic properties.

Research and select a medicinal plant used in Babylonian herbalism. Write a short essay discussing its botanical characteristics, medicinal properties, and how it was utilized in Babylonian healing practices.

Problems:

Analyze the limitations of Babylonian herbalism from a modern scientific perspective. Discuss the challenges they faced and compare their approach to the principles of evidence-based medicine.

Imagine you are a Babylonian herbalist tasked with creating a comprehensive herbal remedy for promoting overall well-being. Identify and justify the selection of five different plants and describe how you would prepare and administer the remedy.

Exercises:

Conduct independent research on the "Medical Diagnostic Handbook" or the "Pharmacopoeia" and summarize the key principles and practices outlined in these texts.

Engage in a group discussion on the similarities and differences between Babylonian herbalism and other ancient healing traditions, such as Ayurveda or Traditional Chinese Medicine. Compare their philosophies, treatment approaches, and use of medicinal plants.

Herbalism in Daily Life

Herbalism in ancient Babylon was not only a practice confined to the realms of medicine and healing but also deeply intertwined with the daily lives of its people. The utilization of medicinal plants extended beyond formal healing rituals and permeated various aspects of Babylonian society, including household remedies, religious ceremonies, and spiritual practices. By exploring the role of herbalism in the daily lives of the Babylonians, we gain a comprehensive understanding of how plants were integrated into their culture, spirituality, and overall well-being.

In Babylonian households, herbalism played a vital role in maintaining the health and wellness of individuals and their families. The Babylonians recognized the value of prevention and often incorporated herbal remedies into their daily routines. For instance, they would use aromatic herbs such as mint, thyme, and rosemary to freshen the air and ward off pests, as well as to promote a sense of calm and tranquility within the home.

Herbal teas and infusions were commonly prepared and consumed for their therapeutic benefits. Families would gather in the evenings to share a cup of chamomile tea, renowned for its soothing properties and ability to promote restful sleep. Such practices were seen as a way to nurture both the body and the spirit, fostering a sense of harmony and balance within the household.

In addition to their medicinal applications, herbs held significant religious and spiritual symbolism in Babylonian society. The Babylonians attributed divine qualities to certain plants and believed that these plants possessed the power to connect with the spiritual realm. The burning of sacred herbs, such as frankincense and myrrh, was a common practice during religious ceremonies and rituals. The fragrant smoke was believed to purify the atmosphere and facilitate communication with the gods.

Furthermore, herbs were utilized in divinatory practices, where their properties were believed to aid in accessing mystical insights and guidance. In the field of divination, the study of celestial omens was closely intertwined with herbalism. For example, herbalists would observe the growth patterns and characteristics of certain plants to interpret messages from the gods and determine the most auspicious times for specific activities.

To fully grasp the significance of herbalism in daily life, it is essential to recognize the cultural and societal context in which it thrived. Babylonian society was deeply agricultural, and the cycle of planting, nurturing, and harvesting was central to their livelihood. The Babylonians closely observed and celebrated the seasonal changes, recognizing the intimate connection between human life and the rhythms of nature.

The use of herbal remedies extended beyond physical well-being and encompassed emotional and spiritual aspects as well. The fragrances of certain herbs were believed to have a profound impact on the mind and emotions. For instance, the aroma of lavender was associated with relaxation and serenity, while rosemary was believed to enhance mental clarity and focus. These scents were incorporated into personal care products, perfumes, and incense to enhance the overall well-being and evoke a sense of spiritual upliftment.

Examples:

Imagine you are a Babylonian household member seeking to incorporate herbalism into your daily life. Create a daily wellness routine that includes the use of herbal remedies for various purposes, such as relaxation, digestive health, and spiritual well-being.

Research and select a Babylonian religious ceremony or ritual that involved the use of herbs. Describe the significance of the herbs used and their role in the ritual.

Problems:

Analyze the practical challenges faced by Babylonian households in integrating herbalism into their daily lives. Consider factors such as availability of herbs, social and economic considerations, and cultural beliefs. Discuss potential solutions or adaptations to overcome these challenges.

Research the use of herbs in modern-day household practices. Compare and contrast the ways in which herbs are incorporated into daily life in ancient Babylon and contemporary society. Identify the similarities and differences, and discuss the factors that have influenced these changes over time.

Exercises:

Engage in a group discussion on the importance of incorporating herbal remedies into daily life. Explore the potential benefits, challenges, and ethical considerations associated with integrating herbalism into modern lifestyles.

Design a practical guidebook for individuals interested in incorporating herbalism into their daily routines. Include tips, recipes, and step-by-step instructions for using herbs in various aspects of daily life, such as cooking, self-care, and spiritual practices.

Cosmological Significance of Plants

Plants held profound cosmological significance in Babylonian society, where they were viewed as conduits between the earthly realm and the celestial spheres. The Babylonians recognized the intrinsic connection between plants, the gods, and the cosmos, attributing divine qualities to specific plant species. By exploring the cosmological significance of plants in Babylonian herbalism, we gain insights into the spiritual and metaphysical dimensions of their healing practices.

In Babylonian cosmology, the universe was believed to be structured in a hierarchical manner, with the gods inhabiting the celestial spheres and exerting their influence on the earthly realm. Plants were considered to be imbued with the essence of the gods, representing their divine power and wisdom. Each plant species was associated with specific deities, and their characteristics were believed to mirror the qualities and attributes of those gods.

For example, the goddess Ishtar, associated with love, fertility, and sensuality, was linked to the sacred plant myrtle. The myrtle plant was regarded as an embodiment of Ishtar's divine essence, and its leaves and branches were used in various rituals and ceremonies dedicated to her. By utilizing the myrtle plant, Babylonian herbalists sought to invoke the blessings and favor of Ishtar, harnessing her energy for healing and spiritual purposes.

Plants were also seen as mediators between humans and the gods, facilitating communication and communion with the divine. The Babylonians believed that through the use of specific plants, they could establish a connection with the gods and receive guidance, protection, and blessings. This belief formed the foundation of various rituals and offerings involving plants, such as the burning of aromatic herbs during religious ceremonies or the placement of specific plants on altars as offerings to the deities.

Moreover, the growth patterns and characteristics of plants were considered to reflect celestial patterns and influences. The Babylonians observed the movements of celestial bodies, such as the sun, moon, and stars, and correlated them with the growth cycles and behavior of plants. They believed that certain celestial configurations and alignments directly impacted the growth, vitality, and healing properties of plants.

For instance, the Babylonians recognized the influence of lunar phases on the growth and potency of medicinal herbs. They observed that plants harvested during specific lunar phases exhibited enhanced healing properties. This understanding led to the development of lunar calendars and the practice of timing herbal harvests and preparations according to the lunar cycle. By aligning their herbal practices with celestial rhythms, Babylonian herbalists sought to harness the optimal energies and maximize the efficacy of their remedies.

To further explore the cosmological significance of plants, the Babylonians also studied the interconnectedness of various elements in the natural world. They believed that plants, along with other natural entities such as animals, minerals, and celestial bodies, were part of a grand cosmic web. This holistic view emphasized the interdependent relationships and the continuous exchange of energies between different realms of existence.

Examples:

Research and discuss the association between specific plant species and deities in Babylonian herbalism. Analyze the qualities and attributes of the plants and the corresponding gods, and explore the significance of these associations in healing and spiritual practices.

Examine the influence of lunar phases on the growth and potency of medicinal plants in Babylonian herbalism. Select a specific plant and explore how its growth and healing properties were believed to be influenced by the lunar cycle.

Problems:

Critically analyze the cosmological beliefs and practices of Babylonian herbalism. Discuss the potential benefits and limitations of incorporating cosmological considerations into herbal healing. Consider different perspectives, including practicality, cultural context, and scientific understandings.

Compare and contrast the cosmological significance of plants in Babylonian herbalism with other ancient traditions, such as Egyptian, Greek, or Chinese herbalism. Identify common themes and divergences in the cosmological frameworks and explore the implications for herbal healing practices.

Exercises:

Engage in a group discussion on the role of plants as mediators between humans and the divine in different spiritual traditions. Compare and contrast the beliefs and practices of Babylonian herbalism with other systems, such as witchcraft, shamanism, or ecospirituality.

Design a ritual or ceremony incorporating plants and celestial symbolism. Consider the cosmological significance of plants and their potential to enhance spiritual connections. Reflect on the intention, symbolism, and practical aspects of the ritual, and present your design to the class.

Interconnectedness with Other Fields of Knowledge

The practice of herbalism in Babylonian society was intricately connected with various other fields of knowledge, reflecting the holistic and interdisciplinary approach to understanding the natural world and human health. By exploring the interconnectedness between herbalism and other fields such as witchcraft, divination, shamanism, ecospirituality, and magic in ancient Babylon, we gain a comprehensive understanding of the multifaceted nature of Babylonian healing practices.

Witchcraft and Herbalism:

In Babylonian society, the boundaries between herbalism and witchcraft were often blurred. Witchcraft involved the manipulation of natural energies and the use of various tools and rituals to bring about desired outcomes. Herbalism played a significant role in witchcraft, as plants were believed to possess inherent magical properties and could be employed for spellcasting, enchantments, and protection.

For example, the Babylonian "Exorcists' Manual" includes instructions on using herbal concoctions and incantations to ward off evil spirits or to heal ailments caused by supernatural influences. The incorporation of herbs in these practices showcased the belief in their inherent powers and the synergy between botanical knowledge and magical practices.

Divination and Herbalism:

Divination, the practice of seeking knowledge about the future or hidden aspects of reality, also intersected with herbalism in Babylonian society. Diviners relied on various methods such as astrology, dream interpretation, and the examination of natural signs to uncover insights and guidance. Herbalism played a role in divination as well, as plants were believed to hold messages and symbolism that could be deciphered by skilled practitioners.

For instance, the Babylonians used plant-related omens as a form of divination called botanomancy. By observing the behavior and appearance of plants, such as their growth patterns, interactions with other organisms, or the presence of certain insects, diviners sought to interpret messages from the divine. These insights were then used to guide decisions, predict outcomes, or provide remedies for existing conditions.

Shamanism and Herbalism:

Shamanism, a practice involving spiritual communication and healing through altered states of consciousness, also shared connections with herbalism in Babylonian society. Shamans, as intermediaries between the physical and spiritual realms, utilized various techniques to navigate these realms and facilitate healing. Plants played a vital role in shamanic practices, acting as allies and sources of power.

Babylonian shamans employed specific plants during their rituals and journeys to induce trance-like states, enhance spiritual perception, or connect with guiding spirits.

The ingestion or application of plant-based substances, such as hallucinogenic herbs or aromatic oils, allowed shamans to access altered states of consciousness and commune with the spirit world. These plant allies were seen as conduits for healing energies and spiritual guidance.

Ecospirituality and Herbalism:

In Babylonian society, the practice of herbalism was deeply intertwined with ecospirituality, which emphasized the sacredness of nature and the interconnectedness of all living beings. Babylonians recognized the divine intelligence and inherent healing power of the natural world, viewing plants as living entities with their own spiritual essence.

The understanding of plants as spiritual beings formed the basis of rituals, ceremonies, and offerings dedicated to nature spirits and deities associated with the natural world. By honoring and harmonizing with the rhythms of nature, Babylonian herbalists sought to cultivate a deeper connection with the plant kingdom and access the healing energies it provided.

Magic and Herbalism:

Magic, as a system of harnessing and manipulating unseen energies, was another realm closely linked to herbalism in Babylonian society. Magical practices often involved the use of plants and their associated properties to achieve desired outcomes. The belief in the correspondence between plants and celestial forces, as well as the use of rituals and incantations, formed the basis for magical workings.

For instance, in Babylonian magic, specific plants were attributed with protective qualities, used to ward off negative influences, or to enhance the efficacy of spells and rituals. By incorporating herbs in magical practices, Babylonian practitioners sought to tap into the inherent energies and metaphysical properties of plants to manifest their intentions.

Exercises:

Compare and contrast the roles of plants in herbalism, witchcraft, divination, shamanism, ecospirituality, and magic in ancient Babylon. Identify commonalities and differences in their approaches to plant knowledge and utilization.

Select a specific plant commonly used in Babylonian herbalism and explore its significance in other fields of knowledge, such as witchcraft, divination, shamanism, ecospirituality, or magic. Present your findings to the class, highlighting the diverse perspectives and applications of the chosen plant.

Engage in a group discussion on the ethical considerations and potential challenges that arise when combining herbalism with other fields of knowledge. Discuss the importance of maintaining cultural sensitivity, respecting traditional practices, and understanding the appropriate contexts for integrating different disciplines.

Reflect on the interconnectedness of herbalism with other fields of knowledge in Babylonian society and its implications for modern holistic healing practices. Discuss how the integration of various disciplines can enhance our understanding and application of herbal remedies in contemporary contexts.

Legacy and Relevance Today

The legacy of Babylonian herbalism extends far beyond its ancient origins, leaving a lasting impact on modern holistic healing practices. Despite the passage of millennia, the wisdom and insights gained from Babylonian herbalism continue to resonate in contemporary approaches to health and well-being. In this section, we will explore the enduring legacy of Babylonian herbalism and its relevance in today's world.

Historical Influence:

Babylonian herbalism laid the foundation for subsequent herbal traditions that emerged in different cultures and civilizations. Its principles and practices influenced the development of herbal medicine in ancient Greece, Egypt, and Rome, which, in turn, shaped the foundations of Western herbalism. Many of the botanical remedies and therapeutic techniques used in Babylonian herbalism were documented and passed down through the ages, contributing to the evolution of herbal healing systems.

Plant Knowledge and Medicinal Properties:

Babylonian herbalism possessed a deep understanding of plants and their medicinal properties. The extensive knowledge of botanical identification, classification, and preparation techniques has persisted throughout history and continues to inform contemporary herbal practices. Today, herbalists and alternative health practitioners draw upon this ancient wisdom to identify and utilize plants with therapeutic potential.

For example, the Babylonians recognized the medicinal properties of plants such as aloe vera, myrrh, and licorice, which are still valued in modern herbal medicine. These plants were employed by Babylonian healers for their anti-inflammatory, antiseptic, and digestive properties. Their usage has endured over time, and scientific research today confirms the effectiveness of these plants in promoting health and treating various ailments.

Holistic Approach to Healing:

One of the key contributions of Babylonian herbalism was its holistic approach to healing, considering the interconnectedness of the mind, body, and spirit. This integrated perspective on health is aligned with contemporary holistic healing systems that emphasize the importance of addressing the whole person and promoting overall well-being.

Babylonian herbalism recognized that physical ailments could be influenced by spiritual, emotional, and environmental factors. This comprehensive understanding of health informs modern holistic practices that seek to address the root causes of illness and promote balance in all aspects of life. By embracing the principles of Babylonian herbalism, practitioners today recognize the importance of a holistic approach to health and healing.

Rituals and Symbolism:

Babylonian herbalism incorporated rituals and symbolism as integral aspects of healing practices. The use of incantations, prayers, and ceremonial offerings aimed to invoke divine forces and establish a connection between humans and the spiritual realm. These rituals were intended to harmonize and align individuals with the healing energies of plants, facilitating the restoration of health and well-being.

In contemporary practices, the use of rituals and symbolism remains significant. Rituals, such as smudging with medicinal herbs or creating herbal-infused oils for massage, are employed to enhance the therapeutic effects of herbal remedies. Symbolism is also embraced, as the meanings attributed to plants can deepen the healing experience and evoke a sense of connection to ancient wisdom.

Cultural Heritage and Preservation:

The study of Babylonian herbalism allows us to appreciate the cultural heritage and intellectual achievements of ancient civilizations. By delving into the practices and beliefs of Babylonian healers, we gain insight into their worldview, spirituality, and relationship with the natural world. Preserving this knowledge is essential not only for historical purposes but also for the enrichment and evolution of modern herbal traditions.

Exercises:

Conduct a research project on a specific Babylonian medicinal plant and its relevance in contemporary herbalism. Investigate its historical usage, current scientific evidence supporting its medicinal properties, and its application in modern herbal remedies. Present your findings to the class and discuss the plant's legacy and continued relevance today.

Explore the influence of Babylonian herbalism on other cultural traditions and healing systems. Choose one specific tradition, such as traditional Chinese medicine or Ayurveda, and identify the ways in which Babylonian herbalism has contributed to its development. Discuss the cross-cultural exchange of knowledge and the enduring impact of Babylonian herbalism on global healing practices.

Engage in a group discussion on the ethical considerations of incorporating ancient herbal knowledge into modern practices. Explore questions such as cultural appropriation, respecting traditional practices, and ensuring sustainability in the use of herbal resources. Analyze different perspectives and develop a set of ethical guidelines for the integration of ancient herbal wisdom into contemporary herbalism.

Reflect on the legacy of Babylonian herbalism and its significance for personal and societal well-being today. Discuss how incorporating elements of Babylonian herbalism, such as holistic approaches, rituals, and symbolism, can enhance the effectiveness and depth of modern herbal healing practices. Consider the potential challenges and benefits of embracing ancient wisdom in a modern context.

By recognizing and embracing the legacy of Babylonian herbalism, we honor the wisdom of the past and enrich our understanding of holistic healing. As students of new-age studies, we have the opportunity to bridge the gap between ancient traditions and modern approaches, cultivating a profound connection to the healing powers of nature and integrating diverse knowledge systems for the betterment of ourselves and our communities.

Knowledge of Medicinal Plants in Ancient Babylon

In ancient civilizations, the utilization of medicinal plants held profound significance, playing a pivotal role in promoting health, well-being, and spiritual connections. This chapter focuses on the importance of medicinal plants in ancient civilizations, with a specific emphasis on the Babylonian society. Through an exploration of their healing power, holistic perspective on health, cultural and spiritual significance, documentation and transmission of knowledge, and historical and contemporary significance, we will gain a comprehensive understanding of the significance of medicinal plants in ancient civilizations.

I. Healing Power of Medicinal Plants

Throughout the annals of history, medicinal plants have been revered for their remarkable therapeutic properties and their ability to alleviate various ailments. From ancient civilizations to modern times, the utilization of medicinal plants has played a pivotal role in healthcare practices, and Babylonian society stands as a shining example of the profound importance placed on these botanical remedies.

In the context of Babylonian society, the use of medicinal plants formed an integral component of their healthcare system. Babylonian healers, known as "asipu" or "baru," possessed a deep understanding of the healing properties of plants and employed them to restore and maintain the well-being of individuals. These healers combined their knowledge of plants with rituals, incantations, and spiritual practices to enhance the efficacy of their treatments. Medicinal plants were considered a primary source of healthcare in Babylonian society, addressing a wide range of ailments and promoting overall wellness.

The recognition of the healing power of medicinal plants was not limited to Babylonian civilization alone. Similar practices were prevalent in other ancient civilizations such as Egypt and China. These civilizations, despite their geographical and cultural differences, shared a universal recognition of the therapeutic potential of medicinal plants. Ancient Egyptian medicine, for example, relied heavily on the use of herbal remedies, employing plants such as aloe vera and frankincense for their healing properties. Similarly, in ancient China, the tradition of herbal medicine thrived, with the discovery and utilization of plants such as ginseng and licorice for their medicinal benefits.

The widespread use of medicinal plants across different ancient civilizations underscores the universality of this practice and highlights the inherent understanding of the healing power of nature. The knowledge and application of medicinal plants were shaped by centuries of observation, experimentation, and accumulated wisdom, which transcended cultural and geographic boundaries. The success and effectiveness of these botanical remedies in diverse civilizations are a testament to their time-honored and proven therapeutic properties.

Furthermore, the utilization of medicinal plants in ancient civilizations serves as a testament to the deep connection between humans and the natural world. Throughout history, humans have sought solace and healing from the abundance of the plant kingdom. The recognition of the healing potential of plants reflects the innate wisdom of ancient cultures and their profound respect for nature's ability to restore balance and promote well-being.

Studying the use of medicinal plants in Babylonian society, as well as in other ancient civilizations, allows us to appreciate the enduring wisdom of our ancestors. It sheds light on the rich heritage of botanical knowledge and emphasizes the importance of preserving and incorporating traditional healing practices into modern healthcare systems. By drawing upon the lessons of the past and embracing the healing potential of medicinal plants, we can continue to unlock the remarkable benefits that nature offers in our quest for optimal health and well-being.

II. Holistic Perspective on Health

Ancient civilizations, including the Babylonian culture, held a deep reverence for the interconnectedness of the body, mind, and spirit in their understanding of health and well-being. Unlike the reductionist approach to health prevalent in some modern medical systems, Babylonians embraced a holistic perspective that recognized the profound influence of mental and spiritual factors on an individual's overall state of health. In this holistic framework, medicinal plants played a pivotal role in addressing not only physical ailments but also in promoting spiritual harmony and balance.

Within the Babylonian healing practices, the selection and application of medicinal plants were guided by the belief in the interdependence of the body, mind, and spirit. The Babylonians viewed human beings as complex entities, composed of physical, mental, and spiritual aspects that were intricately interconnected. Therefore, the treatment of illnesses and the promotion of well-being required addressing the needs of the whole person.

Medicinal plants were seen as powerful allies in achieving this holistic balance. They were believed to possess not only physical healing properties but also spiritual qualities that could restore harmony and equilibrium to the individual. The Babylonians recognized that a state of dis-ease or illness could arise from imbalances not only in the physical body but also in the mind and spirit. By incorporating medicinal plants into their healing practices, they sought to restore harmony on all levels of existence.

The selection of specific medicinal plants was guided by their perceived qualities and effects on the body, mind, and spirit. Certain plants were known for their ability to calm the mind, soothe emotions, or uplift the spirit, while others were renowned for their physical healing properties. The Babylonians carefully considered these qualities when choosing the appropriate plants for each individual and their specific condition.

Moreover, the application of medicinal plants went beyond the physical administration of remedies. Rituals, prayers, and incantations accompanied the use of medicinal plants, creating a sacred context that recognized the spiritual dimensions of healing. These practices aimed to establish a connection between the individual, the healer, and the divine forces associated with the plants. By engaging in these rituals, the Babylonians sought to invoke spiritual assistance and channel divine energies for healing and restoration.

The belief in the interconnectedness of the body, mind, and spirit profoundly influenced the healing practices of the Babylonians. They recognized that addressing only the physical symptoms of an ailment would not lead to lasting healing and well-being. By incorporating medicinal plants into their holistic approach, they aimed to restore balance and harmony on all levels of existence.

Studying the Babylonian perspective on health provides us with valuable insights into the significance of the mind-spirit-body connection in healing. It reminds us of the importance of considering all aspects of human experience when addressing health concerns and encourages us to embrace a more holistic approach to well-being. By integrating the wisdom of ancient cultures with modern medical knowledge, we can aspire to a comprehensive understanding of health that encompasses the intricate interplay between the physical, mental, and spiritual aspects of human existence.

III. Cultural and Spiritual Significance

Medicinal plants held a position of profound cultural and spiritual significance in the Babylonian society, permeating various aspects of their religious beliefs and practices. The ancient Babylonians viewed plants not only as physical entities with medicinal properties but also as conduits for divine energies and symbols of spiritual power. This belief system fostered a deep reverence for the natural world and established a profound connection between individuals, plants, and the divine.

In Babylonian culture, specific plants were associated with particular deities, linking the medicinal properties of the plants to the divine realms. The Babylonians believed that these plants were imbued with the essence and blessings of the gods and goddesses they represented. For example, the plant Akitu was associated with the goddess Ishtar, while the plant Suluppu was connected to the god Ea. By utilizing these plants in their healing practices, the Babylonians sought not only physical healing but also divine favor and intervention.

The use of medicinal plants extended beyond their physical properties. Rituals and ceremonies involving these plants were an integral part of Babylonian religious practices, enhancing the spiritual connection between individuals and the natural world. These rituals were performed with utmost reverence and precision, with the intention of invoking the presence and blessings of the deities associated with the plants.

By incorporating medicinal plants into rituals, the Babylonians sought to establish a direct line of communication with the divine forces, accessing their healing powers and spiritual guidance. The act of using medicinal plants in sacred contexts was seen as a means of harmonizing with the natural order and aligning oneself with the spiritual energies that permeated the world. This practice served to deepen the spiritual connection between individuals and the plant kingdom, reinforcing their understanding of the interconnectedness of all life forms.

The belief in the divine qualities of medicinal plants and their association with specific deities added a spiritual dimension to Babylonian healing practices. The Babylonians believed that by using these plants in a sacred manner, they could tap into the spiritual energies embodied by the deities, fostering a sense of harmony, balance, and well-being on all levels.

Studying the cultural and spiritual significance of medicinal plants in Babylonian society offers us insights into the deep-rooted connection between humans, plants, and the divine. It reminds us of the intricate relationship between spirituality, healing, and the natural world. By recognizing and honoring the spiritual dimensions of medicinal plants, we can foster a greater sense of respect and reverence for the healing power of nature, and cultivate a deeper understanding of the interconnectedness of all living beings.

IV. Documentation and Transmission of Knowledge

Babylonian healers, priests, and scribes held a vital responsibility in the preservation and dissemination of knowledge regarding medicinal plants. Recognizing the importance of documenting this valuable information, they meticulously compiled texts and tablets that contained detailed descriptions, classifications, and applications of medicinal plants. These written records ensured the transmission of knowledge across generations and facilitated the advancement of Babylonian medical practices.

The role of healers, priests, and scribes in documenting medicinal plant knowledge was crucial for several reasons. First and foremost, it allowed for the preservation of accumulated wisdom and experiences related to the use of medicinal plants. By carefully recording their observations and insights, Babylonian practitioners were able to create a repository of knowledge that could be accessed and built upon by future generations.

The compilation of texts and tablets specifically dedicated to medicinal plants enabled the codification of this knowledge. Babylonian scribes meticulously organized and structured the information, creating a systematic approach to the classification and understanding of medicinal plants. Through their efforts, a comprehensive body of knowledge on medicinal plants emerged, enhancing the efficacy and precision of Babylonian medical practices.

These written records not only served as reference materials for practitioners but also played a crucial role in the transmission of knowledge. They were considered invaluable resources, consulted by healers, students, and those seeking remedies and treatments. The texts and tablets ensured the continuity and dissemination of medicinal plant knowledge beyond the lifetime of individual healers, contributing to the overall advancement of Babylonian medical practices.

Furthermore, the codification of medicinal plant knowledge in written form allowed for the exchange and dissemination of information beyond the confines of a particular region or community. Babylonian texts on medicinal plants reached far and wide, influencing and inspiring other ancient civilizations. This cross-cultural exchange facilitated the enrichment and refinement of herbal knowledge and practices across different societies.

The availability of written records also promoted critical analysis and the refinement of Babylonian medical practices. Practitioners and scholars could study and evaluate the effectiveness of different herbal remedies, leading to advancements in the understanding of plant properties, dosage, and treatment protocols. The systematic documentation and codification of medicinal plant knowledge fostered a culture of scientific inquiry and experimentation within Babylonian society.

In conclusion, Babylonian healers, priests, and scribes played a vital role in documenting and preserving knowledge related to medicinal plants. Their efforts in compiling texts and tablets ensured the transmission of this valuable information across generations, leading to the advancement of Babylonian medical practices. The codification of medicinal plant knowledge not only facilitated the dissemination of herbal remedies but also fostered critical analysis, experimentation, and the overall refinement of Babylonian healing traditions.

V. Historical and Contemporary Significance

The ancient Babylonian knowledge and practices surrounding medicinal plants have left a lasting impact on modern herbalism and alternative healing traditions. The identification and utilization of specific plants for various ailments in Babylonian medicine offer valuable insights into the development of herbal remedies that are still employed today. Furthermore, the reverence for nature and the belief in the healing powers of medicinal plants in Babylonian culture resonate with contemporary holistic approaches to well-being.

One of the significant contributions of ancient Babylonian medicine to modern herbalism is the identification and classification of medicinal plants. The Babylonians carefully observed and recorded the properties, effects, and applications of various plants, creating a foundation of botanical knowledge that has endured through the ages. This knowledge has served as a basis for the identification and utilization of medicinal plants in different cultures and healing traditions, including modern herbal medicine.

The specific uses of plants for various ailments in Babylonian medicine offer insights into the development of herbal remedies still employed today. For example, the Babylonians recognized the analgesic properties of opium poppy (Papaver somniferum) and used it to alleviate pain. This plant, along with many others, continues to be utilized in contemporary medicine for its pain-relieving properties. The Babylonian understanding of the healing properties of plants provides a historical and cross-cultural perspective that enriches modern herbalism.

Moreover, the Babylonian reverence for nature and their belief in the healing powers of medicinal plants align with contemporary holistic approaches to well-being. The Babylonians recognized the interconnectedness of humans, nature, and the divine. They viewed medicinal plants not merely as physical remedies but as conduits for spiritual healing and balance. This holistic perspective resonates with the principles of modern holistic medicine, which emphasize the integration of physical, mental, emotional, and spiritual aspects of health.

The ancient Babylonian approach to healing, rooted in the belief that nature holds the key to well-being, continues to inspire contemporary practices. The recognition of the inherent healing properties of plants and the incorporation of medicinal plants into various healing modalities reflect the enduring influence of Babylonian medicine. From herbal teas and tinctures to aromatherapy and plant-based remedies, the use of medicinal plants in modern holistic and alternative healing traditions can be traced back to the wisdom and practices of ancient Babylon.

In conclusion, the knowledge and practices surrounding medicinal plants in ancient Babylon have had a significant impact on modern herbalism and alternative healing traditions. The identification and utilization of specific plants for various ailments in Babylonian medicine offer insights into the development of herbal remedies still employed today. Furthermore, the reverence for nature and the belief in the healing powers of medicinal plants resonate with contemporary holistic approaches to well-being. The wisdom of ancient Babylonian healers continues to guide and inspire those seeking natural and holistic methods of healing and well-being.

VI. Exercises

Research Project: Investigate the role of medicinal plants in another ancient civilization, such as ancient Egypt or China, and compare it to Babylonian practices.

Case Study Analysis: Select a specific ailment commonly treated with medicinal plants in Babylonian medicine and propose a contemporary herbal remedy for the same condition, considering the principles and practices of Babylonian herbalism.

Critical Analysis: Discuss the ethical considerations surrounding the commercialization and appropriation of traditional medicinal plant knowledge, drawing upon examples from both ancient and modern contexts.

Creative Project: Design an informative poster illustrating the significance of medicinal plants in Babylonian society, incorporating images of plants, symbols, and textual explanations.

By delving into the importance of medicinal plants in ancient civilizations, we gain valuable insights into the historical, cultural, and scientific dimensions that shaped their practices. This knowledge not only deepens our understanding of ancient civilizations but also stimulates critical thinking and reflection on the relevance and implications of herbal medicine in contemporary society.

Overview of the knowledge and use of medicinal plants in Ancient Babylon

The ancient civilization of Babylon, situated in the region of Mesopotamia, holds a prominent position in the annals of human history. Renowned for its remarkable advancements in fields such as astronomy, mathematics, and literature, Babylon also made significant contributions to the knowledge and utilization of medicinal plants. In this section, we will provide an overview of the knowledge and use of medicinal plants in ancient Babylon, exploring the cultural, historical, and scientific aspects that shaped their practices.

I. Historical Context of Ancient Babylon

Ancient Babylon, a thriving civilization that flourished from the 18th to the 6th century BCE, stands as a testament to human achievement and innovation. Ruled by influential dynasties such as Hammurabi and Nebuchadnezzar, Babylon became a center of cultural, intellectual, and technological advancements.

The Babylonians developed a sophisticated civilization that left an indelible mark on various aspects of human endeavor. Their governance systems laid the foundation for organized societies, establishing laws and principles that influenced legal systems in the centuries to come. The Code of Hammurabi, one of the most famous legal codes of ancient times, exemplifies the Babylonian commitment to justice and order.

Trade and commerce thrived in Babylon, making it a hub of economic activity. The city's strategic location along major trade routes enabled the exchange of goods and ideas, fostering cultural diversity and innovation. Babylonian merchants engaged in long-distance trade, importing exotic goods and fostering economic prosperity.

Architecture also flourished in ancient Babylon, with grand structures such as the Hanging Gardens of Babylon and the Ishtar Gate showcasing the Babylonians' architectural prowess and artistic sensibilities. These architectural achievements demonstrated the Babylonians' mastery of engineering and their ability to create awe-inspiring structures.

Religion played a central role in Babylonian society, with the worship of numerous deities and the practice of elaborate rituals. The Babylonians believed in the existence of powerful gods and goddesses who governed various aspects of life. These religious beliefs influenced every aspect of Babylonian culture, including their approach to medicine and the utilization of medicinal plants.

The presence of the Euphrates River flowing through Babylon played a vital role in the civilization's agricultural prosperity. The river provided a reliable water source for irrigation, supporting the cultivation of crops and the growth of a fertile natural environment. The abundance of plant life and diverse ecosystems in the region contributed to the Babylonians' knowledge and utilization of medicinal plants.

The favorable agricultural conditions in Babylon facilitated the cultivation of a wide variety of medicinal plants. The fertile soil, combined with the expertise of Babylonian farmers and healers, allowed for the growth of potent medicinal herbs and plants. The availability of such resources played a crucial role in the development of Babylonian healing practices and the incorporation of medicinal plants into their healthcare system.

In conclusion, ancient Babylon was a vibrant and influential civilization that thrived under the rule of prominent dynasties. Known for their advancements in governance, trade, architecture, and religious practices, the Babylonians left a lasting legacy in human history. The presence of the Euphrates River and the fertile natural environment surrounding Babylon fostered agricultural prosperity and contributed to the knowledge and utilization of medicinal plants. This fertile ground, both literally and metaphorically, set the stage for the Babylonians to explore the healing properties of plants and develop their sophisticated understanding of medicine.

II. Significance of Medicinal Plants in Babylonian Society

In the ancient civilization of Babylon, medicinal plants occupied a central and revered position in the daily lives of its inhabitants. Recognizing the therapeutic properties of these plants, the Babylonians integrated them into their healthcare practices and attributed immense importance to their role in promoting physical well-being and spiritual harmony.

Babylonian healers, known as "asipu" or "baru," played a pivotal role in harnessing the healing power of medicinal plants. These skilled practitioners dedicated their lives to the study and application of herbal remedies, diagnosing and treating various ailments using their extensive knowledge. With their deep understanding of the medicinal properties of plants, the asipu and baru served as the primary healthcare providers in Babylonian society.

The knowledge and use of medicinal plants were deeply ingrained in Babylonian cultural and religious beliefs, reflecting their holistic approach to health. The Babylonians believed in the interconnectedness of the body, mind, and spirit, recognizing that well-being extended beyond the physical realm. They viewed illness as a result of disharmony within the individual and the surrounding environment. By utilizing medicinal plants, they sought to restore balance and promote overall wellness.

In Babylonian culture, the use of medicinal plants went beyond mere physical healing. It was intertwined with spiritual well-being and the maintenance of a harmonious relationship with the divine. The Babylonians believed that plants possessed not only medicinal qualities but also divine qualities. Specific plants were associated with particular deities or represented abstract concepts and ideas. By employing these plants in healing rituals and ceremonies, individuals sought to enhance their spiritual connection with the natural world and the divine forces they believed governed it.

The holistic approach to health in Babylonian society is evident in the integration of medicinal plants into various aspects of life. Whether in the form of herbal remedies, spiritual rituals, or daily practices, the utilization of medicinal plants permeated Babylonian culture. This deep-rooted belief system and cultural integration demonstrate the profound significance of medicinal plants in Babylonian society and the holistic understanding of health that underpinned their approach.

In summary, medicinal plants held a central position in the daily lives of the Babylonians, serving as a primary source of healthcare and spiritual well-being. Babylonian healers, the asipu and baru, played a vital role in utilizing medicinal plants to diagnose and treat ailments. The knowledge and use of these plants were deeply rooted in Babylonian cultural and religious beliefs, reflecting their holistic approach to health that encompassed physical, mental, and spiritual aspects. By recognizing the interconnectedness of the body, mind, and spirit, the Babylonians embraced the healing power of medicinal plants as a means to restore balance and promote overall well-being.

III. Herbalism in Babylonian Texts

Babylonian scholars demonstrated a meticulous dedication to the preservation and advancement of knowledge regarding medicinal plants. Their efforts resulted in the creation of invaluable cuneiform texts that provided detailed insights into the practices and understanding of Babylonian medicine. These texts served as essential references for the diagnosis, treatment, and study of diseases and the utilization of medicinal plants.

The most renowned compilation of Babylonian medical knowledge is the "Diagnostic Handbook" (also known as the "Diagnostic Handbook of Physical Examinations"). This extensive text encompassed a comprehensive range of medical information, offering detailed descriptions of various diseases and their corresponding herbal treatments. The Diagnostic Handbook served as a vital resource for Babylonian healers, providing them with a wealth of knowledge to aid in their diagnoses and the selection of appropriate herbal remedies.

Within the Diagnostic Handbook, diseases were meticulously categorized and described, accompanied by specific recommendations for herbal treatments. The text provided detailed instructions on the preparation and administration of medicinal plants, highlighting the expertise and precision with which Babylonian healers approached their craft. This comprehensive compilation of disease descriptions and herbal treatments reflects the Babylonians' dedication to systematically organizing their medical knowledge and their desire to pass it down to future generations.

In addition to the Diagnostic Handbook, Babylonian medicine was enriched by other texts that focused on the specific properties and preparations of medicinal plants. These texts, known as the "Therapeutic Texts," offered insights into the diverse range of plants utilized in Babylonian medicine and the specific applications for which they were employed. Through these texts, Babylonian healers acquired a detailed understanding of the medicinal properties, preparations, and dosages of various plants, enabling them to craft effective remedies tailored to specific ailments.

The meticulous documentation of medicinal plant knowledge in cuneiform texts ensured the preservation and transmission of this valuable information across generations. The codification of Babylonian medical knowledge played a significant role in the dissemination and advancement of herbal remedies, allowing future practitioners to build upon the discoveries and insights of their predecessors. These texts provided a foundation for the development of Babylonian medicine, facilitating the refinement of treatment methods and contributing to the overall progress of medical practices in ancient Babylon.

In summary, Babylonian scholars demonstrated a commitment to preserving and expanding their understanding of medicinal plants through the meticulous documentation of their knowledge. The Diagnostic Handbook, the most renowned compilation of Babylonian medical knowledge, contained detailed descriptions of diseases and their corresponding herbal treatments. Other texts, such as the Therapeutic Texts, provided specific insights into the properties and preparations of medicinal plants. Through these texts, Babylonian healers gained a deep understanding of the diverse range of plants and their applications in treating various ailments. The careful documentation of this knowledge ensured its longevity and facilitated the advancement of Babylonian medicine, contributing to the overall development of herbal remedies and treatment methods in ancient Babylon.

IV. Classification and Application of Medicinal Plants

Babylonian healers possessed a profound understanding of medicinal plants and their properties, which allowed them to develop a sophisticated classification system. This system, based on observable characteristics and perceived therapeutic effects, played a crucial role in guiding the selection and application of medicinal plants in Babylonian medicine.

One aspect of the Babylonian classification system was the consideration of sensory qualities such as taste, appearance, and odor. Healers recognized that these sensory attributes often corresponded to specific medicinal properties of plants. For instance, a plant with a bitter taste might be associated with its ability to stimulate digestion or act as an astringent. Similarly, plants with a strong odor or vibrant colors were believed to possess potent medicinal properties. By observing these sensory qualities, healers could make preliminary assessments of a plant's potential therapeutic effects.

Babylonian healers also categorized medicinal plants based on their perceived actions on the body. Plants were classified into groups such as "cooling," "warming," "binding," and "relaxing." These categories represented the presumed effects that the plants had on the body when used medicinally. For example, "cooling" plants were believed to reduce inflammation, while "warming" plants were thought to increase circulation and stimulate bodily functions. The classification system helped healers determine the appropriate plant to use for a specific ailment, taking into account the desired physiological response.

In Babylonian medicine, the preparation of medicinal plants varied depending on the specific ailment being treated. Different forms of plant preparations were employed, including decoctions, poultices, and ointments. Decoctions involved boiling plant parts, such as roots or leaves, to extract the active compounds, resulting in a liquid that could be ingested or used externally. Poultices, on the other hand, involved mashing or grinding plant materials into a paste and applying them directly to the affected area. Ointments were prepared by combining medicinal plant extracts with other substances, such as animal fats or oils, creating a semi-solid preparation that could be applied topically.

The choice of preparation method was influenced by the desired therapeutic effect and the nature of the ailment. For internal conditions, decoctions were often used to allow the active compounds to be ingested and absorbed by the body. For external conditions, poultices and ointments provided a means of applying the medicinal properties of plants directly to the affected area. Babylonian healers possessed a deep understanding of these different preparation methods and their corresponding applications, ensuring that the medicinal plants were utilized in the most effective and appropriate manner.

In summary, Babylonian healers employed a comprehensive classification system for medicinal plants that considered sensory qualities, such as taste, appearance, and odor, as well as perceived therapeutic effects. The system enabled healers to categorize plants into groups like "cooling" and "warming," guiding their selection and application for specific ailments. Additionally, Babylonian healers prepared medicinal plants in various forms, including decoctions, poultices, and ointments, based on the nature of the ailment being treated. This holistic approach to classification and preparation highlighted the depth of their knowledge and contributed to the effectiveness of Babylonian herbal remedies.

V. Spiritual and Magical Aspects

In Babylonian society, the belief in the interconnectedness of the physical and spiritual realms was deeply ingrained. This worldview influenced the perception of medicinal plants, as they were seen not only as natural resources but also as conduits to the divine. Babylonians attributed divine qualities to medicinal plants, considering them as gifts from the gods and imbued with sacred powers.

The utilization of medicinal plants in Babylonian healing practices was accompanied by rituals and incantations, which served to enhance their effectiveness. These rituals incorporated elements of magic and divination, reflecting the Babylonians' belief in the supernatural forces at play in healing. By performing rituals and reciting incantations, healers sought to harness the spiritual energies associated with the plants, believing that they could channel the divine power into the healing process.

The role of priests was instrumental in the intersection of medicinal plants, religious practices, and healthcare. Babylonian priests, as intermediaries between the human and divine realms, played a significant part in the knowledge and application of medicinal plants. They held the responsibility of performing religious ceremonies, interpreting omens, and conducting magical rituals associated with healing. The priests' involvement in the use of medicinal plants emphasized the inseparable connection between health, spirituality, and the natural world in Babylonian culture.

The rituals and incantations employed alongside medicinal plants were considered vital to the healing process, as they aimed to establish a direct link between the patient, the healer, and the divine. Babylonians believed that through these rituals, they could invoke the gods' favor and intervention, increasing the efficacy of the medicinal plants in restoring health and balance.

Furthermore, the association of medicinal plants with specific deities further underscored their spiritual significance. Babylonian mythology and religious beliefs assigned certain plants to specific gods and goddesses, linking them to particular aspects of healing and well-being. For example, the goddess Gula was associated with medicinal plants and held the role of a healing deity. The identification of plants with specific deities reinforced the belief that using these plants in healing practices was not only a physical act but also a spiritual connection with the divine.

The intertwining of religious practices, spirituality, and the use of medicinal plants in Babylonian society highlights the holistic approach to health and well-being. The Babylonians recognized that physical ailments were not solely confined to the body but also had spiritual dimensions. By incorporating rituals, incantations, and divine associations into the application of medicinal plants, they sought to address both the physical and spiritual aspects of healing.

In conclusion, the Babylonians attributed divine qualities to medicinal plants and integrated rituals, incantations, and religious practices into their use. They believed in the inherent connection between the physical and spiritual realms, emphasizing the interconnectedness of health, spirituality, and the natural world. The role of priests and the incorporation of magical and divinatory elements underscored the belief in the supernatural powers associated with medicinal plants. The Babylonian approach to medicinal plants exemplifies their holistic worldview and their recognition of the multifaceted nature of healing.

VI. Exercises

Comparative Analysis: Compare the knowledge and use of medicinal plants in ancient Babylon with another ancient civilization, such as ancient Egypt or China, focusing on similarities and differences in their practices and beliefs.

Plant Identification: Study and identify five medicinal plants used in Babylonian medicine, describing their properties and potential applications.

Diagnostic Handbook Analysis: Select a disease or ailment mentioned in the Babylonian "Diagnostic Handbook" and discuss the herbal remedies recommended for its treatment, considering the cultural and scientific context of that time.

Ethical Debate: Engage in a class discussion on the ethical considerations surrounding the cultural appropriation of ancient Babylonian medicinal plant knowledge in modern herbal medicine, exploring different perspectives and potential impacts.

In studying the knowledge and use of medicinal plants in ancient Babylon, we gain insights into the historical, cultural, and scientific dimensions that shaped their practices. This understanding not only enriches our knowledge of ancient civilizations but also provides a foundation for critical thinking and reflection on the relevance and implications of herbal medicine in contemporary times.

Botanical Identification and Classification

The ancient civilization of Babylon, situated in Mesopotamia (modern-day Iraq), was known for its remarkable contributions to various fields, including astronomy, mathematics, literature, and medicine. In the realm of medicine, one aspect that stood out was the Babylonians' knowledge and understanding of botanical identification and classification. In this section, we will delve into the fascinating world of botanical identification and classification in Babylonian society, exploring the cultural, historical, and scientific aspects that shaped their practices.

I. Historical Context of Babylonian Botanical Knowledge

The Babylonian civilization, which flourished from the 18th to the 6th century BCE, was a period of remarkable intellectual and cultural development. Amidst this vibrant civilization, Babylonians demonstrated a keen interest in understanding the natural world, including the plants that surrounded them. Through close observation and interactions with the diverse flora in their environment, the Babylonians developed a sophisticated understanding of plants and their classification.

Living in a region with a rich and fertile landscape, characterized by the presence of the Euphrates River, the Babylonians were exposed to a wide variety of plant species. They recognized the abundance and diversity of plants and became astute observers of their characteristics, growth patterns, and medicinal properties. Through their daily interactions with the natural world, Babylonians acquired an intimate knowledge of plants and their interactions with the environment.

Babylonian scholars and healers, known for their meticulous record-keeping and extensive documentation, played a pivotal role in the advancement of botanical knowledge. They systematically recorded their observations and discoveries, developing comprehensive catalogs of plants and their properties. These records included detailed descriptions of plant morphology, growth habits, medicinal uses, and classification systems. The compilation and organization of this botanical knowledge provided a foundation for the Babylonians to understand and categorize the plant kingdom.

The Babylonians recognized that plants exhibited distinct features, such as leaf shape, color, and growth patterns, which allowed for their classification into various groups. They paid careful attention to observable properties like taste, appearance, and odor, as well as the perceived effects of plants on the human body. Through this empirical approach, they established a classification system based on the perceived therapeutic properties of different plants.

Plants were categorized into groups such as "cooling," "warming," "binding," and "relaxing," based on the presumed actions they had on the body. This classification system not only facilitated the identification and selection of appropriate plants for specific ailments but also provided a framework for understanding their broader therapeutic effects. By organizing plants into categories, Babylonians were able to systematize their knowledge and enhance their understanding of medicinal plants.

The Babylonians' understanding of plants and their classification was deeply intertwined with their daily lives, cultural practices, and spiritual beliefs. Plants held profound significance in Babylonian society, serving as a primary source of healthcare and spiritual well-being. The classification of plants allowed healers to navigate the vast array of plant species and select those that were most suitable for specific ailments. This classification system, rooted in their close observation of the natural world, was an essential tool in the practice of Babylonian medicine and played a vital role in their holistic approach to health.

In conclusion, the Babylonian civilization thrived from the 18th to the 6th century BCE, and during this time, they developed a sophisticated understanding of the natural world, including plants. Their knowledge of plants and their classification stemmed from their close observation of the environment and their interactions with the diverse flora surrounding them. Babylonian scholars and healers meticulously recorded their observations, resulting in comprehensive catalogs of plants and their properties. The Babylonians' classification system based on observable properties and perceived therapeutic effects allowed for the identification and selection of medicinal plants. This botanical knowledge, deeply intertwined with their cultural and spiritual beliefs, played a pivotal role in Babylonian society and their holistic approach to health.

II. Significance of Botanical Identification and Classification

Botanical identification and classification held immense importance in Babylonian society, serving multiple purposes that extended beyond their medicinal and healing practices. Let us explore two significant aspects: medicinal and healing practices, and agricultural practices.

Medicinal and Healing Practices:

The Babylonians recognized the therapeutic properties of various plants and relied on them for healing and maintaining well-being. Accurate identification and classification were vital to ensure the selection of the correct plants for specific ailments. The Babylonian healers, known as "asipu" or "baru," relied on their botanical knowledge to diagnose and treat various diseases.

By accurately identifying plants and classifying them based on their observable properties, taste, appearance, and odor, Babylonian healers could determine the potential medicinal effects of each plant. Categorization systems such as "cooling," "warming," "binding," and "relaxing" helped in understanding the plants' perceived actions on the human body. This classification system enabled the healers to choose the appropriate plants for specific health conditions and formulate effective herbal remedies.

Furthermore, botanical knowledge played a pivotal role in the development of Babylonian healing practices. Babylonian scholars meticulously documented their understanding of medicinal plants in texts such as the "Diagnostic Handbook" and "Therapeutic Texts." These texts provided detailed descriptions of diseases and their corresponding herbal treatments. By organizing and codifying this knowledge, the Babylonians ensured the transmission of valuable medical information across generations.

Agricultural Practices:

Agriculture formed the foundation of Babylonian society, and the identification and classification of plants were of utmost importance for successful cultivation. The Babylonians relied on their botanical knowledge to optimize agricultural productivity, ensuring a steady food supply and economic prosperity.

Babylonians classified plants based on their growth habits, water requirements, and suitable growing conditions. They observed the growth patterns, seasons, and environmental factors that influenced plant growth. By understanding these factors, they could select the most suitable plants for different types of soil, climate conditions, and irrigation methods.

Accurate identification and classification of plants also enabled the Babylonians to develop effective agricultural techniques. They learned which plants thrived in certain conditions, such as flood-resistant crops near riverbanks or drought-tolerant varieties in arid regions. This knowledge allowed them to make informed decisions about crop rotation, companion planting, and soil enrichment.

Moreover, Babylonian agricultural practices were deeply connected to their religious and spiritual beliefs. They believed that the gods and goddesses were responsible for the fertility of the land and the success of their crops. Consequently, botanical knowledge played a role in religious rituals and ceremonies related to agriculture, further highlighting the significance of accurate plant identification and classification.

In summary, botanical identification and classification held immense importance in Babylonian society. It served the purposes of both medicinal and healing practices, as well as agricultural practices. Accurate identification and classification of plants ensured the selection of the correct plants for medicinal remedies and facilitated the development of effective healing practices. In agriculture, botanical knowledge played a crucial role in optimizing agricultural productivity, allowing Babylonians to make informed decisions about crop selection, cultivation techniques, and environmental factors. The botanical knowledge of the Babylonians was deeply intertwined with their cultural, religious, and practical pursuits, shaping various aspects of their daily lives.

III. Documentation and Codification of Botanical Knowledge

Babylonian scholars, priests, and scribes played a crucial role in documenting and preserving the botanical knowledge of their civilization. Using the intricate cuneiform script, they meticulously recorded their understanding of plants, creating extensive records and tablets that have survived to this day. These texts provided invaluable insights into the flora of ancient Mesopotamia, including detailed descriptions of various plants, their characteristics, habitats, and uses.

Among the remarkable botanical texts compiled by the Babylonians are the "Catalogue of Medicinal Plants" and the "Catalogue of Trees." These catalogues served as comprehensive references for the identification, classification, and medicinal applications of plants in Babylonian society.

The "Catalogue of Medicinal Plants" contained detailed information about plants that were recognized for their therapeutic properties. It provided descriptions of the plants' physical characteristics, such as their size, shape, color, and growth habits. Additionally, the catalogue documented the parts of the plant used for medicinal purposes, such as leaves, flowers, roots, or seeds. It also included instructions on how to prepare and administer the medicinal remedies derived from these plants.

Similarly, the "Catalogue of Trees" focused specifically on the diverse array of trees found in the region. It provided detailed descriptions of different tree species, including their appearance, size, and the specific habitats where they thrived. The catalogue also documented the practical uses of these trees, such as timber for construction, fruits for consumption, and resins for various purposes.

These botanical texts not only captured the knowledge of plants but also reflected the Babylonians' deep appreciation for the natural world and its significance in their daily lives. The meticulous documentation of botanical knowledge facilitated the dissemination of herbal remedies and advanced Babylonian medical practices. It also contributed to the development of agricultural techniques and the understanding of the ecological diversity of the region.

Furthermore, the survival of these texts allows us to glimpse into the worldview of the Babylonians and their reverence for nature. Their commitment to recording and preserving botanical knowledge showcases their dedication to intellectual pursuits and their desire to pass down valuable information to future generations.

In conclusion, Babylonian scholars, priests, and scribes diligently documented their botanical knowledge using cuneiform writing. The "Catalogue of Medicinal Plants" and the "Catalogue of Trees" are notable examples of the extensive records they compiled. These texts provided detailed descriptions of various plants, their characteristics, habitats, and uses. Their preservation and transmission have allowed us to gain valuable insights into the botanical knowledge of ancient Babylon and its impact on their medical practices, agricultural techniques, and understanding of the natural world.

IV. Methods of Botanical Identification

Babylonian botanists employed various methods to identify and classify plants, combining meticulous observation with comparative analysis. These methods allowed them to discern unique characteristics and establish a systematic classification system for the diverse flora of their region.

One approach used by Babylonian scholars was the observation and documentation of morphological characteristics. They closely examined the physical attributes of plants, paying particular attention to features such as leaves, flowers, fruits, and roots. By noting the shape, size, texture, color, and arrangement of these plant parts, they were able to distinguish between different species. For example, they observed variations in leaf shapes, such as ovate, lanceolate, or palmate, and identified distinctive patterns of veins on the leaves. They also examined the structure and arrangement of flowers, including the number and arrangement of petals, stamens, and pistils. These detailed observations allowed them to recognize patterns and variations among plants, aiding in their identification and classification.

Comparative analysis played a significant role in the botanical practices of ancient Babylon. Botanists made comparisons between different plants, carefully noting similarities and differences in their morphological characteristics. They looked for shared traits, such as similar leaf shapes or flower structures, to group plants into categories. By recognizing common features, they established a system of classification that organized plants into meaningful groups based on their observed similarities. For example, plants with similar leaf shapes and vein patterns were likely grouped together, while those with distinct flower structures formed separate categories. This comparative approach allowed botanists to create a hierarchical classification system, organizing plants into groups that reflected their perceived relationships and shared characteristics.

The methods employed by Babylonian botanists for identifying and classifying plants relied on keen observation, meticulous documentation, and comparative analysis. Their attention to morphological characteristics and the comparative study of plants provided a foundation for their classification system. Through these methods, they were able to navigate the rich botanical diversity of their environment, discern patterns among plants, and develop a systematic understanding of the flora around them. These contributions laid the groundwork for future botanical studies and continue to inform our understanding of ancient Babylonian knowledge of plants.

V. Classification Systems in Babylonian Botany

The Babylonians employed multiple classification systems to organize their botanical knowledge, reflecting their understanding of the medicinal properties of plants and their cultural and religious beliefs.

One classification system utilized by the Babylonians focused on the perceived medicinal properties of plants. They categorized plants based on their effects on the human body, assigning them labels such as "cooling" or "warming." This classification system was rooted in their belief that different plants possessed specific therapeutic qualities and could be used to address various ailments. Plants with cooling properties were believed to alleviate fever and inflammation, while warming plants were thought to promote circulation and stimulate the body. By categorizing plants based on their perceived medicinal properties, Babylonian healers and practitioners could select the appropriate plants for specific health conditions, forming an integral part of their healthcare practices.

In addition to their understanding of medicinal properties, the Babylonians attributed symbolic and mythological significance to certain plants. They believed that plants held divine qualities and were associated with specific deities or represented abstract concepts and ideas. This belief system influenced their classification systems, as plants were categorized based on their symbolic and mythological connections. For example, a plant associated with a particular deity might be grouped together with other plants linked to that same deity. Similarly, plants representing concepts such as fertility or protection might be classified together. This classification approach intertwined their botanical knowledge with their cultural and religious beliefs, providing a comprehensive framework for understanding and interacting with the natural world.

The Babylonian classification systems based on medicinal properties and symbolism and mythology demonstrate the interdisciplinary nature of their botanical knowledge. Their understanding of plants encompassed both practical and spiritual dimensions, reflecting their holistic approach to health and their reverence for the natural world. By organizing plants according to their perceived medicinal properties and their cultural and religious significance, the Babylonians created classification systems that not only facilitated their practical applications but also deepened their connection to the broader cosmological and spiritual realms.

Plant	Medicinal Uses
Thyme	Used as an expectorant and to relieve respiratory issues
Sesame	Believed to have anti-inflammatory and antioxidant properties
Cardamom	Used to aid digestion and relieve gastrointestinal issues
Turmeric	Known for its anti-inflammatory and antioxidant properties
Saffron	Used as an antidepressant and for its potential anti-cancer properties
Poppy	Historically used for pain relief and as a sedative
Garlic	Believed to have antimicrobial and immune-boosting properties
Cumin	Used to aid digestion and as a carminative
Anise	Known for its expectorant and carminative properties
Coriander	Used for digestive support and to alleviate bloating
Silphium	An extinct plant believed to have been used as a contraceptive
Dill	Historically used to relieve digestive issues and as a diuretic
Myrrh	Used for its potential antiseptic and anti-inflammatory properties
Onions	Believed to have antimicrobial and immune-boosting properties
Shallots	Used for their potential antimicrobial and antioxidant properties
Roses	Historically used for their astringent and anti-inflammatory properties
Lilies	Believed to have cooling and soothing effects on the body

VI. Exercises

Plant Identification: Select five plants commonly used in Babylonian medicine and describe their morphological characteristics and medicinal properties.

Comparative Analysis: Compare the Babylonian system of botanical classification with the classification systems of another ancient civilization, such as ancient Egypt or China, discussing similarities and differences.

Herbarium Project: Create a herbarium showcasing ten plants from Babylonian botanical knowledge. Include detailed descriptions, illustrations, and the medicinal uses associated with each plant.

Ethnobotanical Study: Conduct research on the traditional uses of a plant still used in modern herbal medicine. Compare its usage in ancient Babylonian medicine with its contemporary applications.

By exploring the world of botanical identification and classification in Babylonian society, we gain a deeper understanding of the rich botanical knowledge and practices that flourished in this ancient civilization. The exercises provided encourage students to engage in critical thinking, comparative analysis, and hands-on exploration of ancient botanical knowledge. As we continue our journey into the realms of witchcraft, divination, herbalism, shamanism, ecospirituality, and magic in ancient Babylon, we will uncover further insights into the multifaceted nature of this fascinating civilization.

A. Babylonian methods of identifying and categorizing plants

In the ancient civilization of Babylon, located in Mesopotamia (modern-day Iraq), the knowledge and understanding of plants held significant importance. Babylonians developed sophisticated methods of identifying and categorizing plants, drawing upon their close observation of the natural world and their interactions with diverse flora. In this section, we will explore the fascinating Babylonian methods of identifying and categorizing plants, shedding light on their cultural, historical, and scientific dimensions.

I. Historical Context of Babylonian Botanical Knowledge

Babylonian civilization, which spanned from the 18th to the 6th century BCE, was a period of significant advancement in various fields, including botany. The Babylonians, renowned for their achievements in governance, trade, architecture, and religious practices, also displayed a deep appreciation for the natural world and the study of plants.

Agriculture played a vital role in Babylonian society, as the region was blessed with fertile lands nourished by the Euphrates River. The Babylonians relied heavily on agriculture for sustenance and economic prosperity. This dependence on the land led to a keen interest in understanding the characteristics and behaviors of plants, including their growth habits, water requirements, and suitable growing conditions. The study of plants was closely intertwined with Babylonian agricultural practices, enabling them to maximize crop yields and ensure food security.

In addition to their agricultural pursuits, the Babylonians recognized the therapeutic properties of plants and their potential to alleviate ailments. The utilization of medicinal plants formed an integral part of their healthcare practices, reflecting their holistic approach to well-being. The Babylonians believed in the interconnectedness of the body, mind, and spirit, and the use of medicinal plants addressed not only physical ailments but also promoted spiritual harmony and balance. The knowledge of plants and their categorization was essential in selecting the appropriate plants for specific health conditions, ensuring effective remedies and healing practices.

Moreover, Babylonian culture assigned symbolic and mythological significance to certain plants, further influencing their study and categorization. Some plants were associated with specific deities or represented abstract concepts and ideas. Classification systems were influenced by these cultural and religious beliefs, emphasizing the interconnectedness of the natural world, spirituality, and human existence. The Babylonians saw plants as more than mere resources for sustenance and healing; they were regarded as living entities with divine qualities, reinforcing their reverence for the natural world.

The study of plants in Babylonian civilization was not limited to practical and medicinal applications; it also encompassed a broader understanding of the natural world. Babylonian scholars, priests, and scribes meticulously documented their botanical knowledge, using cuneiform writing to create extensive records and tablets. These texts provided detailed descriptions of various plants, their characteristics, habitats, and uses. Notable among these texts are the "Catalogue of Medicinal Plants" and the "Catalogue of Trees," which offer valuable insights into the diverse flora of the region and their significance in Babylonian society.

Overall, Babylonian civilization made significant contributions to the field of botany, driven by their agricultural practices, medicinal traditions, and spiritual beliefs. The study and categorization of plants in Babylonian culture were deeply rooted in their daily lives, reflecting their holistic worldview and their quest for understanding the natural world and its connection to human well-being.

II. Significance of Botanical Identification and Categorization

Botanical identification and categorization held immense importance in Babylonian society, serving multiple purposes that greatly impacted their way of life.

One of the primary reasons for botanical identification and categorization was the utilization of plants for medicinal and therapeutic purposes. The Babylonians recognized the healing properties of various plants and relied on them for healthcare practices. Accurate identification and categorization were crucial to ensure the selection of the correct plants for specific ailments. By understanding the distinguishing characteristics and properties of different plant species, Babylonian healers, known as "asipu" or "baru," could effectively diagnose and treat various ailments using medicinal plants. Botanical knowledge played a pivotal role in the development of herbal remedies and the advancement of Babylonian medical practices.

In addition to their medical applications, plants also played a vital role in Babylonian agriculture. Agriculture formed the backbone of Babylonian society, providing sustenance and economic stability. The identification and categorization of plants were essential for successful cultivation and optimizing agricultural productivity. By understanding the growth habits, water requirements, and suitable growing conditions of different plant species, Babylonians could make informed decisions regarding crop selection, irrigation methods, and land management. This botanical knowledge allowed them to cultivate a diverse range of crops, ensuring food security and economic prosperity.

Moreover, Babylonian scholars and botanists meticulously studied and documented the plant species found in their region. The knowledge of plants' characteristics, habitats, and uses were compiled in texts and tablets, ensuring the preservation and transmission of botanical knowledge across generations. These records provided valuable information about various plant species, including their physical attributes, growth patterns, and potential uses. Notable among these texts are the "Catalogue of Medicinal Plants" and the "Catalogue of Trees," which served as comprehensive references for Babylonian botanists, healers, and agriculturists.

Botanical identification and categorization in Babylonian society also contributed to their broader understanding of the natural world. By studying and categorizing plants, the Babylonians gained insights into the diversity of flora in their region and developed a deeper appreciation for the intricate complexities of the natural environment. This knowledge extended beyond practical applications and contributed to their cultural and intellectual pursuits, enriching their scientific and spiritual worldviews.

In summary, botanical identification and categorization played a crucial role in Babylonian society for both practical and intellectual reasons. The accurate identification of plants enabled effective utilization of their medicinal properties and facilitated the development of herbal remedies. It also empowered Babylonian agriculturists to optimize crop production and ensure food security. The meticulous study and documentation of plants expanded their understanding of the natural world and enriched their cultural and intellectual endeavors. Botanical knowledge was an integral part of Babylonian life, permeating their healthcare practices, agricultural endeavors, and broader exploration of the natural environment.

III. Methods of Plant Identification

Babylonian botanists employed several methods to identify and differentiate plants, allowing them to develop a deeper understanding of the natural world and categorize plant species based on their unique characteristics.

One of the primary methods used by Babylonian botanists was the observation and documentation of morphological characteristics. They meticulously studied the physical attributes of plants, including the shape, size, and texture of leaves, the structure and arrangement of flowers, the appearance and color of fruits, and the morphology of roots. By closely examining these morphological features, they could identify key distinguishing traits that helped differentiate one plant species from another. These observations were recorded in texts and tablets, contributing to the growing body of botanical knowledge in Babylonian society.

Comparative analysis was another crucial approach employed by Babylonian botanists. By comparing and contrasting different plants, they sought to identify similarities and differences in their morphological characteristics. They examined plants side by side, noting variations in leaf shape, flower structure, or fruit morphology. Through this comparative analysis, they were able to group plants based on shared traits and establish a rudimentary system of plant classification. This allowed them to identify patterns and relationships among plant species, laying the foundation for a more systematic understanding of the plant kingdom.

The use of morphological characteristics and comparative analysis served as fundamental tools for Babylonian botanists in their quest to identify and differentiate plants. These methods allowed them to distinguish between various plant species and establish a framework for categorization. It is important to note that their classification system was based on their observations and understanding at the time, and may not align with modern botanical classification systems. Nonetheless, their efforts in documenting and categorizing plants laid the groundwork for future advancements in botanical science.

In summary, Babylonian botanists employed methods such as the observation of morphological characteristics and comparative analysis to identify and differentiate plants. These approaches allowed them to recognize distinctive features and patterns among different plant species, contributing to their understanding of the natural world and the development of a rudimentary classification system. Their efforts in botanical identification and differentiation paved the way for further exploration and contributed to the rich botanical heritage of Babylonian civilization.

IV. Classification Systems in Babylonian Botany

In the study of ancient civilizations, the Babylonian civilization stands out for its remarkable contributions to various fields, including botany. The Babylonians developed a sophisticated understanding of the natural world and recognized the importance of classifying plants for practical, medicinal, and spiritual purposes. This chapter delves into the classification systems employed in Babylonian botany, exploring the methodologies, categorization principles, and cultural influences that shaped their approach to classifying plants.

The classification systems in Babylonian botany held immense significance in practical, medicinal, and spiritual contexts. The accurate identification and categorization of plants facilitated agricultural practices, ensured effective medicinal treatments, and deepened the Babylonians' spiritual connection with the natural world. By employing methodologies such as the observation of morphological characteristics and comparative analysis, Babylonian botanists developed a rudimentary system of plant classification. Cultural influences, including agricultural practices, medicinal traditions, and spiritual beliefs, further shaped their classification systems. Understanding these classification systems provides valuable insights into the complex relationship between the Babylonians and the plant kingdom, offering a glimpse into their sophisticated understanding of the natural world.

The Babylonians developed classification systems to organize their botanical knowledge:

Medicinal Properties:

Plants were categorized in Babylonian botany based on their perceived medicinal properties and effects on the human body. Babylonian healers and scholars believed that plants possessed inherent qualities that could influence the body's well-being. By understanding these qualities, they could select plants with specific therapeutic properties for various ailments. This categorization system played a crucial role in the development of herbal remedies and the practice of Babylonian medicine.

One of the key categories used in Babylonian botany was the classification of plants as "cooling" or "warming." These terms represented the perceived thermal properties of the plants and their effects on the body. The classification was based on the notion that certain plants had the ability to either cool down or warm up the body when consumed or applied externally.

"Cooling" plants were believed to possess properties that could reduce excessive heat in the body. These plants were associated with soothing and calming effects. They were commonly used to alleviate conditions such as fever, inflammation, and skin rashes. Examples of cooling plants included aloe vera, cucumber, and mint.

On the other hand, "warming" plants were believed to have properties that could increase heat and circulation within the body. These plants were associated with stimulating and invigorating effects. They were used to address conditions such as cold-related ailments, poor digestion, and sluggishness. Examples of warming plants included ginger, cinnamon, and black pepper.

It is important to note that the categorization of plants as cooling or warming was not based on their actual thermal properties, but rather on the perceived effects they had on the body. The Babylonians relied on their empirical observations and experiences to determine these classifications. The effectiveness of these plants in treating specific conditions was attributed to their perceived thermal qualities and their ability to restore balance and harmony within the body.

By categorizing plants as cooling or warming, the Babylonians were able to develop a nuanced understanding of their medicinal properties. This classification system provided a framework for selecting and combining plants in herbal remedies to achieve desired therapeutic effects. It allowed Babylonian healers to tailor treatments according to the specific needs of individuals and the nature of their ailments.

Studying the categorization of plants as cooling or warming in Babylonian botany provides valuable insights into the ancient approach to herbal medicine. It highlights the intricate relationship between plants and human health, as well as the sophisticated knowledge and understanding that Babylonians possessed regarding the therapeutic qualities of different plants.

Symbolism and Mythology:

In Babylonian culture, plants held not only medicinal but also symbolic and mythological significance. The Babylonians attributed spiritual and divine qualities to certain plants, associating them with specific deities or representing abstract concepts and ideas. These cultural and religious beliefs played a significant role in the classification systems used to categorize plants in Babylonian botany.

The Babylonians believed that plants were imbued with spiritual energies and were closely connected to the gods and goddesses of their pantheon. Certain plants were considered sacred and were associated with specific deities who were believed to govern different aspects of life and nature. For example, the goddess Ishtar was closely linked to the date palm tree, which was considered a symbol of fertility, abundance, and beauty. The date palm tree held a central place in religious ceremonies and rituals dedicated to Ishtar.

Plants were also associated with abstract concepts and ideas, reflecting the Babylonians' deep understanding of the interconnectedness between nature and human existence. For instance, the sacred tree known as "huluppu" was associated with the goddess Inanna and represented the cycle of life, death, and rebirth. This symbolic tree embodied the eternal nature of the cosmos and played a prominent role in Babylonian mythology.

These symbolic associations and mythological connections influenced the classification systems used to categorize plants in Babylonian botany. The Babylonians incorporated their cultural and religious beliefs into their botanical knowledge, attributing specific properties and qualities to plants based on their associations with deities or abstract concepts.

The classification of plants in Babylonian botany was not solely based on observable characteristics but also encompassed their symbolic and mythological significance. Plants were categorized not only for their medicinal properties but also for their spiritual and metaphysical attributes. This holistic approach reflected the Babylonians' worldview, which viewed the natural world as intrinsically linked to the divine realm.

By integrating their cultural and religious beliefs into their botanical classification systems, the Babylonians sought to understand the deeper meanings and connections between plants and the divine forces that governed their lives. This approach provided a profound understanding of the plant kingdom and emphasized the spiritual dimension of their interactions with nature.

Studying the symbolic and mythological significance assigned to plants in Babylonian culture provides valuable insights into the rich tapestry of their beliefs and the complex interplay between religion, mythology, and botany. It underscores the deep reverence and respect that the Babylonians held for the natural world and the ways in which their cultural and religious perspectives influenced their understanding and classification of plants.

V. Documentation and Transmission of Botanical Knowledge

In the ancient civilization of Babylon, the pursuit of knowledge was highly valued, and this extended to the realm of botany. The Babylonians developed a sophisticated understanding of plants and their uses, which was meticulously documented and transmitted through various means. This chapter explores the methods and practices employed by the Babylonians to document and transmit botanical knowledge, shedding light on the rich heritage of plant wisdom that has been passed down through the ages.

➢ Written Records and Cuneiform Tablets

The Development of Writing in Babylon:

Writing held immense significance in ancient Babylon, serving as a pivotal tool for the preservation and transmission of botanical knowledge. The Babylonians were among the early civilizations to develop a sophisticated writing system known as cuneiform. This remarkable script, characterized by its distinctive wedge-shaped marks, revolutionized communication and documentation.

The cuneiform writing system enabled the Babylonians to record their botanical knowledge on clay tablets, which provided a durable and tangible medium for information storage. These clay tablets were meticulously inscribed with botanical data, including detailed descriptions of plants, their characteristics, medicinal properties, and applications. By committing their understanding of plants to writing, the Babylonians ensured the longevity and accessibility of this valuable knowledge.

The process of creating cuneiform inscriptions involved skilled craftsmanship. Scribes, often trained from a young age, used a stylus made of reed or other materials to impress wedge-shaped marks onto the moist clay tablets. The tablets were then dried or fired, solidifying the marks and preserving the information inscribed on them. This method of writing allowed for a relatively permanent record of botanical knowledge, safeguarding it from loss or alteration over time.

Clay tablets served as the primary medium for recording not only botanical knowledge but also various other aspects of Babylonian culture. Literature, law, mathematics, astronomy, religious texts, administrative records, and more were all documented using cuneiform script. This widespread use of writing demonstrates the central role it played in Babylonian society, enabling the accumulation, organization, and transmission of diverse forms of knowledge.

The preservation of botanical knowledge through writing had several profound implications. Firstly, it facilitated the accumulation and preservation of information, ensuring that botanical insights and practices were not lost to time. This allowed subsequent generations of Babylonian scholars and practitioners to access and build upon the knowledge of their predecessors.

Additionally, the use of writing facilitated the transmission of botanical knowledge beyond the immediate context of Babylon. As ancient trade networks expanded, written records traveled across vast distances, spreading Babylonian botanical wisdom to other regions. This dissemination of knowledge contributed to the cross-pollination of botanical practices and the exchange of ideas among different cultures.

The importance of writing in preserving and transmitting botanical knowledge extended beyond the boundaries of Babylonian society. It paved the way for the development of catalogs, treatises, and specialized texts on botany, providing a foundation for the advancement of herbalism, divination, and other fields related to plant-based practices.

Today, the decipherment and study of cuneiform tablets continue to unveil the botanical wisdom of ancient Babylon. These clay tablets offer glimpses into the complex relationship between the Babylonians and the natural world, shedding light on their understanding of plants, their uses, and their spiritual and healing properties. By engaging with these written records, contemporary scholars and practitioners can delve into the rich heritage of Babylonian botanical knowledge, exploring its relevance to new-age studies, witchcraft, divination, herbalism, shamanism, ecospirituality, and magic.

Catalogues and Texts on Botanical Knowledge:

Babylonian scholars, priests, and scribes dedicated themselves to the meticulous documentation of botanical knowledge, recognizing its significance in various aspects of their society. Through their rigorous observations and systematic approach, they compiled extensive catalogues and texts that continue to serve as invaluable resources for modern scholars.

The "Catalogue of Medicinal Plants" and the "Catalogue of Trees" stand as remarkable compilations of Babylonian botanical knowledge. These texts were meticulously crafted, offering detailed descriptions of numerous plant species, including their physical characteristics, natural habitats, and diverse uses. The Babylonians recognized the importance of accurately recording this information to ensure the preservation and transmission of their botanical wisdom.

In their pursuit of comprehensive botanical understanding, Babylonian scholars employed keen observation skills. They paid meticulous attention to the intricate details of plants, documenting their morphological features, growth patterns, and ecological preferences. By systematically recording such information, they created a foundation for the categorization and classification of plants, facilitating a deeper comprehension of their properties and applications.

The Babylonian catalogues and texts went beyond mere lists of plants. They provided rich insights into the cultural and practical significance of each plant species. Descriptions often included information on the medicinal properties, spiritual associations, and ritualistic uses of specific plants. For example, the Babylonians recognized the healing potential of certain plants and documented their application in the treatment of various ailments. They also attributed symbolic and mythological qualities to certain plants, acknowledging their roles in religious rituals and ceremonies.

These written records were carefully preserved on clay tablets, ensuring their survival over millennia. The Babylonians' dedication to record-keeping, combined with the durability of clay as a medium, allowed their botanical knowledge to endure the passage of time. The discovery and decipherment of these tablets by modern archaeologists and linguists have provided remarkable insights into the botanical practices of ancient Babylon.

The value of these catalogues and texts extends beyond their historical significance. They offer a window into the worldview, beliefs, and practices of the Babylonians, shedding light on their deep connection with the natural world. Additionally, they provide a foundation for comparative studies, enabling scholars to explore the connections and shared botanical knowledge between ancient Babylon and other civilizations of the time.

Contemporary researchers continue to study these Babylonian texts, unraveling the wealth of botanical knowledge they contain. By analyzing the descriptions, classifications, and uses of plants as documented by the Babylonians, scholars gain valuable insights into ancient herbalism, divination practices, and the interplay between plants and spirituality. Furthermore, this exploration encourages critical thinking and encourages discussions on the relevance of ancient botanical wisdom in fields such as new-age studies, witchcraft, divination, herbalism, shamanism, ecospirituality, and magic.

➢   Oral Tradition and Knowledge Transmission

Apprenticeship and Oral Instruction:

In addition to written records, the transmission of botanical knowledge in ancient Babylon relied heavily on oral tradition. Young individuals aspiring to become healers, priests, or scribes would enter into apprenticeships with experienced practitioners. Through this mentorship system, knowledge and skills were passed down from one generation to the next. Apprentices would learn about the identification, classification, and uses of plants through hands-on experiences, guided by the wisdom and expertise of their mentors.

Oral tradition in Babylonian botanical knowledge extended beyond apprenticeships. Rituals, ceremonies, and storytelling played a significant role in the transmission of plant wisdom. During religious and spiritual gatherings, elders and priests would share their knowledge of plants through narratives, myths, and incantations. This oral tradition not only ensured the continuity of botanical knowledge but also imbued it with cultural and spiritual significance, reinforcing the interconnectedness between plants, spirituality, and the human experience.

> ➤ Challenges and Limitations in Transmission

Language and Interpretation:

One of the intriguing challenges faced by modern scholars in the study of Babylonian botanical knowledge lies in the decipherment and interpretation of the cuneiform script. The cuneiform writing system, with its intricate arrangement of wedge-shaped marks, presents a complex puzzle that requires careful unraveling.

The decipherment process involves analyzing the individual signs and their combinations, comparing them with known phonetic and semantic values, and studying the context in which they appear. This task is further complicated by the fact that cuneiform evolved over time, with variations in script styles, linguistic shifts, and regional differences. As a result, the interpretation of cuneiform symbols and their meanings requires a nuanced understanding of the historical and linguistic context.

Decoding the cuneiform script involves a collaborative effort among specialists from various disciplines, including linguistics, philology, archaeology, and botany. Scholars with expertise in these fields come together to share their knowledge, theories, and discoveries, contributing to a more comprehensive understanding of Babylonian botanical wisdom.

By combining textual analysis with archaeological findings and comparative studies, scholars have made remarkable progress in deciphering and interpreting the cuneiform texts related to botany. They have developed dictionaries, grammars, and reference materials that aid in the identification and translation of cuneiform signs, allowing for the reconstruction of ancient Babylonian texts.

Interdisciplinary collaboration plays a vital role in this process. Linguists and philologists provide linguistic expertise, examining the grammar, syntax, and vocabulary of the texts. Archaeologists contribute by uncovering additional tablets and artifacts that offer new insights into Babylonian culture and its botanical practices. Botanists lend their expertise to identify the plant species mentioned in the texts, enriching our understanding of ancient botanical knowledge.

While significant progress has been made, challenges persist. Some cuneiform tablets are damaged, incomplete, or poorly preserved, making the decipherment process more difficult. Additionally, the evolving nature of the cuneiform script means that new discoveries may require reassessment and adjustment of previous interpretations.

Nevertheless, the dedication and collaborative efforts of scholars continue to shed light on the rich botanical knowledge of ancient Babylon. The deciphered texts provide glimpses into the uses, properties, and cultural significance of plants in Babylonian society. They offer a fascinating glimpse into the connections between plants, spirituality, and various aspects of daily life in ancient Mesopotamia.

The ongoing work in deciphering and interpreting Babylonian botanical texts serves as a testament to the importance of interdisciplinary research and the enduring curiosity of scholars. By piecing together the fragments of ancient knowledge, modern researchers are able to unlock the wisdom of the past and bridge the gap between ancient traditions and contemporary studies in fields such as new-age studies, witchcraft, divination, herbalism, shamanism, ecospirituality, and magic.

Fragmentation and Loss:

The passage of time has not been kind to the preservation of Babylonian texts, and unfortunately, the loss and fragmentation of many ancient records have created challenges for understanding the full extent of Babylonian botanical knowledge. Various factors have contributed to this loss, including the destruction of ancient libraries, the decay of clay tablets due to exposure to the elements, and the gaps in archaeological discoveries.

One significant factor in the loss of Babylonian texts was the destruction of ancient libraries, particularly during periods of political instability and military conquests. Conquests by foreign powers, such as the Assyrians and the Persians, often resulted in the destruction or dispersion of valuable texts, leading to irretrievable loss. The Library of Ashurbanipal in Nineveh, one of the most renowned repositories of ancient knowledge, suffered extensive damage and destruction.

Furthermore, the decay of clay tablets over thousands of years has resulted in the loss of countless texts. The vulnerability of clay to physical damage, moisture, and environmental factors has led to the deterioration and disintegration of many tablets. The natural erosion of clay, coupled with human activities and the ravages of time, has resulted in the partial or complete destruction of valuable information contained in these tablets.

Archaeological gaps also contribute to our limited understanding of Babylonian botanical knowledge. The nature of archaeological excavation means that not all areas have been equally explored, and certain periods or regions may be underrepresented in the archaeological record. As a result, there may be gaps in our knowledge of specific botanical practices or the use of certain plant species in ancient Babylon.

Despite these limitations, the surviving texts and fragments provide valuable insights into the botanical practices and wisdom of the Babylonians. The decipherment and interpretation of cuneiform tablets, along with the meticulous study of other historical sources, have allowed scholars to reconstruct aspects of Babylonian botanical knowledge. These surviving texts offer glimpses into the identification, classification, properties, and uses of various plants in the ancient world.

Scholars meticulously analyze and piece together fragments of texts, combining linguistic expertise, contextual understanding, and interdisciplinary collaboration to extract information from these ancient sources. They employ comparative studies, cross-referencing with other ancient texts and traditions, and examining archaeological evidence to fill in the gaps and reconstruct the botanical knowledge of ancient Babylon.

While the loss of texts and the gaps in our understanding pose challenges, the surviving records provide valuable glimpses into the botanical practices and wisdom of the Babylonians. These fragments offer a fascinating window into their cultivation techniques, medicinal applications, spiritual beliefs, and cultural significance of plants. They enable us to appreciate the ancient Babylonians' deep connection with the natural world and their profound understanding of botanical properties and uses.

As ongoing research and archaeological discoveries continue to expand our knowledge, the gaps in understanding are gradually being filled, and our understanding of Babylonian botanical knowledge becomes more comprehensive. The preservation and interpretation of these surviving texts serve as a testament to the enduring importance of the study of ancient civilizations and their wisdom in fields such as new-age studies, witchcraft, divination, herbalism, shamanism, ecospirituality, and magic.

Chapter Summary:

The documentation and transmission of botanical knowledge in ancient Babylon involved a multifaceted approach. The use of written records, such as clay tablets with cuneiform inscriptions, provided a tangible and lasting medium for recording botanical wisdom. Additionally, the oral tradition, through apprenticeships, rituals, and storytelling, ensured the transfer of knowledge from one generation to the next. Despite the challenges of language and loss, the surviving texts and fragments have offered valuable insights into the rich botanical heritage of ancient Babylon. By studying these records, modern scholars can unlock the secrets of Babylonian botany and deepen our understanding of the interconnectedness between humans and the natural world.

➢ Written Records and Cuneiform Tablets

In the ancient civilization of Babylon, the development of writing revolutionized the preservation and transmission of knowledge. Among the various fields that benefited from this innovation was botany, where written records and cuneiform tablets played a pivotal role. This section explores the significance of written documentation in Babylonian botany, focusing on the development of cuneiform writing, the creation of botanical tablets, and their importance in the preservation and dissemination of botanical knowledge.

The Emergence of Cuneiform Writing

Cuneiform writing, a remarkable achievement of ancient Mesopotamia, emerged around the late 4th millennium BCE and became a sophisticated script utilized by various civilizations, including the Babylonians. The term "cuneiform" originates from the Latin word "cuneus," meaning wedge, which accurately characterizes the distinctive wedge-shaped marks made on clay tablets using a stylus. This unique writing system enabled the recording of complex ideas, encompassing a wide range of subjects, including the field of botany, in a relatively permanent and tangible form.

The development of cuneiform writing was a significant advancement in human history. Before the emergence of writing, knowledge was primarily transmitted orally, making it susceptible to loss or distortion over time. With the advent of cuneiform, information could be documented and preserved, ensuring its accessibility to future generations. This revolutionary script enabled the ancient Mesopotamians, including the Babylonians, to communicate, record history, engage in administrative tasks, and explore diverse fields of knowledge, including botany.

The cuneiform writing system consisted of a combination of pictographs (representing objects or ideas), ideograms (representing concepts), and phonetic signs (representing sounds). The script was primarily impressed onto clay tablets, which were then dried or fired to solidify the markings, resulting in a durable medium for written records. The writing process involved the skilled use of a stylus, typically made of reed, to create the distinctive wedge-shaped impressions in the clay.

In the context of botanical knowledge, cuneiform writing provided an invaluable means to document the understanding of plants and their properties. Babylonian scholars, priests, and scribes meticulously inscribed this information on clay tablets, ensuring its preservation over time. These tablets contained detailed descriptions of plants, including their physical characteristics, habitats, medicinal properties, and applications in various spiritual and healing practices.

The ability to record botanical knowledge in a written format facilitated the accumulation and dissemination of information. It allowed for the systematic organization of plant data, facilitating comparisons, classifications, and the development of catalogs and lists of plants. The permanence and tangibility of cuneiform writing also enabled practitioners and scholars to reference and study botanical texts, contributing to the advancement of botany within Babylonian society.

The sophisticated nature of cuneiform writing is evidenced by the vast corpus of surviving texts from ancient Mesopotamia. These texts span a wide range of subjects, providing invaluable insights into the knowledge, beliefs, and practices of the Babylonians and other ancient civilizations. Today, the decipherment and interpretation of cuneiform tablets continue to unlock the secrets of the past, shedding light on the rich botanical heritage of ancient Babylon and its relevance to fields such as witchcraft, divination, herbalism, shamanism, ecospirituality, and magic.

The Creation of Botanical Tablets

Babylonian scholars, priests, and scribes played a crucial role in the meticulous documentation and inscription of botanical information on clay tablets using the cuneiform script. Cuneiform writing, characterized by its wedge-shaped marks impressed onto clay, provided a durable and tangible medium for recording and preserving knowledge.

The clay tablets used for inscriptions varied in size and shape, ranging from small fragments to larger, more comprehensive texts. The process of creating these tablets involved shaping soft clay into a flat surface and then using a stylus or reed to impress the wedge-shaped symbols onto the surface. Once inscribed, the tablets were either left to dry naturally or fired in kilns to increase their durability and ensure long-term preservation.

Each clay tablet contained a wealth of botanical knowledge carefully recorded by the Babylonian scholars. These texts provided detailed descriptions of plants, including their physical characteristics such as the shape of leaves, flowers, fruits, and roots. Moreover, they encompassed information on the medicinal properties attributed to these plants, as well as their applications in various domains relevant to the ancient Babylonian society.

In the realm of witchcraft, Babylonian botanical knowledge offered insights into the magical properties and uses of specific plants. Certain plants were believed to possess mystical powers and were utilized in spells, rituals, and potions by practitioners of witchcraft. The Babylonian clay tablets recorded these plant-based practices, offering guidance on the selection, preparation, and application of plants in witchcraft ceremonies.

Divination, an important aspect of Babylonian culture, involved the interpretation of natural signs and omens for gaining insight into the future. Botanical knowledge played a significant role in divination, as certain plants were associated with specific symbols and meanings. The clay tablets contained information on the identification and interpretation of these botanical signs, enabling diviners to decode messages from the natural world.

Herbalism, as an ancient healing practice, relied heavily on botanical knowledge. Babylonian scholars documented the medicinal properties and applications of various plants, providing a comprehensive understanding of their therapeutic benefits. The clay tablets contained precise instructions on the preparation of herbal remedies, including decoctions, poultices, and ointments, for treating ailments and promoting well-being.

Shamanism, with its emphasis on spiritual and healing practices, also drew upon Babylonian botanical wisdom. Shamans used plants as tools for connecting with the spiritual realm and facilitating healing journeys. The clay tablets recorded the sacred plants and rituals associated with shamanic practices, allowing shamans to harness the power of these plants in their spiritual endeavors.

Ecospirituality, deeply rooted in the reverence for nature and the interconnectedness of all living beings, found expression in Babylonian botanical knowledge. The clay tablets contained information on the spiritual significance of plants, their role in ecological balance, and the rituals and practices associated with honoring the natural world. Babylonian scholars recognized the sacredness of plants and their vital role in the spiritual and ecological fabric of life.

These clay tablets, meticulously inscribed with botanical knowledge, serve as invaluable artifacts that have survived to the present day. Their preservation and decipherment provide modern scholars with a glimpse into the rich botanical traditions of ancient Babylon. The information contained within these tablets contributes not only to the understanding of the historical practices of witchcraft, divination, herbalism, shamanism, and ecospirituality but also offers insights into the broader cultural and spiritual beliefs of the Babylonian civilization.

Importance and Significance

The creation of botanical tablets in ancient Babylon served as a means to centralize and disseminate botanical knowledge throughout society. These tablets were not only repositories of accumulated wisdom but also played a crucial role in the transmission of this knowledge to future generations.

By meticulously inscribing their botanical understanding on clay tablets, the Babylonians ensured the preservation of their knowledge for posterity. These tablets acted as tangible records, safeguarding valuable information about plants and their uses. In a time before the widespread availability of written texts, the tablets provided a tangible source of knowledge that could be consulted and referenced by scholars, priests, and scribes.

The significance of these botanical tablets extended beyond their role as mere archives. They played a pivotal role in the transmission of botanical knowledge to individuals seeking to learn about plants and their properties. Aspiring healers, priests, and scribes could consult these tablets as educational resources, guiding them in their studies and practice.

The standardized and accessible nature of the botanical tablets made them an invaluable tool for learning. Their inscriptions provided a consistent and reliable source of information, ensuring that individuals across different regions and generations had access to the same body of botanical knowledge. This helped establish a common understanding and vocabulary regarding plants and their uses within Babylonian society.

Moreover, the use of clay tablets as a medium for botanical documentation facilitated the dissemination of knowledge. These tablets were relatively easy to produce and transport, making it possible to distribute copies of important texts to various locations within the empire. As a result, botanical knowledge could reach a wider audience and contribute to the cultivation of expertise in different regions.

The availability of botanical tablets also fostered a culture of continuous learning and intellectual exchange. Scholars, priests, and scribes could study and expand upon existing botanical knowledge, building upon the discoveries and insights of their predecessors. This ongoing dialogue allowed for the refinement and improvement of botanical understanding over time.

In summary, the creation of botanical tablets in ancient Babylon served as a means to preserve, transmit, and disseminate botanical knowledge. These tablets acted as repositories of wisdom, ensuring the preservation of valuable information about plants and their uses. They also facilitated the widespread dissemination of this knowledge, providing aspiring healers, priests, and scribes with standardized and accessible resources for learning. The clay tablets played a crucial role in the cultivation of expertise, intellectual exchange, and the continuous refinement of botanical understanding within Babylonian society.

The Content of Botanical Tablets

Catalogues and Lists

In ancient Babylon, the creation of catalogues played a crucial role in organizing and categorizing the vast botanical knowledge of the time. Catalogues were a significant type of botanical tablets, serving as comprehensive inventories of the diverse plant life known to the Babylonians.

One notable example of a botanical catalogue is the "Catalogue of Medicinal Plants." This catalogue provided detailed descriptions of various plants known for their medicinal properties. It included information on the physical features of the plants, such as the shape of leaves, patterns of veins, and the arrangement of flowers. Additionally, it documented the habitats in which these plants could be found and their specific uses in healing practices. By compiling this information, the Babylonians aimed to create a valuable resource for practitioners of medicine and herbalism, ensuring the accurate identification and selection of plants for specific ailments.

Another important catalogue was the "Catalogue of Trees," which focused specifically on trees and their characteristics. This catalogue described the different types of trees, their growth habits, and the environments in which they thrived. It also highlighted the various uses of trees in Babylonian society, such as timber for construction, fruits for food, and sap for medicinal purposes. By categorizing and documenting this information, the Babylonians demonstrated their deep understanding of trees and their significance in both practical and symbolic contexts.

Apart from comprehensive catalogues, the Babylonians also created lists of plants based on specific criteria. These lists categorized plants according to their medicinal properties or symbolic associations. For example, there might have been lists of "cooling" or "warming" plants, reflecting the perceived effects of plants on the human body. Similarly, plants associated with specific deities or representing certain concepts or ideas could be grouped together. These lists served as quick references for practitioners, assisting them in selecting the appropriate plants for specific purposes, such as healing rituals, magical practices, or spiritual ceremonies.

The creation of botanical catalogues and lists in Babylonian society exemplified their meticulous approach to botanical knowledge. By organizing and categorizing plants based on their characteristics, uses, and associations, the Babylonians created valuable resources for practitioners and scholars alike. These catalogues and lists provided a foundation for further exploration and understanding of the natural world, allowing for the systematic study of plants and their diverse applications in various domains of ancient Babylonian culture.

Descriptions and Formulas

Botanical tablets in ancient Babylon served as repositories of detailed information about plants, encompassing various aspects that were crucial for their identification and utilization. The descriptions found on these tablets provided a wealth of knowledge regarding the physical attributes of plants. Babylonian scholars meticulously observed and recorded details about leaves, flowers, fruits, and roots, recognizing distinctive features that aided in the identification and classification of different plant species. By noting the shape of leaves, patterns of veins, and the arrangement of flowers, practitioners could discern specific characteristics that distinguished one plant from another.

Furthermore, botanical tablets provided insights into the growth habits and environmental preferences of plants. Babylonian botanists understood the importance of considering factors such as water requirements, light conditions, and suitable growing environments for successful cultivation. By documenting this information, the tablets enabled practitioners to optimize agricultural practices and enhance the productivity of plant cultivation. For example, understanding the preferred growing conditions of a specific plant species allowed farmers to select appropriate locations and provide necessary care, ensuring the successful growth and yield of crops.

Another significant aspect of botanical tablets was the inclusion of formulas for preparing herbal remedies. These formulas detailed the proper combination and preparation methods of plants to create medicines or potions with specific therapeutic properties. These instructions were crucial in the fields of witchcraft, divination, herbalism, shamanism, and other ancient Babylonian practices. For instance, a tablet might provide a formula for a salve used in witchcraft rituals or a decoction used in shamanistic healing practices. These formulas not only guided practitioners in preparing remedies but also ensured consistency and accuracy in their therapeutic applications.

By combining detailed descriptions of plants with formulas for herbal remedies, botanical tablets provided a comprehensive resource for practitioners seeking to harness the healing properties of plants. These tablets served as practical guides, enabling practitioners to select and prepare plants effectively for various purposes. The meticulous recording and transmission of this botanical knowledge played a pivotal role in the development of ancient Babylonian culture, encompassing a wide range of practices and beliefs related to plants and their therapeutic potential..

Challenges and Interpretation of Botanical Tablets

Challenges in Interpretation

The interpretation of botanical tablets from ancient Babylon presents a unique set of challenges for modern scholars. The passage of time and the inevitable degradation of materials over centuries have left many tablets fragmented, damaged, or lost entirely. As a result, scholars often have to rely on incomplete or partially preserved texts, which can hinder their understanding of the full scope of Babylonian botanical knowledge. Additionally, the decipherment of cuneiform script, the writing system used on these tablets, requires expertise and specialized training due to its complex nature.

One of the primary difficulties in interpreting botanical tablets lies in the language barrier. The tablets were written in ancient Babylonian languages such as Akkadian or Sumerian, which are distinct from modern languages. The linguistic evolution over thousands of years means that scholars must carefully study and analyze the grammar, vocabulary, and syntax of these ancient languages to decipher and translate the texts accurately. This process involves comparing the tablets with other known texts and using linguistic clues to unravel the meaning of unfamiliar words and phrases.

Moreover, the symbolic and metaphorical language employed in some botanical tablets adds an additional layer of complexity to their interpretation. Ancient Babylonians often used figurative language and allegorical expressions to convey concepts and ideas. This symbolic language, intertwined with cultural and religious beliefs, can be challenging to decipher without a thorough understanding of the cultural context in which the texts were produced. Scholars must draw upon interdisciplinary approaches, incorporating insights from fields such as archaeology, anthropology, mythology, and religious studies, to interpret the symbolism and metaphorical language present in the botanical tablets accurately.

To overcome these challenges, scholars engage in meticulous research and collaborative efforts. They combine their expertise in linguistics, archaeology, botany, and other relevant fields to decipher and interpret the botanical tablets. Comparative studies with other ancient texts, cross-referencing of similar themes and motifs, and the use of advanced technologies such as digital imaging and spectral analysis contribute to the comprehensive understanding of these ancient texts.

It is important to approach the interpretation of botanical tablets with caution and recognize the limitations inherent in the decipherment process. Due to the gaps in our knowledge and the subjective nature of interpretation, different scholars may propose alternative readings and interpretations of the same texts. This diversity of perspectives fosters scholarly discussions and debates, contributing to a deeper understanding of Babylonian botany and its cultural significance.

In conclusion, while the existence of botanical tablets provides invaluable insights into Babylonian botany, their interpretation poses various challenges. The passage of time, degradation of materials, language barriers, and the symbolic nature of some texts all contribute to the complexity of deciphering and comprehending these ancient tablets. Nonetheless, through interdisciplinary collaboration and diligent research, scholars continue to make significant strides in unraveling the rich botanical knowledge contained within these ancient texts.

The Role of Modern Scholarship

Modern scholarship plays a crucial role in unlocking the secrets of Babylonian botanical knowledge. Through dedicated research and interdisciplinary collaboration, scholars strive to decipher, interpret, and understand the information contained in the botanical tablets. Their efforts contribute not only to the academic understanding of ancient civilizations but also to the broader fields of botany, history, anthropology, and cultural studies.

One of the primary goals of modern scholarship is to decipher the cuneiform script and translate the ancient texts accurately. Linguists, philologists, and epigraphers work tirelessly to decipher the complex writing system and decipher the meaning of the symbols inscribed on the clay tablets. Their expertise in ancient languages, comparative studies, and meticulous analysis of linguistic structures are instrumental in unraveling the botanical knowledge embedded in the tablets.

Archaeologists and historians play a vital role in contextualizing the botanical tablets within the broader cultural and historical framework of ancient Babylon. They study the archaeological context of the tablets, such as the sites where they were discovered, the associated artifacts, and the broader historical context in which they were created. This contextual information helps scholars understand the purpose, use, and significance of the botanical tablets within Babylonian society.

Botanists and herbalists collaborate with scholars to identify and analyze the plant species mentioned in the tablets. By comparing the descriptions and characteristics provided in the texts with modern botanical knowledge, they strive to identify the plants referred to in the ancient texts. This collaboration between ancient textual evidence and contemporary botanical expertise allows for a more accurate understanding of the plants and their uses in ancient Babylonian society.

Furthermore, the interdisciplinary nature of modern scholarship fosters a holistic understanding of Babylonian botanical knowledge. Scholars from various fields, including anthropology, religious studies, mythology, and folklore, contribute their expertise to shed light on the cultural, religious, and symbolic aspects of the botanical tablets. This multidisciplinary approach allows for a comprehensive interpretation of the texts, considering the socio-cultural contexts in which the botanical knowledge was developed and utilized.

Modern scholarship also benefits from technological advancements that aid in the analysis and preservation of the botanical tablets. Advanced imaging techniques, such as high-resolution photography, multispectral imaging, and digital reconstructions, enable scholars to examine the tablets in greater detail, revealing hidden inscriptions and enhancing readability. These technologies not only facilitate the decipherment process but also contribute to the preservation and conservation of the fragile clay tablets.

In addition to deciphering and interpreting the botanical tablets, modern scholars engage in critical analysis and discussion. They explore different perspectives, challenge assumptions, and present dissenting opinions, fostering intellectual debates and advancing our understanding of Babylonian botany. Through conferences, academic publications, and collaborative projects, scholars disseminate their findings and engage in scholarly dialogue, contributing to the broader academic community and promoting a deeper appreciation of ancient knowledge systems.

In conclusion, modern scholarship plays a fundamental role in unlocking the mysteries of Babylonian botanical knowledge. Through interdisciplinary collaboration, technological advancements, and meticulous research, scholars strive to decipher, interpret, and understand the botanical tablets. Their efforts shed light on the ancient botanical practices, providing valuable insights into the cultural, religious, and medicinal aspects of Babylonian society. By bridging the gap between ancient texts and modern understanding, modern scholarship contributes to the preservation and appreciation of ancient knowledge, while also enriching our contemporary understanding of botany and human history.

The Relevance of Babylonian Botanical Tablets

The study of botanical tablets from ancient Babylon holds great significance in contemporary times, as it provides us with a window into the botanical practices and knowledge of an ancient civilization. These tablets offer a treasure trove of information about the identification, classification, and uses of plants, as well as their role in healing traditions and spiritual beliefs.

For modern practitioners in fields such as herbalism, witchcraft, shamanism, and ecospirituality, the insights gleaned from these ancient texts can be invaluable. They offer a connection to ancestral wisdom and a bridge between past and present practices. By delving into the botanical knowledge of ancient Babylon, practitioners can enhance their understanding of the properties and uses of plants, expand their repertoire of healing remedies, and gain a deeper appreciation for the interplay between nature and spirituality.

Herbalists, for example, can draw inspiration from the botanical tablets to broaden their knowledge of medicinal plants and explore new possibilities for herbal remedies. By studying the descriptions and formulations found in the tablets, modern herbalists can gain insights into the historical uses of plants and potentially discover forgotten remedies that can be adapted and incorporated into their own healing practices.

Similarly, practitioners of witchcraft can find inspiration in the symbolism and magical associations attributed to plants in the Babylonian tablets. The descriptions of plants and their ritual uses can provide a foundation for the development of spells, potions, and rituals that honor the ancient traditions while embracing contemporary perspectives.

Shamans and spiritual practitioners can explore the spiritual and metaphysical dimensions of the plants mentioned in the tablets. By studying the Babylonian understanding of plant spirits, energies, and their relationship with the divine, modern practitioners can deepen their connection with the natural world and develop practices that honor the wisdom of ancient Babylon.

Ecospirituality, which emphasizes the interconnectedness of all living beings and the sacredness of nature, can also benefit from the study of Babylonian botanical tablets. These texts provide insights into the Babylonian worldview, where plants were revered and considered integral to the fabric of life. By reflecting on the Babylonian reverence for nature, contemporary practitioners can develop a greater sense of ecological consciousness and engage in practices that promote sustainability and the preservation of biodiversity.

Moreover, the study of ancient Babylonian botanical knowledge serves as a reminder of the enduring human fascination with plants and their significance in our lives. It encourages us to cultivate a deeper appreciation for the natural world, fostering a sense of wonder and awe for the intricate web of life that surrounds us.

In conclusion, the botanical tablets from ancient Babylon offer contemporary practitioners a wealth of knowledge and inspiration. They provide insights into botanical practices, healing traditions, and spiritual beliefs of an ancient civilization, while also offering a source of guidance for modern practitioners in fields such as herbalism, witchcraft, shamanism, and ecospirituality. By engaging with the wisdom of our ancient predecessors, we can deepen our connection with the natural world, expand our knowledge of plants, and enrich our own practices. The study of these ancient texts invites us to embrace the wisdom of the past while forging a path of growth and innovation in the present.

Exercises and Critical Thinking

Select a specific botanical tablet from ancient Babylon and analyze its contents. Describe the plants mentioned, their properties, and their applications in Babylonian society. Discuss the significance of these plants in the context of witchcraft, divination, herbalism, shamanism, or ecospirituality.

Choose a modern botanical text or catalogue and compare it to a Babylonian botanical tablet. Identify similarities and differences in terms of content, categorization, and purpose. Discuss the evolution of botanical knowledge and classification systems over time.

Imagine you are a Babylonian botanist tasked with creating a new botanical tablet. Select a specific plant and provide a detailed description, including its physical characteristics, preferred habitat, and potential medicinal uses. Justify why you believe this plant should be included in the tablet and discuss its relevance in Babylonian society.

Debate the challenges and limitations of interpreting ancient botanical tablets. Discuss the potential biases, errors, or misinterpretations that can arise when studying these texts. Explore different perspectives and propose strategies to address these challenges effectively.

Reflect on the significance of ancient Babylonian botanical tablets in modern times. How can the wisdom and knowledge contained within these tablets inform and enrich contemporary practices such as herbalism, witchcraft, shamanism, and ecospirituality? Discuss the ethical considerations of incorporating ancient knowledge into modern contexts.

By engaging in these exercises and critical thinking activities, you will deepen your understanding of the role of written records and cuneiform tablets in documenting and transmitting botanical knowledge in ancient Babylon. Furthermore, you will develop a broader appreciation for the diverse fields where this knowledge finds application and its relevance in contemporary spiritual and healing practices.

➢ Oral Tradition and Knowledge Transmission

In the ancient world, before the advent of writing systems, knowledge was primarily transmitted through oral tradition. This method of knowledge transmission relied on the spoken word, where information, stories, rituals, and practices were passed down from generation to generation through verbal communication. The ancient Babylonians, like many other civilizations of the time, relied heavily on oral tradition to preserve and transmit their knowledge, including their understanding of witchcraft, divination, herbalism, shamanism, and ecospirituality.

The Importance of Oral Tradition

Oral tradition played a paramount role in ancient Babylonian society, serving as the primary means of preserving and disseminating knowledge across generations. Within this rich tradition, cultural, religious, and practical information was transmitted orally, ensuring the continuity of Babylonian wisdom and practices. Elders and experts, who possessed invaluable insights and experiences, played a vital role in imparting their knowledge to younger members of the community.

The transmission of knowledge through oral tradition fostered a sense of communal identity and cultural cohesion. It allowed for the preservation of customs, rituals, and beliefs that formed the foundation of Babylonian society. Cultural practices such as the observance of religious ceremonies, the performance of sacred rituals, and the recitation of epic tales were passed down orally, ensuring their preservation and perpetuation.

Religious and spiritual teachings were particularly significant within the realm of oral tradition. Priests, as custodians of religious knowledge, played a pivotal role in conveying divine revelations, sacred myths, and rituals to the next generation. The oral transmission of these teachings served to maintain the connection between the divine and human realms, as well as to uphold the religious traditions and beliefs of the Babylonian people.

Practical knowledge, encompassing various fields such as agriculture, craftsmanship, and healing arts, was also transmitted through oral tradition. Agricultural techniques, for instance, including planting, harvesting, and irrigation methods, were shared orally among farmers. Craftsmen imparted their expertise in metalworking, pottery, and textile production to apprentices through oral instruction and demonstration. Similarly, healers and herbalists passed down their knowledge of medicinal plants, remedies, and healing practices through oral teachings.

Through the oral transmission of knowledge, Babylonian society ensured the continuity and evolution of its cultural heritage. The elders, with their wealth of experience and expertise, mentored the younger generation, nurturing their understanding and skills in various domains. This intergenerational exchange fostered a sense of respect, reverence, and gratitude for the accumulated wisdom of the past, instilling a deep appreciation for the ancestral knowledge that formed the bedrock of Babylonian society.

Exercises:

Reflect on the significance of oral tradition in your own cultural or spiritual background. Consider how knowledge and traditions have been passed down orally in your community. What role does oral tradition play in maintaining cultural identity and transmitting wisdom?

Choose a specific aspect of Babylonian culture, such as religious rituals, craftsmanship, or healing practices, and research how oral tradition contributed to the preservation and transmission of knowledge in that domain. Discuss the specific examples or stories that exemplify the role of oral tradition in maintaining and evolving these practices.

Problems:

Investigate a dissenting opinion regarding the importance of oral tradition in knowledge transmission. Present the opposing viewpoint, providing evidence or examples to support it. Compare and contrast this perspective with the benefits of oral tradition discussed in this chapter.

Analyze the potential limitations and drawbacks of relying solely on written records for knowledge transmission. Consider the challenges posed by the absence of oral tradition in preserving cultural nuances, experiential knowledge, and embodied practices.

Understanding the significance of oral tradition in ancient Babylonian society enables us to appreciate the depth and complexity of their cultural, religious, and practical knowledge. It underscores the value of intergenerational exchange, communal wisdom, and the preservation of ancestral heritage. Exploring the role of oral tradition in knowledge transmission fosters a profound respect for the wisdom of our ancestors and invites critical thinking about the diverse ways in which knowledge is preserved and disseminated.

Challenges and Limitations of Oral Tradition

While oral tradition played a crucial role in knowledge transmission in ancient Babylon, it was not without its challenges and limitations. These factors must be taken into account when considering the accuracy, accessibility, and vulnerability of orally transmitted knowledge.

Accuracy and Consistency:

One of the inherent challenges of oral tradition lies in maintaining accuracy and consistency in the transmission of knowledge. As information was passed from one individual to another, the risk of errors, distortions, or alterations increased. Factors such as memory lapses, subjective interpretations, or personal biases could lead to variations in the transmitted knowledge. Over time, these variations might accumulate and potentially deviate from the original meaning or practice intended by the originators of the knowledge.

For example, in the context of botanical knowledge, the specific details of plant characteristics, medicinal properties, or cultivation methods could be subject to unintentional changes or misinterpretation. This could lead to discrepancies in the understanding and application of such knowledge, potentially affecting the effectiveness or accuracy of traditional healing practices or herbal remedies.

Limited Accessibility:

Another limitation of oral tradition is its inherently limited accessibility. Knowledge transmitted orally often remained within specific communities, lineages, or social groups. This restricted access to individuals who were not part of these circles, resulting in potential gaps in knowledge and understanding among wider populations.

For instance, certain specialized practices or rituals might be passed down only within a specific family or religious order. As a result, individuals outside these circles may have had limited or no access to the associated knowledge and practices. This restricted dissemination of knowledge could hinder the widespread understanding and application of certain traditions or practices, contributing to a fragmented understanding of Babylonian culture and limiting the potential for cross-cultural exchange and enrichment.

Vulnerability to Loss:

Oral tradition, by its nature, is vulnerable to loss. Societal upheaval, natural disasters, or the decline of specific cultural groups can lead to the disappearance of entire oral traditions and the valuable knowledge they encompass. When a community ceases to exist or when its traditions are disrupted, the knowledge transmitted orally within that community may be irretrievably lost.

For instance, the conquest and subsequent cultural assimilation of Babylon by other civilizations could have resulted in the suppression or erasure of Babylonian oral traditions, leading to the loss of valuable knowledge related to various fields, including botany and spirituality. Additionally, the passage of time and the absence of written records to complement or verify orally transmitted knowledge can further contribute to the loss or degradation of ancient wisdom.

In spite of these challenges and limitations, oral tradition played a vital role in the transmission of knowledge in ancient Babylonian society. It served as a living repository of wisdom, fostering a sense of cultural identity and communal cohesion. The knowledge transmitted orally formed the foundation for further exploration and development, inspiring subsequent generations to build upon the accumulated wisdom of their predecessors.

Exercises:

Discuss a specific example or story that exemplifies the challenges of accuracy and consistency in the transmission of oral traditions. Consider how variations or distortions in the transmitted knowledge might have occurred and the potential impact on the understanding or application of that knowledge.

Research an instance in history where the loss of an oral tradition resulted in the disappearance of valuable knowledge. Discuss the potential implications of this loss and reflect on the significance of preserving oral traditions in safeguarding cultural heritage.

Problems:

Explore a counterargument regarding the advantages of oral tradition over written records in the transmission of knowledge. Present the opposing viewpoint, providing evidence or examples to support it. Compare and contrast this perspective with the challenges and limitations of oral tradition discussed in this chapter.

Analyze the role of oral tradition in a specific field of study, such as herbalism, shamanism, or magic in ancient Babylon. Discuss how the challenges and limitations of oral tradition might have influenced the evolution and dissemination of knowledge within that field.

Understanding the challenges and limitations of oral tradition in the transmission of knowledge allows us to critically evaluate its strengths and weaknesses. It emphasizes the importance of multidimensional approaches to knowledge acquisition and preservation, including the integration of written records, archaeological evidence, and interdisciplinary research. By acknowledging these challenges, we can strive to overcome them and ensure the preservation and understanding of the invaluable wisdom embedded within ancient Babylonian oral traditions.

Complementary Relationship with Written Records

In ancient Babylon, oral tradition and written records were not mutually exclusive but rather existed in a complementary relationship. Each form of knowledge transmission played a vital role in the preservation, expansion, and dissemination of knowledge within Babylonian society.

Oral Tradition: The Primary Mode of Knowledge Transmission

Oral tradition served as the primary mode of knowledge transmission in ancient Babylon. Within this context, elders, scholars, priests, and practitioners imparted their wisdom and expertise to younger members of the community through spoken narratives, rituals, songs, and mnemonic devices. Through direct interaction and storytelling, individuals acquired the practical, spiritual, and cultural knowledge necessary for their respective roles in society.

The oral transmission of knowledge allowed for dynamic engagement, fostering a sense of community and continuity. It also facilitated the transfer of experiential knowledge, subtle nuances, and practical skills that might be challenging to convey through written records alone. Furthermore, oral tradition provided an opportunity for interpretation, adaptation, and improvisation, allowing knowledge to evolve in response to changing circumstances.

Written Records: Preserving and Expanding Knowledge

While oral tradition was the primary mode of knowledge transmission, written records, particularly cuneiform tablets, played a vital role in preserving and expanding upon the transmitted knowledge. The development of writing systems, such as cuneiform, enabled the recording of complex ideas, detailed descriptions, formulae, and other forms of knowledge in a tangible and enduring format.

Written records provided several advantages over oral tradition. They ensured the longevity of knowledge by allowing it to be captured and preserved in a more permanent and reliable manner. Unlike oral tradition, which is susceptible to memory lapses or alterations, written texts provided a stable reference for future generations. They allowed for the meticulous recording of precise details, including botanical descriptions, rituals, incantations, and other essential information.

Cuneiform tablets, made from clay and inscribed with wedge-shaped marks, became the medium for recording diverse forms of knowledge, including botanical wisdom. These tablets could be stored in libraries, treasuries, or archives, providing a centralized repository for accumulated knowledge. The dissemination of written records allowed for wider access to information, transcending the boundaries of specific communities or lineages. It facilitated cross-cultural exchange, trade, and the expansion of knowledge beyond individual oral traditions.

Moreover, the existence of written records complemented oral tradition by providing a reference point for subsequent generations. Written texts served as a foundation upon which new insights, interpretations, and discoveries could be built. Scholars, scribes, and practitioners could consult and expand upon existing written knowledge, adding their own contributions and further enriching the collective wisdom of Babylonian society.

Exercises:

Compare and contrast the strengths and limitations of oral tradition and written records as modes of knowledge transmission. Discuss the unique contributions of each and how they can complement one another.

Analyze the role of written records, such as cuneiform tablets, in the preservation and expansion of botanical knowledge in ancient Babylon. Provide specific examples of botanical texts or catalogues found on these tablets and discuss their significance in understanding ancient Babylonian herbalism and medicinal practices.

Problems:

Imagine you are a scholar studying ancient Babylonian culture. Outline a research project that combines the study of oral traditions and written records to gain a comprehensive understanding of a specific aspect, such as magic or divination, within Babylonian society.

Investigate the evolution of knowledge transmission in a different ancient civilization, such as ancient Egypt or ancient Greece. Compare and contrast the roles of oral tradition and written records within these societies, highlighting similarities and differences with ancient Babylon.

➢ Challenges and Limitations in Transmission

The transmission of knowledge across generations is a complex process that involves various challenges and limitations. In the realm of ancient wisdom, including fields such as Witchcraft, Divination, Herbalism, Shamanism, Ecospirituality, and Magic in Ancient Babylon, the transmission of knowledge faced unique obstacles. This section will explore the challenges and limitations inherent in the transmission of ancient wisdom, shedding light on the complexities that practitioners and scholars encounter when seeking to preserve and understand these traditions.

. Challenges in Transmission

Cultural Shifts and Societal Changes:

As the passage of time brings about cultural and societal changes, ancient knowledge faces the risk of being lost, altered, or forgotten. Cultures evolve and adapt to new circumstances, and belief systems undergo shifts as societies progress. This process can lead to the erosion or displacement of ancient practices, which were once deeply ingrained in communities.

One of the primary factors contributing to the loss or alteration of ancient knowledge is the emergence of new beliefs and practices that replace the old ones. As societies evolve, new ideologies, religions, and philosophies may gain prominence, leading to a decline in the relevance or acceptance of ancient wisdom. Practices that were once considered essential may be abandoned or replaced by newer rituals or beliefs that align with the changing cultural milieu.

Furthermore, cultural assimilation and globalization can also contribute to the dilution or loss of ancient knowledge. As different cultures come into contact and exchange ideas, elements of ancient wisdom can become assimilated into new belief systems or diluted to accommodate broader audiences. This process can lead to the fragmentation of ancient practices and a loss of their original essence.

In some cases, ancient knowledge may become misunderstood or distorted as it is passed down through generations. As communities adapt to new circumstances, the original meaning or purpose of ancient practices can become obscured or misinterpreted. Changes in language, societal norms, and cultural contexts can contribute to the misinterpretation of ancient wisdom, leading to a deviation from its original teachings.

Additionally, external factors such as colonization, political upheavals, or the displacement of communities can disrupt the transmission of ancient knowledge. The suppression or erasure of indigenous cultures and practices by dominant powers has historically resulted in the loss of valuable traditions and wisdom. The forced assimilation of marginalized communities can lead to the abandonment or concealment of ancient practices, further contributing to the challenges of knowledge transmission.

To address these challenges, it is crucial to recognize the importance of preserving and documenting ancient wisdom before it is lost or altered beyond recognition. Scholars and practitioners must engage in rigorous research, fieldwork, and cross-cultural collaborations to ensure the accurate recording and interpretation of ancient knowledge. Efforts should also be made to revitalize and reclaim cultural practices that have been marginalized or forgotten.

Exercises:

Reflect on a specific ancient practice, such as divination or herbalism, and analyze how cultural and societal changes may have influenced its decline or transformation over time. Discuss the implications of these changes for contemporary practitioners and their understanding of the ancient wisdom.

Research a case study where ancient knowledge was lost or significantly altered due to colonization or external influences. Analyze the impact of these historical events on the transmission and preservation of the knowledge, and propose strategies to reclaim and revitalize the practices within the affected community.

Problems:

Imagine you are an anthropologist studying the effects of cultural assimilation on a specific ancient practice. Develop a research plan to investigate the extent of assimilation and its impact on the transmission and understanding of the ancient wisdom.

Engage in a group discussion and debate the merits and drawbacks of incorporating modern elements into ancient practices. Consider the potential benefits of adaptation and innovation, as well as the risks of dilution or distortion of the original teachings.

Language and Interpretation:

Language plays a crucial role in transmitting knowledge, but it can also present challenges to accurate comprehension. Ancient texts and oral traditions are often conveyed in archaic languages that differ from modern linguistic conventions. These antiquated languages may contain unfamiliar vocabulary, syntax, and grammar structures that require specialized linguistic expertise to decipher and interpret correctly.

One of the challenges in understanding ancient wisdom lies in the linguistic complexities of the texts. The use of metaphors, symbolism, and figurative language can make the intended meaning of the teachings elusive without a thorough understanding of the cultural and historical context in which they were originally expressed. Metaphors and symbolism are cultural constructs that rely on shared knowledge and associations, which may have evolved or become lost over time. Thus, without a deep understanding of the cultural nuances and symbolic references, it is difficult to grasp the full depth and intended meaning of the ancient teachings.

Moreover, the evolving nature of languages presents another challenge to accurate interpretation. Languages are not static; they change over time due to cultural, social, and technological influences. As languages evolve, certain words may acquire new meanings or fall out of use altogether. This linguistic evolution introduces the potential for discrepancies in the interpretation of ancient texts. The same word or phrase may have had different connotations or shades of meaning in the past, making it necessary to carefully consider the historical context to ensure accurate comprehension.

Additionally, translations of ancient texts can introduce further challenges in understanding. Translating ancient languages into modern ones involves interpretation and decision-making by the translator, which can impact the fidelity of the original message. Each translator brings their own biases, cultural background, and linguistic understanding, which can influence the translation process. Consequently, different translations of the same ancient text may vary in their interpretation and presentation of the knowledge, leading to different understandings among scholars and practitioners.

To overcome these linguistic challenges, scholars and practitioners must engage in rigorous linguistic analysis and research. They must acquire expertise in the ancient languages used in the texts and oral traditions, as well as develop a deep understanding of the cultural and historical context in which they were produced. Comparative linguistic studies, interdisciplinary collaborations, and the use of multiple translations can help mitigate the potential discrepancies and enhance comprehension of the ancient wisdom.

Exercises:

Select a specific ancient text or oral tradition from a particular tradition, such as the Egyptian Book of the Dead or Norse mythology. Analyze the linguistic challenges present in understanding the text and discuss how linguistic expertise and cultural knowledge contribute to accurate interpretation.

Compare different translations of a well-known ancient text, such as the Tao Te Ching or the Epic of Gilgamesh. Examine the variations in language, tone, and interpretation among the translations, and critically evaluate their impact on understanding the ancient wisdom.

Problems:

Analyze a specific metaphor or symbolic element in an ancient text or oral tradition. Discuss its potential interpretations and reflect on how changes in cultural context and linguistic evolution may have influenced its meaning over time.

Form a study group and collectively examine the challenges of translating an ancient text into a modern language. Discuss the potential pitfalls and biases that translators may encounter and propose strategies to ensure accurate and faithful translations.

Transmission Gaps and Loss:

The passage of time can indeed result in transmission gaps, where portions of ancient knowledge become lost or fragmented. Numerous factors contribute to these gaps, hindering our comprehensive understanding of ancient wisdom.

One significant challenge is the physical preservation of texts. Ancient manuscripts, tablets, scrolls, and other written records are susceptible to decay, destruction, or loss over time. Natural disasters, such as floods, fires, earthquakes, or even simple neglect, can lead to the destruction of valuable texts. Additionally, the fragility of materials used in ancient writing mediums, such as papyrus or parchment, further increases the likelihood of degradation or loss. As a result, vast amounts of knowledge may be irretrievably lost, leaving gaps in our understanding of ancient practices, beliefs, and traditions.

Political turmoil and conflicts also contribute to transmission gaps. Wars, invasions, or societal upheavals can disrupt the continuity of knowledge transmission. Libraries and repositories of ancient texts may be targeted, resulting in their destruction or dispersal. The loss of central authority, the displacement of populations, or the decline of specific civilizations can sever the transmission chain, causing valuable knowledge to be scattered or forgotten.

Furthermore, the discontinuation of specific practices or belief systems can contribute to transmission gaps. As societies change, ancient practices and traditions may be replaced or marginalized by new ideologies or cultural shifts. For example, the rise of monotheistic religions in various parts of the world led to the suppression or abandonment of polytheistic belief systems. This transition often resulted in the loss of rituals, practices, and associated knowledge that were central to the ancient traditions.

Transmission gaps not only affect written records but also oral traditions. When a community or lineage ceases to exist or undergoes significant changes, the knowledge held within that group may be lost. This loss can occur through the death of key informants, the disintegration of cultural practices, or the assimilation of communities into larger societies. As the older generation passes away and the younger generation embraces new customs and values, there is a risk of valuable knowledge being forgotten or diluted.

To bridge these transmission gaps and deepen our understanding of ancient wisdom, scholars and practitioners must employ multidisciplinary approaches. Comparative studies, archaeological excavations, linguistic analysis, and cross-cultural investigations can help piece together fragmented knowledge and fill in the gaps. Additionally, collaborations between historians, anthropologists, archaeologists, linguists, and other experts contribute to a more comprehensive understanding of ancient civilizations and their practices.

Exercises:

Research a specific ancient civilization, such as the Mayans or the ancient Egyptians, and identify the transmission gaps that exist in our current understanding of their knowledge and practices. Discuss the possible reasons for these gaps and propose strategies to fill them.

Select a historical event, such as the burning of the Library of Alexandria or the fall of the Aztec Empire. Analyze the impact of these events on the loss or preservation of ancient knowledge and reflect on the implications for our understanding of the past.

Problems:

Imagine you have discovered an ancient artifact, but it lacks any accompanying texts or documentation. Develop a plan to investigate and uncover the potential knowledge and practices associated with the artifact. Consider interdisciplinary approaches and the collaboration of experts from different fields.

Form a discussion group and debate the significance of transmission gaps in the study of ancient wisdom. Discuss the potential consequences of these gaps and propose strategies to mitigate their impact on our understanding of the past.

Contextual and Cultural Limitations:
Ancient wisdom is deeply intertwined with the cultural, social, and historical contexts in which it originated. Without a thorough understanding of these contexts, the true essence of the knowledge may be challenging to grasp fully. Additionally, certain

teachings and practices may be culturally specific, making them less accessible or relevant to individuals from different cultural backgrounds.

Limitations in Interpretation and Application

Subjectivity and Bias:

The interpretation of ancient wisdom is indeed influenced by personal biases and subjective perspectives. When engaging with ancient texts, artifacts, or practices, scholars and practitioners bring their own cultural, social, and intellectual backgrounds, which can shape their understanding and interpretation of the material.

One aspect that contributes to divergent interpretations is the inherent complexity and ambiguity of ancient texts and symbols. Many ancient writings, such as religious scriptures, philosophical treatises, or mystical texts, often employ metaphorical language, symbolism, and allegory. These literary devices can be open to multiple interpretations, allowing individuals to find meaning and relevance based on their own perspectives. As a result, different scholars or practitioners may extract different insights or emphasize different aspects of the same text, leading to varying interpretations.

Furthermore, personal beliefs, values, and ideologies can influence the interpretation of ancient wisdom. Scholars may approach ancient texts through the lens of their own cultural or religious backgrounds, predisposing them to certain biases. For example, a scholar with a strong inclination towards ecospirituality may emphasize the ecological and environmental aspects of ancient practices, while another scholar with a focus on social or political factors may emphasize the socio-political dimensions.

Additionally, disciplinary biases can shape interpretations. Scholars from different academic disciplines may have distinct methodologies, theoretical frameworks, and research interests, which can influence how they approach and interpret ancient wisdom. For instance, an anthropologist may focus on the sociocultural context and rituals associated with ancient practices, while a historian may prioritize chronological analysis and political events. These disciplinary perspectives can result in different interpretations and emphasize different aspects of the same subject matter.

To address these challenges and strive for a more objective understanding, scholars and practitioners must engage in critical self-reflection and acknowledge their own biases. This self-awareness allows for a more nuanced interpretation and encourages the consideration of alternative viewpoints. Engaging in interdisciplinary dialogue and collaboration can also help mitigate personal biases by incorporating diverse perspectives and approaches.

Moreover, it is essential to employ rigorous research methodologies and analytical frameworks when studying ancient wisdom. Critical textual analysis, linguistic studies, comparative studies, and cross-cultural investigations can provide a more systematic and comprehensive understanding of ancient texts and practices. By examining multiple sources, considering various interpretations, and weighing the available evidence, scholars can strive for a more balanced and objective understanding of ancient wisdom.

Exercises:

Select a specific ancient text or artifact from a particular culture, such as the Egyptian Book of the Dead or the Aztec codices. Compare and contrast different interpretations of the material by scholars from different disciplines, such as anthropology, history, and religious studies. Analyze the potential biases and perspectives that influence these interpretations.

Reflect on your own cultural, religious, or disciplinary biases and consider how they might influence your understanding and interpretation of ancient wisdom. Discuss strategies to minimize the impact of these biases and promote a more objective approach to the study of ancient texts and practices.

Problems:

Analyze a controversial interpretation of an ancient text or practice, such as the debate over the meaning of symbolism in alchemical texts or the interpretation of magical spells in ancient Mesopotamia. Critically evaluate the arguments and evidence presented by proponents of different interpretations and form your own well-supported position.

Form a study group with peers from different academic disciplines or cultural backgrounds. Select a specific ancient wisdom tradition or text and analyze it from each participant's perspective. Engage in a dialogue to understand the diverse interpretations and learn from different disciplinary approaches.

Incomplete Information:

The fragmented nature of ancient texts and oral traditions is a significant challenge faced by scholars and practitioners seeking to understand and apply ancient wisdom. Over time, many ancient texts have been subject to damage, deterioration, or loss, resulting in missing sections or incomplete information. These gaps in the textual record can make it difficult to reconstruct the full extent of knowledge and understand the intricate details of rituals, spells, or healing techniques practiced in ancient times.

Missing sections in texts can hinder the comprehensive understanding of specific practices or concepts. For instance, a ritual text may have sections that describe the precise actions, gestures, or incantations to be performed, but if those sections are missing or damaged, it becomes challenging to grasp the complete procedure. This lack of information can lead to ambiguity or uncertainty regarding the correct execution of ancient practices.

Similarly, the absence of certain oral traditions or the discontinuation of specific practices can result in a loss of valuable knowledge. With the passage of time and the evolution of societies, certain rituals, ceremonies, or healing techniques may have faded away or been replaced by new practices. As a result, practitioners today may encounter gaps in their understanding of the original intent, purpose, or methodology of ancient practices.

However, despite these challenges, scholars and practitioners employ various strategies to address the fragmented nature of ancient wisdom and bridge the gaps in knowledge. Comparative studies, cross-referencing multiple texts and sources, and interdisciplinary collaborations can help in reconstructing missing information and filling gaps in understanding.

Comparative studies involve examining similar practices or concepts found in different cultures or time periods. By analyzing similarities and differences, scholars can infer missing information and gain insights into the broader context of ancient wisdom. For example, by comparing similar healing rituals performed in different ancient cultures, scholars can piece together common elements and practices, even if specific details are missing from individual texts.

Cross-referencing multiple texts and sources is another valuable approach to fill gaps in knowledge. By studying various texts and comparing different versions or variations of a particular text, scholars can identify patterns, recurring themes, or shared knowledge. This method allows for a more comprehensive understanding of the subject matter by synthesizing information from multiple sources.

Interdisciplinary collaborations are instrumental in addressing the fragmented nature of ancient wisdom. Scholars from different disciplines, such as anthropology, history, linguistics, archaeology, and religious studies, bring their unique perspectives and methodologies to the table. By combining their expertise and insights, interdisciplinary teams can contribute to a more holistic understanding of ancient practices, rituals, and knowledge transmission.

Exercises:

Select a fragmentary text or an incomplete oral tradition from an ancient wisdom tradition, such as a fragment of a magical spell or a partially preserved healing ritual. Analyze the available information and propose possible reconstructions or interpretations based on comparative studies or cross-referencing with related texts or practices.

Form a study group with peers from different disciplines, such as history, religious studies, and anthropology. Choose a specific topic within ancient wisdom and collectively examine multiple sources and texts. Discuss the challenges posed by fragmentary information and explore strategies to address these challenges in your research.

Problems:

Imagine you have discovered a fragmentary ancient text that contains references to a lost healing technique. Write a short essay outlining your approach to reconstructing the missing information. Include your methodology, the sources you would consult, and the considerations you would take into account when proposing a reconstruction.

Select a particular ancient wisdom tradition and research an aspect or practice that is known to be fragmentary or incomplete. Write a critical analysis of the challenges posed by the fragmented nature of the information and propose potential avenues for further research to overcome these challenges..

Cultural Evolution and Relevance:

Adapting ancient wisdom to contemporary contexts presents a unique set of challenges and considerations. As societies and cultures evolve over time, new frameworks, values, and belief systems emerge, shaping the way individuals perceive the world and approach spiritual or metaphysical practices. These changes may lead to a misalignment between ancient wisdom and modern perspectives, creating a need for careful discernment and adaptation.

One challenge in adapting ancient wisdom is reconciling it with modern scientific and empirical knowledge. Scientific advancements have revolutionized our understanding of the natural world, human psychology, and various phenomena that were once explained through metaphysical or spiritual concepts. Integrating ancient wisdom with modern scientific understanding requires a critical examination of both perspectives, seeking common ground and identifying areas where they can complement each other.

Another challenge lies in addressing cultural and social differences between ancient and modern societies. Ancient wisdom often emerged within specific cultural contexts and was deeply intertwined with the social, religious, and philosophical fabric of those times. Modern practitioners must navigate the cultural nuances and potential cultural appropriation sensitivities when exploring ancient wisdom from different traditions.

Additionally, modern ethical considerations may differ from those prevalent in ancient times. As societies become more inclusive and value-based, it is essential to critically examine ancient practices and teachings through a contemporary ethical lens. Some practices or beliefs may no longer align with modern values such as equality, consent, or respect for diversity. It becomes necessary to discern which aspects of ancient wisdom can be adapted or modified to fit within a contemporary ethical framework.

Furthermore, the language and symbolism used in ancient texts and practices can present challenges in their interpretation and application to modern contexts. Metaphors, allegories, and symbolic language that were deeply meaningful in the original cultural context may require careful analysis and contextualization to convey their intended message in a contemporary setting.

Despite these challenges, the adaptation of ancient wisdom to modern contexts can be a transformative and enriching process. It allows individuals to draw inspiration from the wisdom of the past and apply it in ways that resonate with their contemporary experiences and aspirations. Adapting ancient wisdom involves a balance between honoring the essence and core teachings of the tradition while recognizing the need for evolution, relevance, and inclusivity in modern society.

Exercises:

Select a specific aspect of ancient wisdom, such as divination or herbalism, and critically analyze its relevance and applicability in a modern context. Consider the challenges posed by societal and cultural differences, scientific advancements, and ethical considerations. Propose adaptations or modifications that align with contemporary values while staying true to the essence of the ancient wisdom.

Engage in a group discussion or debate on the topic of adapting ancient wisdom to contemporary contexts. Divide into teams representing different perspectives, such as traditionalists, modernists, and cultural historians. Explore the strengths and weaknesses of each perspective and engage in critical thinking and respectful dialogue to find common ground and potential solutions.

Problems:

Research an ancient wisdom tradition and identify a specific practice or teaching that may pose challenges in adapting to a modern context. Write a reflective essay discussing the ethical considerations and potential adaptations that could make the practice more inclusive and relevant while preserving its core principles.

Explore a contemporary spiritual or metaphysical practice that draws inspiration from ancient wisdom. Write a comparative analysis highlighting the ways in which the practice has been adapted or modified to suit modern sensibilities. Assess the effectiveness of these adaptations and discuss any potential benefits or drawbacks that may arise from the process of adaptation.

By examining the challenges and limitations in the transmission of ancient wisdom, practitioners and scholars can develop strategies to overcome these obstacles and preserve the knowledge for future generations. It is through this critical analysis and adaptation that the rich tapestry of ancient wisdom can continue to inspire and guide contemporary practitioners in their respective fields.

By exploring the world of Babylonian methods of identifying and categorizing plants, students gain a deeper understanding of the botanical knowledge and practices that shaped this ancient civilization. The exercises provided encourage students to engage in critical thinking, comparative analysis, and hands-on exploration of ancient botanical knowledge. As we continue our journey into the realms of witchcraft, divination, herbalism, shamanism, ecospirituality, and magic in ancient Babylon, we will uncover further insights into the multifaceted nature of this fascinating civilization.

B. Role of plant morphology and characteristics in classification

Introduction

Plant diversity is a vast and intricate tapestry of life that encompasses an incredible array of species, each with its own unique characteristics and adaptations. To make sense of this complexity and gain a deeper understanding of the botanical world, scientists and practitioners employ classification systems. Classification is the process of organizing and categorizing plants into distinct groups based on shared characteristics, enabling us to study, identify, and appreciate the diversity of plant life.

A. Understanding Relationships: Classification allows us to discern patterns and relationships among plants. By grouping plants based on their shared characteristics, we can infer their evolutionary histories and genetic relationships. This knowledge helps us unravel the intricate web of life and trace the lineage of different plant groups, shedding light on their evolutionary adaptations and ecological roles.

B. Taxonomic Organization: Classification provides a systematic framework for organizing plant diversity. It helps create a standardized language and nomenclature that facilitates communication among botanists, researchers, and practitioners. By assigning plants to specific taxonomic categories, such as families, genera, and species, we establish a common reference point for studying and discussing plants across different fields.

C. Conservation and Preservation: Classification plays a crucial role in conservation efforts. By identifying and categorizing endangered or threatened plant species, we can focus conservation efforts on preserving their habitats and preventing their extinction. Classification also aids in identifying and protecting plant species with economic, medicinal, or ecological importance, ensuring their sustainable use and conservation.

II. Significance of Plant Morphology and Characteristics in Classification

Plant morphology, the study of external physical structures and traits of plants, forms the basis for their classification. Morphological characteristics include features such as leaf shape, flower structure, stem texture, and fruit morphology. These traits offer valuable clues about a plant's evolutionary history, ecological adaptations, and relationships with other species. Examining and analyzing these characteristics helps us decipher the intricate tapestry of plant diversity and construct meaningful classification systems.

A. Diagnostic Traits: Plant morphology provides diagnostic traits that can distinguish one species from another. These traits, such as leaf arrangement, flower shape, or fruit type, act as key identifiers for different plant groups. For example, the presence of petals fused to form a characteristic shape may be a defining trait for a particular plant family, aiding in its classification.

B. Evolutionary Relationships: Morphological characteristics often reflect shared ancestry and evolutionary relationships among plants. Plants with similar morphological traits are likely to be closely related and share a common ancestor. By examining these shared characteristics, we can infer the evolutionary history and genetic relatedness of different plant groups.

C. Practical Applications: The study of plant morphology and characteristics has practical applications in various fields. For instance, in herbalism, identifying specific plant characteristics helps herbalists distinguish between medicinal and toxic plants, ensuring safe and effective herbal remedies. In witchcraft and divination practices, understanding the symbolism of specific plant characteristics may enhance the potency and efficacy of rituals. Plant morphology also aids in the identification and authentication of plants used in shamanistic practices or the selection of plants for ecological restoration in ecospirituality.

In the following sections, we will delve deeper into the relationship between plant morphology and classification, exploring the key morphological features used in classification, different classification systems, and the role of plant characteristics in identification. Through engaging examples, problems, and exercises, we will develop a comprehensive understanding of how plant morphology and characteristics contribute to our exploration and appreciation of plant diversity.

Exercises:

Visit a local botanical garden or natural area and select five different plant species. Observe their morphological characteristics and create a table documenting the leaf shape, flower structure, stem texture, and fruit type for each species. Discuss any similarities or differences among the species based on their morphological traits.

Research a specific plant family, such as the Asteraceae family (daisy family) or Lamiaceae family (mint family), and identify their key morphological characteristics. Create a visual presentation or poster highlighting these characteristics and their significance in the classification of plants within the family.

Problems:

Given a set of plant specimens, use their morphological characteristics to classify them into major taxonomic categories, such as families or genera. Justify your classification decisions based on the shared traits observed.

Explore the concept of convergent evolution and its implications for morphological classification. Provide examples of different plant species that have evolved similar traits independently and discuss how this phenomenon challenges traditional morphological classification systems.

By delving into the fascinating world of plant morphology and characteristics, we embark on a journey to unravel the intricate connections and stories woven within the botanical realm. Through our understanding of these fundamental aspects, we gain insights into the vast diversity of plant life and cultivate a deeper appreciation for the wonders of the natural world.

II. Plant Morphology and Classification

Definition and Significance of Plant Morphology

Plant morphology is the branch of botany that focuses on the study of the external physical structures and characteristics of plants. It encompasses the analysis of leaf shapes, flower structures, stem textures, root systems, and fruit and seed morphology. Understanding plant morphology is crucial for various disciplines, including witchcraft, divination, herbalism, shamanism, ecospirituality, and the exploration of magic in ancient Babylon. It provides a foundation for plant identification, classification, and the interpretation of their symbolic and practical applications.

A. Significance in Witchcraft and Divination: In the realm of witchcraft and divination practices, the study of plant morphology is an essential tool for discerning the inherent energies and magical properties of plants. It is believed that certain leaf shapes, flower structures, and seed formations carry symbolic meanings and correspondences that align with specific intentions or energies invoked during rituals or spellcasting. By observing and understanding these morphological features, practitioners can tap into the unique qualities of plants and harness their magical potential.

Leaf shapes hold particular significance in witchcraft and divination. Different leaf shapes are associated with distinct energies and qualities, allowing practitioners to select plants that resonate with their desired intentions. For example, plants with pointed or jagged leaf edges, such as hawthorn or thistle, may be associated with protection, warding off negativity, and strengthening boundaries. On the other hand, plants with heart-shaped leaves, like motherwort or violet, are often associated with matters of the heart, emotional healing, and love magic.

Flower structures also play a crucial role in plant morphology and magical practices. Each element of a flower, such as the petals, sepals, and overall arrangement, carries its own energetic properties. Practitioners can select plants with specific flower structures to enhance their rituals and spells. For instance, flowers with star-like shapes, such as those of the evening primrose or starflower, are often connected with celestial energies, cosmic connection, and divination. On the other hand, plants with bell-shaped flowers, like foxglove or bluebells, are believed to facilitate communication with the spirit realm and enhance psychic abilities.

Seed formations, too, contribute to the understanding of plant morphology in witchcraft and divination. Seeds represent potential, growth, and manifestation, and their forms hold symbolic meanings. Some seeds resemble coins, such as the round seeds of fenugreek or lotus, symbolizing abundance, prosperity, and financial success.

Others, like the wing-like structures of maple keys, represent transformation and the ability to transcend limitations.

By studying the morphological features of plants, practitioners can select and work with those that align with their magical intentions. For example, a witch performing a ritual to attract love and romance might choose a plant with heart-shaped leaves, such as rose or jasmine, as well as flowers associated with love, like rose petals or yarrow. These plants and their morphological characteristics are believed to enhance the energetic resonance and effectiveness of the spell or ritual.

Example Problem:

Select three different plants commonly used in witchcraft and divination. Research and describe the specific leaf shapes, flower structures, or seed formations of each plant. Identify the symbolic meanings and correspondences associated with these morphological features, and discuss how practitioners might incorporate these plants into their magical practices to support specific intentions or energies.

By employing the knowledge of plant morphology in witchcraft and divination practices, practitioners can deepen their connection with the natural world and harness the inherent energies of plants to manifest their desires, gain spiritual insights, and create transformative experiences. It is important for practitioners to study and understand the symbolic meanings and correspondences of plant morphology to effectively incorporate them into their magical workings and tap into the profound wisdom of the natural world.

B. Importance in Herbalism:Herbalism, an ancient practice that focuses on the therapeutic use of plants, heavily relies on the understanding of plant morphology to identify medicinal plants and their various parts used for healing. Herbalists recognize that different plant parts, such as leaves, flowers, stems, and roots, possess unique medicinal properties. By studying plant morphology, particularly leaf characteristics such as shape and venation patterns, herbalists gain valuable information about a plant's medicinal properties and potential therapeutic applications.

Leaf shape is an important aspect of plant morphology that herbalists consider in their practice. The shape of a leaf can provide clues about the plant's medicinal properties and guide herbalists in selecting the appropriate plants for specific health conditions. For example, plants with heart-shaped leaves, such as hawthorn or motherwort, are often associated with cardiovascular health and may be used in herbal preparations for supporting heart function or managing high blood pressure. On the other hand, plants with serrated or toothed leaves, like yarrow or chamomile, are commonly used for their anti-inflammatory and analgesic properties.

Venation patterns, which refer to the arrangement of veins in a leaf, also hold significance in herbalism. There are two main types of venation: parallel and reticulate. Plants with parallel venation, such as grasses or corn, are often rich in nutrients and can be used for their nutritive and tonic properties. In contrast, plants with reticulate venation, like dandelion or plantain, are known for their detoxifying and anti-inflammatory properties.

By understanding the relationship between plant morphology and medicinal properties, herbalists are able to create potent herbal remedies tailored to specific health conditions. They carefully select plant parts with the desired medicinal properties and combine them in various formulations such as teas, tinctures, or salves. For instance, if a herbalist wants to create a calming and sleep-promoting herbal blend, they might choose plants with fern-like leaves, such as valerian or passionflower, known for their sedative properties. Combining these plants with other appropriate botanical ingredients can result in a powerful herbal remedy to promote restful sleep.

Example Problem:

Research three medicinal plants commonly used in herbalism. Focus on their leaf characteristics, including shape and venation patterns. Describe how these leaf characteristics relate to the plants' medicinal properties and potential therapeutic applications. Discuss how an herbalist might incorporate these plants into their practice to create effective herbal remedies for specific health conditions.

By utilizing the knowledge of plant morphology in herbalism, practitioners can identify and harness the therapeutic potential of plants for healing and well-being. The understanding of leaf characteristics, such as shape and venation patterns, allows herbalists to select the most appropriate plants for specific health conditions and create targeted herbal remedies. This knowledge, combined with the wisdom passed down through generations, empowers herbalists to support the holistic health of individuals and communities through the gentle and effective use of plant-based medicine.

C. Relevance in Shamanism: In the realm of shamanism, the understanding of plant morphology holds significant relevance as it helps shamans identify and connect with sacred plants that play a vital role in their spiritual journeys, healing rituals, and communication with the spirit world. Plants are seen as allies and sources of transformative power in shamanic practices, and a deep understanding of their morphology allows shamans to navigate the spiritual realms more effectively and access the healing energies and wisdom they offer.

Specific flower structures, root systems, and fruit and seed morphology often hold spiritual significance in shamanic traditions. Shamans observe and interpret these characteristics to discern the energetic properties and spiritual qualities of plants. For example, certain flowers with intricate and vibrant structures, such as the lotus or peyote cactus flowers, are considered sacred and are used in shamanic rituals for their ability to open portals to higher realms of consciousness or facilitate visionary experiences. The unique morphology of these flowers, with their intricate patterns and vibrant colors, is believed to symbolize the divine and evoke spiritual connections.

Root systems also play a significant role in shamanic practices. The roots of plants are often associated with grounding, stability, and connection to the Earth. Shamans may seek out plants with deep and expansive root systems, such as ginseng or ashwagandha, to facilitate a stronger connection to the Earth's energies and aid in grounding during shamanic journeys or healing ceremonies. The morphology of roots, whether they are taproots or fibrous roots, is considered when selecting plants that align with specific shamanic intentions and rituals.

Furthermore, the morphology of fruits and seeds can hold spiritual significance in shamanic traditions. Shamanic practitioners may look for plants with specific fruit or seed structures that symbolize abundance, fertility, or spiritual transformation. For instance, plants with seeds enclosed in protective pods or fruits bursting with seeds, such as pomegranate or passionflower, are associated with fertility, creativity, and the cycle of life and death. Shamans may incorporate these plants into their rituals to invoke the transformative energies of birth, growth, and regeneration.

Example Problem:

Research three plants commonly used in shamanic practices. Focus on their flower structures, root systems, or fruit and seed morphology. Describe how these morphological features are interpreted in shamanic traditions and their spiritual significance. Discuss how shamans might utilize these plants in their ceremonies or spiritual journeys to facilitate healing, transformation, or communication with the spirit world.

The understanding of plant morphology in shamanism allows practitioners to identify and connect with sacred plants that assist in their spiritual journeys, healing rituals, and communication with the spirit world. By recognizing the spiritual significance of flower structures, root systems, and fruit and seed morphology, shamans can select plants that align with their intentions and invoke the transformative powers needed for their practices. The intricate relationship between shamans and plant allies deepens their connection to the natural world and enhances their ability to navigate the realms of spirit, healing, and personal growth.

D. Integration in Ecospirituality: Ecospirituality is a philosophical and spiritual approach that recognizes the interconnectedness and sacredness of all living beings, emphasizing the harmonious relationship between humans and the natural world. In ecospirituality practices, plant morphology serves as a valuable tool for deepening the practitioner's understanding of the intricate web of life and developing a profound connection with the plant kingdom.

By exploring leaf characteristics, flower structures, and fruit and seed morphology, individuals engaging in ecospirituality gain insights into the unique adaptations and ecological roles of plants. Leaf characteristics, such as shape, arrangement, and venation patterns, provide clues about a plant's photosynthetic capacity, water conservation strategies, and its interaction with the surrounding environment. For example, leaves with a waxy cuticle and needle-like shape, as seen in coniferous trees like the pine, are adaptations for reducing water loss in arid environments. Observing and understanding these morphological features allows individuals to appreciate the resilience and resourcefulness of plants in adapting to different ecological niches.

Flower structures play a significant role in ecospirituality as they represent the reproductive and life-sustaining processes of plants. By studying inflorescence types, petal arrangements, and the intricate details of flowers, individuals can gain a deeper appreciation for the diversity and beauty of plant reproduction. For instance, the complex and vibrant flowers of orchids are known to attract specific pollinators through their intricate shapes, colors, and fragrances, showcasing the remarkable co-evolution between plants and their animal counterparts. Exploring flower morphology cultivates a sense of wonder and reverence for the natural world, encouraging individuals to recognize the interconnectedness and mutual dependence between plants and other living beings.

Fruit and seed morphology further contributes to the ecospiritual understanding of plants. Examining the diverse forms of fruits and seeds highlights the plant's role in dispersing its genetic material and sustaining future generations. The various adaptations, such as fleshy fruits, winged seeds, or spiky coverings, facilitate dispersal mechanisms such as animal consumption, wind dispersal, or attachment to fur or feathers. By studying fruit and seed morphology, individuals develop a deep appreciation for the intricate processes of plant reproduction and the ways in which plants interact with their environment.

Through the exploration of plant morphology, ecospirituality practitioners foster a sense of reverence, awe, and stewardship towards the environment. Understanding the ecological roles and adaptations of plants enhances their recognition of the interconnectedness of all living beings and the delicate balance of ecosystems. It encourages individuals to approach the natural world with respect and responsibility, nurturing a deep sense of care for the environment and a commitment to sustainable practices.

Example Problem:

Choose a local plant species and observe its leaf characteristics, flower structures, and fruit or seed morphology. Reflect on the ecological roles and adaptations represented by these morphological features. Discuss how this knowledge deepens your understanding of the plant's place in the ecosystem and how it inspires a sense of stewardship and reverence towards nature.

In ecospirituality, the exploration of plant morphology enhances our understanding of the natural world and fosters a deep connection with plants. By delving into the intricacies of leaf characteristics, flower structures, and fruit and seed morphology, individuals develop a profound appreciation for the diversity and interconnectedness of life, inspiring a sense of stewardship and reverence towards the environment.

II. Relationship Between Plant Morphology and Classification

Plant morphology serves as the foundation for plant classification, which aims to organize and categorize plants into distinct groups based on shared characteristics. By examining morphological features, scientists and practitioners can discern patterns, establish relationships, and develop classification systems that reflect the evolutionary history and genetic relatedness of plants.

A. Clues to Evolutionary Relationships: Morphological traits play a crucial role in understanding the evolutionary relationships among plants. Similarities and variations in leaf characteristics, flower structures, stem textures, root systems, and fruit and seed morphology provide valuable clues about the genetic connections and shared ancestry among different plant species. By studying these morphological traits, scientists can construct phylogenetic trees, which are graphical representations of evolutionary relationships, to depict the evolutionary history and diversification of plant groups.

Leaf characteristics, such as shape, arrangement, and venation patterns, can provide important insights into the evolutionary relationships among plants. For example, plants with similar leaf shapes and vein patterns are likely to share a common ancestor and belong to the same plant family or genus. By comparing the leaf morphology of different plant species, scientists can identify patterns of similarity and divergence, allowing them to infer evolutionary relationships and classify plants into taxonomic groups.

Flower structures are another key morphological trait that aids in understanding plant evolution. The arrangement and structure of petals, sepals, stamens, and pistils can vary among different plant species. Similar flower structures across multiple plant species indicate shared ancestry and evolutionary relationships. For example, plants with similar inflorescence types, such as umbels or spikes, may belong to the same family. By examining the floral characteristics of plants, scientists can unravel the evolutionary history and diversification patterns within plant lineages.

Stem textures and branching patterns also provide valuable information about plant evolution. Certain plant groups may exhibit specific stem characteristics, such as succulent stems in cacti or woody stems in trees, which indicate shared evolutionary adaptations. Furthermore, the branching patterns of plants can reflect their evolutionary history and relationships. For instance, plants with opposite branching, where leaves or branches arise in pairs from the stem, are more likely to be closely related than plants with alternate branching.

Root systems, including the presence of taproots or fibrous roots, offer insights into plant evolution and ecological adaptations. The types of roots a plant possesses can provide information about its ability to access water and nutrients in different environments. Plants with taproots, such as carrots or dandelions, are adapted to penetrate deep into the soil, while plants with fibrous root systems, like grasses, have shallow and extensively branching roots. These root adaptations reflect the evolutionary responses of plants to various environmental conditions.

Fruit and seed morphology also contribute to our understanding of plant evolution. The structure and dispersal mechanisms of fruits and seeds can indicate shared ancestry and evolutionary relationships. Plants with similar fruit types, such as capsules, berries, or drupes, may be evolutionarily related. Similarly, the morphology of seeds, including their shape, size, and surface features, can provide evidence of common ancestry. By comparing the fruit and seed characteristics of different plant species, scientists can trace the evolutionary history and patterns of diversification within plant lineages.

By studying these morphological traits collectively, scientists can construct phylogenetic trees that depict the evolutionary relationships among plant groups. Phylogenetic trees illustrate the branching patterns of evolutionary lineages, showing the common ancestors and the relationships between different plant species. These trees serve as powerful tools for understanding the evolutionary history, biodiversity, and patterns of plant diversification over time.

Example Problem:
Examine the leaf characteristics, flower structures, stem textures, root systems, and fruit and seed morphology of three different plant species. Compare and analyze the

morphological traits to infer their evolutionary relationships. Construct a simplified phylogenetic tree based on the similarities and differences observed in the morphological traits. Discuss the implications of the phylogenetic tree in understanding the evolutionary history and genetic connections among the plant species.

The analysis of morphological traits in plants provides valuable insights into their evolutionary relationships. By examining similarities and variations in leaf characteristics, flower structures, stem textures, root systems, and fruit and seed morphology, scientists can construct phylogenetic trees that reveal the evolutionary history and genetic connections among different plant groups. This understanding of plant evolution not only enhances our knowledge of biodiversity but also informs fields such as ecology, conservation, and agriculture.

B. Diagnostic Features: Certain morphological features play a crucial role as diagnostic traits in distinguishing one plant group from another. Leaf characteristics, including shape, arrangement, and venation patterns, are often key identifiers used in the classification of plants into families or genera. By carefully examining the shape of leaves, their arrangement on the stem, and the patterns of veins that traverse through them, botanists and taxonomists can discern important taxonomic relationships and classify plants into specific groups.

For example, plants with needle-like leaves are typically associated with conifers, while plants with broad, flat leaves are often found in flowering plants. The arrangement of leaves on the stem, such as opposite or alternate, can also provide valuable clues about the plant's taxonomic placement. Additionally, the patterns of leaf venation, such as parallel veins in monocots or net-like veins in dicots, are distinctive features used in classification.

Flower structures are another set of morphological features that aid in determining the taxonomic position of a plant species. The arrangement and characteristics of the inflorescence (the cluster of flowers) can vary greatly among different plant families and genera. For instance, plants in the Asteraceae family commonly have inflorescences composed of many small flowers tightly packed together, forming a flower head, while plants in the Orchidaceae family often have unique and intricate inflorescence structures. By examining these inflorescence types, taxonomists can make informed decisions about the classification and placement of plant species.

The arrangement and characteristics of petals and sepals are also important in plant classification. The number, shape, color, and arrangement of petals and sepals can vary significantly between plant groups. These features can provide valuable information for identifying and differentiating plant species within families or genera. For example, some plant families have distinctive petal arrangements, such as the four-petaled flowers commonly found in the Brassicaceae family. Similarly, the shape and color of sepals can be characteristic of specific plant groups and aid in their identification.

By considering these morphological features, along with other traits such as stem characteristics and fruit and seed morphology, taxonomists can establish a comprehensive understanding of plant classification. The use of such diagnostic traits helps organize plant species into meaningful taxonomic units, enabling effective communication and study of plant diversity.

Example Problem:

Examine the leaf characteristics, flower structures, and other morphological features of several plant species, including a conifer, a monocot, and a dicot. Analyze the observed traits and provide a taxonomic classification for each plant species. Justify your classification by explaining the diagnostic morphological features used in the identification process.

By employing the diagnostic features of leaf morphology, inflorescence types, petal and sepal characteristics, and other relevant traits, botanists can accurately classify and identify plant species. This classification system facilitates the organization and study of plant diversity, enabling researchers to better understand the relationships and characteristics of various plant groups.

C. Practical Applications: The relationship between plant morphology and classification extends beyond scientific research and finds practical applications in various fields, including herbalism. In the realm of herbal medicine, where the use of plant-based remedies is central, understanding the morphological features of medicinal plants is of paramount importance. This knowledge ensures the accurate identification of plants and helps avoid confusion that may arise from similar common names shared by different species.

Proper classification is essential in herbalism to ensure the correct selection and usage of plants for therapeutic purposes. While common names of plants can vary regionally or even within a local community, their scientific names provide a standardized and internationally recognized system for identification. By examining the morphological characteristics of plants, such as leaf shape, flower structure, stem texture, and other diagnostic traits, herbalists can confidently identify the correct species and employ the appropriate remedies.

The precise identification of medicinal plants is crucial as different species often possess distinct chemical compositions and therapeutic properties. Even plants that share a common name may have varying chemical constituents and potential effects on the body. For instance, various plant species may bear the name "Echinacea," but their medicinal properties can differ significantly. By considering the morphological features unique to each species, such as leaf arrangement, flower structure, or fruit morphology, herbalists can accurately differentiate between them and select the most appropriate plant for specific healing purposes.

Misidentification or confusion of plant species can lead to the use of incorrect remedies, potentially resulting in ineffective treatments or adverse reactions. The incorrect usage of similar-looking plants may even pose health risks due to the presence of toxic compounds or unwanted side effects. Therefore, a solid understanding of plant morphology and classification is crucial in herbalism to ensure the safety and efficacy of herbal remedies.

Example Problem:
Examine two plant species commonly used in herbal medicine: Calendula officinalis (Marigold) and Tagetes erecta (African Marigold). Compare and contrast their morphological features, including leaf characteristics, flower structures, and other relevant traits. Discuss how understanding these features can aid in their proper identification and usage in herbal medicine.

By closely examining the morphological features of medicinal plants, herbalists can accurately identify and classify them, ensuring the safe and effective use of herbal remedies. The relationship between plant morphology and classification in practical fields like herbalism underscores the importance of precise identification and the potential risks associated with misidentification.

Key Morphological Features Used in Plant Classification

I. Leaf Characteristics

Leaf shape is a fundamental morphological characteristic that aids in the identification and classification of plant species. The diversity of leaf shapes across different plants allows for the categorization and differentiation of species based on this particular trait. By examining the shape of a leaf, one can gather important clues about the plant's evolutionary adaptations, ecological niche, and taxonomic affiliation.

There are various leaf shapes that botanists and herbalists use to describe and classify plants. Some common leaf shapes include lanceolate, ovate, palmate, pinnate, and lobed, among others. Each shape has distinct characteristics that can help identify and differentiate plant species.

Lanceolate leaves are elongated and taper to a point at the apex, resembling the shape of a lance or spearhead. Examples of plants with lanceolate leaves include willow (Salix spp.) and tulip poplar (Liriodendron tulipifera).

Ovate leaves are generally broad and egg-shaped, with a rounded base and tapering towards the apex. Many fruit trees, such as apple (Malus domestica) and cherry (Prunus avium), exhibit ovate leaves.

Palmate leaves have lobes radiating from a central point, resembling the fingers of a hand. The leaves of maple trees (Acer spp.) are classic examples of palmate leaves.

Pinnate leaves are composed of multiple leaflets arranged along a central axis, resembling a feather. Examples include the leaves of the ash tree (Fraxinus spp.) and the compound leaves of ferns.

Lobed leaves have deep indentations or divisions, creating lobes that give the leaf a distinctive appearance. Oak trees (Quercus spp.) are well-known for their lobed leaves.

Example Problem:
a. Identify and classify the following leaves based on their shape:

A leaf with a long and slender shape tapering to a point at the tip.
A leaf that is broad and rounded, resembling an egg.
A leaf with lobes radiating from a central point, resembling the shape of a hand.
A leaf composed of multiple leaflets arranged along a central axis.
A leaf with deep indentations or divisions, creating lobes.
b. Explain how understanding leaf shape can aid in the identification and classification of plant species in herbalism and botanical studies.

Understanding leaf shape is crucial in herbalism and botanical studies as it allows for the accurate identification and classification of plant species. Different species within the same genus or family may have similar common names, but their leaf shapes can provide valuable clues to distinguish them. For example, while there are several species of Echinacea used in herbal medicine, such as Echinacea purpurea and Echinacea angustifolia, their leaves differ in shape, with Echinacea purpurea having lanceolate leaves and Echinacea angustifolia having ovate leaves.

Leaf shape is also an important characteristic in plant taxonomy and classification. Botanists use leaf shape, along with other morphological features, to determine the relationships between different plant species and group them into families, genera, and species. It helps in constructing taxonomic keys that aid in plant identification.

In addition to identification, understanding leaf shape can provide insights into a plant's ecological adaptations and functions. The shape of a leaf can indicate adaptations to specific environmental conditions, such as drought tolerance or light capture efficiency. For example, plants in arid regions often have small, needle-like leaves to reduce water loss through evaporation.

Overall, leaf shape serves as a valuable tool for plant identification, classification, and understanding their ecological significance. By observing and analyzing the diverse leaf shapes in the plant kingdom, herbalists, botanists, and nature enthusiasts can deepen their understanding of plant diversity

II. Flower Structure

Inflorescence is a term used to describe the arrangement and grouping of flowers on a plant. The study of inflorescence patterns is essential in plant identification and classification, as it provides valuable information about the reproductive structures and strategies of different plant species.

There are several types of inflorescence, each characterized by a specific arrangement and branching pattern of flowers. Some common examples include umbels, racemes, panicles, spikes, and cymes.

Umbels are inflorescence structures where multiple flower stalks arise from a common point, resembling the shape of an umbrella. This arrangement is commonly seen in plants such as dill (Anethum graveolens) and Queen Anne's lace (Daucus carota).

Racemes are characterized by a central stalk with flowers attached along its length, each with its own stalk. Lupine (Lupinus spp.) and foxglove (Digitalis purpurea) are examples of plants with racemose inflorescence.

Panicles consist of a branched cluster of flowers, with each branch bearing smaller clusters or individual flowers. Plants such as oats (Avena sativa) and yarrow (Achillea millefolium) exhibit panicle inflorescence.

Spikes are elongated, unbranched inflorescences with flowers attached directly to the main stalk. Examples include the flowers of wheat (Triticum aestivum) and catmint (Nepeta spp.).

Cymes are compact inflorescences where the central flower opens first, followed by the lateral flowers in a determinate pattern. This type of inflorescence is commonly observed in plants like hydrangea (Hydrangea spp.) and baby's breath (Gypsophila paniculata).

Example Problem:
a. Examine the provided images of different inflorescence types and classify them accordingly:

Image 1: A cluster of flowers arising from a common point, forming a rounded shape.
Image 2: A central stalk with flowers attached along its length, arranged in a sequential pattern.
Image 3: A branched cluster of flowers, with each branch bearing smaller clusters or individual flowers.
Image 4: An elongated, unbranched structure with flowers attached directly to the main stalk.
Image 5: A compact inflorescence where the central flower opens first, followed by the lateral flowers in a determinate pattern.
b. Explain the distinguishing features of each inflorescence type and how they aid in plant identification and classification.

Understanding the different types of inflorescence patterns is crucial in plant identification and classification. By observing the arrangement and branching patterns of flowers, botanists can gain insights into the reproductive strategies and relationships between different plant species.

Inflorescence types help differentiate plants at higher taxonomic levels, such as families and genera. For example, plants in the carrot family (Apiaceae) often exhibit umbel inflorescence, while plants in the mint family (Lamiaceae) commonly have spike or cyme inflorescence. By recognizing these distinctive features, botanists can identify plants and place them within their respective taxonomic groups.

Furthermore, inflorescence characteristics provide clues about pollination mechanisms and adaptations. Plants with umbel inflorescence, for instance, may attract a wide range of pollinators due to the abundant and easily accessible flowers. On the other hand, plants with spike inflorescence may rely on wind pollination, as the exposed flowers facilitate efficient pollen dispersal.

In summary, the study of inflorescence patterns aids in plant identification, classification, and understanding reproductive strategies. By analyzing the arrangement and branching of flowers, botanists can uncover important insights into plant diversity and ecological adaptations.

III. Stem Characteristics

Stem shape is an important characteristic in plant morphology that contributes to the identification and classification of different plant species. The shape of a stem can vary widely among plants, and it is determined by factors such as growth habit, environmental conditions, and genetic traits. Stem shape, along with branching patterns and texture, provides valuable information for distinguishing and categorizing plants.

Cylindrical Stem: A cylindrical stem is rounded and smooth, resembling a cylinder in shape. This type of stem is commonly found in many herbaceous plants, such as grasses (Poaceae) and some annual flowers. The stems of grasses, for example, are typically cylindrical and flexible, enabling them to sway in the wind.

Square Stem: Some plants possess square stems, which have distinct sharp corners or edges. This stem shape is most commonly seen in plants belonging to the mint family (Lamiaceae), including herbs like mint (Mentha spp.) and sage (Salvia spp.). The square shape provides structural support to these plants and helps them withstand external forces.

Angular Stem: An angular stem has pronounced ridges or angles along its length. This stem shape is often observed in succulent plants, such as cacti (Cactaceae) and euphorbias (Euphorbiaceae). The angular shape allows these plants to store water and reduces surface area, minimizing water loss through evaporation.

Branching patterns and texture are additional characteristics that contribute to the identification and classification of plant stems. Branching patterns can vary from simple to complex, with some plants having a single main stem (monopodial branching) and others exhibiting multiple branches (sympodial branching). Texture refers to the surface characteristics of the stem, which can be smooth, rough, hairy, or covered in thorns or spines.

Example Problem:
a. Describe the stem characteristics (shape, branching, texture) of the provided plant specimens and classify them into appropriate categories:

Image 1: The stem is cylindrical, with no visible branches. It has a smooth texture.

Image 2: The stem is square, with multiple branches emerging along its length. It has a rough texture.

Image 3: The stem is angular, with prominent ridges and angles. It has a hairy texture.

b. Classify the plant specimens based on their stem characteristics:

Image 1: Cylindrical Stem, Simple Branching, Smooth Texture

This specimen exhibits a cylindrical stem shape with no visible branches. The smooth texture suggests it belongs to a herbaceous plant or a young woody plant with a relatively soft stem.

Image 2: Square Stem, Sympodial Branching, Rough Texture

The square stem shape, along with multiple branches, indicates a member of the mint family (Lamiaceae) or a closely related group. The rough texture may be due to small hairs or trichomes present on the stem surface.

Image 3: Angular Stem, Monopodial Branching, Hairy Texture

The angular stem shape with prominent ridges and angles suggests a succulent plant, possibly belonging to the cactus family (Cactaceae) or a related group. The hairy texture could be an adaptation for water conservation or protection against excessive sunlight.

By observing and classifying stem characteristics, botanists and plant enthusiasts can gain valuable information about plant identity and classification. Stem shape, branching patterns, and texture contribute to the overall understanding of plant diversity and evolutionary relationships.

IV. Root System

The root system of a plant plays a crucial role in its overall growth, nutrient uptake, and stability. Root systems can be classified into two main types: taproot and fibrous roots. Understanding the characteristics and significance of these root systems is essential for plant identification and provides insights into a plant's growth habit and ecological adaptations.

Taproot System: A taproot system consists of a single primary root that grows deep into the soil, serving as the main anchor for the plant. From the primary root, lateral branches, known as secondary roots, emerge. Taproot systems are commonly found in dicotyledonous plants, including trees, shrubs, and many herbaceous plants. Examples of plants with taproot systems include carrots (Daucus carota), dandelions (Taraxacum officinale), and oak trees (Quercus spp.).

The taproot system offers several advantages to plants. First, the primary root's deep penetration into the soil allows the plant to access water and nutrients from deeper layers, making it more resilient to drought conditions. Second, the taproot provides stability and anchorage, especially for taller plants like trees, preventing them from toppling over in strong winds or storms. Additionally, taproots can store nutrients and water, providing a reserve for the plant during periods of limited resources.

Fibrous Root System: In contrast to taproots, fibrous root systems consist of numerous thin and highly branched roots that spread out horizontally in the upper soil layers. Fibrous root systems are typically found in monocotyledonous plants, such as grasses, wheat (Triticum aestivum), and lilies (Lilium spp.). The primary root in fibrous root systems is short-lived and quickly replaced by a dense network of fine roots.

Fibrous root systems offer several advantages suited to the ecological needs of these plants. The dense network of fine roots enhances water and nutrient absorption from the shallow soil layers, allowing efficient utilization of available resources. The extensive branching also contributes to the plant's stability, ensuring it remains firmly anchored in the ground.

Example Problem:

a. Examine the root systems of various plant specimens and classify them as taproot or fibrous roots. Explain the significance of each type:

Image 1: The plant specimen exhibits a central primary root extending deep into the soil, with lateral branches growing horizontally. This is a taproot system.

Significance: The taproot system allows the plant to access water and nutrients from deeper soil layers, enhancing its resilience to drought conditions. The central primary root provides stability and anchorage.

Image 2: The plant specimen features a dense network of fine roots spreading horizontally in the upper soil layers. There is no clear central primary root. This is a fibrous root system.

Significance: The fibrous root system allows efficient water and nutrient absorption from the shallow soil layers. The dense network of fine roots provides stability and prevents soil erosion.

Image 3: The plant specimen shows a single dominant root extending deep into the soil, but with few or no lateral branches. This is a taproot system.

Significance: The taproot system enables the plant to access water and nutrients from deeper soil layers, offering resilience in drought conditions. The single dominant root provides stability and anchorage.

By examining and classifying root systems as taproot or fibrous, botanists and plant enthusiasts can gain valuable insights into a plant's growth habit, ecological adaptations, and nutrient acquisition strategies. The root system type contributes to the overall understanding of plant diversity and plays a significant role in plant identification and horticultural practices.

V. Fruit and Seed Morphology

The study of fruit types is an important aspect of plant morphology and classification. Fruits are mature ovaries that contain seeds and play a crucial role in the reproductive cycle of flowering plants. They exhibit a wide range of forms, each with its distinct characteristics and classification significance. Understanding fruit morphology aids in plant identification, classification, and the study of reproductive structures.

Berries: Berries are fleshy fruits that develop from a single ovary and usually contain multiple seeds. They have a soft or juicy texture and are often brightly colored to attract animals for seed dispersal. Examples of berries include tomatoes (Solanum lycopersicum), grapes (Vitis vinifera), and bananas (Musa spp.).

Capsules: Capsules are dry fruits that consist of multiple chambers or compartments, each containing seeds. They typically split open at maturity to release the seeds. Capsules can vary in size, shape, and texture. Examples include poppy capsules (Papaver somniferum) and the fruit of the hellebore plant (Helleborus spp.).

Drupes: Drupes are fruits with a fleshy outer layer, called the mesocarp, and a hard, stony endocarp surrounding a single seed. They often have a single, central pit or stone. Common examples of drupes include peaches (Prunus persica), cherries (Prunus avium), and olives (Olea europaea).

Nuts: Nuts are hard-shelled fruits that do not split open at maturity. They have a single seed enclosed within a hard, woody or stony pericarp. Examples of nuts include acorns (Quercus spp.), hazelnuts (Corylus avellana), and almonds (Prunus dulcis).

Seed Characteristics:

Seeds are reproductive structures that contain the genetic information necessary for plant propagation. Their morphology can vary significantly among different plant species and serves as a valuable tool for plant identification and classification.

Seed characteristics that can be used for classification include size, shape, surface texture, and the presence of appendages or structures like wings, hooks, or hairs. For example, seeds of certain plants have distinct patterns or sculpturing on their surfaces, which aids in identification.

Example Problem:

a. Analyze the provided images of different fruit types and seed characteristics. Classify them accordingly and explain the distinguishing features of each type:

Image 1: The fruit in the image is a fleshy berry. It is small, round, and has a smooth skin. It contains multiple small seeds embedded in the flesh.

Classification: Berry

Distinguishing Features: Small, round shape; smooth skin; fleshy texture; multiple seeds.

Image 2: The fruit in the image is a dry capsule with several compartments. It has a elongated shape and a rough, textured surface. It splits open to release the seeds.

Classification: Capsule

Distinguishing Features: Elongated shape; rough, textured surface; multiple compartments; splits open at maturity.

Image 3: The fruit in the image is a drupe. It is spherical with a fleshy outer layer and a hard, stony pit at the center.

Classification: Drupe

Distinguishing Features: Spherical shape; fleshy outer layer; hard, stony pit enclosing a single seed.

Exercises:

Select five plant specimens from different families and identify their morphological characteristics using a field guide or botanical resources. Classify each specimen based on the observed traits and explain the reasoning behind your classification.

Research a specific plant family and create a visual presentation or poster highlighting its key morphological features. Discuss how these features contribute to the classification of plants within the family.

By exploring the intricate world of plant morphology and understanding its role in classification, we unlock the door to a deeper understanding of the plant kingdom. Through careful observation and analysis of leaf characteristics, flower structures, stem features, root systems, and fruit and seed morphology, we gain insights into the evolutionary relationships, diagnostic traits, and practical applications of plants. This knowledge enhances our abilities in fields such as witchcraft, divination, herbalism, shamanism, ecospirituality, and the exploration of ancient Babylonian magic, enabling us to forge deeper connections with the natural world and harness the wisdom of botanical allies.

III. Classification Systems

A. Overview of different classification systems

Traditional Classification Systems

Traditional classification systems have been employed for centuries to organize and categorize plants based on their observable characteristics. These systems were developed before the advent of molecular biology and genetic analysis, relying primarily on morphological features and other visible traits for classification. One prominent example of a traditional classification system is the Linnaean system, created by the Swedish botanist Carl Linnaeus in the 18th century.

The Linnaean system introduced a hierarchical structure that organizes plants into progressively more specific categories, enabling a systematic approach to plant classification. This hierarchy includes the following levels: kingdom, division, class, order, family, genus, and species. Each level represents a different level of relatedness and shared characteristics among plant groups.

The Linnaean system revolutionized the study of taxonomy, providing a standardized framework for identifying and classifying plants. One of its most significant contributions is the implementation of a consistent and universal system of nomenclature. Linnaeus introduced the use of binomial names, where each plant is identified by a unique combination of genus and species names, often based on Latin or Greek words. This standardized nomenclature allows for clear communication and precise identification of plants across different scientific disciplines and cultures.

The Linnaean system remains widely used in botany and provides a foundation for plant classification. It serves as a common language for scientists, facilitating the exchange of information and knowledge about plant species. Moreover, the Linnaean system's hierarchical structure allows for the classification of plants into broader categories, aiding in the organization of vast amounts of plant diversity.

For instance, practitioners of Herbalism and Ecospirituality often refer to plants using their Linnaean names to ensure accuracy and avoid confusion. The use of standardized scientific names enhances clarity in discussions and helps in the proper identification of plants with specific medicinal or spiritual properties. By employing the Linnaean system, herbalists and ecospiritual practitioners can effectively communicate about plants and their associated characteristics, facilitating the sharing of knowledge and experiences within their respective fields.

In summary, traditional classification systems, such as the Linnaean system, have played a pivotal role in organizing and categorizing plants based on their observable characteristics. The Linnaean system's hierarchical structure, standardized nomenclature, and reliance on morphological features have greatly influenced the field of taxonomy and provided a robust framework for plant classification. Its widespread use ensures consistent communication and identification of plants across scientific disciplines and cultural contexts..

Phylogenetic Classification Systems

In recent years, phylogenetic classification systems have emerged as powerful tools for understanding the evolutionary relationships among plants. These systems, such as cladistics, incorporate not only morphological traits but also genetic data and molecular analysis to reconstruct the evolutionary history of organisms and establish their evolutionary relatedness. Unlike traditional classification systems, which focus primarily on observable traits, phylogenetic systems provide a more comprehensive understanding of the evolutionary dynamics of plants.

Cladistics, in particular, has gained prominence as a widely used phylogenetic classification method. It employs a principle known as shared derived characteristics, or synapomorphies, to group organisms into clades. Synapomorphies are unique, derived traits that are present in a specific group of organisms but not in their ancestors or other groups. By identifying these shared derived characteristics, cladistics allows for a more precise and objective classification, based on evolutionary relationships rather than subjective interpretations of morphological similarities alone.

Phylogenetic classification systems provide valuable insights into the evolutionary history and patterns of diversification in plants. By analyzing genetic sequences and molecular markers, researchers can construct phylogenetic trees that illustrate the branching patterns of plant lineages and the degree of relatedness between different taxa.

These trees not only reveal the common origins of plants but also shed light on the processes that have driven their evolution and adaptation to different environments.

The incorporation of molecular data and genetic analysis in phylogenetic classification systems has revolutionized the field of plant taxonomy. It has enabled researchers to uncover previously unrecognized relationships between plant species and revise existing classifications based on robust scientific evidence. Moreover, phylogenetic classification systems facilitate a more comprehensive understanding of plant evolution, helping researchers unravel the intricate web of connections among different plant groups and providing a foundation for further investigations into their biology and ecology.

It is worth noting that while phylogenetic classification systems offer numerous advantages, they also have their limitations. For instance, they heavily rely on available genetic data, which may be lacking for certain plant groups or species. Additionally, the construction of phylogenetic trees can be influenced by the choice of molecular markers and the methods used for analysis, leading to potential discrepancies in the resulting classifications. Nonetheless, phylogenetic classification systems continue to advance our understanding of plant diversity and evolutionary history, complementing the insights provided by traditional classification systems.

Example Problem:

a. Using a molecular dataset and cladistic analysis, construct a phylogenetic tree that depicts the evolutionary relationships between different plant families. Identify the synapomorphies that define each clade and explain their significance in understanding the shared ancestry of the taxa involved.

Exercises:

Compare and contrast the Linnaean system and cladistics in terms of their approach to plant classification. Discuss the advantages and limitations of each system.

Choose a specific plant group (e.g., orchids, conifers) and investigate the evolutionary relationships within that group using phylogenetic analysis. Present your findings in a visual format, such as a phylogenetic tree or cladogram.

Debate the importance of incorporating molecular data into plant classification. Discuss the implications of relying solely on morphological traits versus integrating genetic information in understanding plant evolution and diversity.

Section B: Application of Plant Morphology in Classification Systems

Use of Morphological Traits to Group Plants into Taxa

One of the primary applications of plant morphology in classification systems is the grouping of plants into taxonomic categories. Taxonomists, scientists who study the classification of organisms, utilize the morphological traits of plants to identify similarities and differences and determine their placement within taxonomic ranks, such as families, genera, and species. Morphological traits provide valuable clues about the evolutionary relationships and shared characteristics among different plant groups.

Leaf characteristics, such as shape, arrangement, and venation, play a significant role in the classification of plants. Taxonomists examine the shape of leaves, such as lanceolate, ovate, palmate, or lobed, as well as their arrangement on the stem and the pattern of veins. These leaf traits can be key identifiers in distinguishing plants within families or genera. For example, plants with similar leaf shapes and venation patterns may indicate a closer evolutionary relationship, suggesting a shared ancestry.

Flower structures are another essential aspect of plant morphology used in classification. The arrangement and form of flowers, including inflorescence types, petal arrangements, and sepal shapes, provide valuable information for taxonomists. Different flower structures may indicate taxonomic relationships, as plants within the same family or genus often exhibit similar floral characteristics. By studying flower morphology, taxonomists can categorize plants based on their reproductive structures and gain insights into their evolutionary strategies.

Stem shape, along with branching patterns and texture, is another morphological trait used in plant classification. Stems can have various shapes, such as cylindrical, square, or angular. The branching pattern, whether it is alternate, opposite, or whorled, also contributes to the classification process. Taxonomists analyze stem characteristics to determine the similarities and differences among plant species and assign them to appropriate taxonomic groups.

The root system of a plant, including the classification of taproot or fibrous roots, is also significant in taxonomy. Taproots consist of a primary root with lateral branches, while fibrous roots form a dense network of fine roots. The classification of root systems aids in understanding a plant's growth habit and ecological adaptations. For instance, many plants with taproots belong to the family Asteraceae, while plants with fibrous roots are commonly found in the grass family, Poaceae.

Fruit and seed morphology provide additional insights into plant classification. Fruits exhibit diverse forms, such as berries, capsules, drupes, and nuts, each with distinct characteristics. Seeds vary in size, shape, surface texture, and the presence of appendages. By examining these traits, taxonomists can distinguish plant species and group them based on their reproductive structures.

The use of morphological traits in plant classification extends beyond scientific research. In practical fields like Herbalism, understanding the morphological features of medicinal plants is essential for their proper identification. Different species may share similar common names, but their morphological traits allow for accurate classification, ensuring the correct selection and usage of plants for therapeutic purposes. This prevents potential harm or ineffective treatments and underscores the importance of accurate plant identification in herbal medicine.

Example Problem:

a. Identify and classify the following leaves based on their shape: lanceolate, ovate, palmate, pinnate, lobed. Describe the distinguishing features of each leaf shape and provide examples of plants that exhibit these leaf shapes.

Exercises:

Choose a plant specimen and examine its leaf characteristics, flower structures, stem shape, and root system. Use these traits to classify the plant into the appropriate taxonomic ranks, explaining your reasoning for each classification.

Compare and contrast the leaf characteristics and flower structures of two plant species from different families. Discuss how these traits contribute to their classification and potential ecological roles.

Investigate the seed morphology of various plant species and analyze the significance of different seed characteristics in terms of dispersal mechanisms and survival strategies.

Importance of Shared Morphological Characteristics in Determining Evolutionary Relationships

Shared morphological characteristics are key indicators of evolutionary relationships among plants. When multiple plant species display similar morphological traits, it implies a common ancestry and evolutionary history. These shared characteristics suggest that the species in question have undergone similar adaptations and may be linked through a shared lineage.

By examining shared morphological traits, scientists can construct phylogenetic trees, also known as cladograms or phylogenies, which visually represent the evolutionary relationships and interconnections between plant groups. Phylogenetic trees depict the branching patterns and evolutionary divergence of different lineages, providing a framework to understand the evolutionary processes that have shaped plant diversity over time.

Morphological traits, such as leaf shape, flower structure, stem texture, root system, and fruit type, are essential in constructing phylogenetic trees. Similarities in these traits among different plant species indicate a closer evolutionary relationship, suggesting a shared ancestry. For example, if two plant species have similar leaf shapes, it suggests that they may belong to the same family or share a common ancestor. Similarly, plants with similar flower structures or fruit types may be classified within the same genus or higher taxonomic category.

Phylogenetic trees are constructed based on the principle of shared derived characteristics, also known as synapomorphies. These are unique traits that are present in a specific group of organisms but not in their ancestors or other groups. By identifying and analyzing these synapomorphies, scientists can determine the relationships between plant species and assign them to appropriate clades or branches on the phylogenetic tree.

Advances in molecular biology and genetic sequencing techniques have enhanced the accuracy and reliability of phylogenetic classification. Scientists now incorporate molecular data, such as DNA sequences, into their analyses, along with morphological traits. Molecular phylogenetics allows for a more precise understanding of evolutionary relationships, as it reveals genetic similarities and differences that may not be apparent from morphological observations alone.

It is important to note that while morphological traits provide valuable insights into evolutionary relationships, they have certain limitations. Convergent evolution is one such limitation, where different species independently evolve similar traits due to similar environmental pressures, rather than through a shared evolutionary history. This can lead to misleading similarities in morphology, making it challenging to accurately assess evolutionary relationships based solely on morphological characteristics.

Nevertheless, the use of shared morphological characteristics remains a vital tool in determining evolutionary relationships among plants. By combining morphological observations with molecular data and other lines of evidence, scientists can construct robust phylogenetic trees that shed light on the complex history and diversification of plant life on Earth.

Example Problem:

a. Analyze the morphological traits of two plant species and construct a simplified phylogenetic tree depicting their evolutionary relationship. Explain the shared derived characteristics that support their placement in specific clades.

Exercises:

Choose a plant family and investigate the shared morphological characteristics that define the family. Construct a visual representation, such as a diagram or infographic, highlighting these traits and their significance in classifying plants within the family.

Research a group of plants known for convergent evolution, such as cacti and euphorbias. Compare and contrast their morphological traits, highlighting the convergent features and discussing the challenges they pose in determining their evolutionary relationships.

Limitations of Morphological Classification

While plant morphology provides a wealth of information for classification, it also has certain limitations. One significant limitation is the occurrence of convergent evolution, where unrelated species independently develop similar morphological traits due to similar ecological pressures. For example, cacti from different plant families have evolved succulent stems as an adaptation to arid environments. This convergence of morphological traits can complicate classification based solely on observable characteristics.

Additionally, morphological traits alone may not capture the full complexity of evolutionary relationships, as they do not account for genetic variations and molecular data. In such cases, phylogenetic classification systems that integrate genetic and molecular information become essential for achieving a more accurate understanding of plant evolution and classification.

Despite these limitations, morphological classification remains a valuable approach for plant identification and categorization. It serves as a foundation for understanding the diversity of plant species and their relationships, both within scientific research and in various practices and belief systems, such as Herbalism, Shamanism, and the study of Magic in Ancient Babylon.

In conclusion, plant morphology plays a crucial role in classification systems by providing insights into the relationships, evolutionary history, and diverse characteristics of plant species. Traditional classification systems, such as the Linnaean system, utilize observable morphological traits to organize plants into hierarchical categories. Phylogenetic classification systems, on the other hand, integrate genetic and molecular data to establish evolutionary relationships among organisms. While plant morphology is a valuable tool, it has limitations, such as the potential for convergent evolution and the need for complementary genetic and molecular analysis. By exploring these concepts, students will gain a comprehensive understanding of the importance of plant morphology in classification and its relevance in various fields of study, including New Age practices and ancient belief systems.

IV. Role of Plant Characteristics in Identification

In the vast realm of plant diversity, accurately identifying and classifying species is of paramount importance for various fields, including Witchcraft, Divination, Herbalism, Shamanism, Ecospirituality, and the study of Magic in Ancient Babylon. Plant characteristics provide essential clues for species identification, enabling practitioners and researchers to discern between different plants and understand their unique qualities. By examining key morphological features, such as floral morphology, leaf characteristics, stem and bark features, and fruit and seed traits, individuals can unlock the secrets held within the plant kingdom.

Use of Diagnostic Characteristics for Plant Identification

Floral Morphology:

Floral morphology plays a significant role in identifying different plant species. It involves studying the various features of a flower, such as its color, petal arrangement, shape, size, and the presence of reproductive structures like stamens and pistils. These characteristics provide valuable information for distinguishing between plants and understanding their unique qualities.

Floral color is easily noticeable and helps in recognizing different flower species. Colors can range from vibrant to subtle shades, each carrying symbolic meanings and energetic properties. For instance, in Witchcraft, specific flower colors are associated with particular qualities or intentions. White flowers may represent purity, while red flowers might signify passion or vitality. In Divination, interpreting flower colors can provide insights into the energies and influences surrounding a situation or individual.

The arrangement of petals is another crucial aspect of floral morphology. Petals can be arranged in various patterns, such as radial (actinomorphic) or bilateral (zygomorphic) symmetry. This arrangement is used to identify plant species. Herbalism practitioners, for example, associate specific petal arrangements with medicinal properties. A flower with five symmetrical petals arranged radially might indicate the presence of balancing compounds or qualities. On the other hand, a flower with a unique bilaterally symmetrical shape could be linked to specialized pollination methods or specific energetic properties.

Flower shape and size also aid in species identification. Flowers exhibit a wide range of shapes, from simple to complex, and vary in size from small to large and showy. In Shamanism, certain flower shapes or sizes are considered representations of spiritual beings or used in rituals to connect with specific energies or entities. Understanding the diverse range of flower shapes and sizes allows practitioners to align their practices with desired energetic qualities.

Reproductive structures, such as stamens and pistils, are important factors in floral morphology. These structures are responsible for pollen production and the fertilization of ovules, leading to seed formation. The number, position, and arrangement of stamens and pistils vary among plant species and provide valuable information for identifying plants and understanding their reproductive strategies. In Ecospirituality, observing and interpreting reproductive structures deepens the connection with the natural world and provides insights into plant life cycles and reproductive potentials.

Example Problem:

a. Examine the provided images of flowers and classify them based on their floral morphology. Identify the distinguishing features that aid in their identification.

Image 1: The flower displays bright yellow petals arranged in a radial symmetry. The petals are elongated and tapered, resulting in a star-like shape. The center of the flower contains numerous stamens and a single, prominent pistil.
Distinguishing features: Bright yellow color, radial symmetry, elongated and tapered petals, star-like shape, numerous stamens, prominent pistil.

Image 2: The flower exhibits a deep purple, almost black color and has a bilateral symmetry. It consists of five petals arranged in a distinctive lip or pouch shape. The center of the flower contains a single large stamen and a prominent pistil.
Distinguishing features: Deep purple color, bilateral symmetry, lip or pouch-shaped petals, single large stamen, prominent pistil.

By carefully analyzing the floral morphology of these images, we can classify the flowers and identify their distinctive characteristics. This exercise provides students with a hands-on approach to understanding the significance of floral morphology in plant identification.

Note: The examples and exercises presented in this section are designed to encourage critical thinking and foster discussions on the importance of floral morphology in fields such as Witchcraft, Divination, Herbalism, Shamanism, Ecospirituality, and the study of Magic in Ancient Babylon.

Leaf Characteristics:

Leaf characteristics play a crucial role in the identification of plant species. By examining features such as leaf shape, margins, venation patterns, and surface textures, one can gather valuable information about a plant's identity and its unique qualities.

Leaf shape is a prominent characteristic that varies significantly among plant species. Leaves can be narrow and elongated, broad and ovate, lobed, or palmate, to name a few examples. The diverse range of leaf shapes provides important clues for plant identification. In the study of Divination, leaf shape may be linked to specific symbolic meanings or used as a tool for interpreting signs and omens. Certain shapes may be associated with qualities such as strength, adaptability, or balance. By understanding the symbolism associated with different leaf shapes, practitioners can gain deeper insights into their divinatory practices.

Leaf margins, or the edges of a leaf, also contribute to plant identification. Margins can be smooth, serrated, toothed, lobed, or wavy, among other variations. These distinct margin patterns are observed in different plant species and aid in distinguishing between them. In Ecospirituality, the margins of leaves are sometimes revered for their unique characteristics, believed to hold spiritual teachings or represent the interconnectedness of nature. By paying attention to leaf margins, individuals can cultivate a deeper appreciation for the wisdom contained within the natural world.

Venation patterns refer to the arrangement of veins on a leaf. Some leaves exhibit parallel venation, where the veins run parallel to each other, while others have a netted or reticulate venation, forming a complex network of veins. Venation patterns are highly characteristic of plant species and can be used as a reliable tool for identification. In the field of Herbalism, practitioners often rely on venation patterns to identify medicinal plants and distinguish between species with similar appearances. The unique arrangements of veins provide valuable information about a plant's identity and its potential medicinal properties.

Surface textures of leaves also offer insights into plant identification. Leaf surfaces can be smooth, rough, hairy, glossy, or textured. These textures, along with other leaf characteristics, are utilized by botanists and enthusiasts to differentiate plant species. In Shamanism, for example, certain plants with specific leaf textures may be regarded as sacred or used in rituals to connect with particular energies or entities. By exploring the various leaf textures, individuals can deepen their understanding of plant diversity and the ways in which different species interact with their environments.

Example Problem:

a. Examine the provided leaf specimens and classify them based on their leaf characteristics. Discuss the significance of each trait in identifying the plant species.

Leaf Specimen 1: The leaf is broad, ovate in shape, with serrated margins and a smooth surface. The venation pattern exhibits a netted arrangement.

Distinguishing features: Broad ovate shape, serrated margins, smooth surface, netted venation.

Leaf Specimen 2: The leaf is long and slender, lanceolate in shape, with wavy margins and a hairy surface. The venation pattern shows parallel arrangement.

Distinguishing features: Long slender shape, lanceolate shape, wavy margins, hairy surface, parallel venation.

Through careful observation of these leaf specimens, we can classify them based on their distinctive characteristics. This exercise allows students to develop their skills in leaf identification and appreciate the significance of leaf traits in various fields of study.

Note: The examples and exercises presented in this section are designed to encourage critical thinking and foster discussions on the importance of leaf characteristics in fields such as Divination, Ecospirituality, Herbalism, Shamanism, and the study of Magic in Ancient Babylon.

Stem and Bark Features:

Stem and bark features play a crucial role in the identification of plant species. These characteristics include texture, color, presence of thorns or spines, and overall shape of the stem or trunk. They become especially valuable when flowers or leaves are not readily available for examination. Let's explore these features in more detail:

Texture: The texture of stems and bark provides important clues for plant identification. It can be smooth, rough, corky, peeling, or covered in hairs or bristles. By carefully observing and feeling the texture, one can distinguish between different plant species. In practices such as Witchcraft and Shamanism, the texture of stems and bark may influence the selection of plants for rituals or ceremonies, as specific textures can be associated with desired energetic qualities or symbolic meanings.

Color: The color of stems and bark varies across plant species. It can range from green to brown, gray, red, or even vibrant hues. These color variations serve as valuable indicators for identifying plants. In Shamanism and related practices, the color of stems and bark holds symbolism and significance. Different colors may represent different aspects of nature or correspond to specific spiritual intentions. By understanding the symbolic meanings of colors, practitioners can deepen their connection with plants and enhance their spiritual practices.

Thorns and Spines: Many plants possess thorns or spines on their stems. These structures serve as adaptations for defense against herbivores or as aids for climbing. The presence or absence of thorns or spines can aid in the identification of plant species. In the context of Shamanism and other belief systems, certain plants with thorns or spines may be utilized for protective purposes or to establish energetic boundaries during rituals. The unique characteristics of these structures add depth to the practitioner's understanding and interaction with the plant realm.

Overall Shape: The overall shape of stems and trunks refers to their form and growth habit. Stems can be erect, trailing, climbing, or exhibit specific growth patterns. Understanding the growth habits and overall shape of stems contributes to the identification of plant species. In the field of Herbalism, knowledge of stem shapes assists in differentiating medicinal plants with similar foliage. Familiarity with the growth habits and overall shape of stems enables the proper identification and utilization of plant species.

Example Problem:

a. Analyze the provided stem and bark samples and classify them based on their distinctive features. Explain the significance of each trait in the identification process.

Stem and Bark Sample 1: The stem is rough and covered in fine hairs, while the bark peels off in thin strips. The color is grayish-brown.

Distinguishing features: Rough texture, fine hairs, peeling bark, grayish-brown color.

Stem and Bark Sample 2: The stem is smooth and adorned with long, sharp thorns evenly distributed along its length. The bark has a dark brown color with deep furrows.

Distinguishing features: Smooth texture, long sharp thorns, dark brown bark, deep furrows.

By carefully examining these stem and bark samples, you can classify them based on their distinct features and discuss the significance of each trait in the identification process. This exercise promotes critical thinking and cultivates an appreciation for the role of stem and bark characteristics in various practices, such as Witchcraft, Shamanism, and the study of Magic in Ancient Babylon.

Note: The examples and exercises provided aim to engage you in active learning and facilitate discussions on the importance of stem and bark features in plant identification within different fields of study.

Fruit and Seed Traits:

Fruit and seed traits provide valuable insights into the identification of plant species. These characteristics include size, shape, color, and dispersal mechanisms. Let's explore the significance of fruit and seed traits in plant identification and their applications in different fields:

Size: The size of fruits and seeds can vary greatly among different plant species. Some plants produce large, conspicuous fruits or seeds, while others have smaller ones. By examining the size of fruits and seeds, practitioners and researchers can differentiate between plant species and gain insights into their life cycles and ecological roles. In the realm of Herbalism, the size of fruits and seeds may indicate the readiness and potency of medicinal plant material. It helps Herbalists determine the appropriate time for harvesting and utilizing plants for therapeutic purposes.

Shape: The shape of fruits and seeds is another distinguishing characteristic. They can be round, elongated, flattened, or have unique structures. Different plant species exhibit distinct shapes, aiding in their identification. In the study of Magic in Ancient Babylon, seeds with specific shapes may hold symbolic meanings and be utilized in magical rituals or incorporated into talismans. The shape of fruits and seeds contributes to the symbolism and energy associated with these practices.

Color: Fruits and seeds come in a wide array of colors, ranging from vibrant and eye-catching to more subdued hues. The color of fruits and seeds is influenced by pigments and serves as an important characteristic for identification. By observing and comparing the colors of fruits and seeds, practitioners and researchers can differentiate between plant species. In various fields, such as Herbalism, specific colors may be associated with certain properties or energetic qualities of plants, guiding their selection and use in rituals or remedies.

Dispersal Mechanisms: Plants have evolved various mechanisms to disperse their fruits and seeds, ensuring the survival and propagation of their species. Dispersal can occur through wind, water, animals, or mechanical means. The presence of structures or adaptations for dispersal can aid in plant identification. Understanding dispersal mechanisms is crucial in fields like Ecology and Botany, as it provides insights into plant adaptations and ecological interactions. It also guides the selection of appropriate plant species for ecological restoration or landscaping projects.

Example Problem:

a. Examine the provided images of fruits and seeds and classify them based on their distinctive traits. Discuss the significance of each characteristic in plant identification and their potential uses in different fields.

Fruit and Seed Sample 1: The fruit is small and spherical with a bright red color. The seeds are tiny and dark brown.

Distinguishing features: Small and spherical fruit, bright red color, tiny and dark brown seeds.

Fruit and Seed Sample 2: The fruit is elongated and segmented, resembling a capsule. The seeds are numerous, flat, and have a white feathery appendage for wind dispersal.

Distinguishing features: Elongated and segmented fruit, numerous flat seeds, white feathery appendage.

By carefully examining these fruit and seed samples, you can classify them based on their distinctive traits and discuss the significance of each characteristic in plant identification and their potential uses in different fields. This exercise promotes critical thinking and encourages students to explore the multifaceted applications of fruit and seed traits in disciplines such as Herbalism, Shamanism, Ecology, and the study of Magic in Ancient Babylon.

Role of Plant Characteristics in Field Identification and Botanical Keys

Plant characteristics play a crucial role in field identification, allowing individuals to identify species directly in their natural habitats. Field guides and botanical keys are valuable resources that aid in this process. They provide detailed descriptions and illustrations of plant characteristics, enabling users to navigate the diverse world of plants. These resources utilize a combination of morphological traits, often focusing on easily observable features, to guide individuals through the identification process.

Field guides are comprehensive references that contain information about various plant species found in specific regions or ecosystems. They provide descriptions of plant characteristics such as floral morphology, leaf traits, stem and bark features, and fruit and seed traits. These guides are often organized in a user-friendly manner, allowing users to quickly access relevant information and compare it with the plants they encounter in the field.

Botanical keys are tools designed to facilitate the identification of plants based on their characteristics. They consist of a series of dichotomous choices that lead users to the correct identification. Each choice presents a pair of contrasting characteristics, and users select the option that best matches the plant they are trying to identify. By systematically progressing through these choices, users arrive at the correct identification of the plant species. Botanical keys often highlight key diagnostic features that distinguish one species from another, making the identification process more efficient and accurate.

Example Exercise:

a. Using a botanical key or field guide, identify five plant species based on their floral morphology, leaf characteristics, stem and bark features, or fruit and seed traits. Describe the specific diagnostic features used for each identification.

Plant Species A:

Diagnostic Features: The flowers are yellow with a tubular shape and arranged in clusters. The leaves are lanceolate with serrated margins, and the stems have thorns.

Plant Species B:

Diagnostic Features: The flowers are purple and bell-shaped with a distinctive floral scent. The leaves are heart-shaped with smooth margins, and the stems are smooth and green.

Plant Species C:

Diagnostic Features: The fruits are small, round berries with a bright red color. The leaves are compound with serrated leaflets, and the bark is smooth and gray.

Plant Species D:

Diagnostic Features: The flowers are white and star-shaped, arranged in umbels. The leaves are palmately lobed with toothed margins, and the stems have a reddish-brown color.

Plant Species E:

Diagnostic Features: The seeds are enclosed in a dry, elongated capsule. The leaves are needle-like and arranged in clusters, and the bark is rough and fibrous.

By engaging with botanical keys and field guides, students can develop their skills in plant identification. This exercise challenges students to utilize their knowledge of plant characteristics and apply them in real-world scenarios. It encourages critical thinking and observation skills, allowing students to deepen their understanding of plant diversity and the importance of specific diagnostic features for accurate identification.

Through these exercises, students can appreciate the significance of plant characteristics in various fields and belief systems, such as Witchcraft, Divination, Herbalism, Shamanism, Ecospirituality, and the study of Magic in Ancient Babylon. The ability to identify plants in their natural habitats enhances our connection to the natural world and opens up a world of exploration and discovery.

C. Examples of commonly known medicinal plants in Babylon

III. Medicinal Properties and Uses of Plants

A. Understanding the therapeutic properties of plants in Babylonian medicine

In the ancient civilization of Babylon, plants held great importance in the practice of medicine. The Babylonians believed that the natural world contained valuable healing properties, and their medical system heavily relied on plants for treating various ailments. This chapter delves into the understanding of plant-based healing in Babylonian medicine, examining their historical context, the role of plants, and specific examples of plant-based remedies.

Section 1: Historical Context of Babylonian Medicine

Ancient Babylonian Medicine:'

Ancient Babylonian medicine was a sophisticated and comprehensive system of healing that emerged in the region known as Mesopotamia, now modern-day Iraq, during the third millennium BCE. It was influenced by the rich cultural and intellectual traditions of the Babylonian civilization, which flourished along the banks of the Tigris and Euphrates rivers. Babylonian medicine encompassed a wide range of healing practices, including herbal medicine, and demonstrated an advanced understanding of the therapeutic properties of plants.

The Babylonians believed in the interconnectedness of the natural world and human health, viewing illness as a disruption of harmony within the body. To restore balance and promote healing, Babylonian physicians utilized a combination of spiritual, magical, and empirical approaches. Their medical knowledge was documented in cuneiform tablets, which provided detailed instructions on diagnosis, treatment, and prescriptions.

Within the Babylonian medical system, plants held a central role as sources of medicinal remedies. The Babylonians recognized the diverse therapeutic properties that different plants possessed, and they carefully observed and recorded the effects of various botanical substances on the human body. This profound understanding of the medicinal potential of plants laid the foundation for the development of herbal remedies in Babylonian medicine.

The knowledge of plant-based medicine in ancient Babylon was acquired through empirical observation, experimentation, and the accumulation of practical wisdom passed down through generations. Babylonian physicians carefully studied the characteristics, habitats, and growth patterns of plants, considering these factors in the diagnosis and treatment of diseases. They believed that specific plants held the power to alleviate symptoms and restore health.

The use of herbal remedies in Babylonian medicine was not limited to treating physical ailments alone. The Babylonians recognized the interconnectedness of the body, mind, and spirit, and understood the importance of holistic healing. Therefore, plants were also employed to address psychological and spiritual afflictions, as well as to promote overall well-being.

By incorporating a wide range of botanical substances into their medical practices, Babylonian physicians developed a repertoire of herbal remedies for various ailments. These remedies included plant-based potions, poultices, ointments, and teas, carefully prepared to extract the medicinal properties of the plants. The efficacy of these remedies was often enhanced through the combination of different plant substances and the addition of other natural ingredients.

The understanding of the therapeutic properties of plants in Babylonian medicine not only contributed to the treatment of diseases but also played a significant role in the cultural and spiritual aspects of Babylonian society. Plants were associated with deities and spiritual forces, and their use in healing rituals and ceremonies was considered a sacred practice.

Overall, the integration of herbal medicine in ancient Babylonian medicine reflects the Babylonians' deep appreciation for the natural world and their recognition of the healing potential that plants possess. This knowledge and understanding continue to resonate in various contemporary belief systems, including Witchcraft, Divination, Herbalism, Shamanism, and Ecospirituality, where plants are revered for their medicinal and spiritual properties. By studying the ancient Babylonian approach to plant-based healing, students can gain a profound appreciation for the historical and cultural significance of herbal medicine and its enduring relevance in different fields of study.

Evidence of Plant-Based Healing:

Cuneiform tablets, unearthed in the ancient region of Mesopotamia, provide a remarkable window into the medical practices of the Babylonians. These texts, including notable works such as the "Diagnostic Handbook" and the "Therapeutic Handbook," offer valuable insights into the extensive use of plants within Babylonian medicine. The tablets serve as a testament to the meticulous recording and preservation of medical knowledge by ancient scribes.

The Diagnostic Handbook, written in the ancient Akkadian language, outlines the diagnostic methods employed by Babylonian physicians. It describes various symptoms and their interpretations, providing a framework for understanding diseases and their causes. This text emphasizes the importance of careful observation and examination, highlighting the vital role of plant-based therapies in restoring health.

The Therapeutic Handbook, another essential Babylonian medical text, offers detailed instructions on the use of plants in the treatment of specific ailments. It provides a comprehensive list of medicinal plants, along with their preparations and dosages, showcasing the Babylonians' extensive knowledge of botanical remedies. The text includes descriptions of plants such as juniper, licorice, coriander, and myrrh, indicating their use in addressing a wide range of medical conditions.

These cuneiform tablets reveal that the Babylonians recognized the therapeutic potential of numerous plants and understood the importance of selecting the appropriate botanical substances for specific diseases. For example, they prescribed the use of willow bark, which contains salicylates, as an analgesic for pain relief—a precursor to modern-day aspirin. The Babylonians also employed aromatic plants like thyme and cypress for their antiseptic properties in treating infections and wounds.

Moreover, the Babylonians attributed certain plants with magical and spiritual qualities. They believed that incantations and rituals, combined with the use of specific plants, could invoke the assistance of deities or spiritual forces to aid in the healing process. This blending of medical and spiritual practices is exemplified in the incorporation of plants such as frankincense and myrrh in rituals associated with purifying spaces and promoting spiritual well-being.

The meticulous documentation of plant-based remedies in cuneiform tablets provides valuable insights into the medicinal practices of ancient Babylonian society. These texts demonstrate a comprehensive understanding of plant properties and their applications in treating a diverse array of ailments. The knowledge preserved in these tablets has influenced various fields of study, including modern Herbalism and the exploration of plant-based therapies in complementary and alternative medicine.

Example Exercise:

a. Translate and analyze excerpts from a cuneiform tablet describing the use of plants in Babylonian medicine. Discuss the significance of these botanical remedies and their potential therapeutic applications in the context of modern herbal medicine.

By delving into the historical roots of Babylonian medicine and exploring the use of plants in healing practices, students gain a deeper appreciation for the ancient wisdom that continues to shape contemporary approaches to herbal medicine. Understanding the therapeutic properties of plants in ancient Babylonian medicine allows students to critically evaluate the historical, cultural, and scientific aspects of botanical remedies and their enduring relevance in different fields of study.

Section 2: The Significance of Plants in Babylonian Medicine

Identification and Classification of Medicinal Plants:

Babylonian physicians possessed a profound understanding of plants, which they acquired through meticulous observation, classification, and documentation. They recognized that plants exhibited distinct physical characteristics, growth patterns, and geographical distributions that could provide valuable insights into their medicinal properties. This knowledge allowed them to diagnose illnesses and prescribe appropriate treatments based on their understanding of plants' therapeutic qualities.

Babylonian physicians carefully observed the external features of plants, such as their leaves, stems, flowers, and fruits, noting variations in color, shape, texture, and size. By documenting these characteristics, they could identify specific plant species and correlate them with their medicinal properties. For example, they might have recognized that plants with specific leaf shapes or flower colors were associated with particular healing properties. This observation-based approach formed the foundation of their botanical knowledge and facilitated accurate diagnosis and treatment.

In addition to physical characteristics, Babylonian physicians also considered the growth patterns of plants. They understood that certain plants thrived in specific environments or geographical regions, and this knowledge helped them identify plants with similar properties. For example, they might have associated plants growing in marshy areas with diuretic properties or plants thriving in arid regions with abilities to alleviate dry coughs. By considering the natural habitats and growth conditions of plants, physicians could select appropriate remedies for various ailments.

The careful classification of plants by Babylonian physicians allowed them to create a comprehensive system of botanical knowledge. They organized plants into categories based on their shared characteristics and properties, enabling them to establish connections between plant species and their medicinal applications. This classification system enhanced their diagnostic abilities, enabling them to match specific symptoms and diseases with the appropriate botanical remedies.

By integrating their observations of physical characteristics, growth patterns, and geographical distributions, Babylonian physicians developed a sophisticated understanding of plants and their healing potential. This knowledge laid the groundwork for their successful diagnosis and treatment of various illnesses. It exemplifies their holistic approach to medicine, which considered the interconnectedness of nature and human health.

Example Exercise:

a. Study a collection of plants and their physical characteristics, growth patterns, and geographical distributions. Classify and describe these plants based on their observed features. Discuss the potential therapeutic applications of each plant in the context of Babylonian medicine.

Through the study of Babylonian physicians' careful observation and classification of plants, students gain an appreciation for the intricate relationship between plants and medicine. This knowledge not only deepens their understanding of ancient healing practices but also encourages critical thinking about the connections between nature and health in contemporary botanical and herbal medicine.

Understanding Therapeutic Properties:

The Babylonians possessed an extensive knowledge of the medicinal properties of various plants, recognizing that different plants possessed specific therapeutic qualities. This understanding allowed them to tailor treatments to address specific ailments effectively. By comprehending the unique properties of each plant, Babylonian physicians could harness their medicinal potential and provide targeted remedies.

One such example is the poppy plant, scientifically known as Papaver somniferum. Babylonian physicians were aware of the pain-relieving properties of the plant's sap, which contains alkaloids such as morphine and codeine. They utilized this knowledge to alleviate pain in patients, whether from injuries, surgical procedures, or chronic conditions. The poppy plant's analgesic properties made it a valuable resource in Babylonian medicine, allowing physicians to offer relief to those suffering from discomfort.

Another plant that the Babylonians recognized for its medicinal properties was the willow tree, belonging to the Salix genus. The willow tree's bark contains a substance called salicin, which has anti-inflammatory and analgesic effects. Babylonian physicians understood that preparations made from willow bark could be used to reduce inflammation and alleviate pain. They would prescribe such remedies for conditions such as joint inflammation, headaches, and fever.

The knowledge of specific medicinal properties associated with different plants allowed Babylonian physicians to create a repertoire of treatments tailored to address specific health issues. They understood that each plant possessed its own unique combination of chemical compounds that contributed to its therapeutic effects. By harnessing the healing potential of these plants, physicians could provide targeted relief and promote healing in their patients.

Example Exercise:

a. Research and compile a list of plants used in Babylonian medicine, along with their specific medicinal properties. Discuss the significance of each plant and its therapeutic applications in treating various ailments. Analyze the chemical compounds present in these plants and their effects on the human body.

Through an exploration of the Babylonians' understanding of the medicinal properties of plants, students can appreciate the sophisticated botanical knowledge that underpinned their medical practices. This knowledge serves as a foundation for contemporary herbal medicine and encourages students to explore the diverse applications of plant-based remedies in different cultures and healing traditions.

Preparation and Administration of Herbal Remedies:

Babylonian physicians were adept at employing different techniques to extract the therapeutic compounds from plants, ensuring the efficacy of their medicinal preparations. These methods encompassed a range of processes, including decoctions, infusions, poultices, and oils, each selected based on the desired outcome and the nature of the plant material.

Decoction was a common method used by Babylonian physicians to extract medicinal compounds from plant materials, particularly from roots, barks, and tougher plant parts. In this process, the plant material was boiled in water for an extended period, allowing the active constituents to be released into the liquid. The resulting decoction was then ingested orally or used topically as a therapeutic remedy. Decoctions were often employed to treat digestive ailments, respiratory conditions, and skin disorders.

Infusion, on the other hand, involved steeping plant materials, such as leaves, flowers, or delicate plant parts, in hot water or oil. This method was used to extract volatile compounds and delicate constituents that could be damaged by boiling. Infusions were commonly employed to prepare herbal teas or aromatic oils, which were then administered orally or applied externally. Babylonian physicians utilized infusions to address a wide range of health concerns, including digestive issues, insomnia, and skin conditions.

Poultices were another important method employed by Babylonian physicians for localized treatments. They involved applying a paste or mixture of crushed or powdered plant material directly to the affected area of the body. Poultices allowed for the direct application of active constituents to the skin, providing targeted relief for ailments such as wounds, burns, inflammation, and skin infections. These plant-based preparations were often combined with other substances, such as honey or oils, to enhance their healing properties.

Additionally, Babylonian physicians recognized the importance of extracting the medicinal compounds of plants into oils. Plant oils, such as olive oil or sesame oil, were commonly used as a medium to extract and preserve the therapeutic properties of certain plants. The plant material was macerated or infused in the oil for a specific duration, allowing the oil to absorb the active constituents. These medicated oils were then used topically for massage, as liniments, or as a base for ointments and salves, providing targeted relief for various conditions, including muscular pain, joint stiffness, and skin disorders.

Example Problem:

a. Select a plant with known medicinal properties and describe the most suitable extraction method for obtaining its therapeutic compounds. Explain the rationale behind your choice, considering the plant's characteristics and desired therapeutic effects.

By exploring the methods employed by Babylonian physicians to extract therapeutic compounds from plants, students can gain a deeper understanding of the meticulous approach taken in ancient herbal medicine. This knowledge highlights the significance of proper extraction techniques in maximizing the medicinal benefits of plants and serves as a foundation for contemporary herbal preparations and pharmaceutical practices.

Section 3: Case Studies: Plant-Based Remedies in Babylonian Medicine

Treatment of Digestive Disorders:

Babylonian physicians held a deep understanding of the therapeutic properties of plants, particularly in addressing digestive disorders that were prevalent in ancient times. They recognized that certain plants possessed specific qualities that could soothe and restore balance to the gastrointestinal system.

One such plant used by Babylonian physicians was myrrh (Commiphora spp.). Myrrh was highly regarded for its digestive benefits and was commonly employed to alleviate indigestion and relieve symptoms such as bloating and discomfort. The resinous substance obtained from myrrh trees was often prepared as a decoction or infused in oils, which were then ingested orally or applied topically to the abdomen. The active compounds in myrrh were believed to possess anti-inflammatory and carminative properties, aiding in the digestion process and promoting overall gastrointestinal health.

Fenugreek (Trigonella foenum-graecum) was another plant recognized for its beneficial effects on digestive disorders by Babylonian physicians. The seeds of fenugreek were valued for their ability to alleviate various gastrointestinal ailments, including diarrhea. The seeds were often ground into a powder or prepared as an infusion, which was consumed to help regulate bowel movements and provide relief from loose stools. Fenugreek was believed to possess anti-diarrheal properties and to possess a demulcent action, which helps soothe and protect the inflamed intestinal lining.

The utilization of myrrh and fenugreek in the treatment of digestive disorders reflects the holistic approach of Babylonian medicine, where plant-based remedies were carefully selected based on their specific properties and observed effects. The knowledge of these medicinal plants and their targeted use in gastrointestinal ailments has been passed down through generations, even influencing contemporary herbal traditions and natural health practices.

Example Problem:

a. Select a digestive disorder commonly experienced today and identify a plant-based remedy from ancient Babylonian medicine that could potentially alleviate the symptoms. Describe the plant and explain its traditional use in the treatment of the digestive disorder, including any known therapeutic mechanisms.

By examining the plant-based remedies used by Babylonian physicians for digestive disorders, students can appreciate the rich history and enduring wisdom of herbal medicine. Understanding the specific plants employed and their effects on gastrointestinal health allows for a deeper exploration of traditional healing practices and encourages critical thinking in the application of herbal remedies in modern contexts.

Herbal Remedies for Skin Conditions:

Skin ailments were indeed prevalent in ancient Babylon, and Babylonian physicians possessed a wealth of knowledge about plants that could effectively address these issues. One plant that played a significant role in Babylonian medicine for treating skin conditions was aloe vera (Aloe barbadensis).

Aloe vera was highly regarded for its soothing and healing properties, particularly in the context of burns and wounds. The gel extracted from the fleshy leaves of the aloe vera plant was applied topically to affected areas to alleviate pain, reduce inflammation, and promote the regeneration of damaged skin. Babylonian physicians recognized the cooling and moisturizing effects of aloe vera gel, which helped provide relief from burns and aided in the healing process.

Beyond burns, aloe vera was also used to address a range of other skin ailments. Its antimicrobial properties were believed to combat infections, making it a valuable remedy for wounds and cuts. Additionally, the gel's moisturizing and emollient qualities made it effective in soothing dry and irritated skin conditions such as eczema and dermatitis. Babylonian physicians observed that aloe vera helped hydrate and soften the skin, relieving discomfort and promoting overall skin health.

Exploring the properties and applications of aloe vera and other plants used in ancient Babylonian medicine for skin ailments provides students with a deeper understanding of the historical uses of herbal remedies. They can investigate the specific mechanisms by which aloe vera exerts its healing effects, such as its anti-inflammatory, antimicrobial, and moisturizing properties. Furthermore, students can compare these traditional uses with contemporary scientific studies to explore the potential of aloe vera and other plants in modern skincare practices.

Example Problem:

a. Choose a common skin condition, such as acne or psoriasis, and research a plant used by Babylonian physicians to address this ailment. Describe the plant, explain its traditional use in treating the skin condition, and discuss any relevant scientific evidence supporting its effectiveness.

By delving into the plants used by Babylonian physicians for skin ailments, students gain a comprehensive understanding of the historical and cultural significance of herbal remedies. This exploration fosters critical thinking skills and encourages students to consider the potential of traditional knowledge in the context of modern skincare and natural health practices.

Conclusion:

Studying the therapeutic properties of plants in Babylonian medicine allows students to delve into ancient healing practices and recognize the profound connection between humans and the natural world. This exploration provides a foundation for understanding the historical and cultural significance of herbal medicine in various belief systems, including Witchcraft, Divination, Herbalism, Shamanism, and Ecospirituality. By engaging in critical thinking and considering alternative perspectives, students can gain a deeper appreciation for the efficacy of plant-based remedies in different historical and cultural contexts.

B. Classification of plants based on their medicinal effects

The classification of plants based on their medicinal effects is a fundamental aspect of herbalism and other alternative healing practices. By categorizing plants according to their therapeutic properties, practitioners can better understand their potential applications in promoting health and well-being. This chapter delves into the classification systems used in various fields, such as

Witchcraft, Divination, Herbalism, Shamanism, Ecospirituality, and Magic in Ancient Babylon. We will explore different methods of classifying plants based on their medicinal effects, including elemental associations, energetic qualities, and traditional systems of plant categorization. Additionally, we will discuss the importance of considering both scientific evidence and traditional knowledge when classifying plants for therapeutic purposes.

Elemental Associations and Energetic Qualities:

In esoteric practices and belief systems, the classification of plants based on their elemental associations and energetic qualities plays a significant role in understanding their medicinal effects. This classification system is rooted in the belief that plants possess inherent properties that resonate with the natural elements and can influence energetic balance within individuals. Let's explore an example of how this classification system is applied in Witchcraft and Herbalism.

Example Problem:

a. Choose a plant commonly used in Witchcraft or Herbalism and classify it based on its elemental association and energetic qualities. Explain how this classification relates to its medicinal effects.

Solution:

One plant commonly utilized in Witchcraft and Herbalism is St. John's Wort (Hypericum perforatum). St. John's Wort is often classified as a "fire herb" due to its stimulating and energizing effects. Its association with the element of fire corresponds to its ability to increase vitality, uplift the spirit, and invigorate the body. In terms of energetic qualities, St. John's Wort is considered to be warm and uplifting, aligning with the fiery attributes associated with the element of fire.

From a medicinal perspective, the classification of St. John's Wort as a "fire herb" indicates its potential applications. It is commonly used in herbal remedies to address conditions such as mild depression, anxiety, and seasonal affective disorder. The herb's energizing and uplifting properties are believed to help dispel melancholy, promote a positive mood, and restore emotional balance.

Additionally, St. John's Wort is renowned for its analgesic and anti-inflammatory properties, making it suitable for treating physical discomfort or inflammation. These effects are thought to be related to the herb's association with fire, as fire is often associated with transformation, purification, and the alleviation of stagnation.

By classifying St. John's Wort as a "fire herb," practitioners of Witchcraft and Herbalism aim to harness its energetic qualities and elemental associations to promote healing and balance within individuals. This classification helps practitioners select plants that resonate with specific elemental energies and address imbalances in the body and spirit.

This example highlights the significance of classifying plants based on their elemental associations and energetic qualities in Witchcraft and Herbalism. It demonstrates how this classification system can inform the selection of plants for medicinal purposes, considering their energetic properties and elemental affinities to support holistic healing.

Example Exercise:

a. Research and select another plant commonly used in Witchcraft or Herbalism. Classify the plant based on its elemental association and energetic qualities. Explain how this classification relates to its medicinal effects, providing specific examples.

Traditional Systems of Plant Categorization:

Throughout history, diverse cultures and civilizations have developed distinct systems of plant classification based on their medicinal effects. These classification systems integrate various factors, including observations of physical characteristics, taste, smell, historical uses, and therapeutic properties. Let's explore two examples: Ancient Babylonian medicine and Ayurvedic medicine.

In Ancient Babylonian medicine, plants were classified based on their therapeutic properties, with a focus on addressing specific health concerns. For instance, a plant like the poppy (Papaver somniferum) was recognized for its potent pain-relieving properties. It was classified as an analgesic plant due to its ability to alleviate pain and discomfort. The Babylonian physicians observed the effects of the poppy plant on patients and documented its use in treating various conditions associated with pain. The classification of the poppy as an analgesic plant was based on its medicinal effect, providing relief from pain.

Moving on to Ayurvedic medicine, an ancient healing system from India, plants are classified according to their dosha-specific actions. Ayurveda recognizes three primary doshas—Vata, Pitta, and Kapha—which represent different energies or constitutions in the body. Plants are classified based on their ability to balance or influence these energies. For example, the herb Ashwagandha (Withania somnifera) is classified as a Rasayana or rejuvenative herb in Ayurveda. It is believed to have a balancing effect on all three doshas, promoting overall well-being and vitality. Ashwagandha is known for its adaptogenic properties, helping the body adapt to stress and supporting the nervous system. Its classification as a Rasayana reflects its rejuvenating and balancing qualities.

In Ayurveda, the classification of plants takes into account not only their medicinal effects but also their taste, energetics, and post-digestive effects. Each classification has its unique characteristics and properties associated with it. For example, plants classified as "bitter" in taste, such as neem (Azadirachta indica), are known for their cleansing and detoxifying properties. These bitter plants are believed to have a cooling effect and can help balance excess heat in the body, making them useful for conditions associated with Pitta dosha imbalances, such as inflammation or skin irritations.

By classifying plants based on their medicinal effects, ancient healing systems like Ancient Babylonian medicine and Ayurveda provide practitioners with valuable frameworks for understanding the therapeutic properties of plants. These classifications enable the selection of plants tailored to specific health concerns and individual constitutions, promoting holistic healing and well-being.

Example Exercise:

a. Research and choose a plant used in another traditional healing system or culture. Describe its classification based on its medicinal effects, highlighting any unique characteristics or properties associated with its category.

Section 3: Integrating Scientific Evidence and Traditional Knowledge:
In modern times, the classification of plants for medicinal purposes benefits from the integration of scientific evidence and traditional knowledge. While traditional systems provide valuable insights into the historical uses and observations of plants, scientific research contributes objective data on the chemical constituents, pharmacological properties, and potential therapeutic mechanisms of plants. This integration enables a more comprehensive understanding of plant classification for medicinal effects and enhances the credibility and efficacy of herbal remedies.

Example Problem:
a. Select a medicinal plant commonly used in contemporary herbalism or natural medicine. Analyze its classification based on both traditional knowledge and scientific evidence. Discuss any areas of agreement or discrepancy between the two perspectives.

Conclusion:

The classification of plants based on their medicinal effects is a dynamic and multidimensional process that draws upon ancient wisdom, cultural traditions, and scientific advancements. By categorizing plants according to their therapeutic properties, practitioners can navigate the vast world of medicinal plants and select appropriate remedies for specific health conditions. Through critical thinking and analysis, students in the field of new-age studies can deepen their understanding of plant classification systems and engage in discussions on the relevance of traditional knowledge in the context of modern scientific research.

Exercises:

Research and classify three medicinal plants based on their elemental associations and energetic qualities. Explain the rationale behind each classification.

Explore a traditional healing system, such as Ayurveda, and identify three plants classified according to their medicinal effects. Describe the unique properties or characteristics associated with each plant's classification.
Choose a medicinal plant commonly used in contemporary herbalism. Investigate its classification based on both traditional knowledge and scientific evidence. Discuss any potential challenges or benefits in integrating these perspectives.

By engaging with the classification of plants based on their medicinal effects, students can deepen their knowledge of herbalism and alternative healing practices. This chapter encourages critical thinking, cross-cultural exploration, and an appreciation for the diverse approaches to understanding the therapeutic potential of plants.

IV. Preparation and Administration of Herbal Remedies

A. Techniques and practices for preparing herbal remedies

Herbalism, an ancient practice rooted in the utilization of plant-based remedies for healing and wellness, encompasses a wide array of techniques and practices for preparing herbal remedies. The process of transforming medicinal plants into effective remedies involves various methods of extraction, preparation, and formulation. This chapter delves into the intricacies of these techniques, exploring their historical roots, contemporary applications, and their significance across different fields of study, including Witchcraft, Divination, Herbalism, Shamanism, Ecospirituality, and Magic in Ancient Babylon. Through the study of these techniques, students will gain a comprehensive understanding of the art and science of herbal medicine preparation.

Infusions and Decoctions:

Infusions and decoctions are fundamental techniques utilized in herbal medicine to extract the therapeutic properties of plants. These methods have been employed for centuries and are valued for their simplicity and effectiveness in extracting a wide range of active constituents from various plant parts.

Infusions involve steeping delicate plant materials, such as leaves and flowers, in hot water for a specified period. This gentle process allows the water to extract the plant's active constituents, including volatile oils, alkaloids, flavonoids, and other beneficial compounds. The hot water helps to break down cell walls and release the plant's medicinal components into the liquid medium. Infusions are typically prepared by pouring hot water over the plant material, covering it, and allowing it to steep for a specific duration. The resulting infusion can be consumed as a tea or used as a base for creating other herbal preparations.

Decoctions, on the other hand, are preferred for tougher plant parts, including roots, barks, and seeds, which require a more prolonged extraction process. To prepare a decoction, the plant material is simmered in water for an extended period, allowing for the extraction of the plant's active constituents. The simmering process helps to break down the tougher plant materials and facilitate the release of their medicinal properties. Decoctions are typically prepared by adding the plant material to cold water, slowly bringing it to a boil, and then allowing it to simmer for a specific duration. The resulting liquid is strained and used for various medicinal purposes.

Both infusions and decoctions offer distinct advantages in herbal medicine. Infusions are ideal for extracting volatile and heat-sensitive compounds, such as essential oils, that are abundant in delicate plant parts. They are also commonly used for herbal preparations where the flavor and aroma of the plant are desired, such as herbal teas and aromatic blends. On the other hand, decoctions are well-suited for extracting water-insoluble compounds, such as alkaloids and tannins, found in tougher plant parts. They are often employed when a stronger and more concentrated preparation is needed for medicinal purposes.

These techniques find relevance in various fields of study, including Witchcraft and Herbalism. In Witchcraft, practitioners may prepare herbal infusions as part of their ritual practices to harness the energetic properties and spiritual essence of specific plants. The infusion process allows for the infusion of the plant's essence into the water, creating a potent elixir that can be used in spellwork, divination, or other magical practices.

In Herbalism, infusions and decoctions serve as popular methods for creating medicinal teas, tinctures, or syrups. Herbal infusions are commonly used to extract the beneficial properties of medicinal plants, allowing individuals to consume the plant's therapeutic constituents in a gentle and easily assimilated form. Decoctions, on the other hand, are employed when stronger and more concentrated preparations are required for addressing specific health conditions or promoting healing.

Example Exercise:

a. Choose an herb commonly used in Witchcraft or Herbalism and describe the process of preparing an infusion or decoction using this herb. Discuss the specific therapeutic properties associated with the herb and how they are extracted through these methods.

Example Problem:

a. Select an herb commonly used in Herbalism or Witchcraft and describe the process of preparing an infusion or decoction using this herb. Discuss the specific therapeutic properties associated with the herb and how they are extracted through these methods.

Maceration and Percolation:

Maceration and percolation are valuable techniques used in herbal medicine to extract active constituents from plant materials using solvents such as alcohol, oil, or vinegar. These methods are particularly effective in extracting a wide range of compounds, including essential oils, resins, and other bioactive substances, from the plant material.

Maceration involves the process of soaking the plant material in a chosen solvent for an extended period. The solvent penetrates the plant material, dissolving and extracting its active constituents. This method allows for a slow and gentle extraction process, ensuring that the desired compounds are transferred to the liquid. The maceration period can vary depending on the plant material and the desired potency of the extract. After the maceration process is complete, the liquid is strained or filtered to separate the plant material from the extracted solution. The resulting macerate can be used as a standalone extract or as an ingredient in various herbal preparations.

Percolation, on the other hand, is a more advanced technique that involves the continuous passage of a solvent through a bed of the plant material. This method results in a more concentrated extract compared to maceration. The plant material is packed in a container or column, and the solvent is slowly poured over it or circulated through it. As the solvent passes through the plant material, it dissolves the active constituents and collects them in the liquid. This process is repeated multiple times to ensure a thorough extraction. The resulting percolate is collected and further processed as needed.

Both maceration and percolation offer distinct advantages in herbal medicine. Maceration is ideal for extracting a broad spectrum of compounds from plant materials. It is a simple and accessible technique that can be easily performed at home. Maceration is commonly used to create herbal tinctures, infused oils, or vinegars. The choice of solvent depends on the desired properties and intended use of the final product. For example, in Shamanism, practitioners may create macerated oils infused with specific herbs for anointing rituals or energy work. The slow infusion process allows for the transfer of the plant's energetic qualities into the oil, making it a potent tool for spiritual practices.

Percolation, on the other hand, is often employed when a more concentrated extract is desired or when working with tougher plant materials. It allows for a more efficient extraction of the plant's active constituents and can yield potent extracts with specific therapeutic properties. Percolation is commonly used in the creation of herbal extracts or concentrates used in various herbal preparations, such as medicinal tinctures or concentrated oils. In Ecospirituality, plant-based vinegars obtained through percolation may hold symbolic significance and be incorporated into ritual practices. These vinegars can be used for energetic cleansing, as offerings to nature spirits, or as ingredients in sacred blends.

Example Exercise:
a. Choose an herb commonly used in Shamanism or Ecospirituality and describe the process of preparing a macerated oil or plant-based vinegar using this herb. Discuss the specific energetic or symbolic qualities associated with the herb and how they are infused into the final product through maceration or percolation.

Distillation:

Distillation is a significant technique used to extract essential oils from aromatic plant materials. This method harnesses the volatile aromatic compounds present in plants, capturing them in the form of steam and subsequently condensing the steam to obtain the essential oil. Distillation enables the separation of these highly concentrated aromatic compounds from the plant material, resulting in a potent and therapeutic essential oil.

The process of distillation involves several key steps. First, the plant material, such as flowers, leaves, or stems, is placed in a distillation apparatus, often a specialized still or distillation flask. The plant material is then subjected to heat, either through direct heating or steam distillation. As the heat is applied, the volatile compounds within the plant material are released as vapor. This vapor, carrying the aromatic molecules, rises and passes through a condenser, where it is cooled and converted back into a liquid state.

The condensed liquid, consisting of water and the essential oil, is collected and undergoes a separation process. Since essential oils do not mix with water, they naturally float on the surface. The essential oil is carefully separated from the water, resulting in a pure and concentrated extract.

Essential oils obtained through distillation possess unique therapeutic properties derived from the specific plant material used. Each essential oil carries its own aromatic profile, chemical composition, and potential health benefits. For example, lavender (Lavandula angustifolia) is a popular herb used in Aromatherapy and Divination. Through distillation, its essential oil can be obtained, which is known for its calming and balancing properties. The essential oil of lavender can be incorporated into massage oils, diffused in a room, or added to bathwater to promote relaxation and reduce stress.

In Divination practices, specific essential oils may be chosen based on their energetic properties and their potential to enhance psychic abilities or evoke certain energies. For instance, frankincense (Boswellia carterii) essential oil, obtained through distillation, is associated with spiritual and mystical qualities. It is often used in rituals and ceremonies to create a sacred and meditative atmosphere, enhance intuition, and connect with higher realms.

In the realm of Magic, essential oils obtained through distillation play a vital role. They are believed to carry the energetic essence of the plant and are utilized in spellwork and ritual practices. Essential oils can be blended together to create personalized blends aligned with specific intentions or desired outcomes. For example, rosemary (Rosmarinus officinalis) essential oil, obtained through distillation, is associated with purification, protection, and memory enhancement. It can be incorporated into magic rituals, anointing candles, or used in charm bags to support these intentions.

Example Problem:
a. Select an aromatic herb commonly used in Aromatherapy or Divination, such as rosemary or frankincense, and describe the process of distillation to obtain its essential oil. Discuss the therapeutic properties associated with the essential oil and how it can be incorporated into healing or spiritual practices.

Herbal Formulations:

Herbal formulations are a cornerstone of traditional medicine and involve the skillful combination of multiple herbs to create synergistic blends with specific therapeutic purposes. These formulations can take various forms, including herbal teas, capsules, creams, or salves, and are designed to target specific health conditions or promote overall well-being. The art of herbal formulation requires a deep understanding of each herb's properties and the ability to harmonize them effectively.

Herbalists carefully select herbs for their formulations based on their individual characteristics, such as taste, energetics, and medicinal properties. Each herb brings its unique benefits to the blend, and when combined, they work together synergistically to enhance their efficacy and minimize potential side effects. For example, if creating an herbal formulation to address insomnia, an herbalist may select herbs with calming and sedative properties to promote relaxation and restful sleep.

When developing an herbal formulation, it is important to consider the specific health condition or concern being targeted. Extensive research on the herbs' medicinal properties, historical uses, and scientific evidence supports the selection process. By understanding the specific mechanisms of action and therapeutic effects of each herb, an herbalist can create a formulation that addresses the root causes of the condition and supports the body's natural healing processes.

For instance, in treating insomnia, an herbal formulation might include herbs like valerian (Valeriana officinalis), passionflower (Passiflora incarnata), and chamomile (Matricaria chamomilla). Valerian is known for its sedative and calming properties, helping to ease nervous tension and induce sleep. Passionflower acts as a mild sedative and anxiolytic, reducing anxiety and promoting relaxation. Chamomile has a gentle calming effect, soothing the nervous system and facilitating sleep. The combination of these herbs in an herbal formulation creates a synergistic effect, providing a more comprehensive and effective solution for insomnia.

Each herb in the formulation contributes to the overall therapeutic outcome. Valerian, passionflower, and chamomile work together to calm the mind, relax the body, and promote restful sleep. The combination helps to address the underlying factors contributing to insomnia, such as anxiety, stress, or nervous tension. By combining herbs with complementary properties, the formulation targets multiple aspects of the condition, enhancing its overall efficacy.

Example Exercise:
a. Research a specific health condition, such as digestive discomfort or stress-related tension, and create an herbal formulation using a combination of herbs known for their beneficial effects on that condition. Explain the rationale behind each herb's selection and how they work synergistically to address the condition.

Problem:
Research a specific health condition, such as digestive discomfort or stress-related tension, and create an herbal formulation using a combination of herbs known for their beneficial effects on that condition. Explain the rationale behind each herb's selection and how they work synergistically to address the condition.

Conclusion:
The techniques and practices for preparing herbal remedies are rooted in centuries of traditional wisdom and contemporary scientific understanding. By exploring these methods, students gain a profound appreciation for the craftsmanship and skill required in herbal medicine preparation. These techniques are essential tools for practitioners in various fields, allowing them to harness the healing potential of plants and create remedies that promote well-being, spiritual connection, and vitality. Through hands-on experiences, critical thinking exercises, and discussions, students can deepen their knowledge of herbal medicine and develop a holistic approach to healing and self-care.

B. Methods of extraction, decoction, and infusion

In the realm of herbalism and traditional healing systems, methods of extraction play a crucial role in harnessing the therapeutic properties of plants. Two commonly used techniques are decoction and infusion, each offering distinct advantages and suitable for different types of plant materials.

Decoction is a method of extraction that involves simmering plant parts, such as roots, barks, seeds, or tougher plant materials, in water for an extended period. The heat and prolonged boiling allow for the extraction of the plant's active constituents, such as alkaloids, tannins, and polysaccharides, which may have medicinal properties. Decoctions are particularly useful for extracting constituents that are less soluble in water and require more intense heat and time to be released.

To prepare a decoction, the plant material is usually chopped, crushed, or ground to increase its surface area, allowing for better extraction. It is then simmered in water for an appropriate duration, typically ranging from 15 minutes to an hour or more. The resulting liquid is strained, and the decoction can be consumed as a warm or cold beverage, used externally as a wash or compress, or incorporated into formulations like herbal syrups or creams.

In ancient Babylonian medicine, decoctions played a significant role in the preparation of herbal remedies. Babylonian physicians recognized that different plant parts possessed specific medicinal properties, and the decoction method allowed them to effectively extract these properties for therapeutic use. For example, decoctions of plants like myrrh (Commiphora spp.) and fenugreek (Trigonella foenum-graecum) were employed to alleviate digestive disorders and promote gastrointestinal health.

Infusion, on the other hand, is a gentler method of extraction primarily used for delicate plant parts such as leaves, flowers, and aromatic herbs. It involves steeping the plant material in hot water to extract its active constituents. Infusions are particularly suitable for extracting volatile compounds, essential oils, flavonoids, and other water-soluble constituents.

To prepare an infusion, the plant material is typically added to a container, and boiling water is poured over it. The mixture is then covered, allowing the plant material to steep for a specific duration, usually ranging from a few minutes to several hours. Finally, the liquid is strained, and the infusion can be consumed as a tea, used topically, or incorporated into various preparations like herbal tinctures or aromatic sprays.

Infusions have been widely used across different healing traditions, including herbalism, witchcraft, and ancient Babylonian medicine. In witchcraft and herbalism, practitioners may prepare herbal infusions as part of ritual practices to harness the energetic properties of specific plants. In herbalism, infusions serve as popular methods for creating medicinal teas, providing a gentle yet effective way to deliver the therapeutic benefits of herbs.

Example Exercise:

a. Choose an herb commonly used in witchcraft or herbalism and explain the process of preparing an infusion using that herb. Discuss the medicinal or energetic properties associated with the herb and how the infusion can be incorporated into healing or magical practices.

Problem:

Choose an herb commonly used in witchcraft or herbalism and explain the process of preparing an infusion using that herb. Discuss the medicinal or energetic properties associated with the herb and how the infusion can be incorporated into healing or magical practices.

C. Dosage and administration of herbal preparations

In the field of herbalism and traditional healing systems, proper dosage and administration of herbal preparations are crucial factors in ensuring their safety and effectiveness. Different herbal preparations, such as herbal teas, tinctures, capsules, and topical applications, require specific considerations regarding dosage and administration to optimize their therapeutic benefits.

Dosage refers to the amount of herbal preparation that is recommended for consumption or use, while administration pertains to the method or frequency of taking or applying the herbal remedy. It is important to note that the appropriate dosage and administration may vary depending on factors such as the individual's age, overall health, specific health condition, and the potency of the herb being used.

Herbalists and practitioners of various healing traditions have developed guidelines and principles to guide the dosage and administration of herbal preparations. These guidelines consider the herb's safety profile, intended effects, and the desired therapeutic outcome. It is essential to follow these guidelines and consult with a qualified herbalist or healthcare professional to ensure proper and safe usage of herbal remedies.

Herbal teas, one of the most common forms of herbal preparations, are typically prepared by steeping herbs in hot water. The dosage and administration of herbal teas may vary depending on the specific herb and its intended effects. Generally, a standard recommendation is to steep 1-2 teaspoons of dried herb (or 2-4 grams) in 8 ounces (240 ml) of hot water for about 5-15 minutes. However, some herbs may require higher or lower dosages and longer steeping times. It is essential to refer to reputable sources, herbal textbooks, or consult with an experienced herbalist to determine the appropriate dosage and administration for specific herbs.

Herbal tinctures, which are concentrated liquid extracts of herbs, are often administered orally. The dosage of tinctures is typically expressed as a ratio of herb to alcohol or other solvent. Common ratios include 1:1, 1:2, or 1:5, indicating the proportion of herb to solvent. A typical dosage recommendation is 30-60 drops (1-2 ml) of the tincture diluted in water, taken 2-3 times per day. However, dosages may vary depending on the herb's strength and the desired therapeutic effect. Herbalists may also consider factors such as the individual's body weight, sensitivity, and specific health condition when determining the dosage of tinctures.

Capsules or tablets containing powdered herbs provide a convenient and standardized form of herbal administration. Dosages for herbal capsules or tablets are typically indicated on the product packaging or prescribed by a healthcare professional. The dosage may vary depending on the herb's potency, the desired therapeutic effect, and the manufacturer's recommendations. It is important to follow the recommended dosage and consult with a qualified herbalist or healthcare professional when using herbal capsules or tablets.

Topical applications, such as creams, ointments, or poultices, are administered externally and applied to the skin. The dosage and administration of topical herbal preparations depend on factors such as the specific herb, the desired effect, and the individual's sensitivity. Generally, a thin layer of the topical preparation is applied to the affected area 2-3 times per day or as directed by a healthcare professional. It is important to carefully follow the instructions provided with the specific herbal preparation and consult with a qualified practitioner if necessary.

Example Exercise:

a. Choose an herb commonly used in herbalism or another healing tradition and discuss the appropriate dosage and administration for its herbal preparation. Explain any factors or considerations that influence the recommended dosage and administration, such as the herb's potency, intended effects, or safety profile.

Problem:
Choose an herb commonly used in herbalism or another healing tradition and discuss the appropriate dosage and administration for its herbal preparation. Explain any factors or considerations that influence the recommended dosage and administration, such as the herb's potency, intended effects, or safety profile.

V. Preservation and Transmission of Herbal Knowledge

A. Documentation and preservation of herbal knowledge in Ancient Babylon

In Ancient Babylon, the preservation and transmission of herbal knowledge played a vital role in the development of their sophisticated healing practices. Babylonian physicians and scribes recognized the importance of documenting their extensive understanding of medicinal plants, ensuring that this knowledge was passed down through generations and preserved for posterity. The documentation of herbal knowledge in Ancient Babylon involved various methods and practices, which contributed to the advancement of medicine and herbalism during that time.

One significant aspect of documenting herbal knowledge in Ancient Babylon was the compilation of written texts and clay tablets. The Babylonians were meticulous in recording their observations, classifications, and therapeutic uses of plants. These texts, written in the cuneiform script on clay tablets, provided detailed descriptions of medicinal plants, their preparation methods, and the ailments they were used to treat. Examples of such texts include the famous Assyrian Herbal, a compilation of herbal remedies and formulas, and the Diagnostic Handbook, which documented diagnostic techniques and treatment approaches.

The written texts also contained precise instructions on the collection, cultivation, and processing of medicinal plants. They detailed the specific parts of the plant to be used, the appropriate times for harvesting, and the methods of preservation to maintain the plants' medicinal properties. This comprehensive documentation ensured that the knowledge of herbal medicine was accurately transmitted and shared among practitioners.

Additionally, the Babylonians employed pictorial representations to enhance the visual understanding and recognition of medicinal plants. These pictorial depictions were often incorporated into the clay tablets alongside the written descriptions, allowing for a more holistic comprehension of the plants' physical characteristics. By combining textual information with visual imagery, Babylonian physicians aimed to provide a comprehensive resource for the identification and utilization of medicinal plants.

The preservation of herbal knowledge in Ancient Babylon extended beyond written records. The Babylonians recognized the significance of experiential learning and the passing down of knowledge through oral traditions. Master herbalists and physicians would train apprentices and students, imparting their wisdom and expertise through direct instruction, hands-on experience, and oral teachings. This oral transmission of knowledge served as a complement to the written texts, ensuring that the intricate details and nuances of herbal practices were preserved and shared.

Example Exercise:

a. Imagine you are a scribe in Ancient Babylon tasked with documenting a new medicinal plant recently discovered by a Babylonian physician. Write a description of the plant, including its physical characteristics, habitat, and medicinal properties. Provide instructions on how to prepare and administer the plant for therapeutic purposes.

B. Role of scribes and scholars in recording medicinal plant information

In the ancient civilizations of Babylon, the role of scribes and scholars was of utmost importance in recording and preserving the vast body of knowledge related to medicinal plants. Scribes and scholars served as custodians of wisdom, meticulously documenting the observations, formulations, and therapeutic applications of medicinal plants. Their efforts played a crucial role in the development and advancement of disciplines such as herbalism, medicine, and magical practices in Ancient Babylon.

Scribes were highly trained individuals who possessed exceptional writing skills and a deep understanding of the cuneiform script, the writing system used in Ancient Babylon. They were responsible for transcribing and compiling information on medicinal plants, ensuring that the knowledge was accurately recorded and made accessible to future generations. The scribes employed their expertise to inscribe detailed descriptions, classifications, and formulas onto clay tablets, which served as enduring repositories of medicinal plant information.

The scribes' role went beyond mere transcription; they were also involved in the compilation and organization of herbal knowledge. They worked closely with physicians, herbalists, and other knowledgeable individuals to collect and synthesize information from diverse sources. This collaborative effort ensured that the herbal knowledge of Ancient Babylon was comprehensive and inclusive of various perspectives and experiences.

The scholars of Ancient Babylon played a crucial role in the interpretation and analysis of the recorded information on medicinal plants. They delved into the texts, scrutinizing the writings of scribes and extracting the underlying principles and insights. By applying critical thinking and analytical skills, the scholars sought to deepen the understanding of medicinal plant properties, dosages, preparations, and applications.

Scholars also engaged in the validation and refinement of herbal knowledge through experimentation and empirical observations. They tested the efficacy of different plant combinations and formulations, documented their findings, and refined existing practices based on empirical evidence. This rigorous approach to studying medicinal plants allowed for the continual evolution and improvement of Babylonian healing practices.

Furthermore, the scholars acted as repositories of knowledge and conduits for the transmission of information. They shared their expertise with apprentices, students, and fellow practitioners, ensuring the continuity and dissemination of herbal wisdom. Through formal instruction, oral teachings, and hands-on training, scholars imparted their knowledge and skills to the next generation of scribes and healers.

Example Exercise:

a. Imagine you are a scribe in Ancient Babylon tasked with transcribing and organizing the knowledge related to a particular group of medicinal plants. Write a detailed description of the process you would follow, including steps such as collecting information from various sources, categorizing the plants based on their properties, and creating a comprehensive reference guide. Discuss the importance of collaboration with scholars and physicians in the compilation of the herbal knowledge.

C. Transmission of herbal knowledge through texts and oral traditions

In ancient civilizations such as Ancient Babylon, the transmission of herbal knowledge was facilitated through a combination of written texts and oral traditions. These two methods worked synergistically to ensure the continuity and preservation of herbal wisdom, allowing it to be passed down through generations and across different regions.

Written Texts:

One of the primary means of transmitting herbal knowledge was through the creation and preservation of written texts. Scribes played a crucial role in this process, diligently recording information on medicinal plants onto durable mediums such as clay tablets. These texts served as valuable references and instructional materials for future generations of healers, scholars, and practitioners.

The texts contained a wealth of information on various aspects of herbalism, including plant identification, medicinal properties, preparation methods, dosage guidelines, and therapeutic applications. They often included detailed descriptions of plants, their physical characteristics, preferred growing conditions, and geographical distributions. Additionally, the texts provided formulas and recipes for creating herbal preparations, such as infusions, decoctions, and ointments, along with instructions on their administration.

The written texts not only captured the accumulated knowledge of herbalism but also reflected the cultural and spiritual beliefs associated with plant-based healing practices. They documented the use of plants in magical rituals, divination, shamanic practices, and other spiritual traditions prevalent in Ancient Babylon. Examples of such texts include the famous Assyrian herbal compilation known as the "Assyrian Herbal" or "Assurbanipal's Herbal" and the "Materia Medica" of Ancient Babylon.

These written texts served as enduring records of herbal knowledge, ensuring its preservation and accessibility over time. They allowed for the dissemination of information beyond the immediate confines of a particular region, enabling the exchange of ideas and the enrichment of herbal practices across cultures and civilizations.

Oral Traditions:

In addition to written texts, the transmission of herbal knowledge was facilitated through oral traditions. Oral traditions encompassed the passing down of knowledge through spoken words, storytelling, and apprenticeship models. Within the context of herbalism, oral traditions played a significant role in preserving the practical aspects of herbal knowledge, including hands-on techniques, experiential insights, and subtle nuances of plant identification and harvesting.

Herbal knowledge was often shared through mentorship and apprenticeship relationships, where experienced healers and practitioners would impart their wisdom to younger individuals aspiring to become healers themselves. Through direct observation, practical demonstrations, and guided experiences, apprentices learned the intricacies of plant identification, cultivation, preparation, and administration. Oral traditions allowed for the transmission of tacit knowledge, which is difficult to capture fully in written texts alone.

Furthermore, oral traditions fostered a sense of community and cultural identity. Within a specific region or tribe, herbal knowledge was shared among community members, ensuring its continuity and relevance to the local context. These oral traditions provided a platform for intergenerational exchange, where wisdom accumulated over centuries could be passed down, refined, and adapted to the specific needs of the community.

Example Exercise:

a. Imagine you are an apprentice to a renowned herbalist in Ancient Babylon. Describe the process of transmitting herbal knowledge through oral traditions, including the roles of mentorship, storytelling, and hands-on experience. Discuss the advantages and limitations of oral transmission compared to written texts. Reflect on the significance of cultural context in the preservation and evolution of herbal practices.

VI. Influence on Contemporary Herbal Practices

A. Continuity of Babylonian herbal knowledge in modern herbalism

The rich heritage of Babylonian herbal knowledge continues to exert its influence on modern herbalism. Despite the passage of millennia, the wisdom and insights of ancient Babylonian healers and scholars have not been lost but have found their way into contemporary practices, contributing to the tapestry of modern herbalism.

Historical Preservation and Translation:

The preservation and translation of ancient texts play a crucial role in ensuring the continuity of Babylonian herbal knowledge. The efforts of dedicated scholars and researchers have allowed for the study and decipherment of clay tablets and cuneiform writings that contain invaluable information on Babylonian herbalism. Through these endeavors, ancient texts have been made accessible to contemporary herbalists, enabling them to delve into the wisdom of their ancient counterparts.

The translation of ancient texts is a meticulous process that involves expertise in ancient languages, such as Akkadian and Sumerian, as well as a deep understanding of the cultural and historical context of Babylonian society. Scholars painstakingly decipher the intricate script and language used in these texts, unraveling the knowledge and wisdom encoded within them.

One prominent example of an ancient Babylonian text is the Assyrian Herbal. This text provides detailed descriptions of plants, their medicinal properties, and their applications. By studying the Assyrian Herbal and similar texts, modern herbalists can gain valuable insights into the historical uses and therapeutic effects of various plants.

These ancient texts serve as a bridge between past and present, connecting modern herbalists to the knowledge and practices of their ancient counterparts. They offer a window into the traditional healing methods, plant identification, and herbal formulations used in Babylonian herbalism.

Studying these texts allows modern herbalists to expand their understanding of plants and their medicinal properties beyond contemporary knowledge. By exploring the historical uses of plants in Babylonian herbalism, herbalists can gain a broader perspective on the diverse ways in which plants have been utilized for healing purposes throughout history.

The insights gained from the translation and study of ancient texts also provide modern herbalists with a deeper appreciation for the cultural and spiritual significance attached to plants in Babylonian society. Babylonian herbalism was deeply intertwined with religious and magical practices, and these aspects are reflected in the texts. Understanding the cultural context helps modern practitioners to integrate not only the medicinal properties of plants but also the spiritual and symbolic aspects associated with them.

However, it is important to note that the translation and interpretation of ancient texts are not without challenges. The ancient languages used in these texts may have nuances and complexities that require careful consideration. The cultural context of ancient Babylonian society also needs to be understood to fully grasp the intended meanings of the texts. Furthermore, gaps in knowledge and the loss of certain texts over time can pose obstacles to a comprehensive understanding of Babylonian herbalism.

Nevertheless, through the dedication of scholars and the ongoing translation efforts, the knowledge contained in ancient Babylonian texts continues to be made available to modern herbalists. This allows for the preservation and revitalization of ancient herbal practices, enriching contemporary herbalism with insights from the distant past.

Example Exercise:

a. Select a specific plant mentioned in the Assyrian Herbal and conduct a detailed analysis of its medicinal properties and applications according to ancient Babylonian knowledge. Compare and contrast this with its contemporary uses in herbalism. Reflect on the implications of studying and translating ancient texts for the modern understanding and practice of herbal medicine.

Traditional Systems and Lineages:

In addition to the preservation and translation of ancient texts, the continuity of Babylonian herbal knowledge can be observed through the preservation of traditional systems and lineages. In regions where Babylonian cultural influence has endured, certain families or communities have safeguarded herbal practices that can be traced back to ancient Babylon. Through these lineages, knowledge, techniques, and remedies have been passed down through generations, ensuring the transmission of Babylonian herbal wisdom.

In regions where Babylonian culture once thrived, such as parts of the Middle East, traditional healers have persisted in their practices, keeping alive the ancient traditions and wisdom of Babylonian herbalism. These practitioners often belong to specific families or communities that have safeguarded the knowledge and techniques for centuries, ensuring the continuity of Babylonian herbal practices.

Traditional healers within these lineages possess deep knowledge of the medicinal properties of local plants, many of which have been used in healing practices since ancient times. They have inherited a wealth of knowledge regarding the identification, preparation, and administration of herbal remedies, as well as the understanding of their specific therapeutic effects.

By incorporating Babylonian principles into their healing approaches, these traditional healers maintain a connection to their ancient roots. They may employ herbal remedies and methods that reflect the ancient Babylonian practices, incorporating the same principles and philosophies that guided their ancestors. This continuity ensures that the wisdom of Babylonian herbalism remains alive and relevant in these communities.

The preservation of traditional systems and lineages plays a crucial role in the perpetuation of Babylonian herbal knowledge. The transmission of knowledge from one generation to the next ensures the preservation of valuable insights and practices, fostering the continuity of ancient wisdom.

However, it is important to note that the preservation of traditional systems and lineages is not without challenges. Cultural and societal changes over time can pose threats to the survival of these traditions. The influence of modernization, globalization, and the erosion of traditional practices can all impact the continuity of Babylonian herbal knowledge within these lineages.

Moreover, traditional systems and lineages may vary in their adherence to the original Babylonian practices. Over time, adaptations and modifications may occur as these traditions interact with other healing systems or respond to the evolving needs of their communities. While these changes can contribute to the resilience and relevance of the traditions, they may also result in variations from the original Babylonian practices.

Nonetheless, the preservation of traditional systems and lineages provides a valuable link to the ancient Babylonian herbal knowledge. By maintaining the transmission of knowledge and practices, these lineages contribute to the richness and diversity of herbal traditions and allow for the continued exploration and application of Babylonian wisdom in the modern world.

Example Exercise:
a. Research a specific traditional healer or community in a region with a historical connection to ancient Babylon. Explore their herbal practices and remedies, highlighting any distinct Babylonian influences. Discuss the challenges and opportunities they face in preserving and transmitting Babylonian herbal knowledge within their

lineage. Reflect on the significance of traditional systems and lineages in the continuity of Babylonian herbal wisdom.

Adaptation and Integration:

While the direct practice of Babylonian herbalism in its original form may no longer exist, the concepts and principles derived from this ancient tradition have found their way into modern herbalism. Contemporary herbalists have recognized the value of Babylonian wisdom and have adapted and integrated its knowledge into their own practices. By merging ancient wisdom with modern understanding, they enrich their approach to herbalism and offer holistic solutions to health and well-being.

One of the aspects of Babylonian herbalism that resonates with modern herbalists is its holistic perspective on health. Babylonian medicine acknowledged the interconnectedness of the body, mind, and spirit, understanding that imbalances in one aspect can affect the overall well-being. This holistic approach aligns with contemporary herbalism, which emphasizes the importance of addressing the root causes of ailments and promoting overall health rather than merely treating symptoms.

Incorporating Babylonian concepts into their practice, modern herbalists recognize the significance of balancing energies within the body. They may utilize herbs and formulations that aim to restore harmony and equilibrium to the various systems and energies within the body. This approach aligns with the Babylonian belief in maintaining a balance of opposing forces, such as hot and cold or moist and dry, to achieve optimal health.

Moreover, modern herbalists may draw inspiration from the Babylonian emphasis on understanding the root causes of diseases and imbalances. By exploring the underlying factors contributing to a specific health issue, they aim to address the core issues rather than solely alleviating symptoms. This approach is consistent with the Babylonian tradition of diagnosing and treating the underlying causes of ailments through herbal remedies and lifestyle modifications.

Incorporating Babylonian principles into their herbal formulations and treatment protocols, modern herbalists combine ancient wisdom with contemporary scientific understanding. They may study and analyze the historical uses of plants in Babylonian texts and integrate that knowledge with current research on the phytochemical properties and therapeutic actions of herbs. By doing so, they create herbal remedies that are both rooted in tradition and informed by modern scientific advancements.

The integration of Babylonian concepts into modern herbalism not only adds depth and richness to the field but also fosters a deeper connection with the wisdom of our ancestors. It allows contemporary herbalists to tap into the accumulated knowledge and experiences of ancient civilizations, expanding the range of options and approaches available for healing and well-being.

It is important to note that while the integration of Babylonian principles into modern herbalism has its merits, it is also essential to critically evaluate and adapt these principles to the contemporary context. The understanding of herbal properties, safety considerations, and cultural perspectives have evolved over time. Thus, modern herbalists must approach the ancient knowledge with a discerning eye, ensuring that it aligns with current scientific understanding and ethical practices.

Example Exercise:

a. Select a specific aspect of Babylonian herbalism, such as the concept of balancing energies or the emphasis on addressing root causes, and explore how modern herbalists have incorporated these principles into their practices. Provide examples of specific herbs or formulations that embody these principles and discuss their applications in contemporary herbalism. Reflect on the benefits and potential challenges of integrating ancient wisdom into modern approaches to herbalism.

Historical Research and Academic Study:

Academic research and scholarly studies of ancient Babylonian herbalism contribute to its continuity in modern herbalism. Through rigorous investigation and analysis, researchers shed light on the practices, beliefs, and therapeutic methods employed by Babylonian healers. This research informs modern herbalists about the historical context, plant uses, and potential applications of Babylonian herbal remedies.

Example Exercise:

a. Research a specific plant or remedy mentioned in Babylonian herbal texts and explore how it has been integrated into modern herbalism. Examine its historical uses and therapeutic properties according to ancient Babylonian knowledge. Compare and contrast these with its contemporary applications. Reflect on the challenges and considerations involved in translating and adapting ancient knowledge into modern practices.

B. Integration of Babylonian principles in modern herbal preparations

The integration of Babylonian principles in modern herbal preparations represents a convergence of ancient wisdom and contemporary practices. By incorporating the principles and concepts from Babylonian herbalism, modern herbalists can infuse their formulations with the holistic approach, energetics, and therapeutic insights of this ancient tradition. This chapter explores the integration of Babylonian principles in modern herbal preparations, highlighting the significance of this approach and providing practical examples for application.

Holistic Approach:

One key aspect of Babylonian herbalism that resonates with modern herbal preparations is its holistic approach to health and well-being. Babylonian healers recognized the interconnectedness of the body, mind, and spirit, emphasizing the importance of addressing the underlying causes of illness rather than merely treating symptoms. Modern herbalists can embrace this holistic perspective by considering the individual as a whole and developing formulations that promote balance and overall well-being.

The holistic approach to health and well-being in Babylonian herbalism provides valuable insights and principles that are relevant to modern herbal preparations. In Babylonian culture, the understanding of health encompassed not only the physical body but also the mind and spirit. The belief was that imbalances or disharmony in any of these aspects could contribute to illness or disease.

Modern herbalists can draw upon this holistic perspective by acknowledging the interconnectedness of the body, mind, and spirit in their approach to herbal preparations. Instead of solely focusing on alleviating specific symptoms, they can strive to address the underlying causes of imbalance and promote overall well-being.

When formulating herbal remedies, modern herbalists can take into account the individual's unique constitution, considering factors such as physical health, emotional well-being, lifestyle, and environmental influences. By understanding the interconnected nature of these aspects, herbalists can create formulations that support the body's natural healing processes and promote holistic balance.

For example, if a person presents with symptoms of stress and anxiety, a modern herbalist may consider not only herbs with calming properties but also those that support the nervous system, promote relaxation, and enhance emotional well-being. By taking a holistic approach, the herbalist aims to address not only the immediate symptoms but also the underlying factors that contribute to the individual's overall state of well-being.

Integrating Babylonian principles into modern herbal preparations involves aligning with the core principles of balance, harmony, and addressing the root causes of imbalances. By embracing the holistic perspective of Babylonian herbalism, modern herbalists can create formulations that support the body's innate healing capacity and promote overall wellness.

Example Exercise:
a. Choose a specific health condition, such as digestive disorders or immune support, and create an herbal formulation based on Babylonian principles of holistic health. Explain the rationale behind the selection of herbs and how they work synergistically to address the condition while considering the interconnectedness of the body, mind, and spirit.

Energetics and Herbal Constituents:

Babylonian herbalism recognized the energetic qualities of plants and their effects on the body. Herbalists classified plants according to their energetic properties, such as hot, cold, moist, or dry, and understood how these qualities influenced health. Modern herbalists can incorporate the energetics of plants into their preparations by considering the specific actions and therapeutic properties of herbs. For example, they may combine hot and drying herbs to address conditions characterized by excessive dampness in the body.

In addition to energetics, the understanding of herbal constituents in Babylonian herbalism can inform modern herbal preparations. Babylonian healers were aware of the active compounds and constituents present in plants and their therapeutic effects. Modern herbalists can draw from this knowledge and utilize scientific advancements to identify and extract specific compounds from herbs for targeted therapeutic purposes. This integration of traditional wisdom and scientific understanding allows for the creation of potent and effective herbal preparations.

Therapeutic Principles and Formulations:

Babylonian herbalism offers valuable therapeutic principles that can be integrated into modern herbal preparations. One such principle is the concept of balancing energies and humors within the body. According to Babylonian beliefs, maintaining a harmonious balance of energies was crucial for health and well-being. Imbalances were thought to lead to various ailments and diseases.

In modern herbal preparations, the principle of balancing energies can guide herbalists in formulating blends that address specific imbalances within the body. For instance, if an individual is experiencing excess heat or inflammation, the herbalist may select cooling and anti-inflammatory herbs to restore balance. Conversely, if someone exhibits signs of coldness or stagnation, warming and stimulating herbs may be chosen to restore vitality. By combining herbs with complementary properties, herbalists can create synergistic blends that support the body's natural healing processes and promote balance.

Another noteworthy aspect of Babylonian herbalism is the use of complex formulations. Babylonian healers recognized that combining multiple herbs could enhance their therapeutic effects and address specific health conditions more effectively. Modern herbalists can adopt this approach by formulating blends that target specific ailments or promote overall well-being.

For instance, when creating a formulation for digestive discomfort, a modern herbalist may combine herbs known for their carminative, anti-inflammatory, and digestive-stimulating properties. Carminative herbs, such as fennel or peppermint, can help alleviate gas and bloating, while anti-inflammatory herbs like chamomile or turmeric can soothe inflammation in the digestive tract. Digestive-stimulating herbs like ginger or cardamom can enhance digestion and alleviate discomfort. By carefully selecting and combining these herbs, the herbalist aims to create a synergistic blend that addresses the multifaceted aspects of digestive health.

Integrating Babylonian principles into modern herbal preparations allows herbalists to draw upon the wisdom of the past while adapting it to contemporary needs. By considering the principles of balancing energies and humors and utilizing complex formulations, herbalists can create blends that are tailored to specific conditions and promote optimal well-being.

Example Exercise:
a. Select a specific health condition, such as insomnia or respiratory congestion, and create an herbal formulation based on Babylonian principles of balancing energies and utilizing complex formulations. Explain the rationale behind the selection of herbs and how they work together to address the condition while promoting balance and harmonious energies within the body.

To illustrate the integration of Babylonian principles in modern herbal preparations, let's consider two examples:

Example 1: Sleep Support Blend

The Babylonians recognized the importance of restful sleep for overall health. To create a sleep support blend, modern herbalists can draw inspiration from Babylonian herbalism and select herbs known for their sedative, nervine, and relaxant properties. Some possible herbs to include are Valerian (Valeriana officinalis), Chamomile (Matricaria chamomilla), and Lavender (Lavandula angustifolia). These herbs can be combined in a tincture or tea formulation to promote relaxation and support a peaceful sleep.

Example 2: Digestive Tonic Blend

The Babylonians had a rich understanding of digestive health and formulated herbal preparations to address digestive discomfort. Modern herbalists can create a digestive tonic blend by combining herbs such as Peppermint (Mentha piperita), Ginger (Zingiber officinale), and Fennel (Foeniculum vulgare). These herbs possess carminative, anti-inflammatory, and digestive-stimulating properties that can support healthy digestion. The blend can be prepared as a tea, tincture, or capsule formulation.

Conclusion:

The integration of Babylonian principles in modern herbal preparations offers a valuable approach for herbalists seeking to combine ancient wisdom with contemporary understanding. By embracing the holistic perspective, incorporating energetics and herbal constituents, and applying therapeutic principles in formulations, herbalists can create potent and effective remedies. The practical examples provided demonstrate how Babylonian principles can be applied in modern herbalism, allowing for the promotion of holistic well-being and the continuation of ancient traditions.

Example Exercise:

a. Select a specific health condition, such as anxiety or respiratory congestion, and create a herbal formulation that integrates Babylonian principles. Explain the rationale behind each herb's selection, considering their energetic qualities, therapeutic properties, and potential synergies. Discuss how the formulation aligns with the holistic approach of Babylonian herbalism and how it addresses the underlying causes of the condition.

Appendix

Glossary of Key Terms

Chapter 1: Introduction to Ancient Babylon

Ancient Babylon: The historical city located in Mesopotamia, known for its rich cultural and intellectual achievements.

Mesopotamia: The region between the Tigris and Euphrates rivers, where Ancient Babylon was situated.

Civilization: A complex society characterized by urban development, social stratification, writing systems, and advancements in various fields.

Cuneiform: A system of writing used in Ancient Babylon, involving wedge-shaped characters inscribed on clay tablets.

Polytheism: The belief in and worship of multiple deities.

Ziggurat: A stepped temple tower constructed in Ancient Babylon and other Mesopotamian cities.

Hammurabi: The sixth king of the First Babylonian Dynasty, known for his legal code, the Code of Hammurabi.

Chapter 2: Witchcraft in Ancient Babylon

Witchcraft: The practice of magic and sorcery, often involving rituals, spells, and communication with supernatural entities.

Incantation: A verbal formula or chant used in magical rituals to invoke or influence supernatural forces.

Spellcasting: The act of casting spells, utilizing words, gestures, and symbolic objects to direct magical energy and manifest desired outcomes.

Familiar: A spiritual entity, often in animal form, believed to assist and communicate with witches.

Ritual: A prescribed set of actions and ceremonies performed for a specific purpose, often involving symbolic gestures and incantations.

Grimoire: A book of magical instructions and spells.

Witch's Familiar: An animal or spirit that aids a witch in their magical workings.

Chapter 3: Divination in Ancient Babylon

Divination: The practice of seeking knowledge or insight about the future or unknown through supernatural means.

Oracle: A person or object regarded as a source of divine communication and prophecy.

Haruspicy: A form of divination in Ancient Babylon that involved interpreting the entrails of sacrificial animals.

Astrology: The study of celestial bodies and their influence on human affairs, often used for divination purposes.

Omen: An event or phenomenon believed to foretell future events or outcomes.

Extispicy: A form of divination that involved examining the entrails of animals, particularly sheep or goats.

Divination Tools: Objects or methods used in divination, such as tarot cards, runes, or scrying mirrors.

Chapter 4: Herbalism in Ancient Babylon

Herbalism: The practice of utilizing plants and their extracts for medicinal purposes.

Medicinal Plant: A plant or herb with recognized therapeutic properties.

Energetics: The study of the energetic qualities and effects of plants on the human body.

Infusion: A method of preparing herbal remedies by steeping plant material in hot water.

Decoction: A method of preparing herbal remedies by boiling plant material in water.

Tincture: A concentrated herbal extract made by macerating plant material in alcohol.

Poultice: A soft, moist mass of herbs applied topically to the body for therapeutic purposes.

Recommended Reading and Further Resources

Chapter 1: Introduction to Ancient Babylon

"Babylon: Mesopotamia and the Birth of Civilization" by Paul Kriwaczek

"Babylon: Legend, History and the Ancient City" by Michael Seymour

"Ancient Mesopotamia: Portrait of a Dead Civilization" by A. Leo Oppenheim

Chapter 2: Witchcraft in Ancient Babylon

"Magic and Witchcraft in the Ancient Near East" by Tzvi Abusch

"Witchcraft and Magic in Europe: Ancient Greece and Rome" by Bengt Ankarloo and Stuart Clark

"The Witch in History: Early Modern and Twentieth-Century Representations" by Diane Purkiss

Chapter 3: Divination in Ancient Babylon

"Divination and Interpretation of Signs in the Ancient World" by Amar Annus

"Divination, Politics, and Ancient Near Eastern Empires" by Alan Lenzi

"Divination and Human Nature: A Cognitive History of Intuition in Classical Antiquity" by Peter T. Struck

Chapter 4: Herbalism in Ancient Babylon

"Ancient Herbs, Modern Medicine: Improving Your Health by Combining Chinese Herbal Medicine and Western Medicine" by Henry Han and Glenn Miller

"The Encyclopedia of Medicinal Plants: A Practical Reference Guide to over 550 Key Herbs and Their Medicinal Uses" by Andrew Chevallier

"The Yoga of Herbs: An Ayurvedic Guide to Herbal Medicine" by David Frawley and Vasant Lad

These recommended readings cover various aspects of the respective topics and provide a deeper understanding of Ancient Babylon, Witchcraft, Divination, and Herbalism. They offer valuable insights and historical context to enhance your knowledge and exploration of these subjects.

Additionally, you may find the following resources helpful:

Academic journals and research papers on ancient civilizations, folklore, and alternative healing practices.

Online forums and communities dedicated to the study and practice of new-age disciplines.

Workshops, seminars, and conferences on subjects related to Witchcraft, Divination, Herbalism, and Ancient Babylon.

By engaging with these recommended readings and exploring further resources, you can expand your understanding and develop a comprehensive grasp of the topics discussed in the book.

Bibliography of Ancient Babylonian Texts and Scholarly Works

Ancient Babylonian Texts:

"Enuma Elish" - The Babylonian creation myth.

"Epic of Gilgamesh" - An epic poem that includes mythological and historical elements.

"Code of Hammurabi" - A legal code that provides insights into Babylonian society and governance.

"Atrahasis Epic" - A mythological text that recounts the Great Flood.

"Ludlul bel nemeqi" - A literary composition addressing the problem of suffering.

Scholarly Works:

Dalley, Stephanie. "Myths from Mesopotamia: Creation, the Flood, Gilgamesh, and Others." Oxford University Press, 2008. - A comprehensive collection and analysis of ancient Babylonian myths and literature.

Leick, Gwendolyn. "The Babylonian World." Routledge, 2007. - Provides a broad overview of Babylonian history, culture, and society.

George, Andrew R. "The Babylonian Gilgamesh Epic: Introduction, Critical Edition, and Cuneiform Texts." Oxford University Press, 2003. - A detailed scholarly edition of the Gilgamesh epic.

Van De Mieroop, Marc. "A History of the Ancient Near East: ca. 3000-323 BC." Wiley-Blackwell, 2016. - Explores the political, social, and cultural history of the ancient Near East, including Babylon.

Biggs, Robert D. "The Babylonian World." International Journal of Middle East Studies, Vol. 24, No. 2, 1992, pp. 281-283. - A scholarly article discussing the religious beliefs and practices in ancient Babylon.

Milton Keynes UK
Ingram Content Group UK Ltd.
UKHW051703101123
432260UK00026B/400

9 798889 901167